CIRCLE WAYS

CIRCLE WAYS

PEDAGOGY IN THE ROUND

JOE PROVISOR

THIRD PRESENCE PUBLISHING

Published in the United States by Third Presence Publishing

Hardcover ISBN: 9798993097121

Paperback ISBN: 9798993097107

ePub ISBN: 9798993097114

Library of Congress Control Number: 2025919622

Cover design by Anna Berzovan

Interior design and layout by Maria Giovanna Brauzzi

Visit the author's website at www.circleways.org

PRAISE FOR JOE PROVISOR

"Joe's book links the conceptual framework of circle practice to daily activities that allow the building of new neural pathways in adults and students. These neural pathways can lead us to cultural transformation toward a culture of belonging and agency for everyone. This is the urgent call of our time. The book is bursting with examples of activities, prompts, and strategies to support educators in bringing the circle to life in schools."
Kay Pranis, Circle trainer, coauthor of *Circle Forward: Building a Restorative School Community*

"For years I have witnessed the transformative power of Joe Provisor's circle practice. His pioneering work in California and beyond has not only shaped my own journey as a theater and ritual practitioner but has offered thousands of students and teachers a path back to the heart of learning: connection, story, and community. *Circle Ways* arrives at a moment of profound educational and planetary crisis—as both map and medicine. This book is not merely a manual; it is a legacy, crafted with humility and courage, for the seventh generation. Joe's life-long commitment to healing and transformation shines through every page, inviting us all to remember that we belong to one another—and that no one is expendable."
Héctor Aristizábal, theater artist, psychologist, and founder of *Re-Conectando*

"In an era when schools are asked to do more than ever, *Circle Ways* provides a timely and compassionate model for meeting children's academic, social, and emotional needs. Refined through Joe Provisor's decades of practice in diverse schools, this book is a practical resource that addresses the real-world challenges educators face while fostering belonging, resilience, and hope."
Susan Kaiser Greenland, author of *Real-World Enlightenment*, *Mindful Games*, and *The Mindful Child*

"Joe Provisor's book could not be more timely, essential and profound in giving concrete tools for a circle-based pedagogy—one based on connection to self, others, and the greater good. The book offers critical and creative insights that Provisor lives and downloads from his vast and rich experience. He offers how to formulate prompts ranging from biblical verse, poetry, prose and the seemingly mundane. Naming rituals and shared purpose, he hits the mark on how to foster a sense of shared identity and belonging. Teaching children to listen deeply he makes clear that Circle not only develops crucial skills for resolving conflicts but also capacity for creating relationships that satisfy the need to be safely seen without judgement, rejection, or shaming. This is an essential book for anyone interested in social change and community building."
Deborah Heifetz, PhD, social anthropologist, mediator, and educator who developed the *Human Needs Matrix as a Map to Compassion*

"This is an important book for those interested in education and a must-read for anyone in the growing movement to re-imagine the way we educate our young ... This includes teachers, administrators, parents and those students who are ready to reflect more consciously on their educational lives. Joe Provisor introduces the circle practices that lie at the heart of every traditional culture in remarkably deep, comprehensive and personal ways, that engage one's imagination profoundly. Beyond the great learning benefits of circle practices, Provisor's extensive experience connects these practices to many dimensions of a school's curriculum—both philosophically and practically. Page after page, the reader becomes more tangibly engaged in *Circle Ways*'s potential for playing a primary role in a school community."

Jack Zimmerman, PhD, coauthor of *The Way of Council*

"I am in great gratitude for this long-awaited offering from Joe Provisor and his dedication to the ways of council over so many years. The experience shared within I trust—and, dare to say, pray—will touch the hearts and minds of many and will become even more part of the education and healing needed for our shared future. Such an essential gift for many who need to engage with this book and awaken, offer, learn, and carry support for circle ways in their schools, their communities, and their everyday lives in the times ahead."

Virginia Coyle, community activist, coauthor of *The Way of Council*

"The circle is one of humanity's oldest symbols of wholeness, belonging, and renewal. In this book, Joe Provisor draws on decades of holding circles in schools and communities to demonstrate how this ancient, yet simple, practice can transform the lives of students and teachers. Amid systems of power and hierarchy, the circle offers a radical alternative: listening and speaking with the whole self—body, mind, and heart—fostering connections within oneself, with others, and with the larger, living world. This book reminds me that circles, indeed, can save our world!"

Betsy Perluss, PhD, retired professor of Counseling, CSULA, and wilderness guide with *The School of Lost Borders*

CONTENTS

ACKNOWLEDGEMENTS

I first wish to acknowledge the Tonga/Gabrielino people of this place, now called Los Angeles, where I am a guest. I am also grateful to the Chumash people who brought their ceremonies to the land in the Upper Ojai Valley of California. That spirit drew many to return to that land again and listen to each other and the natural world. I also acknowledge all indigenous, earth-cherishing peoples, who have been victims of colonization and genocide, who have lost their languages, their ceremonies, their ways of staying in right relation with all living things. We turn now to what has endured: their timeless wisdom, their healing ways, their resilience, and their knowing that we belong to each other, that no one is expendable, and where there is harm, there must be healing.

This book could never have been produced without the students of Thomas Starr King Junior High and Palms Middle School in Los Angeles. They tolerated my presence in *their* circles as I learned to listen and to follow their lead.

I acknowledge my teachers on this path to a circle-based worldview: Benjamin Saltman, Helen Lodge, Michael Meade, Wayne Liebman and the Lost Dogs Men's Council, Jane Wheatley, Robert Bly, Jack Zimmerman, Virginia Coyle, Mahaleena Payson, Leon Berg, Lola Ray Long, Marlow Hotchkiss, Leslie Roberts, Leon Berg, Shinzen Young, Anna Halperin, Joanna Macy, Lauren Abramson, Beverly Title, Hector Aristizabal, Jill Townsend-Sorel, and Brent Blair.

The school leaders who said, "Yes! Let's do this!:" Lana Brody, Paul Cummins, Hugh Gottfried, Merle Price, Gene Rubin, Marcia Haskin, Guillermina Jauregui, Stu Bernstein, John Leichty, Tom

Nolan, Kristy Mack-Fett, Betsy Perluss, Don Wilson, Michelle King, Sherre Vernon, Judy Utvitch, Angel Beamer, Debra Duffin Coaloa, Danna Lomax, Kelly Hatton, Michael Rosner, Marni Parsons, Joyce Dara, Susan Canjura, Barbara Locker-Halmy, and Carmina Osuna.

The persistent pioneers, facilitators, teachers, and volunteers at Palms Middle School and other early adopters: Sylvia Thomas, Susan Fisher, Jerry Smith, Elliot Stillman, Deana Estrada-Wu, Maricarmen Cardena-Igarashi, Ann Kelly, Davia Rivka, Monica Chinlund, Ray Tucker, Bonnie Tamblyn, Natalie White, Lori Austein, Carol Kurland, Dan Brumer, Judy Gantz, Justine Bloomingdale, Ronit Rinat, Michelle Pilar Mansfield, Valerie Wildman, Kate Lipkis, Lisa Ransdell, Carol Kurland, Camille Ameen, Diane Bulens, Carmen Wurgel, Ruth Souza, Lynn Henderson, Cheryl Macon-Oliver, Judith Hall, Stefani Valadez, Adam Bendell, Susan Harris, Roxanne Steinberg, Patty Factor, Cricket Wingfield, Andel McCoy, Lynda Hoffman, Jodi Margaram Bell, Jill Murray, Chris Norris, Chrissy O'Grady Martin, Zahava Weiss, Kenzo Bergeron, Monique Marshall, Jill Valle, Jane Raphael, Julia Wasson, Robert M. Contreras Peters, and Tara Contreras Peters.

Our benefactors: Rona Sebastian, The Herb Alpert Foundation, The Annenberg Foundation, The Burton Bettingen Foundation, The Windsong Foundation, Justine Bloomingdale, The Stuart Foundation, The S. Mark Taper Foundation, The Employees' Community Fund of Boeing, California, The Wilson-Thornhill Foundation, The Tawney and Jerry Sanders Foundation, Michael J. Olsen, Ruth Ziegler.

Special thanks to Monica Chinlund, who, in addition to negotiating a cubicle built for one but shared by two on the 25th floor of the school district headquarters, passed the rose quartz heart with me every morning to ground ourselves from that height as we navigated bureaucratic roadblocks to get to schools and do the work we loved.

Special thanks to Marc Rosner, who leapt into the breach and was my partner when we moved our endeavors from the school district to an independent entity, and who brought so much heart and calm centeredness to that, which balanced my sometimes-overheated enthusiasm. Sail on, brother.

Deep gratitude to those who took the time to read the manuscript and offer editorial suggestions: Doug Adrianson, Kate Lipkis, Lori Austein, Kay Pranis, Amy Lignitz Harken, Jennifer Wilhoit, and Maria Giovanna Brauzzi, whose manuscript midwifery took the book across the threshold.

To my daughter, Hannah Michelle, who, in addition to exemplifying the ability to enter the imaginal world of every child she encounters, resulting in fairy houses and the transformation of trauma into art, challenges me every day to walk my talk and not fall blindly back into the patriarchal solipsism that defined my cultural upbringing.

To my son, Aaron Michael, who, in addition to being able to wake the gods from their emotional slumber with his music, provides an exemplar of what it means to live in one's truth.

And to my partner, wife, and friend, Abbe, for her ability to find humor in darkness, for matching my flights of fancy with practicality, for living with someone for whom good enough never is and who considers it all a giveaway. Your love sustains me.

INTRODUCTION

THIS BOOK IS A MANIFESTO, a memoir, and a map. Educators have always faced the challenge of imagining what their students will need in the future. The reality now, in 2025, is that the pace of cultural, technological, and environmental change vastly outpaces our ability to predict the future from year to year. Our curricula are obsolete the moment they are conceived. How do we keep up?

With the availability of the internet, information (and misinformation) of all kinds is accessible to all, and tracking reliable sources and research is becoming an advanced skill. Facts and truth are now matters of debate. The cascade of news and media-produced images preclude our ability to reflect, to ask ourselves, "How does this information touch my lived experience?" Now with AI, the work of gathering and processing information appears to be done for us! We might say that humanity is being coded. In addition, the glut of images from media crowds out the ability to exercise our own imagination. As John Dewey said, "We do not learn from experience but from reflection upon experience." How do we create more opportunities for imagination and reflection?

The former United States Surgeon General noted that there is an "epidemic of loneliness." We have just emerged from a global pandemic. Who could have predicted the emotional tolls this caused for families, schools, and communities? Teachers report a decrease in social skills as a product of isolation. Even if they are not exposed to it directly, children sense the anxiety of adults around them—their concerns about survival and safety, adequate housing, the availability of clean water and healthy foods, environmental degradation, a lack of healthcare, future possibilities for employment, ongoing wars, and polarized politics. How do we as educators sustain our vision of a better world for the children? How do we embrace the reality of these issues and build a community of "active hope" as Joanna Macy puts it?

This book offers suggestions for how to meet this moment through building connections—within the self, within and around the school community, and between lived experience and academic knowledge. It is a memoir, offering one educator's experience with a circle-based pedagogy, providing anecdotes of the joys and challenges of what is being proposed. In doing so, I encourage the reader to bring an attitude of compassion for yourself and your students as you face inevitable resistances and setbacks that arise with this shift of paradigm and perspective. When you suggest that students can listen and speak "from the heart," they will rightly ask, "What world are you living in?" They see no exemplars of such compassion for self and other in their world. This is why all stakeholders in the school community must walk the talk.

As a manifesto in the manner of Paulo Freire's *Pedagogy of the Oppressed*, it offers a radical shift in the relationship of student to teacher and a revisioning of how curriculum is determined, developed, and delivered. It suggests a paradigm that shifts the culture of schools from a vertical axis of authority and dominance to a horizontal axis of collaboration, from a pre-determined, curriculum-based education to one embodying flexibility and relevance to meet the pace of change. It also suggests a worldview, a way of being, and a way of teaching and learning that values each being as essential, unique, and irreplaceable. A circle view honors people and the natural world. Every living thing has a voice worthy of our compassionate listening. In circle, leaders emerge when there is a common need, and, when that need has been met, they return to a coequal place as simply one among many. In circle, knowledge is not commodified; it is shared. We acknowledge circle "ways" because every culture has developed unique circle practices. We honor, rather than appropriate these, noting commonalities that can serve within many traditions and unique circumstances. *A circle-based pedagogy* is one based on connection—to self, others, and the greater good. It respects the unique perspectives and experiences of all participants; engages all learners in the co-creation of meaning; acknowledges the teacher in the student and the student in the teacher; and links academic, relational (social-emotional), and student-directed learning. It aligns process with content and creates relevance by linking both to the experiences and needs of learners. It encourages ownership, responsibility, and agency in the process and application of learning.

As a map, this book gives extensive guidance to readers to initiate and sustain circle-based practices with students, administrators, counselors, and parents/caregivers. Rather than providing a curriculum for the reader to follow by rote, I hope that you will see how to apply circle practice to the existing curriculum within traditional "disciplines"; as a foundation for what is now called social-emotional learning and skills; and how to shape facilitation to serve students' needs in the immediate moment. I hope that the examples and anecdotes given will encourage you to shape your pedagogy to the unique circumstances of your classrooms, including how to apply circles to support deeper understanding of whatever curriculum you are charged with delivering.

This book is also about a return of schools to the village spoken of in the African maxim, a return of the place where the community gathers with a focus on posterity, addressing the challenging pan-cultural, indigenous wisdom: *May all of our decisions be made with awareness of their impact on the children—for seven generations.* It is from the village that we re-learn a lesson we and our ancestors knew so well: *We belong to one another. No one is expendable.*

Chapter 1 begins by placing a circle-based pedagogy in broad pancultural contexts, reminding the reader that every culture has some form of structured dialogic practice. The first chapter also orients the reader to rationale for the uses of circles not only to build *social-emotional competencies* but also for the delivery and processing of content in every *academic* discipline as well for creating a context for students to explore *what is important to them*.

Chapter 2 considers the inner work required of an educator who adopts a circle-based pedagogy. Having been raised in a culture focused on individual achievement, I emphasize the challenges of developing a circle-based worldview and becoming a facilitator of circles. Schools that adopt a circle "program" must begin with the educators experiencing the value of the practice *for themselves*. As exemplars of authentic expression and compassionate listening are few in the lives of students, *educators must live the practice*, exploring the possibilities with each other, so that they are not, once again, asking students to do something that the teachers themselves don't do. I suggest how a reader might approach bringing authenticity and humble authority to circle facilitation.

Chapters 3, **4**, and **5** emphasize the basics of circle facilitation and the art of forming prompts that elicit stories of *lived experience* from participants. **Chapter 6** explores circle forms and modes. There are many forms to adapt practice to large groups, limited time and space, multiple perspectives, and conflict. Modes, based on Gardner's "intelligences," offer various ways to engage students through art, movement, music, meditation, process, and intuition. This addresses the common, inaccurate expectation that circles are just about sitting around talking.

Chapter 7 describes many ways a teacher of any subject can use circles to welcome students, develop class norms, assess prior knowledge, celebrate achievements and special moments, collaborate and persevere, develop study skills, set intentions, create accountability, make course corrections, and meaningfully acknowledge transitions. **Chapter 8**, then, looks at how to apply a circle-based pedagogy in service of content delivery in all the traditional academic disciplines: language arts, social studies, math, and science.

Chapter 9 focuses on what I call "relational arts," including social-emotional learning and skill-building, counseling, and restorative justice. Educators learn to read the "interactive field" of the classroom to discover relational dynamics and turn towards them to strengthen agency and heal from harm. **Chapter 10** explores how we hand facilitation over to the students. Circle practice is a "portable" skill that students can take into every aspect of their lives: personal relationships, business and other collaborative ventures, and creative pursuits.

Chapter 11 addresses what I call "institutional realities," the challenges that will likely come up as we try to bring circle practice to all school stakeholders. The chapter looks at how we might meet pushback; how a horizontal axis of authority (the circle) can flourish within the vertical axis (hierarchy) of an institution; how to manage not having enough time, space, and too many students; how to sustain a program internally without reliance on outside agencies; and how we care for our emotional well-being when we bear witness to the complex and often traumatic inner lives of students.

Chapter 12 brings the reader back to a vision of the culture shift possible when all school stakeholders embrace circle practice. The chapter considers how circle practice addresses issues of underutilization of school premises, community healthcare, co-parenting (or "village" parenting), sustainable human and environmental practices, and deepening the practice to bring engaging relevance to the rapidly changing circumstances that students will confront in an uncertain future. It is a vision of hope informed by recognizing and turning towards the complex realities of our time.

My Journey to the Circle

My journey of return to the circle is a most unlikely story, and that is why I consider circle practice a way of healing and why I am writing this book. For me personally, and from what I absorbed from my culture and environment, being simply *one among many, one among equals* is a sign of failure. It symbolizes a lack of independence, a surrender of autonomy and choice. To be a man, I thought, meant not needing anyone and being entirely self-reliant. To this day, I find it hard to ask for help. Perhaps the thing I long for most is the thing I most resist.

We all turn away from circles at some time in our personal and cultural development. We leave the mother, the community, a home, a path, a workplace, a relationship. We individuate. At some point, the circles feel confining. I can tell only my own story with any degree of authenticity, and mine involves a somewhat enclosed childhood in a mostly Jewish, middle-class neighborhood in Los Angeles.

Several early incidents stand out in my journey toward the circle. I knew very little about people who were not just like me, and my only exposure to diversity came through the TV. As usual in August of 1965 in our house, the TV was on in the living room. What I saw scared me: images of police and military confronting people in the streets of Los Angeles. The people were Black. Pictures flashed of Black people running wild, smashing store windows, looting, and setting fires. At nine years old, all I knew was that this was happening somewhere south of where we lived. The TV images lasted for days. On one of those days, I climbed up on the roof of our apartment with my toy BB gun and aimed it south across Venice Boulevard, prepared to defend my home from invaders. The imprints from those TV images still haunt me.

Although I was unaware of it, I probably heard a call to the circle when I was 12 years old. I distinctly remember thinking that my goal in life was to smile at and have conversations with as many people as I could. I imagined being the kind of person who would listen to the stories of others. I didn't feel such a need to tell my own story, but I did want to find out what other people were interested in, what they loved and what their concerns were. I tried to do this, but deep culturally ingrained fears limited my capacity to do more than smile at strangers, and to condemn those who did not smile back! Perhaps more than a compassionate streak, this was my own desire to be seen.

In contrast to my fantasy, fear of *the other*, particularly the Black other, was seared into me. My school experience continued to be relatively segregated in West Los Angeles. In 1968, when I was 13, along with nightly images of soldiers fighting another *other* in Vietnam, I became aware of the presidential campaign of Robert F. Kennedy. I had seen pictures of him with Dr. Martin Luther King. Images of him seemed to convey a compassionate, concerned listener. Here was a man, it seemed, who embraced all people, and at the time I was not aware of any such leaders. And he was running for president!

This, I believe, gave me a surge of hope and optimism, so much so that on a school night I stayed up late into the early morning hours of June 5, 1968, to watch the results of the California presidential primary. When Kennedy took the stage in the ballroom of the Ambassador Hotel, after making a joke about his dog Freckles and thanking his wife Ethel, he acknowledged "the Black community" for helping him win the primary. This was a moment full of possibility, holding the promise of a better world with people of all races and nations working together for peace.

It was a scene quite unfamiliar to me. The moment and the feeling were short-lived. There was a commotion and then the news that Kennedy had been shot.

I count that moment as the beginning for me of a turning away from the circle inherent in that vision of peace, a circle where I felt engaged and included, one where the seeds of awareness of others and compassion could grow. I was turning towards a more selfish view. Nothing could be done for the world, so I had to focus on my own pleasure and my own small circle of peers.

In 1970, when I started at Alexander Hamilton High School, students had just begun to be bused to the campus. Although these were the "hippie" years, and "rap groups" were a thing, there was no protocol instituted to help students get to know one another. Suddenly, there were Black students in our classes, but there was *no opportunity* for us to hear each other's stories. South LA was still another and completely alien world to us.

Another experience that I consider formative occurred over a two-year period in 1978–79 when as a part of my teacher training program at CSU Northridge, I was a volunteer writing tutor at Camp David Gonzales, a maximum-security boys detention facility in Malibu Canyon. Most of the young men there were Black or Brown.

One night stands out. Another student and I were working in "Zuma," the solitary confinement wing. These 16–17-year-old boys had a choice: either stay in their cells alone or come to see us! We had designed what we thought was an engaging lesson. I would pretend to be from (Vonnegut's) planet Tralfamadore. Knowing nothing about life on Earth, I needed advice from its inhabitants because my planet was in chaos. We were to design an ideal community, a model for reform. It would have all the elements for safe, creative, and fulfilling lives.

On a large sheet of paper, we started to draw a map and to brainstorm what should be included in the community: housing, schools, businesses. When we suggested that there should be *a park*, there was unanimous disagreement over the idea. I was baffled. The boys explained that the park would only become turf for gang wars. Such public, open spaces would bring about violence, they told us, and the community would be better off without them.

This led to the boys revealing that they were all involved in gangs. They informed us that although they were cool with each other in the camp, those from rival gangs would have to kill each other if they met up on the outside. One young man said, "Like this guy right here," pointing to another young man sitting on the other side of the table, "if I saw him outside, I'd blow him away, and I know he would try to do the same to me." I could not comprehend or believe what I was hearing and at the time wrote it off as a boast. I came to find out that this was not just bravado. Over my two years at Gonzales, several recently paroled students I had worked with turned up dead only days or weeks after their release.

It was not until I began teaching at two remarkably diverse schools, Thomas Starr King Junior High in 1983 and Palms Junior High, my alma mater, in 1990, that I really met students not only of different racial, ethnic, and cultural backgrounds, but also from across the globe. At King, my beginning ESL classes were filled with children whose families had fled war or strife in El Salvador, Guatemala, Mexico, Nicaragua, Cambodia, Laos, Iran, Pakistan, and Afghanistan. My job was not only to teach them English but also to shape a respectful, cooperative classroom. As I began to hear their stories through pictures and their emerging English, my world broadened, and I believe my heart opened. It was in this context in 1989 that I first offered the circle, talking piece and all, in my classroom.

The Ojai Foundation, Robert Bly, and Mythopoetic Men's Groups

In late October of 1985, I attended a weekend gathering for men with poet Robert Bly and mythologist-storyteller Michael Meade on the land at The Ojai Foundation retreat center a couple hours north of LA. It was still a personal, intellectual interest that motivated me. Bly's poetry was the subject of the master's thesis I had just begun, so, I told myself, this was about gathering information for that purpose. I was not interested in hanging out with a bunch of men. In fact, at the time the thought of doing so was quite off-putting. I did not talk about matters of the heart with other men.

I soon found myself in the Dharma Yurt, a large round structure nestled amid the oaks and sage, with about 100 men. In that room I heard something I had never had before. It was *more the tone than the actual content*—men speaking, as we say, *from the heart*. Men speaking of love, loss, and longing, of absent fathers, missed opportunities, and dreams deferred, men weeping, consoling one another, and acknowledging the soft places in themselves without this revelation diminishing their strength and wild delight. And there was in that place, for me, a yet unfamiliar and extraordinary quality of listening. As men told their stories, the silence of the listeners was embracing and encouraging. Men not only did not interrupt one another: there were silences *after* each speaker as his words were felt and considered. This quality of listening awakened in me a longing for something I had only experienced in the company of women.

While I felt the need for deeper connection, I still felt uneasy about this kind of intimacy. I returned for a men's gathering with Bly in 1986. I had heard that men from these gatherings were forming local groups to continue what Bly called "mythopoetic" work. Bly and Meade used myths, fairy tales, and poetry to help men make connections between these expressions and their own *lived experience*. After this gathering, when a friend told me about a local men's group, not associated with Bly's events, I steeled myself and went. When I entered the location, I found credit card machines ready for the initiates to sign up. Then came a high-pressure sales pitch for facilitated how-to-become-a-man trainings! That sealed it for me. I was convinced that there was always a catch to these groups. My return to the circle was again thwarted.

I did, however, return to The Ojai Foundation in late October 1988. At the conclusion of this workshop, Bly asked if any of us would like to form local groups. Despite my long-standing reservations, I raised my hand and found myself connected with eleven other men who lived close to me in Los Angeles. We committed to meet every other week in a "leaderless" group to explore mythology, poetry, dreams, and topics of interest and concern to us as men.

We learned about the use a "talking piece" from members of *The Lost Dogs Men's Council,* the group that had sponsored the event with Bly in Ojai. One member of the Lost Dogs, Wayne Liebman, later published *Tending the Fire: The Ritual Men's Group* (*1991*), which contains circle practices that influenced how we would conduct our meetings. Our biweekly meetings consisted of three parts: an "outer" check-in, an "inner" check-in, and a topic of meaning to the group "leader" for the night. The "outer" check-in was a time to share details about work, relationships, local and world events that might be affecting us. This was usually done without a talking piece and in no prescribed order. After a ceremonial move to another space, the "inner" check-in involved an opportunity for each of us to reflect on the stirrings of our hearts, to speak of these or to access them silently. For this we used a talking piece. During the third phase of the meeting, the evening's leader would bring us something that for him was charged with meaning—a myth, a poem, a fairy or folk tale, a question, a dream, or a dilemma. We each in turn, with the use of the talking piece, spoke of what was alive for us in these archetypal renderings, where we "entered" the poem, myth or dream, what touched the truth of our direct experience. I speak of my "journey" to the circle, because nothing in my experience had prepared me for the kind of honesty, empathy, and brotherhood I felt in those gatherings and in that group.

Poetry Council

My training as a teacher in the early 1980s focused on benevolent control—having the students *think* that they were making the discoveries I had carefully placed in their path. In those days, before the current prescribed scripting of lessons, we prepared plans using a "t-sheet." The left column was "what the teacher does" and the right was "what the students will do." Teacher questions and directions were on the left and *acceptable* student responses and actions were on the right. My training supervisor at that time, Dr. Helen Lodge, to whom I am deeply indebted for instilling in me the rigor, craft, and seriousness of teaching, even had me note what she called "heavy cuing" in the left column of the plan—what I would say and do if students failed to give those predetermined responses. I later discovered that I was being acculturated in what Paulo Freire called "the banking model" of education.

In May of 1990, in my one "honors" ninth-grade English class at Thomas Starr King Junior High, I announced that now that state testing was finished, I had "saved the best for last." We were going to focus our last unit on poetry! My excited offering inspired a chorus of groans. I was crestfallen. This was the reaction of my students to *poetry*, the highest aesthetic expression of language! What was it about this form of expression that my students found so off-putting?

I determined that it must have been something about the way poetry had been presented to them in school. I thought about the unit I was about to present, the preconceived insights I would lead the students to "discover," including the "heavy cuing" I would employ if they stumbled on their journey to those insights. I believed that by teaching about poetic form and figurative language, I would give my students the keys to unlock the mysteries of meaning.

Realizing that the way I was about to *teach* is exactly the reason for my students' revulsion, I dropped my carefully crafted lesson plans for the unit and decided instead to see if we could find a way to *enjoy* poetry. My experience with the men's group pointed a way.

The next day I took the class to the library. Every book of or about poetry was arranged on tables. My instruction to my students was simple: "Find something that speaks to you." It might be just a word, a phrase, or an image that draws your attention. If they couldn't find something in the library, they might think about the lyrics from a favorite song. To earn extra credit all students had to do was memorize a poem or lyric and present it to the class *as a gift*. That is, they should feel that the words would in some way be meaningful to others in the class. This gift, I told them would be presented in a "poetry council."

I crafted a talking piece for the occasion: a piece of driftwood from a local beach that I decorated with colorful stones collected in my travels. I took the class outdoors to a grass area where we sat in a circle. The protocol for the circle was this: holding the talking piece, one student would recite the poem *twice*; listeners took the words in, not trying to analyze or understand, just listening. Once students heard the poem twice through, the speaker passed the talking piece to the left. There was no requirement to speak. Students could "pass" (with a bit of encouragement to check in internally long enough to see if they had anything to say). They were instructed to simply listen for words, phrases, or images, or passages that sparked some interest for them. And they were explicitly told *not* to try to remember the whole poem or to determine what it meant. Then, we had a "speed round," where students simply said the word, phrase, or image that stayed with them. Next, we conducted a "story round." Students were encouraged to recall a *personal experience* that *in some way* (even tangentially) connected to the word, phrase, or image they remembered from the poem. If there was a mountain in the poem, a student might, upon receiving the talking piece, tell of an experience in the mountains; if there was mention of a father, a student might offer a story that comes to mind about their father. After a round of such stories, the speaker would recite the poem a third time.

Our first volunteer, a young woman whose choice perhaps was influenced by familiarity from a previous English class, offered Robert Frost's "The Road Not Taken." After hearing the poem twice, the speaker passed the talking piece and students first shared recalled words, phrases or images, and then, in the second round, they told their stories. There were stories of family camping and road trips, playing in grassy fields, getting lost in the woods, even an early memory of getting lost in a supermarket. There were stories of choices and decisions and stories of regret.

When the talking piece came around the circle and back to her, the young woman recited the poem *a third time*. What I witnessed next changed my life as an educator.

As she spoke, I saw students in the circle lean in. They were listening, I thought, with new ears. They were *receiving* the poem in a new way. They were listening not only for the words that prompted their stories the first time around but also for the words that elicited stories from their classmates. They were actively engaged in creating relevance, seeing where the poem touched the lived experience of their peers, and in gaining a deeper understanding of the whole poem through collaborative awareness. The poem was no longer a specimen to be dissected. It was alive, evolving, current, and meaningful. The "poetry council" became a regular end-of-year activity in my English classes.

Palms Middle School

In 1990, as we were expecting our first child, I moved closer to home and accepted a position at Palms Middle School, where I had been a student at from 1968–1970. Several of my teachers were still on the faculty!

At the end of my first year, I took each of my seventh-grade classes out to the grassy quad area in the middle of the school. We sat in a circle and conducted poetry councils. During one such session, the assistant principal, Lana Brody, came up behind me and tapped me on the shoulder. "Please see me in my office after school," she said and walked away toward the administrative building. I thought, "Uh oh! Busted." Had I failed to comply with a permission protocol to conduct class on the quad? Were we the target of a noise complaint? Was it something about the circle? Something about "Native American" spiritual practice in a public school?

I entered her office with these paranoid concerns swirling. When she saw me, she asked, "Were you doing a *council*?" Yes, as a matter of fact, I was. She asked, "Do you know Jack Zimmerman and Paul Cummins?" I said that I knew of them ... Jack as a director at The Ojai Foundation and Paul as the founder of Crossroads School in Santa Monica—but I had not met them. Then she said, "I sit *in a council* every month with Jack and Paul and other private and public-school administrators." She explained that they had established a group called New Visions for Educators to provide a place for administrators to "speak the truth about what was going on in their schools." They, too, used the protocol of the talking piece to allow for more considered expression and more attentive listening. I was completely knocked out by this striking alignment of fates (and the degree to which I allowed myself to misjudge her simple request to meet in her office).

Two years later, this meaningful coincidence came back into focus. On May 1, 1992, as we were celebrating my son Aaron's first birthday, we could smell the smoke from the uprisings in Los Angeles that came with the news of acquittals of police officers charged in the beating of Rodney King, a Black motorist, an incident videotaped and widely viewed. News of the acquittal of a Korean shop owner in the shooting of 15-year-old Latasha Harlans was also still fresh. These events pervaded the atmosphere at Palms the next day. Students clumped in racially defined groups and moved around campus anticipating and preparing for trouble. There was a palpable fracturing of the usual calm of this highly socio-economically and culturally diverse Los Angeles Unified School District campus.

When Lana arrived at the next New Visions council, she spoke of her deep concern over this fracturing and the powerlessness of the system to address it, other than through the usual means of punishing students responsible for reactive violence or misconduct on campus. Her tone was uncharacteristic for the woman Palms faculty lovingly referred to as "Poly-Lana." At that meeting Jack and Paul determined to try the first public-school experiment with the council practice that had become the cornerstone of Crossroads' human development program called "Mysteries." After a series of meetings with staff and parents—and Lana's declaration "This will happen!"—the Palms Council Project launched.

At its peak in the years 1997–2005, every student, over 2,000 at that time, experienced a weekly hour-long circle with time allotted from Social Studies or Language Arts classes. There were literally 100 circles occurring every week. With no set curriculum for these sessions, teachers and facilitators were free to integrate circle practice with the content and instructional goals of their classes; to use the time to facilitate bonding, sharing, self-reflection, respect, intention setting, as well as accountability and "restorative" practices when relational norms were broken. Often, the sessions would include play, movement, music, art making, and mindfulness. This variety of applications in an educational setting produced rich monthly "curriculum shares" among staff. There were weekly lunchtime drop-in circles for all staff, monthly staff and parent circles, and community circles involving all school stakeholders—neighbors, local businesspeople, and service providers, including local police. The children themselves regularly led these as they were becoming experts in facilitation and in modeling what it means to listen and speak "from the heart."

By the time of the Columbine school shooting tragedy, Palms had become a go-to site when the press wanted to know about proactive violence prevention efforts in the Los Angeles Unified School District (LAUSD), although we were only one of one thousand schools in the District.

Two other Palms Council Project components should be noted here and will be more fully discussed in later chapters. Students in our special education and special day classes were regularly "mainstreamed" for circles. That is, students who would normally all be together with one teacher for most of the instructional day were integrated into "regular" classes for the hour. This brought deeper awareness to the school community that everyone, no matter what their personal or educational challenges, has a story to tell. You do not have to be a member of the academic decathlon team or even to be a "successful" student to participate in a circle.

Another critical factor that gave great vitality to the program involved the inclusion of "community participants" in the classroom councils. The vision was to return local elders to the school community, to invite adults living close to the school to become "listening presences" in the youth councils. We wanted the children to know that if they were going to have the courage to bring their truths to the circle, the *community* would be listening.

LAUSD/CPC/Circle Ways

After 14 years of successful implementation at Palms, in the spring of 2006, The Herb Alpert Foundation provided The Ojai Foundation with a three-year grant, authored by Jack Zimmerman, to establish an office in the school district's headquarters to spread the practice to the LAUSD's nearly 1,000 schools.

For eight years, 2006–2014, the Council Practitioners Center was housed in LAUSD's Office of Curriculum, Instruction, and School Support (OCISS). My longtime partner in the Palms project, Monica Chinlund, and I staffed the office. We were grateful to have a circle of 15 council "mentors" who worked as independent contractors to bring training and mentoring into the schools. Together we developed a "mentor model," which paired experienced circle facilitators with classroom teachers, counselors, and administrators.

After I retired from the District in 2016, Marc Rosner, who devoted himself to circle practice after having experienced it as a parent in one of our schools, and I established Circle Ways to carry on the work independently of both the school district and The Ojai Foundation.

Circles, of course, belong to no one and to everyone. There are many other organizations that provide training in the use of circles in schools. I like to think that the success and spread of circles in the schools is coming about now because there is another cultural paradigm shift in operation, brought about by a growing consciousness of our interdependence, with each other and with the natural world. It is perhaps a shift brought about by knowing that the survival of our species requires that we remember that *we belong to one another*. No one is expendable. No one can be exiled or expelled from this classroom we call Earth. We will learn to collaborate, or we will perish. The circle is where we begin and where we must return.

My hope is that you will hear this invitation to return to the circle, and that you will have the courage to rearrange the furniture in your classroom, your meeting spaces, and your common areas from time to time. See what happens! The story I tell myself is that I am writing this book because *circle practice is my medicine*. The disease is the illusion of separateness. I am still in recovery. My journey to the circle continues. Old habits are hard to break.

1

INVITATIONS TO THE CIRCLE: HISTORY AND RATIONALE

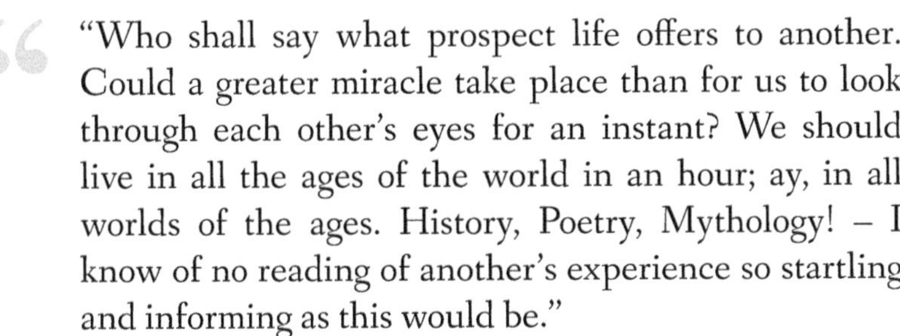

> "Who shall say what prospect life offers to another. Could a greater miracle take place than for us to look through each other's eyes for an instant? We should live in all the ages of the world in an hour; ay, in all worlds of the ages. History, Poetry, Mythology! – I know of no reading of another's experience so startling and informing as this would be."
>
> —Henry David Thoreau, "Economy," *Walden*

A Brief Amnesia

THIS BOOK IS an invitation to bring circles first into your own life and then perhaps to extend the invitation to others and to your students. For many of you, this will be an invitation to a place with which you are already deeply familiar, as there is really nothing new in this old way. Personally, I believe that our familiarity with circle technology is a matter of recovering from a mild case of brief amnesia, say about 200–300 years. Our ancestors gathered around the central fire. For most of human history we learned in circles. Your DNA already knows how to be in circles!

What is Circle?

I define "circle" as anything we do with a heightened awareness of self and other (people and elements of the natural world). By this definition you can have a circle with yourself as in meditation or other forms of self-inquiry. A circle can be just two individuals who commit to listen deeply to self and other. And a circle can include the whole community. In circle, we turn towards each other and issues of interest, concern, or celebration. In addition, we note that circle is a worldview gifted to us from people who lived close to the earth and close to each other. In that worldview, everyone is precious and essential; no one is expendable. When harm or transgressions of norms occur, there must be healing (restoration or transformation).

What is a "Circle-Based" Pedagogy?

A circle-based pedagogy is a view of education based on connection—to self, others, and the greater good. A circle-based pedagogy respects the unique perspectives and experiences of all participants; engages all learners in the co-creation of meaning; acknowledges the teacher in the student and the student in the teacher; and links academic, relational (social-emotional), and student-directed learning. It aligns process with content and creates relevance by linking both to the experiences and needs of learners. It encourages ownership, responsibility, and agency in the process and application of learning.

In this chapter, I want to invite you to remember and to imagine. I want to remind you of the universality of circle practices in all cultures and show you that these practices are very much alive in our *modern* world—in education, business, science, social science, psychology, spirituality, government, and the arts. I want to invite you to re-imagine the school as a nexus, a hearth; a place for body, mind, heart, and spirit; a *new commons*, a place where all generations gather—to celebrate, to learn, to mark transitions, to dream, to plan, and to act. I invite you to consider circles as a practice of community building, of creating what my friend Hector Aristizabal calls "a sudden village." Finally, I invite you to imagine how peace, creative engagement, and prosperity rest on this practice of connection, where our differences are not just tolerated but celebrated. As educators, our stock in trade is *a vision of a better world for our students*. If we lose that vision the youth will not want to learn from or with us.

Worldwide Dialogical Practices

Circle practices are ubiquitous and pancultural. Every culture has some form of structured dialogue practice. The term "council"—from the Latin to "summon together," and originally applied in English to ecclesiastical assemblies—is the term used in North America by Benjamin Franklin to designate what he witnessed in meetings of the Haudenoshaunee (Iroquois).[1]

The basic forms and elements of circles are found worldwide in what are called "cultural dialogic practices." Each culture, it seems, has discovered the need for certain formalities in public discourse on issues of meaning and importance. Although circle practices are often associated with Native American spirituality, governance, and deliberation, talking and listening practices are rooted worldwide—in both sacred and secular traditions. Every culture has taken up the question of what agreements and structures are needed to have meaningful meetings. Out of this inquiry *every culture has developed some form of circle practice.*

A few examples of cultural dialogic practices include the *Kikundi* in Kenya, *Daré* in Zimbabwe; *Legotla* in Botswana; the *Imbizo* among the Zulu; the *Indaba* of South Africa; *Wayamou* among the Yanomami of Southern Venezuela and Northern Brazil; *Dadirri* for Australian Aboriginals; *Omnichye* among the Lakota; *Match-comaco* among the Haudenosaunee; *Loya Jurga* in Pakistan and Afghanistan; the Arabic *Sulha* and *Dawaniya*; the *Panchayat* in India; *Recuerdos* in Latin America; the old Germanic practice of *Ting* or *Ding*; the Russian *Sovet*; *Veche* in old Slavic countries; the *Farbrengen* (story telling gathering) in Yiddish-speaking Eastern Europe; and the practice of *Ho'oponopono* among indigenous Hawaiian peoples.

Many religions also employ circle practices, among them the Islamic *Sobhet*, "sincere and egalitarian talking practice;"[2] the Hindu *Satsang*; Jewish *Havurah, Hevreh,* and *Avruta* (deep dyadic listening and speaking); Christian *Listening Circles*; and Quaker *Friends Meetings* where participants listen in silence, sometimes for the entire duration, until someone hears "the call" and speaks. One of the spiritual practices of St. Ignatius of Loyola is called "desolation and consolation," where on a daily basis family members share what has been challenging and what has given them strength.

Structured circle practices are also present in contemporary decision-making processes, organizational and business contexts, and certainly, in education. Circle processes must stretch back to the beginning of human history.

I mention these references to dispel the notion that circles are something strange and new, an appropriation of Native American or other spiritual practices, or a form of psychotherapy practiced without a license. Circles are indeed "spiritual" in that they are practices that connect.

Circles are in the lineage of indigenous, earth-based practices. They are "therapeutic" in the original sense of that word, as "care for the soul." Zimmerman and Coyle say, "Our aim has always been to practice a form of council that honors the spirit of ancient ceremonies without the pretense of being traditional. We believe that the many forms of council belong to all people who gather in the circle to embrace the challenge of listening and speaking from the heart."[3]

Circles and Literacy: Reading, Writing, Speaking, and Listening

Listening and speaking comprise 50 percent of the standards for language arts instruction. The other 50 percent are standards for reading and writing. In my 30-plus years as a language arts instructor, I have yet to see the standards scaffold the development of listening and speaking skills. The standards do indicate tasks that are to be completed such as, "Listen to a story and then recall the major events in the plot," but there is no indication of *how* we are to teach such listening or how we are to *motivate* the desire to do so. The same is true with the speaking standards. Students are required to "Tell a story with a beginning, middle, and end," or to "orally summarize the content of research findings using several secondary sources," or to "give an oral report, modulating tone to fit a particular audience," but there is no indication of *how* to do these things, let alone inspire students to *want* to speak.

We all know that the most successful students come from what is called a "language-rich environment." Students do well when they have caregivers who talk to them and ask them to speak of their experiences and feelings. Students do well when they see others, particularly in the home, engaging in give-and-take conversation where various perspectives are invited and honored, and when they see others reading for pleasure. In fact, reading for pleasure ranks highest as an indicator of academic success. We know, however, that many of our students do *not* come from such an environment, and there is a necessity to recreate it in the classroom.

We as teachers can provide direct reading instruction. We can teach phonetics, word recognition, decoding, vocabulary, literary devices, and even the more complex skills of logic, semantics, and deep textual analysis. Likewise, we can assist students to develop as writers. We can teach sentence structure and transformation, the writing process, rhetorical forms, and ways to develop syntactic fluency and style. But how do we create the conditions wherein students will *want* to read and *want* to communicate in writing? To do this we must address listening and speaking skills. Reading *is* listening, and writing *is* speaking. When we learn to listen, we learn to *receive* information. When we learn to express ourselves either by speaking to others or through inner dialogue and reflection, we learn the basis of communicating through writing.

Expressing and receiving, speaking and listening, are *social* constructs, and as such they can only be developed *in the presence of others*—others who are listening to what we say and who are speaking in a way that will evoke our desire to listen. This is the domain of circles. In circles, we are encouraged to "speak from the heart," to tell our stories, our lived experience. When people do speak in this way, we tend to listen more deeply.

When someone lectures us, gives opinions unsupported by personal experience, attempts to manipulate, lie, or condescend, we rightly tend to shut down our listening. Likewise, when we speak or write into critical or judgmental listening, our tendency is to stop attempting to communicate. We all have known students who have stopped raising their hands to answer questions when they fear our judgment or the judgment of peers.

In circles, we learn that each of us has a story to tell. I have had middle-school students tell me, "I don't have any stories. Stories are only in books or in the movies." To acknowledge that we are all *carriers of story,* we first must feel our own agency to be observers of our own experience, and furthermore, we must feel that our story matters. When students are encouraged to tell their stories in circles, with others "listening from the heart," they are empowered as active agents in the world, and they *want* to tell their stories. As Maya Angelou says, "There is no agony like an untold story inside you." Furthermore, when you are sitting in circles and you hear these stories of the heart, you *want* to listen.

To truly *understand* what we read, we must listen from the heart, suspending judgment long enough to receive the writer's message. Once we do this, we can bring all our critical faculties to bear on the information, but if we can't suspend those faculties temporarily, we will never be able to understand what we read. How can I, a white, middle-class male living in Southern California in 2026, understand the experience of Maya Angelou, conveyed in *I Know Why the Caged Bird Sings*, about being a Black woman growing up in Stamps, Arkansas, in 1944? I can only understand, I submit, by listening from the heart as I read. This same quality of listening for understanding, reading for understanding, is true of material that is not only foreign to my experience and cultural referents but also material toward which I harbor deep disagreement. Nonetheless, if I am to bring a critical eye to my reading, I must first understand what I'm reading.

Listening from the heart does not mean that we agree but that we are *willing to receive* the information fully before we respond. To paraphrase Thoreau's quote in the epigraph to this chapter, there is nothing more powerful and informing as the experience of deep presence with another, of looking through another's eyes. We begin with a recognition that we have a story to tell and with the discovery of the beauty and enrichment that comes from listening to the stories of others.

From Experience to Knowledge: The Spiral of Circle Learning

The Spiral of Circle Learning. Artwork by Hannah Michelle Provisor.

Let's consider the place of circles in *academic* learning. All learning begins with *experience.* Our first task as educators is to provide a wide range of relevant experiences. Taking students to the forest is more impactful than showing them a picture of the forest. A trip to the museum will make a deeper impression than looking at the same art online.

After experiences, we must create time for *reflection*—opportunities to recall and consider what occurred during an experience. In the internet age, it is so easy to access vast troves of information on every conceivable topic. The problem is that we tend to flit from topic to topic, source to source, site to site, without taking the time to reflect on that information. The result is that we accumulate a great deal of information but very little deep understanding or wisdom. As a writing teacher, I can provide opportunities for reflection by assigning a paper that will demonstrate what students have acquired from a text or experience. This is an opportunity for *private* reflection. Simply asking a question and then pausing before taking answers is an opportunity for private reflection. When, however, such reflection is *only* shared in writing with the teacher, the learner can remain within the echo chamber of their own perception. Even in classroom discussions we often only hear the reflections of a few, usually those who are quick to raise hands to respond, often with little consideration, and we rarely hear the reflections of *all* students in the class.

When we allow students to narrate their experiences in the compassionate listening of a circle, we multiply the opportunity for reflection on a particular topic, calling in *multiple perspectives* that give each listener a chance to compare their perceptions with those of others. Even a brief circle after an experience provides for deeper reflection. For example, after a museum visit, we might offer the prompt: *Say one thing you remember from what you observed today in the museum.* As students recall, one by one, what they noticed, the entire group has an opportunity to walk through the museum again in memory. Teachers don't often ask *simple* recall questions, but such questions provoke reflection, and they also create the foundation for higher-level thinking.

Even more importantly, as educators we must help students *to value the truth of their own experience.* Students must learn to trust their perception and intuition. *They must believe that they have a story to tell, and that story is as valid as any found in books or movies.* The capacity to *narrate* their stories is one of the core curricular skills in language arts standards. When students in a circle each narrate their experiences fully and confidently, *everyone learns*. Furthermore, the information shared in personal stories is *primary data* for research. Primary data comes from direct observation, interviews, and letters.

Active listening is mostly what we do in circles. When we cross the threshold to being in circle, we are committing to deeper, more compassionate listening, suspending judgments. Often in a circle, before we close, we ask for a *witnessing round.* This can be a simple echo of a word, phrase, or image heard in the sharing of someone else in the circle. Later in this book, we will discuss deeper forms of *witnessing*, but even this simple recall of something another person said in the circle exercises what I like to call the *paraphrase muscle.* Such sharing gives the students and the facilitator a sense of what made an impression, what was most resonant in the stories told.

Providing students with an opportunity to recall what they heard deepens their capacity to listen (as they know a witnessing round is coming) and to exercise the valuable academic skill of summarizing what they have taken in, whether from a story, lecture, book, or any other source of information.

After we close the circle and return to our usual modes of classroom discourse, there is an opportunity for *harvesting*. The usual harvesting prompt is something like: *Given the stories we just heard, what can we say about* (the topic). For example, if we have been exploring experiences of "love," sharing stories of times we felt this thing we call "love," either for someone or something, or when we felt it coming towards us from another being, the harvesting prompt could be: *Given the stories we just heard about love, what can we say about it?* This elicits generalizations based on the personal experiences shared in the circle. In academic terms, we might consider these generalizations to be *hypotheses* or *thesis statements*. The *primary data* of the stories told serve as support examples.

Upon the foundation of the lived experience of the students, the teacher can *extend* the learning by offering *secondary sources*, say in this case with a Shakespeare sonnet. This, of course, is the same method Paulo Freire used to support indigenous peoples in Brazil to learn to read and write. First, they told their stories. Then, to bring in additional perspectives, they were motivated to learn to read, to know the stories of others outside of their circle. Extended learning leads to new experience, and the spiral begins again.

Circles create a foundation of *relevance* that stimulates curiosity and receptivity for additional resources outside the immediacy of the circle. Usual classroom practice reverses this process. The text is offered first, and then students are asked to find its meaning or relevance.

The referents for that meaning rely on each student's individual experience. With the addition of a circle in the learning process, and the *primary sources, the lived experience, the stories* elicited there, students are afforded a much broader range of perspectives, which allows them to reflect on their own experience and views more fully, and to expand their understanding of whatever the topic may be.

The combination of primary and secondary sources leads to the possibility of meaningful exposition. Now students can connect their own tangible experience and that of others with the research and reflections outside the classroom community through both informational and literary texts and other media. The result, if all goes well, might just be what we call knowledge, understanding, and ultimately wisdom.

Social-Emotional Learning and Resilience

Imagine two students, both coming from conditions of economic and relational poverty, multiplied by the trauma of loss, violence, and inadequate educational experiences. One succeeds and one does not. Research shows that the single most significant factor contributing to the capacity of one to overcome these adverse childhood experiences is *a relationship with one adult who sees the best and expects the best from that child.*[4]

I suspect that if you are reading this book, you have been that caring adult for many children. The challenges, of course, are number and time. If you are an elementary school teacher, you have 30 or so students in your class; in middle and high school the number jumps to 150 plus, and if you are a school counselor your caseload is often more than 600. How can we possibly give this quality of attention to each child in our care? And where would we find the time?

While there is a certain insanity to a model of education that puts one adult teacher in a roomful of children—and one counselor in charge of an entire auditorium—you might find an ally in circles.

When we learn to listen and speak from the heart in a circle, what Zimmerman and Coyle call "a third presence," or the "wisdom of the circle," manifests. When the children feel safe with you and with each other, it is as if another, bigger, wiser adult is also present. In circles, the circle itself becomes an adult presence, the collective consciousness of the group. The role of the facilitator/teacher is critical in bringing this about, as they must model the values and qualities of circles and well as create safety through structure. The circle can itself become a caring presence that sees and expects the best of each participant. In this way, accountability is always to a circle. I can have "high expectations" of my students, and research has shown that doing so contributes significantly to their development.

What happens, though, when the children hold high expectations of one another? As you will see in the chapter on what students want to know and student-led circles, when intentions and goals are set in the context of a caring circle, chances for *adherence*, following through on them, are exponentially higher.

In addition, if we think about the variety of creative ways students seek our attention, the so-called "attention-getting behaviors," we begin to understand such behaviors as demonstrating a basic need to be seen. To see, to know and trust our perceptions, and to be seen by others are primary needs that fill our moment-to-moment experience once our physiological needs for nourishment and warmth are met. I like to think of circles as providing a kind of *inoculation of attention*, and the beauty of it is that the whole group provides this medicine, not just you!

As Dr. Gabor Maté says, with reference to the explosion of cases of attention-deficit disorder, drug-addiction, and violence in our society, "What the problem reflects is the loss of the community and the neighborhood. We must recreate that. So, the schools must become not just places of pedagogy, but places of emotional connection. The teachers should be in the emotional connection game before they attempt to be in the pedagogy game."[5]

For Reflection and Imagination

1. Choose a concept you teach and map it onto the "spiral of circle learning" (p. 25).

- What foundational *experiences and activities* do you offer students at the start?
- When and how do you invite private student reflection?

- How do you create space for students to "witness" the perspectives of others?
- What new experiences and resources help extend and deepen their understanding?

2. Reflect on your own experiences of "circle."

   - In what circumstances have you been able to speak from the heart into compassionate listening?
   - And where and with whom have you provided that listening to others?

3. Reflect on a situation where you wished this kind of authentic speaking and compassionate listening could have occurred.

4. Imagine the lights go out and the internet goes down. You are sitting with a group of friends or people from your neighborhood.

   - What do you see yourself doing, and if you find yourselves in a circle, what topic might you be discussing?

5. Imagine your ancestors of 300 years ago sitting around the fire.

   - What do you imagine they were discussing?
   - What kinds of stories were they telling?

Chapter 1:
Invitations to the Circle: History and Rationale

1 **Remember our Roots**

Circle practice is not new: it's a return to ancient, global ways of learning through presence, storytelling, shared reflection, durable decision-making, and meaningful, accountable action.

2 **Define Circle Broadly**

A circle begins with heightened awareness. Whether with oneself a group, or the natural world, it centers connection, equality, and collective meaning-making.

3 **Adopt a Circle-Based Pedagogy**

Design learning around relationships: align process with content, honor each voice, and connect academics to lived experience.

4 **Build Literacy Through Listening**

Listening and speaking are foundational to reading and writing. Use circle to cultivate the desire and skills to express and receive meaning.

5 **Move from Experience to Knowledge**

Start with lived stories (primary data), then scaffold academic learning with texts and secondary sources. Circle anchors reflection and relevance.

6 **Support SEL and Resilience**

Circle creates belonging, recognition, and emotional safety: key for student growth, especially in trauma-informed education.

7 **Let the Circle Hold the Expectations**

When the group sets intentions and expectations together, accountability and motivation increase. The circle itself becomes a caring adult presence.

2

REARRANGING THE FURNITURE

"If we change the chairs, we can change the world. How we set the chairs sets our expectations about who speaks and who listens—whose voice carries weight or whose voice is missing. The arrangement of chairs can determine what kind of society we live in—whether leaders stand in front or are imbedded in the rim where shared purpose is held and collaboration can emerge."

—Christina Baldwin and Ann Linnea, *The Circle Way: A Leader in Every Chair*

Triangle Culture, Circle Culture

THIS BOOK BOILS down to one recommendation: rearrange the furniture and see what happens. In her book *Calling the Circle,* Christina Baldwin suggests that circles belong to the earliest, or "first" cultures, that it is a natural form for gathering and sharing information. The "second" cultures emphasize a triangle or hierarchical structure, with a teacher standing in front of rows of students. The "third" culture, she suggests, will bring a reintegration of the circle into a culture that relies most predominantly on the triangle model.[1] Former Palms Parent and longtime collaborator, Ray Tucker and I played with this idea when we were asked to introduce council to 50 boys at an in-school "retreat" for the Wildwood private school in Los Angeles. We found ourselves on a stage in front of the group who were sitting in rows on the carpet below us.

"Pretty cool, Ray, standing up here, looking down on these guys. What should we do?"

"I don't know, Joe, maybe a little tap dance, tell a few jokes."

"Let's ask these guys. So, when you see us standing up here, what do you think is going to happen? What do you expect from us?"

"You're gonna teach us something," replied one student.

"We expect that you know something, and you are going to explain it to us."

Ray turned to me and said, "Yeah, we *do* know a lot, don't we, Joe? We must have about a hundred years of knowledge up here on this stage. A few college degrees, fathers raising families, lots of life experience. Seems appropriate, us *up here* and those guys *down there.*"

"Darn right, Ray. We worked hard to get here. And what do you expect of yourselves?" I prompted, "as we provide you with all of this valuable information?"

"We are going to listen."

"We're supposed to pay attention."

"We're supposed to learn something."

"Right," I acknowledge, "and it's going to be ... "

"BORING!" offered one courageous soul.

We came down off the stage and asked the boys to form three concentric circles. Without any explanation, we set up a center with a bell and a few talking pieces. Once we had all settled into our places, I asked, "Where's the teacher?"

The students looked around. Three Wildwood teachers raised their hands. One student said, "You are the teachers."

"That's right," Ray acknowledged. "We are the teachers because we are older, smarter, bigger, better looking."

"We are the teachers!" shouted one of the students, perhaps the same "coyote" who said it was all going to be "boring."

"What do you mean, *you* are the teachers?"

"When we are in the circle, we are all teachers. No one is more important than anyone else. I might not have as many experiences as you have, but no one else knows my life like I do."

"Right!"

This book does not in any sense propose to do away with triangle culture. Direct instruction from a knowledgeable source will always be of great value and will likely continue to be the dominant shape of pedagogy, but from time to time *even the sage should turn over the talking piece.*

Rearranging the Furniture

I like to suggest, only half-jokingly, that people who come to our circle trainings try an experiment: *The next time you have a party, before the guests arrive, arrange the chairs in a circle, and see what happens.* People know that the guests will likely avoid the circle, pull chairs out to sit, or go into other rooms.

I had a direct experience of this when my wife Abbe and I called together relatives, some who had not seen each other for many years, for my mother's eightieth birthday.

After a meal outdoors on the deck, and much catching up in the usual way—recounting the same stories repeatedly to each person or to a small group—we began to arrange the furniture in our living room into an approximation of a circle. As we did so, I heard my cousin David say,

"Takes a therapist to ruin a good time."

There was clearly an air of discomfort, and not just from Cousin David. People continued to chatter. Some had not yet taken a seat. I moved to the center, turned towards my mother and said, "I dedicate this council to you, Mom, on this, your eightieth birthday." I lit the candle, saw her smile, and then moved back to my seat.

My son Aaron, seven years old at the time, perhaps sensing that he would need to demonstrate how this is done, moved to the center to retrieve the rose quartz heart I had placed there for a talking piece, returned to his seat and began: "Grandma, I really like it when you play with me and read me books like Amelia Bedelia and when we go for walks. You are really funny, and I like you a lot." Barbara beamed at him and said, "That Amelia Bedelia, I never get tired of reading that, and I love you, too!"

Aaron passed the heart to my mother's brother, Uncle Teddy, who told a story of their growing up in the Sheepshead Bay neighborhood in Brooklyn. As Barbara was the youngest of eight, the brothers had to protect her out in the streets and that, it appears, put a crimp in Uncle Teddy's social life. As the heart went around the circle, more stories were shared along with wishes and statements of love. Although people continued to comment and react to each speaker, I decided not to intervene as the chatter usually diminished when the heart was passed.

Then, the piece came to Cousin David. I braced myself for another cynical comment. As he held the heart, I saw a change in his face. Usually stoic and inscrutable, he softened. Tears came as he recalled: "When I was very young, I spent a lot of time alone in my room practicing magic tricks. I didn't want to show them to anyone, but when you came over, you always asked to see what I was doing. You always laughed and at least pretended to be amazed and said the tricks were 'wonderful!' I always felt comfortable showing you my stupid tricks. I want to thank you for that."

His tears flowed steadily as he passed the talking piece to his left, to my seven-year-old nephew, Ben. The day before the party, Ben had been riding in the back seat of my car with my son Aaron as my brother and I were talking in the front. Apparently, Ben overheard me recalling an unpleasant story from when I was a teenager. He took the opportunity of the circle to let it fly: "I remember a time when Grandma came into Uncle Joey's room and tore all of the pictures off his wall and made him clean it up!" He then passed the heart ... to me! After a few more speakers, Barbara received the heart, commented on a few of the stories, and thanked everyone. We closed the council by *passing the pulse,* holding hands and gently passing a squeeze from one to the next around the circle.

There is a deep longing for and resistance to intimacy, and old patterns of communication are hard to break, especially in such a public setting. On this most significant day for Barbara, however, the gifts came in the form of cherished memories.

Rearranging the Furniture in Oneself

Circle practice is *not* simply a learning strategy we use with children. It must be something we *do*, and if we do it well enough, we may consider bringing it to the children, with humility because so many of us, like me, are *circle immigrants*. We were not born into a circle-based worldview. So, *circles must first become a personal practice,* and the first person you call to the circle is yourself. Self-reflection, self-witnessing, this is where we begin.

Imagine—or better yet, *actually have*—a circle with yourself. Create a space that honors who *you* are. Make it tidy and comfortable. Have a few objects there that carry meaning for you, perhaps a candle, a bell, a flower, a book of inspiration, or a photograph. Have some way to begin, some way to signal that you are now going to pay attention to yourself more fully: ring a bell, light a candle, say a prayer, recite a line, sing a song. Listen carefully, not only to the language of internal dialogue but to the images and body sensations that arise. You might even take note of what you notice in the environment. Employ active self-witnessing, noting what stays with you of what occurs. After a prescribed time (if only a few minutes), find a way to conclude, to honor what you have done with this time. You might write down what came to you and reflect on it. Journaling is certainly a kind of circle with self. You might even draw an image or be moved to dance. Simply find a way to honor this *sacred* (set-apart) time.

Can we be honest with ourselves? Can we listen to that honesty? When we say, *listen* and *speak* from the heart, this is a relatively limited metaphor. More abstract but closer to the fullness of what it is to be *in circle*, we might ask, "Can we *express* and *receive* from the heart?" Our capacity to receive is the basis of all social action as well as cognitive processing. This is the first rearranging of furniture—*to face yourself.*

The ethos/spirit/nature of the circle has everything to do with "mindfulness," or gently focusing one's awareness in a non-judgmental way. Mindfulness practices are becoming more commonplace in many settings, including schools. In circles, the "object" of meditation is each person, as we shift our complete attention to one and then another.

When we developed internships at Palms Middle School and began the training adult interns to hold circles with the students, we were explicit about the need for each to have a way to develop their own self-awareness. Without an active practice of self-awareness, one cannot hope to bring full presence to a circle. Safety in the circle ensues from your capacity to *really be there* for others, and to do this for others we have to develop our capacity to be present with *all aspects of ourselves.*

Accessing the Student Self

In the summer of 1998, I was privileged to participate in a week-long workshop with Anna Halprin at the Esalen Institute. Anna was 83 at the time I met her. One evening near the end of our time together, she treated us to a performance she choreographed to celebrate her 80th birthday. As the music began, Anna moved into the space and said, "When I was five, I did the dance of five!" I saw her body movements transformed into those of a five-year-old girl, dancing joyfully through the space, filled with wonder. Her movements were quick, with arms open, head up, whirling ecstatically around the space, encountering everything with the awe of first exposure. Tears came unbidden as my usual categories of perception were shattered. Then she said, "And when I was 12, I danced the dance of 12!" Her form elongated, taking on the ambiguity of confident recklessness and insecurity as well as budding sexuality. With each announced age, Anna re- inhabited the body she bore at that time of life. At seventeen she moved with strength and independence. "When I was 25 and had my first child," she said as her movements became other-directed, those of love flowing outwards, of being in service. "At 50, in the height of my activism" she manifested a complete empowered presence, directing action with assured authority. As she somatically recalled the body of 80, movements conveyed her compassionate embrace of others, the present moment, and her aging body. She continued through 90, 100, 110, 120, and with each age her movements became more ethereal, approaching pure spirit, weightless, effortless. She concluded with a prayer to the gods of longevity: "May I continue to move through all the ages."

I was so moved by this performance; it became a turning point in my circle practice. My sense was that in the presence of Anna, a group of five-year-olds would relax and allow for fully expressive physical movement and emotional expression. A group of twelve-year-olds, 17, 25, 40, 50, elders in their 80s and beyond, would all have the same experience, that of being so comfortable with Anna and fully at home in their own feeling bodies. This comfort derives from the fact that Anna has kept in touch with *all* of her selves—deeply, physically in touch. As she has not exiled any of these selves from her conscious awareness, others sense that in her presence they can be fully who they are.

Similarly, a circle facilitator should remember and reintegrate their childhood selves. Try the exercise of relaxing and recalling a memory from childhood, of being the age of the students you teach, as fully as possible. Once you have clarity about the details of the memory, think about the *topic or topics inherent in the memory*. What was this memory *about?* Was this a memory of adventure, of curiosity, of joy? Was this a memory of loss or fear or self- consciousness? A recent workshop yielded the following topic harvest of childhood memories:

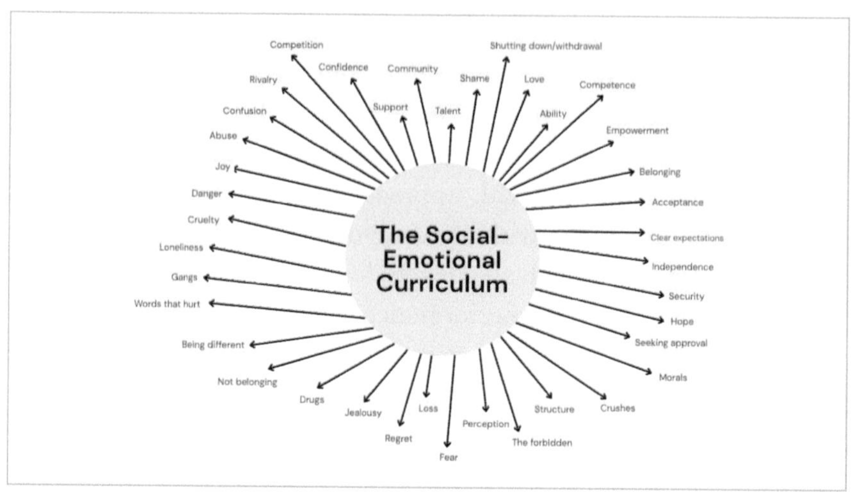

A topic cluster from recalled childhood experiences

In this case, there was a somewhat equal distribution of memories carrying positive and negative charges. Topics marked with an asterisk came up more than once in the recollection of participants. Looking over this list now, can you see anything here that you did *not* experience? It is rare that anything on the chart falls outside of our spectrum of experience. With few exceptions, we find that today's youth are experiencing many of the same social-emotional issues that we did.

In circles we often speak of our *lived* experiences, telling our stories rather than giving our opinions. As adults, our capacity to tell *age- and context-appropriate stories* serves as a model for young people to do the same. If we are not estranged from our memories of childhood, our students will feel this, and the circle will feel *safe* to them.

Look again at the above list and try to recall stories on these topics from *when you were the age of the children you teach*. Can you *tell about a time when you ...* felt confused, lonely, or in danger; a time when you felt secure, empowered, independent, accepted; a time when you did something you were not supposed to do; a time when having structure and clear expectations was helpful; a time when you felt confident and a time when you did not. Then, imagine how you might convey a story as simply and clearly as possible to your students. The story you tell four- year-olds will likely be quite different from the one you tell twelve-year-olds. Also, please note that if the memory is one of an unprocessed emotional wound, do not bring this to a circle of children. They are not there to help you process trauma. A useful mnemonic is, *Share the scar but not the wound.*

If you are so inclined, use a journal to recall these stories. I and others have found that having a store of what we call *facilitating* stories, *stories that enable students to tell their own*, is an asset for adults who facilitate circles with youth.

Rearranging the Furniture with Others

Upon reflection, many people who have an experience of circle will say, "I've done this before! We used to sit in circles like this in the Girl Scouts!" Or "This is very similar to the way we conduct ourselves in our sacred study group." This recognition might even be an atavistic remembering of the way our ancestors conducted their public gatherings. Some of you might have read *The Way of Council,* or this book might be your first exposure to the practice. Some of you might have experienced circles as a teacher or parent at your child's school. Some of you might have had the opportunity to attend a Council training at The Ojai Foundation, through the European Council Network, or through the Magal Hakshava in Israel. Others might have experienced circles firsthand with native peoples.

Council trainings at The Ojai Foundation, now called the Topa Institute, have occurred for 40 years on a verdant ridge overlooking the Ojai Valley surrounded by the Topatopa Mountain range in California. This 40-acre plateau served as a Chumash ceremonial site for thousands of years, and Chumash descendants continue to bless the work done there. Purchased in 1927 by Annie Besant, who envisioned the site as a place to "establish an educational center that would nurture spiritual, artistic and intellectual growth as well as physical and mental well-being," this was to be "the birthplace of the new civilization."

Over the years, people from around the world came to The Ojai Foundation, including teachers representing diverse spiritual, intellectual, artistic, and ceremonial traditions. This was the land that called forth and nurtured the experiences reported by Zimmerman and Coyle in *The Way of Council.*

At so many of these trainings in this beautiful place as well as the events we have in the city, people say that the experience of the circle is something they have been looking for all their lives. Finally, a way to cut through superficial conversation! Finally, a way to learn how to really listen! There is often an experience of going very deep very fast, of satisfying a longing for authentic, honest, compassionate communication, of coming home to a community. I have seen people become instant circle practice converts! They have connected not only with other participants but also with the land itself and perhaps even with their ancestors from the not-so-distant past sitting around the ceremonial fire. Students who return from circle-based retreats often speak of the *Ojai glow* and say that they feel a special bond with the classmates who went with them, that they can never see each other in the limited way that they had before the retreat. And then, they leave the mountain.

I use the metaphor of *the mountain* as an emblem of that rarefied place where conditions are not as they generally are in our day-to-day lives. Usually, our spaces are not set up in circles. Our classrooms are square or rectangular. The chairs are in rows. In our meeting rooms, there is a giant, oblong central table separating us. We rarely set aside special or *sacred* time for our conversations. We frequently don't listen to each other without interrupting or thinking about what we will say in response. When we return from the mountain, we return to an environment that does not value compassionate listening, where it may be dangerous to speak our truth or to show any vulnerability. We return to an environment where others might interpret this vulnerability as a sign of weakness to be exploited. The safety we felt in the context of the circle on the mountain is nowhere to be found.

When we return from the mountain after an experience of circles, we often feel the glow of having found something long sought: our need to see and to be seen. At first, we may want to stay connected to the people at the training. We gather emails and promise to stay in touch. Although this continued connection may be possible for students who come from the same school, particularly if they return to a school that has a circle program where they can continue and deepen this connection, for many continuing the circle as it was at the retreat or training is not possible.

Many leave the mountain and report having had a beautiful connection to others. Then, after a few weeks they begin to doubt the value of what happened at the circle, the retreat, or the training. They start to think, "Well, that was great, but it was because of that particular group of people in that particular setting. It can't be replicated here in the real world!" They start to wonder whether they were hypnotized by the training. They return to a context where such compassionate listening and authenticity just don't happen—not in the family, not in the workplace, not in the world. Some might even wish they had *not* had the experience. It showed them a possibility of connection that they longed for, but the world just doesn't operate like that!

Likewise, when you introduce your students to circle practice, especially if it is late in their school experience, they might wonder what world you are living in as they see no exemplars of this listening and speaking from the heart. This is another critical reason for you to have a circle practice with colleagues. Sometimes, I like to say that to root a systemic circle practice at your school, you must create opportunities for students to *discover* their teachers in circle, doing exactly what we are asking them to do.

Partnership: Co-Practicing, Co-Mentoring, and Circle Friends

Circle is a practice of partnership—with self, with others, and with the natural world. Riane Eisler, author of *The Chalice and the Blade,* speaks of a "partnership paradigm vs. a dominator paradigm." Circles are clearly a technology of the former. After your return from the mountain, when you find yourself back in a world that generally does not practice listening and speaking from the heart, it is best to find at least *one willing partner with whom to carry on a personal practice.* It may seem off-putting to suggest that teachers must practice with other adults to be able to facilitate circles with students. But can we imagine a reading teacher who does not read, a writing teacher who does not write, a math teacher who is averse to equations, a science teacher who does not observe the world? The same is true for circles. If you walk into your class and say, "OK, children, we are now going to listen and speak from the heart!" they will instantly smell a rat and distrust the process. However, if you have learned to walk your talk, to have personal experiences of circle, of the practice of listening and speaking from the heart, you will bring this *authenticity* to your offering.

Circle practice is rooted in the earth, originated by people who lived in partnership with the natural world. Whether you see this as honoring a creator's creation, finding the spirit in nature, or bowing to the complex biomechanical systems that through random chance produced you, the rhinoceros, the hummingbird, and the chrysanthemum—carefully observing and listening to nature is immensely informative and keeps the council fires lit. What might this look like? Native peoples bring us the notion of a *medicine walk*. This involves simply going out into a natural setting with no predetermined goal or direction and allowing yourself to notice what you notice: this rise of the path, an excrescence of rock, the sudden appearance of an animal, a change in the wind or weather. After the walk, reflect on what these things have to say to you as if they were friends speaking to you in circle. Where in your life is there a rise in the path, something happening that requires a bit more effort? What at this moment is emerging as solid, rock-like, in your life? What does the lizard have to say to you as a co-traveler on this planet at this moment in time? In what ways are the winds shifting, the clouds clearing, the shadows lengthening, for you at this moment? Reflect on this *medicine*; write about it, draw it, allow it to move you. This is being in circle, bringing a heightened awareness to yourself and the natural world.

Your *circle friend* could be a teaching colleague, a friend, or spouse. What to do in this pairing? You can explain that you would like to try an exercise—having a conversation with the use of a talking piece. You will see that *a conversation with or without the talking piece is distinctly different.* Without the piece, even if we are listening well to the other, we are also thinking about how we might respond, to concur or disagree, to add, or to change the subject if it is uncomfortable. We are listening for junctures where we might interject. With the talking piece we are challenged to suspend judgment, to listen fully, not only to the words but the tone, the energy of the speaker, the body language.

You can use your two-person circle, or dyad, simply to check in, talking about what is occurring in your lives, and you can add an *inner check-in* to name thoughts and feelings that arise in the present moment. Your dyad can determine topics to discuss, such as those in the cluster above or whatever is present for you now. Circle with your spouse, partner, or significant other can explore *what the relationship needs from you* to thrive. After each partner checks in, place the talking piece in the center and ask, internally, what does the relationship need from us, what is it asking for to sustain its health and wellbeing? Listen deeply. Then, if you heard something, express it.

Forming a men's group[2] or a women's group[3] is ideal for deepening your practice. Groups that include both men and women can deeply explore gender issues, even more so when queer, nonbinary, gay, lesbian, and transgender people are involved.

Intercultural and interracial groups provide extraordinary opportunities. Intergenerational groups can explore stages of life.

The guidelines for practice groups are simple:

- Set a regular time: weekly, biweekly, monthly, etc.
- Select a place conducive to the practice.
- Rotate leadership. Each member of the group should take on responsibility of *holding the container*. To do so, the leader considers what topic or activity might serve the group. In a group of eight people, for example, meeting every other week, each person has four months to prepare. That person is then responsible for creating the space, watching the time, as well as beginning and ending the circle.

A common sequence for a 2- to 3-hour meeting is the following:

- Gathering and chatting.
- An outer check-in. This is a time for participants to catch one another up on what is happening in their outer lives: relationships, work, etc. This can be done casually or after opening a formal circle.
- Transition to formal council. Sometimes participants will literally cross a physical threshold, moving from a casual conversation space to the circle itself. The transition can also involve taking time for silence, singing a song, playing drums, using sage to smudge, or other ways to signal the shift.
- Dedicate the circle.
- An inner check-in. This is a time for each participant in turn to hold the talking piece and express what is happening for them at this moment.
- The leader may choose to follow a thread from the check-in if it appears that the group needs to go in a particular direction given the feelings evoked during that round. If nothing seems to be particularly resonant or urgent, the leader presents the topic or activity they prepared.
- With 10 or so minutes remaining, the leader calls for a witnessing round, where people can note what was resonant for them in the sharing of others.
- Close the circle.

While the above guidelines are for what we might call an *open* group, your practice can also be structured around the interests, vocations, or needs of a particular group. If you are an educator, you can explore the issues and experiences you encounter in your classroom. If your group shares a spiritual practice, the circle might involve the recitation of teachings from that practice followed by the sharing of stories. A writers' group can share and comment on pieces in development. At Palms, we called all the teachers and circle facilitators together every month. The prompt was almost always the same: *What is coming up for you as you try to bring this practice to the children?* Even though the stories were often about the struggles, we would all leave a little lighter, feeling connected in our quixotic quest, and willing to return to give it another go.

Every time you create an opportunity for yourself and others to experience the practice, you keep alive the feeling that drew you to the circle in the first place. Your return from the mountain will not be so jarring as you build a mountain, a set-apart (sacred) space, *exactly where you are.* And in that space, rearrange the furniture so that everyone, sitting equidistant from a beautified center, is embraced and honored by the circle.

For Reflection and Imagination

1. Have a circle of one, as described in *Rearranging the Furniture in Oneself* (p. 37). Afterwards, note what you noticed.

2. Find a comfortable, quiet space. Close your eyes and try to see the students you teach—their appearance, how they move, their affect, their energy, their speech.

- Then, allow a memory to return from when you were their age. Don't judge. Just notice what experiences come to mind.
- Linger long enough to note the environment, the feelings, the dialogue if there were others there. Write down as much as you can recall.
- Then, ask yourself, "What is this experience about? What is the topic at its heart: fear, excitement, loneliness, accomplishment, loss, etc.?"
- Reflect on why this memory revealed itself.

3. Invite one person who might be willing to use a talking piece to have a dialogue.

- Have something alive and beautiful between you.
- Find a way to signal a beginning.
- You can use a topic or simply check in with what is happening in your life.
- Resist the habit of feeling you must immediately respond to the other person.
- When you receive the piece, pause and allow yourself to let the words just spoken by your partner settle in you, and then patiently listen for what is calling to be expressed.
- When your partner has the piece, listen for understanding, not response, suspending judgment. Listen not just to the words but the non-verbal physical, tonal, and energetic content.
- When you both reach a time to conclude, find a way to mark the moment.

Chapter 2: Rearranging the Furniture

1. **Rearrange the Furniture, Rethink the Power**
   How we set up a space shapes expectations. Circles invite equity, presence, and participation, which are essential for collaborative learning.

2. **Balance Triangle and Circle Cultures**
   Triangle (hierarchical) and circle (collaborative) approaches can coexist. Use each intentionally, and know when to shift from one to the other.

3. **Listen Before You Lead**
   Let students experience circle's power before explaining it. They'll feel the difference and often name it themselves: "We are all teachers here."

4. **Bring Circle into Daily Life**
   Circle isn't just for school. Practice it with family, friends, or yourself. Rearranging the chairs at home can spark meaningful connection and healing.

5. **Start with the Inner Circle**
   Cultivate self-awareness and mindfulness through personal practices and journaling. A strong personal practice supports authentic facilitation.

6. **Reconnect with the Student Self**
   Access age-appropriate memories to build trust and empathy. Share authentic, context-appropriate, facilitating stories (not wounds) that help students feel seen and safe.

7. **Sustain the Practice Beyond the "Mountain"**
   After powerful retreats or trainings, create sacred (set-apart) space and community where you are. Build a local practice to carry the glow into daily life.

3

COMMONALITIES: CIRCLE BASICS

Ritual and Ceremony

ALTHOUGH RITUAL AND ceremony are not in themselves circle basics, they are inherent in the practice. Ritual elements such as the talking piece and a decorated center appear to distinguish circle practice from a simple discussion in a circle. As I noted previously, just the sight of a circle of chairs can freak people out. When they see shells, rattles, bells, and flowers in the center, people get worried about the crossing of church-state boundaries. I recall a teacher at a workshop who refused to touch the talking piece, a fossil shell found on the land at The Ojai Foundation. Her reason was that she did not believe in investing objects with special power or significance. The person sitting before her in the circle would simply place the shell in front of her when she spoke, and when she finished the next person to took up the shell.

A friend who was teaching in a small district in Southern California told me the following story: at her middle school, she had accepted an administrator's request to conduct a class for students who mid-year were all failing. She used circle to develop an atmosphere of mutual respect where students could reflect on their own behavior and the challenges they were facing at school. So thrilled by their progress, she and her administrator invited the district superintendent to visit the class. She recalled that the session went beautifully, with the students clearly demonstrating their ability for self-reflection and respectful listening. Afterwards, when she asked her visitor what he thought, he responded, "Well, you know, the circle *is* a pagan symbol." That was the end of the conversation. Sometimes we can't see what we can't see.

While it is true that you can have a circle without a talking piece or a beautified center, there are still ritual aspects to the practice. Ritual pervades most everything we do in our personal lives and in the classroom. What are your classroom rituals? What kinds of ceremonies does your school practice? What ritual do you use to indicate that it is time for students to pay attention? What about the ringing of bells? What is the agreement in your classroom about who speaks when? Are there any ceremonies you use to acknowledge student success or to remind students of what needs to be changed or improved? Is not the graduation ceremony a rite of passage?

Our understanding of the English word "ritual" comes to us by way of the Latin root for "rite:" "ritus." It was applied originally to the rites performed in the church, *a repeated series of actions* done in accordance with church tradition, and that is probably the beginning of our Western association of ritual with religion. "Ceremony" also comes from Latin and has its origins in church activities, particularly those that mark a certain occasion. In the modern context, a ritual can be *any activity undertaken repeatedly*. Going to the gym or having a cup of coffee every morning can become a ritual. The term "ceremony" also carries the idea of an activity done consciously to mark an occasion, whereas a "ritual" might occur without conscious awareness.

In our work with circles, we often talk about the *co-creation of ceremony* and the group's capacity to mark its own occasions, such as the beginning of something new, the accomplishments of an individual or the group itself, commitment to a certain action, or the ending of the group.

The issue of conscious versus unconscious action is significant when we think about circles. We do want to guard against circle fundamentalism. The only fundamental is the circle itself, and perhaps the mutual respect that the shape implies. Ultimately, the group co-creates and evolves its rituals and ceremonies.

The Circle

The first basic is the circle. The form itself creates a sense of equality. It provides the basic condition for the practice of democracy, the practice of hearing each voice. The circle evokes a certain reverence for those who share it with us, a responsibility and receptivity, the joy and fear that comes with seeing and being seen. When we create what we call a *strong circle*, participants should be equidistant from the center and be able to see one another's eyes. As you will soon see, there are many circle forms—some that involve different arrangements or that have participants moving around doing various activities—but we always return to this strong circle as our foundation.

The requirement of the circle form in a contemporary classroom may itself provide a formidable challenge for teachers. You might be saying, "I can barely cram my 36 students into what desks I have!" We will take up this and other challenges later in Chapter 11 ("Circles and Institutional Realities") but for now, *imagine* the possibility of a circle. If possible, desks should be moved or stacked to open a space on the floor. Sitting on the floor relaxes us, brings us all closer to the *rug time* of our kindergarten experience and to the earth itself. If they are available, carpet squares, cushions, or backrests can be used to provide a bit more comfort. If making such a floor space is impossible, the next best arrangement is a circle of freestanding chairs. Circle practice is not meant to be a test of physical endurance. However, we do ask students to be in a position that supports alertness.

Ideally, we build the circle *container* in a clean, beautiful space, free from distractions and interference. Children will readily get involved with sweeping up, arranging the room, and placing an *In Council: Do Not Disturb!* sign on the door.

No Walls
The clear bead at the center changes everything. There
are no edges to my loving now.
I've heard it said, there's a window that opens from
one mind to another. But if there's no wall,
there's no need for fitting the window,
or the latch.
—Rumi

Whether we consciously define one or not, every circle has a center. If there is time and the inclination, in our classroom circles—we acknowledge this center by making it beautiful. Students bring objects to decorate it. Often a few will oversee its creation. We might place items from the natural world—a plant, some flowers, stones, etc. —in the direct center. Talking pieces and anything else the children offer surround this center.

In classroom circles, the center can also contain an item that represents the focus of a particular session. For example, a photo of a historical figure might occupy the center if that person is the springboard for the council. I recall visiting a seventh-grade US history class on a January 15, where we placed a photo of Dr. King in the center along with a laptop. Through the computer's speakers, his "I Have a Dream" speech emanated from the center. The prompt for the council was a report to Dr. King: *If he were with us here in the council, what would you tell him about your experience of the dream? How far have we come?*

Taking care with the center is a vital aspect of the practice. With Rumi, I now acknowledge that "the clear bead at the center" does indeed change everything. When we train the staff at a particular school, I often ask the question: *When the staff of this school comes together, what is at the center?* While some may name the literal objects placed there, someone eventually will note something to the effect of the *well-being of the children.* At some point we might even ask: *If the school itself, the center, had a voice, what might it say about what it needs to be healthy and in service to the children?* Zimmerman and Coyle refer to the center as the place of "the third," the whole that is more than the sum of its parts. In a dyadic council with two individuals, the center is *the place of the relationship itself.* When we beautify the center, we honor what is alive at the nexus of the individuals involved.

Opening the Circle

Every learning experience is a ritual. To learn something new involves the wonder of transition from a state of not knowing to a state of knowing and then, usually, to a state of re- evaluation and extension of what is known. Passing though this transitional doorway is a ritual practice. Circle is also a ritual practice in that its form acknowledges moving from one state of being (not in council) to another (in council), and then to leaving this state and returning to our usual mode of discourse. We signal this transition by sitting in silence, offering a dedication, ringing a bell, lighting a candle, pouring water, clapping hands, singing a song—some way to mark the threshold, the shift into council.

When the time is right, we mark the beginning. This is a way of indicating that we are about to do something set apart from our usual ways of being together. The classroom bell was perhaps originally intended for such a purpose, especially when the teacher rang it by hand. It marks the beginning of a time when we become more attentive, both within ourselves and toward others.

Some groups are ready to jump right in as soon as they form the circle. Others might need to enter into discussion to clarify an intention or the topic of the day. Try asking students: *Are we ready to go into council?* A quick glance around will tell me whether this is the time to begin, whether we need to continue informal discussion, or to scrap the circle that day.

Here are a few images of openings:

- One by one, kindergarteners drop small stones in a bowl of water.
- In a group of sixth graders, one student turns to another, hands apart. The pair attempt to clap at the same moment. Then, the receiving student turns to the student on her left and *passes* the handclap. This continues all the way around the circle.
- High school special education students use a small hand drum. Each student plays a brief rhythm, a statement of how they are feeling that day, and then passes the drum on.
- College students, when they are moved to do so, come into the center of the circle, ring a small brass bell, and offer a *dedication* (*something in their heart/mind that they want to bring into the awareness of others in the circle*).

A few other ways to begin:

- Silence. After a period, when someone is moved to speak, he or she picks up a talking piece and begins.
- One student rings a bell at the center. All listen for the moment when they can no longer hear the sound and raise hands to indicate that moment.
- Everyone claps at the same moment.
- Light a candle. If fire laws don't permit the lighting of candles, use a battery- operated one.
- After the signal of a bell, everyone tracks the cycle of three breaths.

Dedications are thoughts, spoken or offered in silence. They can involve a wish for the health of a sick friend or relative; the *bringing in* of an awareness of a situation in the school, the community, or the world; or a simple offering such as *I dedicate this council to our having a good council* or *I hope everyone does well on the algebra test next period!* Students love the opportunity to dedicate. It is a way for them to bring the awareness of the group to something they are holding in mind and heart. Some adults get a little squeamish with the similarities between a dedication and a prayer. A *prayer*, generally, is directed to someone's conception of a higher power, while a dedication is a statement directed to the group. In the context of a religious school, the opening of a circle can certainly involve a prayer. And in secular, public schools, students will sometimes dedicate the circle to their conception of a higher power. In the latter context, the line is drawn only for the teacher.

Like every other aspect of circle practice, the ritual used to begin is entirely in the hands of the group. It is useful to ask the students: *How shall we mark the beginning of our council?* They will find unique and meaningful ways to indicate that we are about to listen a bit more deeply and actively than usual to ourselves and to others in the circle.

The Talking (or Listening) Piece

Like the traditional classroom ritual of raising a hand to be recognized, the talking piece is a tool for focusing attention. Holding the piece encourages authentic expression. Noticing where it is, and who has it, supports attentive listening. When the talking piece goes around the circle, we are reminded that we can't cut someone off, and we are challenged to monitor our own reactivity and judgments when someone else has it. We say to participants, *If you are ever confused about what to do in council, or you discover that your mind has been wandering, look for who has the talking piece, and place your attention on that person.*

The use of a talking piece can powerfully shift the dynamics of a group or even two people in discussion. When our son, Aaron, was four years old, he taught me a lesson about the value of using a talking piece.

Two months after our daughter, Hannah, was born, I was in the living room of our home when I heard an alarming combination of sounds coming from the bedroom: my wife, Abbe, yelling, "Will you stop? Stop right now," Hannah wailing ... and the sound of bedsprings compressing and releasing.

I dashed into the room and surveyed the situation. Aaron was jumping on the bed, gritting his teeth, and directing mocking cries toward Hannah. My assessment: there was nothing I could do about the crying baby as she was already in the arms of her mother. There was no way for me to temper Abbe's frustration. But I certainly *could* stop this little guy. I could remove him from this equation.

"Aaron, get in your room!" I intoned in my big daddy way, pointing a finger first at him and then in the direction I intended him to go. Boing, boing, boing, a few more bounces and Aaron leapt off the bed and headed toward his room. I stomped in after him, my finger outstretched, ready to deliver my homily on his responsibilities towards the new addition to our family. As I looked down at him from my height, Aaron, sitting on the floor, looked up at me and said, "Dad, I think we need the talking piece for this."

I was stopped short. A dose of my own medicine! I stopped my momentum and sat on the carpet as Aaron brought out his talking piece, a special one I had carved for him on a trip to Yosemite. Holding the piece, Aaron began to speak. For the first time, he spoke of missing his mother and me since Hannah had come home, of wanting us to spend more time with him instead of giving all our attention to the baby. I *had* to listen. He had the talking piece! I, too, had my say, but it was a completely different message than the one I had intended, and it was delivered without the anger and frustration.

We passed the piece for about twenty minutes, acknowledging how much we both wanted to be with each other and how life and our responsibilities have changed now that we were a family of four. With the intervention of a piece of whittled High Sierra pine, in this case it was the four-year-old who reminded the forty-year-old about the importance of listening and speaking respectfully.

Anything can serve as a talking piece. Natural objects such as feathers, stones, pieces of wood, flowers, etc. can be used. Stuffed animals and small toys are favorites with younger children (although a little pink bunny has been a hit with middle schoolers!). Items that make noise—like rattles, rain sticks, and hand drums, things the children can, with a shake or a tap, use to punctuate their sharing—also work well. Sometimes students will construct their own talking piece, decorating it with found objects or small items from their homes. Some classes have one student each week take the talking piece home to *live* with for a week. Trainer Kate Lipkis harvests large bamboo, cuts one-foot lengths, hollows out the inside, has students write their intentions for the group on scraps of paper, and then seals these intentions inside the bamboo by securing bits of cloth over the ends. There should also be some *soft* pieces such as beanbags and Hacky Sack balls that can be tossed from person to person.

Sometimes the talking piece will have a particular significance for a group. With one gathering of students who were identified as those who were in danger of not culminating, we passed a copy of a middle-school diploma. A sports team passed a trophy. A group beginning a writing project passed a blank sheet of paper and a pencil. Another that had finished a long-term research project passed their final drafts.

Once we have had the experience of councils using a talking piece, brief class councils might invoke the use of an *invisible* talking piece. This request reminds all that we will listen a bit more deeply to the one who has the floor. Teachers who were able to meet students in person during the COVID-19 pandemic used the invisible talking piece idea, and students would transform it into whatever they wanted it to be through mime. We have even asked experienced students to look around the room to see who *should* have the invisible piece next. This is a fascinating way to shift responsibility to the students for respectfully handing off the floor, a powerful step towards more civil discourse.

Benjamin Franklin noted that in the councils of the Iroquois (Haudenosaunee), the speaker would rise as the rest observed a "profound silence." Having members of your circle rise to address the group is also a powerful way to have them *stand* in their truth.

One common phenomenon with students is that of the flying talking piece. This is where the piece is passed from hand to hand as if it were a hot potato. We use two reminders when this happens. First, we remind students that *silence is honored* in the circle, that they never *have to* speak, and they are free to pass. Next, we suggest that they *hold the piece long enough to check in with themselves* and to see if there is anything to add, anything that will serve them and the circle. While we are culturally conditioned to value a speedy response, clever repartee, and calling on the first hand raised, find a way to encourage students to slow down, to consider the question or topic without concern about how their silence might be perceived.

One of the values of circle practice in school is that it trains attention and concentration. Like a focusing object of meditation, such as the breath, the body, or a mantra, the talking piece gently returns our awareness to others in the circle, and to ourselves when we are holding it. With younger students, as they become distracted, you might gently ask them, "Who has the talking piece?"

Circle Intentions

Unlike a "rule," an "intention" is something we make up our minds to try our best to do, but we are also aware that it may be very difficult to achieve.

Agreed upon intentions are what we *practice* in the circle. We determine them together and do them as well as we can. One way to elicit intentions from the group is to ask a question such as this: *What would you need from others and from yourself to feel safe to be fully who you are in this circle?* Every group must have agency to make its own agreements, and these should be posted and revisited from time to time. We have found that the responses tend to cluster around what Zimmerman and Coyle call "the four intentions."

As Jack Zimmerman tells the story, when he was headmaster, children at the Heartlight School in Calabasas, California, formulated the first three of the following intentions in 1980 as they described what they were doing to a group of parents who came to witness their circles:

- Speak from the heart
- Listen from the heart
- Speak spontaneously (and only when you have the talking piece)
- Speak leanly

We notice in the first two intentions that the children knowingly added the phrase "from the heart." We can surmise from this that they recognized the special, *embodied* qualities of listening and speaking in circles. They relocated the listening center from the ears and the head, and the speaking center from the mouth to a deeper place less reliant on words alone. Although children seem to get these ideas without much explanation, a few words are appropriate here.

My students developed silent signals for each of the intentions. To show *speak from the heart* they would touch their mouth, extend their hand, and then touch their heart. For *listen from the heart* they would touch both hands to their ears and then touch their heart with both hands.

The sign for *speak spontaneously* was a snapping of fingers. To convey the concept of *leanness* they would touch both hands to their mouth, then extend their hands from a center point to show a thin line. Doing this at the beginning of a circle, helps the group remember what we *aim* to do together.

Speak from the Heart

> "If you bring forth what is within you, what you bring forth will save you."
>
> —Gospel of Thomas

To speak from the heart means to speak as honestly as you can, with a fullness not bound by the desire to project a certain image of self. The children say that it is to *tell the truth and not try to impress anybody*. It is about recognizing and letting go of preconceptions.

Sometimes this "speaking" is what is expressed in our silences, our stillness, our movement, and our songs.

In a sense, speaking from the heart is connected to the intention of spontaneity. In our competitive, rapid-fire lives, we often feel compelled to craft what we will say well before it is our turn to speak and to deliver our messages in "sound bites." We often don't speak from the heart because we don't feel that we have the time to do so, or we don't believe that others will afford us that time. As noted above, witty repartee is highly valued in our culture. Deliberative silences sadly are not.

Circles provide us with an opportunity to get off the wheel briefly, to take time for reflection. In classrooms, it is often the student whose hand shoots up first who gets the opportunity to speak while the more deliberate child is still considering the question. In circle, we encourage everyone to hold the talking piece, take a breath, conduct an internal check-in, internally repeat the question that the group may be considering, and see if there is anything to add. We also remind students that speaking from the heart always takes precedence over speaking to any "topic" that the council or the teacher might have suggested. When we give a circle prompt, we often tag at the end the phrase "*or anything else.*" For example: *Tell a story* about a time when you realized you had a true friend ... or anything else (you wish to say in the moment).

Trainer Monica Chinlund reminds us that when we speak from the heart, we also need to speak *with heart* for those who are listening. To speak from the heart does not mean to dump anything and everything that comes to mind in the moment. We are to remember the generosity of those who offer us the gift of their listening. Trainer Marlow Hotchkiss suggests a fifth intention: *Speak only what serves the self, the group, and the greater good.*

Some people think that being in circle means that you will have to spill your guts, share your feelings, be entirely vulnerable, hold nothing back, tell your deepest, darkest secrets. *Trust yourself to say only what you trust can be heard.* You always have a choice about what to share. Emphasize to the students that while you hope they will speak, they *never have to* speak, and remind them that it is in their power to decide what they want to say.

Listen from the Heart

How do I listen to others?
As if everyone were my master speaking to me
their cherished last words.
—Hafiz (1320–1389)

To listen from the heart is to listen while suspending judgment, to listen with an open heart/mind, even if you disagree with what a person is saying. You simply try to take in what the person is saying, to hear it completely. When we listen from the heart, we also practice monitoring our emotional reactivity. We naturally tend to categorize what others say to us, almost instantaneously determining whether we agree or disagree. We often busy ourselves constructing a response or an addition. We tend to look for small inaccuracies in what another is trying to express, a chink in the argument, so that we can assert ourselves by denying or modifying what has been said. One young man said, quite perceptively, "Cynical distancing is the default communication style of our age." We are somehow not oriented toward attentive listening, and it takes real practice.

Complicated and challenging as this kind of deep listening may be, students readily understand the difference, and circle gives them an opportunity to practice. As one fourth grader put it, "When you are listening to the teacher give directions, you might be thinking at the same time 'Oh, I have a really good idea for that' or 'I don't understand,' but when you are listening from the heart, there's nothing else in your mind except for what that person is saying."

The Way of Council suggests that we imagine a large ear in the middle of the chest through which we take in what is being expressed —the words, the non-verbal aspects of communication, and the energy. You can also try this: close your eyes. Bring your awareness to the area of your heart. Notice how long you can linger there. If you start telling yourself a story about what you are doing or why, or you start to think about something you must do later today, or a memory asserts itself into the moment—then you have moved away from the heart and into the head. Gently return to the heart. There is nothing wrong with thinking, but we are attempting to expand our capacity to stay in the immediacy of the heart. The heart only beats in the present moment.

There is some difference between listening from the heart and what Carl Rogers called "active listening." In active listening, one is aware that there will be a need to restate or paraphrase what has been said to demonstrate empathy or understanding. When one listens from the heart, even these requirements can be suspended.

As teachers, we are trained to anticipate the responses of our students. We look for certain correct answers, and we plan the next layer of questioning even as we are listening. For us, listening from the heart can be more difficult than it is for our students! Even the most experienced circle facilitators are challenged to listen, to take stock of the whole group ("to read the field") and guide the process simultaneously. We will take up this issue of multilayered attention again in Chapter 4.

Listening from the heart does not mean never having opinions, responses, and reactions, but when we practice this intention, we *suspend* them and wait for the talking piece before we check in and see if they are still present. We explain to students that practicing this intention involves trusting yourself: *Trust yourself to listen deeply to others. Trust that when it is your turn you will know what you need to say.*

For a truly advanced practice, trainer Monica Chinlund challenges us to take our listening to an unprecedented level. She says that in council you never interrupt the person who is speaking ... *even with your thoughts!*

Spontaneity

The third of Zimmerman and Coyle's intentions is to speak spontaneously. We try to wait until the talking piece comes before we decide what we want to express. There are very good reasons for this. First, if you are thinking about what you are going to say, then you are not listening completely to the person who is speaking. Second, when you don't pre-plan what you are going to say, you will often be surprised with what comes to you when you are holding the talking piece. This is sometimes called the *magic* of council.

In some traditions, the center of the circle is called "the children's fire." The center reminds us that whatever we do, it must ultimately be in service of the children and of future generations. It also reminds us of the idea that *children do not lie until they learn to fear*. Parents, pre-school, and elementary educators know well the ability of young children to speak the unvarnished truth in the moment (in supermarkets and at park playgrounds, I am often reminded that I am bald!). As we grow more concerned with projecting a certain image in the world, our ability to be spontaneous decreases, and we find ourselves mouthing rehearsed phrases, oft-told tales, and positions that seem to be acceptable, appropriate, or attention-getting. Exercises in improvisation (such as those suggested by Viola Spolin and Augusto Boal) and movement help older students and adults rejuvenate their spontaneity.

Generally, school is not a place that encourages spontaneity. In addition to the fear we have about loss of control when everybody is doing their own thing, we teachers rely on a certain predictability in classroom discourse. We are constantly rephrasing our questions to lead students toward a predetermined position. It is important to remember that we are not suggesting that teachers encourage a free-for-all. To the contrary, circle processes have *highly formalized structures*. We are, however, strongly advocating you provide students with an opportunity to practice spontaneity in the context of the circle. Goal- or standard-oriented learning will always be a mode of operation in the classroom, but we are suggesting that this orientation be *suspended* during circle time. If, as the myths suggest, the creative impulse arose out of chaos and darkness, to encourage this impulse we must provide opportunities for spontaneity.

Being of Lean Expression

> Brevity is the soul of wit.
> —William Shakespeare, *Hamlet*

The last intention articulated in *The Way of Council* is to speak leanly. This is a practical intention that keeps us mindful of how many people are in the circle and how much time we have together. To speak leanly is to try to not let your stories go on and on, just long enough to say what needs to be said. We are challenged to maintain our awareness that the talking piece is not a soap box but that we are addressing a group, and that everyone would like a chance to participate.

The Spanish expression *ir al grano*, "go to the grain," or the English *get to the heart of the matter* conveys the idea more fully than the instruction to *be brief*. Brevity may be the soul of wit, but that wit may be lacking in heart.

One might think that this intention contradicts those of speaking from the heart and speaking spontaneously. What if my heart wants to go on and on? What if my spontaneity knows no bounds? Leanness of expression does not mean limiting what is shared to a sound bite or a quick quip. It means rather to develop an awareness of *when* you have delivered the essence of your message and to leave it there.

As teachers, we know that to get our message across in class often requires a clever phrasing, a rephrasing, a complete paraphrase of what we have already said, and then calling a student to state to the class what we have just stated! In circle, we try to develop trust that the first expression is, for the time being, the best expression.

When someone in a circle is not following this intention, the group has many subtle and not so subtle ways of letting the speaker know. A group of third graders reminded a student who was going on and on, "Don't be fat!" The feedback we receive from yawns, stretches, and withdrawal of attention, is often enough to remind us to practice this intention. We have even noticed that students who have a loquacious tendency gain a corrective self-consciousness in the circles, and likewise those who tend to be extraordinarily lean sometimes stretch out in the attentive atmosphere.

Closing the Circle

Just as it is important to mark the beginning of our time in circle, we also bring awareness to when we conclude. It is important for the facilitator to keep an awareness of time so that the closing can be meaningful rather than the abrupt jolt of the school bell. One technique is to use *leader's piece* (*or pause piece*), an object the facilitator can raise during the circle to signal that time is nearly up and to acknowledge what has been done and what remains unfinished. If there is time, it is a good practice to call for a *witnessing round*, where each student has an opportunity to say what stayed with them from the sharing of others. Another good practice is for the facilitator to do a kind of general witnessing, as objectively as possible noting the broad outlines of what has been shared. Actual closings can take many creative, playful, and ceremonial forms:

- A group of kindergarteners takes hands and sings, "Goodbye, Travon, goodbye, Lucia, goodbye, Steven, goodbye, Kalia ... we'll see you again next week!"
- Fourth graders stand and come close to the center of the circle. They turn bodies to the left and stretch right hands out, thumbs extended, toward the center. Each puts their thumb in the closed palm of the student to their left. This forms an interlinked circle of hands. We witness the beautiful circle of hands within our circle of bodies, and one says, *That's our circle for today.*
- The helicopter: sixth graders turn their left hands palm up and extend to their left. They put their right index finger facing down into the center of the palm of the student to their right. On the count of three, they try to grab the finger in their left palm and escape the grab of the hand on their right.

- Eighth graders sit with both hands extended left and right, palms facing up. Left hands go underneath the right hand of the student to the left. One student begins to pass a "five," tapping the right hand of the student to the left and then replacing their hand where it was. The "five" travels around the circle.
- A group of high schoolers take hands and pass a "pulse" around the circle, a gentle squeeze that moves from hand to hand.
- Graduate students take hands and hold a silence until the time is right and all squeeze hands simultaneously.

I want to make special note of a beautiful closing created by kindergarteners in Jane Raphael's class at Wonderland Avenue School. They call it the *respect closing*: to begin, two students in the circle face one another. They put both arms up and clap both hands against their partner's (a double high-five). Then, with hands still touching, they wiggle their bodies for a few moments. Finally, they each put their hands together at their heart and bow to one another. The student to the left in the pair then turns to the next student on her left and repeats the process, a double high-five, a wiggle, and a bow. Try this with an adult circle. It's a riot!

The helicopter with Ray Tucker

Thumb holding hand circle closing

There are often three ancillary intentions that emerge to support the four described above: an acknowledging expression, confidentiality, and witnessing.

An Acknowledging Expression

In circle we speak into a listening silence. The usual ways we acknowledge that we are listening in normal conversation are suspended. We don't say, *Yeah, I get it. I had a similar experience*, or *Yeah, but* ... There are times, however, when it is important to let a speaker know that they have been heard, to signal agreement or understanding.

Each group can determine how this can be done through a word or some other gesture of acknowledgment. Sometimes the whole group will spontaneously be moved to signal the speaker in acknowledgment. Sometimes just one or a few will do so. Here are a few popular expressions:

- "Jazz hands," where hands are raised and wiggled.
- "Twinkle fingers" or sign language applause, where hands are raised and fingers wiggled.
- The Tibetan sign of acknowledgment: hands are gently rubbed together.
- A touch of one hand to the heart.
- A snapping of fingers.
- The shaking of a rhythm egg, shaker, or rattle.

- Words spoken once, such as "word" or "Axé" (pronounced "ah-SHAY"), a Yoruba word meaning "primordial confidence."

Each group can bring its creativity to the signal. It has come to my attention that with some groups, an acknowledging expression can become a popularity contest. Some students get the signal, and others do not. This, I think, is a call for a more judicious use, as when something truly touches your heart, not just that you agree or like what was said.

Confidentiality

"Confidentiality" is a term with legal implications for therapists, doctors, clergy, and attorneys. It is also regarded as essential in support groups such as Alcoholics Anonymous. Its purpose is to create a sense of safety and trust in these relationships, so that people feel free to disclose what might be difficult, embarrassing, or illegal, and still be able to get the help they need. The cultures from which we receive circle practices, however, would find the notion of confidentiality unfathomable. When the well-being of every individual is seen as the responsibility of every member of the community, *secrets serve no purpose.*

The parameters of confidentiality often depend on the purpose and intentions of the group. A psychotherapeutic group, for example, which functions to unearth repressed material for participants, needs very strict rules around confidentiality. A school board meeting might require considerably less.

Often, in confidential settings we hear, "*What's said in here stays in here.*" The meaning is that, within certain limits, such as an explicit threat to the physical safety of self or other, we promise not to tell anyone outside the confidential relationship what is said within its confines. With circles, however, it is not so simple, and it is therefore worthwhile to explore our cultural and clinical assumptions about confidentiality.

In its indigenous forms, circle practice reflects the entirely open system of village life. An "open system" is one that invites feedback and reflection from all constituents. All members of the community, young and old, participated. No experience was too embarrassing, no dream too dark to be told.

A public-school classroom is unique. Teachers don't generally think about confidentiality in the classroom. In general, teachers agree not to reveal any personal biases, and students are not expected or required to reveal anything about their personal lives. While it is valuable for teachers to be aware of personal information about students, it is considered secondary to the process of curriculum delivery.

Circle practice, in contrast, relies for its health on the assumption that all participants will bring the truth of their experience to the circle. The feedback provided in such a way allows teachers to determine the needs of individual classes, assess for understanding, evaluate the need for course corrections, and, in the case of prescribed curriculum, revise delivery strategies. What we call *probing for background knowledge or prior experience* is essential to creating *relevance*, a link between the subject matter and a student's lived experience. Teachers still must consider their primary role as facilitators of discussion and be aware that by dint of their authority, students experience the teacher's comments and beliefs as significant.

So, regarding confidentiality, the classroom (or staff or parent) circle lies somewhere on the continuum between the entirely open system of the village, the limited exchange of personal information in a traditional classroom, and the strict confidentiality of the professional and support group associations mentioned above. There are also developmental considerations to keep in mind. Don't expect the youngest students to keep *anything* confidential. Expect teens (and most adults) to be challenged to hold emotionally charged stories. There will be times when a story told in the circle will be shared without the teller's permission and hurt will ensue. This becomes an opportunity for circles on the topic of gossip and *information we must protect and information we must share.*

In upper elementary and above, it is good to be explicit about the limits of confidentiality and the necessity of mandated reporting. I like to say to these groups that there are things that I must report if students choose to talk about them. If they don't want me to report, then don't mention these things. I have found the acronym DASH useful. "D" is for drug and alcohol *sales*. When students speak of their personal use, the school must have a protocol and resources to address this, and procedures must be clearly understood and articulated to staff, students, and parents, but use is not technically something we are mandated to report. If you suspect that the use is at a dangerous or suicidal level, then it is mandatory to report. (In Chapter 9, we will look at circle prompts that explore underlying causes for the perceived need to alter our moods.) "A" is for physical, sexual, or psychological abuse. Students need to know that if they speak of these things, you are required to take steps to protect them. "S" is for suicide or self-harm. "H" is for imminent physical harm to others. With older students, all these limitations should be discussed, and students should be reminded of them from time to time. When a school adopts systemic circle practice, it is essential to know the protocols when students reveal any sort of harm to self or others. Lists of community resources, such as support groups, shelters, counseling, and medical providers must be compiled and updated regularly. In my experience, this is rarely the case, but if we create conditions where students, staff, and parents are encouraged to speak from the heart, we must be prepared to respond. All stakeholders must be clear about the protocols.

While each group may develop its own agreements regarding confidentiality, in general, those that have emerged in our experience with students include the following:

- It is fine to tell people outside the group about the *topic* discussed *or the activity* done in circle if no one in the group would be hurt by this telling.
- It is fine to tell others what *you* did, shared, thought, or felt in the circle.

- It is *not* okay to tell another person's story outside of the circle.
- Don't say anything about another person you would not be willing to say to them directly.
- Don't speak negatively of people who are not present to respond. If you must tell a story involving a negative experience with someone, tell it in such a way that the person is not identifiable.
- If you have an issue with someone in the circle, ask that person whether they would be willing to let you talk about the issue to the whole circle. If that person says no, then wait until after the circle to speak of it and perhaps ask for a neutral mediator.
- Expressed threats of harm to self or imminent harm to others must be reported by the teacher/facilitator.

It is fruitful for circle facilitators to explore the issue of confidentiality, and the underlying themes of trust and safety, with their groups. Some facilitating questions might include:

Without revealing names or details, tell about a time you:

- *discovered you could really trust someone.*
- *felt trusted.*
- *trusted someone with personal information and that person kept your trust.*
- *trusted someone, and that person broke your trust.*
- *were trusted with personal information that was difficult to keep.*
- *had to tell a secret to keep someone safe.*

Rather than being entirely prescriptive about the rules of confidentiality with our circles, explore with students the circumstances in which confidentiality should be strictly applied and when it should be limited. It is best to *have the group generate a list of agreements*, refer to it regularly, and revise it when necessary.

"What is the difference between a 'witness' and a 'judge?'" the teacher asks her fifth-grade class. "A witness sees things. And hears things. A judge says if you are guilty or innocent and if you are right or wrong."

In a group of 30, each student spends about 97% of circle time listening. The intention to listen from the heart calls us to adopt the perspective of a witness and to monitor any judgments that might arise and get in the way of our listening. Witnessing develops empathy, a social-emotional skill, and paraphrase/conceptualization, an academic skill. We often suggest that the students conduct a *witnessing round* to develop these skills. After a "story round," the simple instructions for witnessing are offered: *When the talking piece comes, say one thing you remember that another person shared*, or *Share what stayed with you from what others have said*, or *Share what you heard, not what you thought about it.* This is a basic form called "echo witnessing."

We ask students not to explain why they think information stayed with them, just to recall it. We also emphasize that this is not a *memory game*, but just a way of checking in about what was retained by group members. Teachers often ask students to say *one thing you "learned"* today or from the reading. This is a complicated request. What does it mean to have *learned* something? Rather, if we simply ask them to say one thing they *remembered* from the circle, or from the lecture, reading, or experience, we lower the *affective filter* (the screen that goes up when a student is asked to produce something beyond their capacity). If, for example, we have taken a museum field trip, before we board the bus to return to school, circle the students and ask them to recall *one thing they remember* from the day. This simple sharing will review and reinforce the experience, and you will learn what stayed with them as well as what was missed.

In exercises suggested later in the book, I show how the teacher can take the information elicited from witnessing to find resonances to refocus and deepen the group. The art of witnessing can be a great deal more complex as we deepen our experience in the circles, involving noting non-verbal occurrences, questions that arise, as well as what was missing from the exchange. For now, consider *witnessing* as simply recalling what has been said or done in the circle. That includes self-witnessing. Because of the presence of attentive others in the circle, there is a heightened quality of noticing both of what one says and does and what others say and do. Attending to what others say has an obvious educative effect. Witnessing your own speaking from the heart enlarges perspective and sometimes brings about a revision of your own story. As Los Angeles poet Jorge Monterrosa put it: "If I listen, my ignorance reveals itself to me."

Objective witnessing requires a great deal of practice. As Marshall Rosenberg points out in his course on Nonviolent Communication, we naturally combine observation and evaluation[1]

Philosopher Jiddu Krishnamurti says, "The highest form of intelligence is observation without evaluation." Again, if we feel rushed in our communication, we are compelled to generalize our observations. We say, *You're mean*, rather than, *I was upset when I saw you yelling at Alice for not bringing her homework.* When we ask students to take their time in circle and to tell their stories, we are encouraging them to become witnesses to their own lives.

Witness consciousness is the ability to bring a certain equanimity and objectivity to the flow of experience. Socially, this is important so that we can relate to others free from the influence of our own emotional reactions. Academically, witnessing is important as we try to take in and retain new information, suspending critical analysis until the information has been fully received, the text fully read, the speaker fully heard. Circle practice becomes a laboratory for the development of this kind of consciousness.

Circle Topics

What are the topics for a circle and how do we determine them? Sometimes topics are related to the class *atmosphere*—creating the conditions for learning, establishing and maintaining norms and procedures, building relationships—making agreements, expectations, and responsibilities explicit and co-determined. Sometimes topics focus directly on *the academic curriculum*—processing new information, projects, pre-reading, and pre-writing activities, historical or literary themes, and checking for understanding.

Sometimes we deal with the issues about which everyone is aware, but few are acknowledging—on the campus, in the community, in the world. Since circle practice is a *proactive* measure, it is there when we need it. We have dealt with topics including deaths of students and teachers, climate crisis, earthquakes, blackouts, and war. On the morning of September 11, 2001, at Palms Middle School, almost every class, even those who didn't regularly do so, used circles to share what we knew and what we were thinking and feeling.

Sometimes we teachers bring in issues that have come to our attention—teasing, fighting, put-downs, misunderstandings, unfulfilled responsibilities, and unacknowledged accomplishments. School administrators can also request that a topic of concern be taken up by the circles. Sometimes we just *check in* to find out what's *up* for the children and then fashion a prompt around what comes from that. As circle facilitators, we must monitor our own expectations of what makes for a *good circle* and a *good topic*. Asking students to share their preferences for cheese can bring about as much heartful sharing, attentive listening, and deep connection as far more *serious* topics.

Circles revive the oral tradition. Storytelling is often at its core, even if the story is the one of what is occurring in the present moment or of a vision of what may come to pass. I say, *Opinion is story robbed of its narrative*. We share our opinions, generalized from experiences, because we might not trust that anyone will take the time to listen to our stories, our lived experience. Opinions can conflict. Stories do not. No matter the topic, we encourage participants to go beneath their opinions to the experiences that shaped them. One of the most prevalent circle prompt stems is *tell about a time when* ... We recognize that our tendency toward opinion is another symptom of feeling that we must compress our experience, for there is not enough time and there are too few willing to listen.

A protocol for determining topics of immediate relevance to students, staff, parents, and others is called "the mysteries process," and it will be covered thoroughly in Chapter 10. Sometimes we play, sing, move, create art, improvise, debate, or sit silently. Always, as facilitators and teachers, *we read the field*, staying alert to what the children themselves are calling for.

All this said, don't overcomplicate the process or cling to these guidelines as if they were brought down the mountain on stone tablet. The commonalities in all cultural dialogic practices are simply: circle, center, intentions, opening, and closing. Or as one high school science teacher put it, "One person speaking, everyone else listening."

For Reflection and Imagination

1. To explore the notion that "an opinion is a story robbed of its narrative:"

- Consider an opinion you hold, especially one about something being right or wrong or someone being good or bad.
- Trace the experiences you had that led you to this opinion.
- If the experience that led to your opinion occurred just once, is it possible that a second experience might have altered your opinion?
- If you wish, use the same line of inquiry to source a "belief" you hold. Where did it come from?

2. Imagine some ways you might ...

- choose a talking piece
- beautify a center
- open a circle
- choose a topic related to interpersonal issues you have noticed in your classes
- choose a topic from a concept you teach
- close a circle

Chapter 3: Commonalities: Circle Basics

1. **Understand the Circle's Core Elements**
   All circle practices share five basics: the circle form, a center, opening and closing rituals, shared intentions, and a talking/listening piece.

2. **Honor Ritual and Ceremony with Intention**
   Rituals help mark transitions and elevate attention. Circles use simple, co-created ceremonies to open, hold, and close space respectfully, without dogma or prescription.

3. **Create and Care for the Center**
   A physical center offers symbolic focus and shared grounding. Beautifying the center reminds students of shared purpose, connection, and respect.

4. **Use the Talking Piece to Train Attention**
   The talking piece teaches presence, listening, and patience. It invites authentic expression and gives each student uninterrupted time to speak or pass.

5. **Establish and Practice Shared Intentions**
   Circle intentions (e.g., speak and listen from the heart, be spontaneous, speak leanly) create a culture of compassion, authenticity, and reflection.

6. **Cultivate Witness Consciousness**
   Witnessing—recalling what others said without evaluation—builds empathy, memory, and emotional intelligence. It's a foundational academic and relational skill.

7. **Let Topics Emerge with Relevance**
   Whether curriculum-based, relational, or responsive to current events, circle topics should connect to students' lives and experiences to create a foundation for receiving new information and meaningful engagement.

4

CIRCLE FACILITATION

Shifting Roles

BECOMING a circle facilitator involves a fundamental shift in teacher consciousness, if only for the duration of the circle itself. That shift is from what Paulo Freire calls the "banking" concept of education, where the teacher or counselor has the information to be "deposited" into the student, to a "problem-posing" pedagogy, where *the distinctions between teacher and student disappear* as both are engaged in the process of understanding. Freire says: "Through dialogue, the teacher-of-the-students and the students-of-the-teacher cease to exist and a new term emerges: teacher-student and student-teachers."[1]

To achieve this kind of open communication and respect in the classroom, the teacher must serve as a model of authenticity and deep listening. As we facilitate circles with the children, we must be fully present, walking our talk, practicing the same agreements we ask of them.

How well do students handle our shifting roles, from the open, personal sharing in the circle to the focused curriculum delivery of the classroom? Quite well, actually! Although some teachers fear that they will lose their "authority" by participating openly in circles, we find that students often develop a deeper respect for their teachers because they are willing to show their "human side." As one eighth grader expressed, "When I'm with my teachers and I actually see how they are when they are not assigning homework or giving us work, and I just see them on an equal level as a person, it makes me feel more comfortable with them, and also sometimes it helps me to pay attention to them in class because I understand what they are like when they are not teaching." Middle school Leadership and English teacher Sylvia Thomas puts it this way: "I can be *Sylvia* in circle, and five minutes later I can walk back into the classroom and be *Mrs. Thomas.* There isn't even a bat of the eye."

Like Sylvia, many teacher facilitators indicate their shifting role by asking students to address them by their first names in circle and more formally in the regular classroom. While a few students will take advantage of this new freedom, most respect the distinction and even come to see the value of having *both* a Sylvia *and* a Mrs. Thomas. All of us must learn to negotiate the shifting circumstances of "triangle" (hierarchical-vertical) and "circle" (egalitarian-horizontal) pedagogies. There are times when we need instruction from the experts and other times when we need to rise to our own expertise.

This shift in the teacher-student dynamic parallels that of the administrator-teacher or manager-staff. Can an administrator, one with oversight responsibilities, participate fully in a circle and still retain authority when making critical staffing decisions? Can a teacher who has to make evaluative and disciplinary decisions retain authority after sitting on the rug in circle with students? The answer is a qualified "yes." The capacity to move seamlessly between these two axes of authority, the circle and the triangle, depends on one's sense of self. That is, if you feel secure in your position, you won't need to demonstrate that. You can receive and consider feedback about your performance—the teacher from the students and the manager from the staff—and not take it personally but as information to promote professional growth. Some people say the vertical and horizontal axis of authority cannot co-exist, but one need only look at the *earthrise photo* taken from space to see that they can dance together quite beautifully!

Telling Our Own Stories

After food and shelter, *telling stories* is a basic need, even before love and belongingness. As facilitators of circles, we are challenged to tell *stories that are authentic, appropriate, and facilitating* (making it easy for others to tell their stories). *Authentic* stories come from actual experience, what we have lived, felt, and dreamed. To be effective circle facilitators we must live reflective lives. For many of us living in this fast-paced world, the time to reflect and remember our stories is rare, so the practice of slowing down and doing so in adult circles is most valuable.

I recall telling a story in circle that allowed students to access the completeness that comes from recognizing a polarity present in all of us. I had been preparing my eighth graders for our yearly trip to the Museum of Tolerance. This museum houses a historical walk-though of the Holocaust. At the beginning everyone receives a card with the name and picture of a child who lived during the time of the Holocaust. The tour progresses through the history, and before the exhibits on the liberation, we find ourselves inside a replica of a gas chamber. On screens around the room are changing images of piles of corpses and scenes from the camps, and so visitors are exposed to the extremes of human cruelty. At the exit of the exhibit, we put the card with the child's image into a reader to reveal that child's fate.

I knew that this experience would be painful and profoundly moving for many of them. I wanted to prepare them to deal with the extraordinary cruelty to which they would bear witness. As we often do in circle, I used a prompt that encompassed the polarity implicit in the topic of how people treat each other: *Tell a story about a time when you treated someone with kindness or when you found yourself being cruel to someone. See which story comes when you receive the talking piece.*

In the circle, I began by recalling a recent moment driving through my old neighborhood with my wife on our way to the movies when I saw a man walking his dog, a man whom I immediately recognized as a boy I knew from my elementary school days. Adam was different, I told them. He was physically different from most of us, shorter and heavier, with a sloping forehead, close-set eyes, and thick glasses. He could not do the class work that we all did. He behaved differently, and the teacher treated him differently. When someone said hello to him, he would turn red, hide his face, and either freeze or run away.

I told my students how I—and my group of friends—used to torture Adam by calling him names, chasing him, and threatening him, until he shook with fear, and then we would spread our arms and fly away, laughing at our power to cause such a reaction in him.

I told them how my heart sank as I passed him that day in my car and how the pain of recalling *my own cruelty* was still fresh. There I was, going out for an evening of diversion, and Adam appeared to be likely still living in the house where he grew up.

The not so simple guideline for adult sharing in circle is that our stories must be *authentic, appropriate, and facilitating*. The story of Adam fits all those requirements. It is relatively simple in terms of the details. If we give too many details, students might feel that they cannot match that level of specificity. It is *authentic*; that is, there is real feeling in it still for me, and it is the truth. It is also *age- and context-appropriate*. This reflection is about a time when I was quite young, a time when such indiscretions might be forgiven. Telling such a personal story in the context of the public-school classroom is appropriate since the details are not so graphic, there is enough distance from the event, so it is no longer psychologically charged for me, and I have processed and come to terms with the feelings associated with it. The story is also *facilitating*; that is, *it serves as a model and makes it easier* for students to tell their own stories.

While there were a few stories of kindness in the circle, it appeared that my story created an opportunity for students to share the often-unexpressed sides of their humanity as well. And the stories all had a quality of self-reflection and remorse, rather than the dismissive joking about the suffering of others we often hear from middle schoolers. Recognizing the potential for cruelty and kindness in all of us provided a degree of context for the students to understand the unspeakable violence as well the selfless acts of compassion they would encounter in their museum experience.

I am not suggesting that teachers and facilitators bring all the details of their personal lives to circles with children. In fact, teachers must be vigilant about not dumping unprocessed emotional material on the students. As I heard someone say, *it is okay to share the scar but not the wound.*

It is valuable for us to consider why a group of young people would even want *us* in *their* circle! Our presence provides two useful elements for the children: we model active listening, and we model storytelling, the capacity to honestly articulate personal experience. In general, teacher self-disclosure should be "facilitating" in effect, making it "easy" ("facile") for students to express themselves. When we facilitate circles in our classrooms, we are sitting in at least two seats: that of the guide and that of the participant.

Creating a Safe Container

Sometimes we speak of the circle as a *container*, the thing that holds our stories. From the work of Stephen Krashen, teachers are familiar with the concept of the "affective filter." Its symptoms are the blank stare, lack of participation, and sometimes acting out to shift the power dynamic. When there is an atmosphere of evaluation and hypercorrection, students shut down. Circle time must hold the promise of being *non-evaluative* and at the same time provide the safety that comes from structure, boundaries, and familiarity. And this safety can lead to new structures, the expansion of boundaries, and excursions into the unfamiliar.

Safety is a product of trust, of the environment and of those with whom we share it. The facilitator's role in creating a safe space involves the following:

1. Establish norms and encourage participant "ownership"

Early circles should involve students in creating agreements. As I noted in Chapter 3, these agreements generally align with "speak from the heart" and "listen from the heart," but it is best to have the students articulate the intentions in their own way. Beginning in around third grade, I ask students: *What do you need to feel safe in the circle to bravely speak your truth?* Find out what they need from others, including you, and what they need from themselves. With older students, this kind of *norm setting* can go into additional detail about what can and cannot be shared and what to do when certain things are shared. Write these norms down and post them in the room. Revisit them as needed.

2. Clarify confidentiality and its limits

Remind participants that they can choose what to share and what to keep private. If they choose to share something that indicates to you the potential for self-harm or harm to others, then as a mandated reporter you are required to take this information outside the circle. Remind students that we agree *not* to tell each other's stories outside the circle. Each of us is free, however, to tell others what the topic was and the story *you* chose to tell. See Chapter 3 for more details.

3. Clarify norms around conflict

The general rule is that we don't speak ill of anyone not present who can be identified by others in the circle. If a student wants to tell a story about someone who they feel has caused harm, the experience can be expressed without identifying terms. This can be tricky because participants might want to tell stories about others even if they are not identified by name. We especially do not want to invite "bagging" (complaining) about others. Instead, encourage students to speak directly to those people or to request a circle or restorative process. If the conflict is with someone present in the circle, the protocol is to ask that person whether they would be willing to have the story told publicly. If the answer is "no," then encourage those students to have a dyadic or mediated circle to work through the issue.

4. Help students to state needs and *ask* for advice

The ability to state one's needs with clarity and without blame or expectation is the aim of Nonviolent (compassionate) Communication.[2] See Chapter 9 for processes to identify feelings and needs. At any time, a student can call for a *response council* when they have a particular question or are looking for advice. See Chapter 8 for details.

5. Refrain from giving advice unless it is specifically requested

When we hold awareness of the circle as a *container*, we increasingly trust *it* to provide what everyone needs. "Advice" may come from a *story* told by another student. Sometimes all a participant needs is to be heard. The telling of the story will activate the *inner adviser*. If someone directly asks for advice, use the *response circle* form discussed in Chapter 8. Furthermore, as circle participants bond, they learn to trust the "braided" or collective knowledge that comes from hearing all the stories. Then, the advice comes from the circle rather than any one person.

6. Diminish distractions and interruptions

Clear space in the center. Turn down the lights. Post a sign on the door: Circle in session; do not disturb. Keep circle practice consistent, weekly at the same time.

7. Create continuity

Traditional circles are not ruled by the clock, but classrooms typically are. You can create a sense of continuity or timelessness by providing a recollection of what occurred and where the group left off, both in terms of content and feeling, in the previous circle. This assures the group that from circle to circle, you carry their stories.

8. Model emotional regulation

Reflect back to the group what you have heard, as much as possible without judgment or spin. When you receive the talking piece as a participant, say what emotions come up for you but refrain from reactivity. Near the end of the circle, provide a kind of meta-witnessing, objective summary of what has occurred. In Chapter 11, we will look at tactics when a circle goes off the rails. In essence, practice objective reflection without conveying anger or disappointment. A personal note here: For the first 10 years of my circle practice with students, I would try to "vibe," or silently encourage, students to tell the stories I was hoping to hear or to say more. I know for a fact that when I didn't get what I was hoping for, non-verbal communication betrayed my disappointment. Suspending expectations for outcomes is a hard habit to break!

9. Respect the talking piece

When you don't have it, you don't speak. Use a facilitator's piece, an additional talking piece to be used only when there is a need for a *process intervention. Process interventions* or *process checks* are designed to remind participants of agreements that have been made and to note if things have changed, such as the group having moved away from the prompt or the need to move to another circle form. You are *checking* (not chiding) to see if this is what the group wants to do. You might also call for a process check if the group members are showing signs that they no longer want to be in circle. *Process* interventions can also be simple reminders, for example that there is five minutes remaining in the allotted time.

10. Allow students to sit out when necessary

Try not to stigmatize a student's need or choice to sit out a session or when it becomes clear that the student cannot participate without disrupting or is clearly uncomfortable. Provide an alternate assignment. There should always be an invitation to rejoin the circle when they are ready and able to respect the agreements.

11. Don't require students to speak

Sometimes under the guise of *encouragement,* we push students to speak: "Tell us more." "What else happened?" Some students will choose *never* to speak in circle. I have had students who made this choice demonstrate at the end of the year that they had indeed been listening! Do encourage students to hold the talking piece and to check in with themselves before passing it on. Sometimes the more "considerate" students will pass quickly because they feel they don't have time to formulate their thoughts.

12. Don't grade or evaluate participation

We certainly do not want our students to feel that they must give us what we want or tailor their stories to please us. When we are disappointed or displeased with what a student shares, we can't allow this to carry over when we are wearing our instructor hat. The challenge in circle is to re-spect, to literally *re-see* each student every time they hold the talking piece, abiding in the absolute conviction that they will connect with and rise to their best self. Even if this conviction goes unfulfilled continually with some students, the practice is to *gently return* to this kind of respect and expect the best next time.

13. Keep time

Note how much time is allotted for each activity. If the time to close is near, signal this with a process intervention. You might note, for example, that there are five minutes remaining and that ten students have yet to speak. There is nothing more jarring than having the bell ring and students jump up before you can close the circle.

14. Beautify the space

As I Walk with Beauty
As I walk, as I walk
The universe is walking with me
In beauty it walks before me
In beauty it walks behind me
In beauty it walks below me
In beauty it walks above me
Beauty is on every side
As I walk, I walk with Beauty.
—*Traditional Navajo Prayer*

We have all heard the stories of students in other countries who rise before dawn to arrive at school and spend the first hour or more cleaning the campus before the instructional day begins. While this is still rarely the case in the US, we have found that students love to "practice the Beauty Way" when it comes to readying a space for circle, and sometimes the skill transfers to other times and settings. The Beauty Way is simply to notice where you are and make the space more beautiful, especially when you leave it for others to enjoy.

Creating a beautiful space is conducive to circle. If possible, move the tables and desks to create an open space in the center for floor-sitting. Most of my classes had upwards of 30 students, so we needed to move desks to the periphery and stack one on top of the other. On circle day, students often saw me sweeping the floors—even if they didn't particularly need sweeping—and soon they would ask to take over. Asked why, I would say something about my wanting to make the space beautiful for the important work they do in circle. There are various types of chairs that rest directly on the floor. These are preferable for circle as they bring everyone a bit closer to the earth and to the same level. Whenever your anatomy allows, sit on the floor with the students. If your room is carpeted, you can sit directly on the floor, but it can become challenging to remain seated for extended periods if students don't have something to lean against. If you have freestanding chairs, these can also be used. If it is impossible to move the furniture, you can use the "flower" orientation simply by asking students to turn their chairs or just their bodies to face the center of the room.

Creating a beautiful center is an aspect that is not common in other forms of circle-based, group dialogue. Aside from the circle itself and the use of a talking piece, the center is the thing that most often raises fears in some adults and generates interest among students. The center appears to be an altar, and indeed it is—one that honors the circle itself rather than any single tradition. In public schools, we refrain from placing objects in the center that might have religious significance to participants—no Buddhas, crosses, stars of David, Native American or other indigenous ritual objects. Of course, having these things in the center at a religious school would be entirely appropriate. In general, we abide by Education Code that limits the ability of adults in a public school from overt expressions of their own religious traditions, and this includes bringing in objects that signify that tradition. An exception is when a child chooses to bring such an object as a representation of their own tradition. Such an object, however, should not be used as a talking piece because doing so requires its handling by all participants.

As noted in Chapter 3, the center can be very simple, consisting, for example, of a single fresh flower. It can involve various objects from nature and objects that hold a personal meaning for students. If you are reading a book together and the topic for the circle comes from the book, it can reside in the center. Whenever possible, engage the students in creating beauty at the center. As a facilitator, though, we recommend that you consider the value of creating a beautiful, meaningful center. It represents the place where all participants meet, the heart of the circle.

When the circle concludes, leave time for the important work of reconfiguring the space for regular classroom activities. This is another way of clarifying the threshold between circle and classroom.

15. Create *liminal* space: Honor the change from conversation to formal circle

How do we know when we are "in" council? How do we distinguish council from discussion, dialogue, debate, or other forms of respectful group engagement? "Liminal" means having the quality of crossing a line, a border, or a threshold in time and space. While ultimately, we hope to "live council," to listen deeply and speak with and from the heart in all situations, it is helpful for the mere mortals among us to have some clear boundaries as to when we are in or out of council. The primary difference between being in or out of council has to do with the commitment of the group to practice the intentions. To be in council is to commit, for a given period, to speaking and listening from the heart. In the classroom, this commitment can be assessed simply by asking, "Are we ready to go into council?" Look around and you will know whether students are ready. If your question is greeted by groans, yawns, and the sound of air leaking out of a tire, they are probably not ready and you should change course to, perhaps, an informal discussion, writing to the topic, or something to get them ready like a game or a mindfulness practice. It is a serious rookie mistake to have a council just because it is time for council. When we converse (literally to "turn with") or "discuss" (literally to "shake apart"), we listen in part to understand and in equal part to respond when it is our turn. In circle, we practice listening to understand fully, suspending the need to assess or to respond. In dialogue (literally to "talk through"), there is generally an attempt to move toward some kind of conclusion, whereas in council even this goal is suspended, replaced by the intention to allow the process to move where it needs to go. Not being attached to outcomes is also a critical aspect of "restorative" justice and restorative practices.

16. Develop and encourage comfort with silence

Last, perhaps one of the most challenging aspects of facilitation is developing a degree of comfort with *silence*. When things go silent, we tend to think that we have done something wrong, that we need to rephrase the prompt or go in another direction entirely. If we take listening from the heart seriously, then we are not pre-planning what we will say when others are speaking. As facilitators it is important that we model *consideration*; that is, we hold the talking piece in silence to consider what we have to say and what will serve the circle. Sometimes we just hold the talking piece in silence and then pass it on. We encourage our students to do the same. The silences are the clear lines *between* expressions. In contrast, sometimes the talking piece flies around the circle and *no one speaks*. Sometimes facilitators will just send it around again or let the silence stand as its own expression.

Developing a Circle Habit of Mind

A classroom circle facilitator develops a way of thinking about education and praxis, and this way over time becomes a habit. Essentially, those who become habituated to circle see its application in three areas:

1. Prescribed curriculum
2. The immediate, interpersonal, interactive field of the classroom, school, community, world
3. What students themselves *want* to know (what we will later call "mysteries of the heart")

Once you have the habit, you will see how to use circles to create relevance and deepen understanding in all curricular areas; to address interpersonal issues that regularly arise in the little village of the classroom as well as those that arrive in the classroom through the *global* village; and to elicit and turn towards the issues, concerns, and dreams that each individual group of students wants to engage and pursue.

Once we allow ourselves to think in terms of teaching and learning in circles, we seem to do so with increasing frequency. The symptoms of being a true circle *carrier* include but are not limited to the following:

- Stopping in the middle of an otherwise enjoyable activity —reading, playing a game, eating a meal, watching a movie—and wondering how you could turn it into a circle.
- Finding yourself utterly dissatisfied with normal conversation, particularly in situations where you find yourself repeating the same story over and over to different people.
- Imagining that it would be of great value to have your adult basketball team sit down with the other team after a match to process the game in circle.
- Upon hearing a piece of news, rather than reacting with judgment, thinking instead about how you could turn the essence of the issue into a circle prompt.
- Becoming frustrated with lectures or gatherings where an "expert" conveys information without providing an

opportunity for listeners to speak of how that information strikes them and relates to their lived experience.

- Really wanting to introduce circles to your partner, spouse, friends, family, colleagues, the bank teller, cold call salespeople, etc.
- Having all these thoughts in the middle of the night!

You will notice quite quickly that anything and everything can feed and inspire a circle. A true carrier of circle is one who seizes the opportunity when the time is right. The chart below shows a very simple process for thinking about moving from any topic or any experience to a circle that deepens understanding, insight, and collective wisdom:

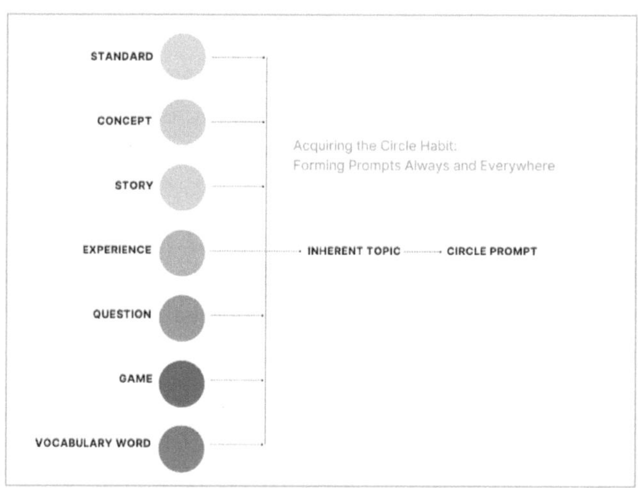

Anything can become a source for circle.

No matter the stimulus, the circle facilitator first asks, *What is this about?* and then looks for a way to phrase a prompt that will allow and encourage all participants to tell stories. While Chapter 5 will more fully discuss the prompt-forming process, here are some examples for each of the categories listed in the chart above:

- **Standard:** "Students will distinguish facts from opinions." (This is a common learning standard for

Language Arts.) *Name something that you believe to be true, but you don't have proof. Then tell about how you came to believe that.*

- **Concept:** "Time is subjective." *Tell about a time you were enjoying yourself so much that you didn't realize how many hours had passed or tell about a time when a brief experience felt like it took forever!"*
- **Story:** The myth of Phaethon. *Tell about a time you wanted to do something, but you couldn't or were not allowed to do it.*
- **Experience:** A walk in the woods: *Tell about one thing you remember from your time in the woods.*
- **Question:** What is my purpose in life? *Tell about a time you were in the right place, at the right time, doing exactly what was needed.*
- **Game:** Hide and seek. *Tell about a time you had to hide, either physically or emotionally. Tell about a time you went looking for something, tangible, like an object, or intangible, like adventure, and you either found it or you did not.*
- **Vocabulary word:** "Justice." Before the circle, cluster students' associations with the word "justice." These might include law, courts, police, fairness, etc. *Tell about a time you had an experience with one of these things.*

Witnessing and Reading the Field

As I mentioned in Chapter 3, a quote attributed to philosopher Jiddu Krishnamurti sums up the challenge of what we call *witnessing*: "To observe without evaluating is the highest form of intelligence." How is this so, and if it is, how do we do it? When we bring our preconceptions to the act of observation or to our listening, these will inevitably filter, shape, and color what we take in. Circle trainer Marlow Hotchkiss suggests that facilitators must become like a "hollow bone;" that is, empty of preconception and personal agenda while at the same time open and fully present.

This requires a great deal of practice. As Marshall Rosenberg points out in his course on Nonviolent Communication, we naturally combine observation and evaluation.[3] It is a survival mechanism. If we feel rushed in our communication, we are compelled to generalize our observations. We say "You're mean," rather than, "I was upset when I saw you yelling at Alice for not bringing her homework." As we ask students to take their time in circle, to pause and check in before speaking, and to tell their stories, we are encouraging them to bear witness to their own lives.

Witness consciousness is the ability to bring a certain equanimity and objectivity to the flow of experience. Socially, this is important so that we can relate to others, free from the influence of our own emotional reactions. Academically, this quality is important as we try to take in and retain new information, suspending critical analysis until the information has been fully received, the text fully read, the speaker fully heard. The circle is a laboratory for the development of this kind of consciousness.

In a group of 30, each student spends about 97 percent of circle time listening. The intention to listen from the heart calls us to adopt the perspective of a witness and to monitor any judgments that might arise and get in the way of our listening. Doing so develops empathy and simultaneously exercises our capacity to paraphrase and conceptualize, which are academic skills.

At its most basic level, witnessing is just exercising recall of what another person has said in circle. We often suggest that the students conduct a "witnessing round," with the simple directions: *When the talking piece comes, say one thing you remember that another person shared,* or *Say what stayed with you from what others have said,* or *Share what you heard, not what you thought about it.* Initially, we ask students *not* to explain why they think this information stayed with them, just to recall it. We also emphasize that this is not a memory game, but just a way of checking in as to what was retained by group members.

On the part of the facilitator, however, witnessing is a more subtle and inclusive process. This involves developing our capacity to *read the field,* a concept we get from social scientist Kurt Lewin, who also coined the term "group dynamics." The "field" as Lewin describes it is the dynamic interplay between the person and the environment. The environment includes the place, whether that is out in nature or in a classroom, and the people present.[4] As we have already noted, simply rearranging the furniture to create a circle affects the dynamics of what occurs with the people in that space. And, of course, everyone brings their own influences into the field—their energy, attitudes, prior experience, values, physical attributes, etc.

To *witness* or *read the field* is to bring awareness to how all the variables present in the people *and* the place interact at any given moment. While this seems nearly impossible, if you are a teacher (or a parent or a sensitive human being) you are *always* reading the field. You know when the collective energy is low, when attention is distracted or focused, when it is time to press on or time to let up. When you are facilitating circle, a way to think about the interactive field is to consider its four basic aspects: *non-verbal, verbal, energetic, and marginal.* As we look at each part, keep in mind that our attempts to "read" the field are always colored and influenced by our own subjectivity. So, when looking outward into the field, it is also important to stay mindful of subjective states: body sensations, thoughts, mental images, and emotions (which are largely a combination of thought and sensation). Since your subjectivity is also a part of the field, it's valuable to sort it out and see its contribution to the totality.

The *non-verbal* field involves the physical environment as well as the physical expressions of those in it. If there is clutter, distractions, temperature changes in the room, or the circle takes place outdoors or in an unfamiliar space, for example, these conditions will influence what occurs. With people, the non-verbal includes body language, posture, eye contact, etc. As an experiment, the next time you are in a group let go of the content of what people are saying and limit your awareness to the non-verbal occurrences taking place. On an even more subtle level, you might become aware of a breeze that kicks up at a particularly opportune moment, the visit of a hummingbird or butterfly, things that might be meaningful coincidences or synchronicities.

Reading the *verbal* field involves tracking the spoken content of the circle. Look for patterns of content, emerging topics and themes, similarities and differences in what is shared, as well as verbal nuances such as tone, phrasing, pitch, etc. It is often useful for the facilitator to do a kind of *meta-witnessing* of the verbal field from time to time. You might summarize the content at the end of a circle or *link circles* by reminding the group of what they talked about in a prior gathering. You might also be picking up on subtle connections between the stories and you determine that it would serve the group to make these explicit.

Although *energetic* is an imprecise term, we know when the "energy" waxes or wanes in a group! There are some ways to develop sensitivity to this aspect of the field. For example, allow the verbal content to be sound *unencumbered of meaning*. That is, play with hearing speech as if it were music. Try to hear the song of a bird, for example, without identifying it as "song" or as the sound coming from a "bird." Imagine sound as merely frequencies striking the eardrum. Sometimes the labels we put on things keep us from really seeing them. How many times have we passed by a tree, perhaps calling it by its species name but missing the texture of the bark or how the wind ruffles the leaves? Also, *try not to interpret* visual events. I find it helpful sometimes to gaze at the center of the circle in soft focus. Sometimes the energetic field defies description. It may be just a sensation, a change in temperature, a flash of color, or an internal image.

Last, to read what is *marginal* in the field is to become aware of words unspoken, questions unanswered, expressions withheld or not embodied, issues unaddressed, or the many dim manifestations of "the elephant in the room." These inklings can come through persistent thoughts or images, even those seemingly disconnected from what is happening in the circle, like remembering your mother's birthday in the midst of things! Being a deeply subjective category of noticing, what is perceived to be *marginal* needs to be checked internally before you share this aspect of the field with the group. If you determine that this material is coming out of your own needs, is completely irrelevant to the group, or that sharing it will *not serve,* then don't share it. You might find yourself deeply moved or angered by what you are noticing in the field. If so, note this internally with a degree of non-reactive equanimity and determine whether the group needs to hear what you feel, whether it would serve to make this explicit or held silently.

To *read the field* is to put all four (and probably more) aspects together, with a continued awareness of our human limitations as readers. One way to think of this *field* is to see the circle itself as an organic, energetic being. It is the totality that is "more than the sum of its parts." To say that the circle has a life of its own, something more than the sum of the verbal, non-verbal, energetic, and marginal contributions of each individual, is to approach the idea of the interactive field. Once we read the field, as facilitators we are responsible to respond to it in service of the group.

As you work with students to develop *their* skills at witnessing and reading the field, trainer Bonnie Tamblyn suggests that there are five approaches:

- **Echo witnessing:** Asking the group to say what stayed with them from the expressions of others, without commenting as to why. (Trainer Camille Ameen often uses an extension of this form by asking students to tell a story from their own experience that connects with what they mentioned in their mirror witnessing.)
- **Resonance witnessing:** Ask the group what appears to be "up" with the group given what has been shared. (This is connected to what I call "harvesting.")
- **Thematic witnessing:** What seem to be the themes or main points that have emerged from what the group has shared?
- **Questions:** What questions do we have given what we have heard?
- **Prompts:** What prompts might we use to go deeper into the issues, themes, and questions we have heard?

Just as we are challenged in circle to shift our perspective from teacher or counselor to facilitator, so we are challenged to *re-see* the students who come to us with "special needs." I recall one student diagnosed with Asperger's Syndrome who during class would get up from his seat, exit the door, and then return, over and over, crossing the threshold again and again. While it appeared that he was in his own world and was not paying attention, he could, in fact, say exactly what was on a page of text after having glanced at it only momentarily. When we were in circle, he did the same. When the group grew comfortable with the strangeness of this behavior, when it was, so to speak, *embraced* by the circle, this young man brought us an amazing gift. At the end of our circles, he would witness everything that had passed from his position at the doorway, and he would do so with exquisite, non-reactive objectivity, holding a mirror up to the group so we could see ourselves!

Another student of mine was so painfully shy that he would cringe when anyone would simply greet him. In circle, he often just held the talking piece for a moment and then passed it on. After a while, he began to speak but barely in a whisper. When he did, the circle deepened their silence and their listening even though it was nearly impossible to hear what he was saying. Somehow, he must have sensed that we were listening to *him*, not just to the content of his words, because as the year went on his voice became more distinct. By the end of the year, he too stood up to give the results of a yearlong research project!

Students with diagnoses of Autistic Spectrum Disorders (ASDs), from mild "attention deficit" to the seemingly complete withdrawal of extreme autism, are coming into our world and our classrooms in ever increasing numbers. Perhaps these children with so-called "relational disorders" are here to teach *us* something about how to relate differently to one another and to the environment. Jack Zimmerman, in the concluding chapter of Jaquelyn McCandless's book *Children with Starving Brains,* puts it this way:

> The special children have truly become canaries in the mines of our culture; they are compelling, not only because we come to love them so much for who they are individually, but also because they are here to catalyze the expanded awareness needed to change our culture—and sooner rather than later.

> The vast and increasing numbers of ASD children are messengers reflecting critical unbalances in the ways we live our lives. In their silences and explosions of feeling, in the disruption of their biochemical makeup, in their obvious incompatibility with our established educational system and traditional medical paradigm, they are literally asking us to see how out of balance we have become, collectively and individually. They are a wake-up message, a desperate eleventh-hour call for us to realize the insanity of our priorities and the many dangers in our present courses of action.[5]

In their own journey with an autistic grandchild, Jack and Jacqueline discovered the value of "aquatic therapy," now widely used for children and adults living with autism. Children who would never look you in the eye on dry land will do so underwater. It has been suggested that the water, warm and containing, provides an experience of being *held* in a *tangible relational field*. In water, when we are close enough, we feel each other's movements. Perhaps being in water, as we were in the womb, reminds us that *we are all connected*. When the relational field of circle is strong, it is like being in such a warm bath.

At Palms Middle School, our coordinator of special education, Chris Norris, suggested that students participating in what were called "special day classes," self-contained classrooms for children with exceptional needs, be mainstreamed for circle. These students, with labels from "emotionally disturbed" to "autistic," were integrated, no more than two at a time, into high- functioning classes where strong *relational fields* had developed in circle. There were no special accommodations. This worked exceptionally well for everyone.

In LAUSD, when we trained special education high school teachers to use circle in social skills classes for ASD students, they hit upon a very powerful strategy. Each identified student was paired with a neurotypical buddy for circle. The result was a much stronger relational field than what existed with segregated special needs groups.

The reality for all our students is that they live in a world with a highly fractured relational field. There are so few exemplars of heartful, compassionate communication. Consider how often you see examples of people deeply engaged in compassionate dialogue, really listening to one another, not just trying to make points and one-up each other. We have the illusion of connection through the internet and social media, but when we put even the most adept web surfers in the same room, they don't know how to relate to one another. So, this *problem* of what to do with students who are challenged to relate is a culture-wide problem, as Jack Zimmerman notes above.

We must begin with ourselves. When we practice listening and speaking from the heart, our students will feel safer around us. When they know that we can compassionately take in what they are expressing—even if those expressions frighten or disturb us, then they are more likely to continue to reach out. Once again, I strongly believe that when the adults on a campus practice circle with one another, this creates what biologist Rupert Sheldrake calls a "morphogenetic field," which the children will feel.[6] Many people tell me that when they walk onto a campus where circle is practiced in an authentic way, they can *feel* this relational field.

Students on the spectrum are often highly anxious, always feeling unsafe, and are highly sensitive to the onslaught of stimuli that barrage our environments. Perhaps we have more attention-deficit disorders because there is so much calling for our attention!

In addition to creating a strong relational field in our classrooms by walking our talk, there are steps we can take to adapt the environment and our approach to better serve all our students, including those with "special needs:"

- Limit distractions in the environment by taking the steps noted above about how to *create a safe container*.
- Limit clutter in the environment. If possible, have a designated circle space in the school with soft lighting, comfortable seating, elements from nature, etc.
- Actively teach practices for calming and self-regulation, including meditation and guided imagery.
- Actively teach a vocabulary of feelings and needs.
- Vary circle modalities, using art, movement, rhythm, etc.
- Develop a set of visual and verbal cues to help students gently return to the intentions of circle. For example, I use a giant plastic sunflower as a "leader's piece." Students know that when I raise it, this bloom is a sign for the group to re- focus. Consider writing instructions and prompts on the board or a small, portable white board you can carry into the circle.
- Use activities that bring about a sense of *collective mastery*, where the group feels that they have accomplished something *together*. This can be as simple as a simultaneous handclap, or the use of a prompt that requires only a brief or single- word answer.
- Most of all, heed the advice offered by trainer Camille Ameen: "*Just go slowly, calmly, and lovingly.*"[7]

Facilitator Self-Awareness and Self-Care

We should apply Camille's advice meticulously to ourselves! If we welcome the *whole* child in ourselves and we choose to welcome the whole child in every child in our classroom, we can easily become overwhelmed. You are to be commended if you have even considered bringing circles to your classroom. In terms of self-awareness, staying true to your own body, mind, heart, and intuition is the first step. If you are feeling the weight—the burden and the honor—of offering circle in your classroom, this physical feedback is critical to your growth and the expansion of your capacity to hold the circles. Try to welcome the feelings with a degree of equanimity and then look for the causes. Was it a particular student's sharing or behavior that acted as a trigger? Was it the messages you are receiving from the institution that this way of being with students is undervalued? Was it something you were carrying into the circle from your personal life? I can say in all honesty that a full day of holding circles in my classes was significantly more exhausting than teaching a lesson on grammar! The exhaustion, I believe, was the result of my own limitations to contain all that was shared as well as my instinct to try to shape it and do something about it.

And there is one more thing to keep in mind: it is likely that many of us have not received the quality of attention that we propose is possible in circle. In other words, we have not had many opportunities in our daily lives to enact and to receive the compassionate listening and speaking promised in circle. To people who have been raised in listening cultures, this is a complete non-issue. For us, however, *we may be trying to give what we never got.* And that is a recipe for burnout. So, for now, just a few tips on self-care:

- Practice deep council with other adults, particularly those who are also attempting to offer the practice to others.
- Let go of the idea of a "good circle." What you experience with the youth will very likely look quite different from what you experience with like-minded adults.
- Embrace the small victories.
- Remember that this is a transitional time, that what you are doing is radically countercultural—that is, counter to a culture that values independence over interdependence. You are operating at the beginning of a new paradigm, and such transitions are rarely easy.
- Find a way to sustain a degree of joy, playfulness, lightness, celebration, and appreciation in your circles even as you embrace the reality of loss, struggle, and grief.

- Make allies of humor and the unexpected.
- Find ways to nourish body, mind, spirit, and psyche. Not simply to *soothe* yourself but to get what you need to thrive. Explore what these might be in a circle of peers and then support each other to follow through!
- Protect what brought you into this noble endeavor in the first place: the possibility of a better world for future generations.

For Reflection and Imagination

1. An exercise in "witnessing:" Once you finish reading this chapter (or any chapter), pause and ask yourself, "What did I just read?"

- Note what you remembered.
- Skim back through the chapter and note what you did not recall.
- Ask yourself, "How does the information in this chapter touch my lived experience?"
- Note the questions you still have about the information.

2. Consider the story about The Museum of Tolerance and the circle about cruelty and kindness.

- What story might you tell your students about receiving or giving an act of kindness?
- What story might you tell about an act of cruelty committed against you or one that you witnessed?
- What story might you tell that acknowledges your own capacity for cruelty?

3. To develop a "circle habit of mind," in reference to any experience or information, we must ask, "What is this about?" and try to see the implied topics. Consider the topic(s) inherent in ...

- a game you like to play
- a recent news story
- a question you have
- a song or poem you love
- an experience you have had
- a standard you teach

Chapter 4: Circle Facilitation

1 **Shift From Authority to Authenticity**

Circle facilitation invites a move from "expert" to co-learner. Educators model presence, humility, and deep listening, holding both participant and instructional roles with care.

2 **Tell Stories That Are Authentic and Facilitating**

Effective stories are honest, age-appropriate, and offered in service of students' self-reflection, not for catharsis. Share scars, not wounds.

3 **Create a Safe Container Through Clear Agreements**

Collaboratively establish and revisit norms. Clarify boundaries around conflict, confidentiality, and participation to ensure students feel seen, heard, and safe.

4 **Read the Field, Don't Just Lead It**

Skilled facilitators learn to witness not only what is said, but also what is unsaid. Pay attention to verbal, non-verbal, and energetic cues to guide the circle responsibly.

5 **Adapt Practice for Diverse Needs**

Circle creates belonging for all. Thoughtful design, sensory support, and relational cues can open space for neurodiverse students and those with anxiety or trauma histories.

6 **Support Your Own Inner Teacher**

Facilitating deep connection is demanding. Tend to your energy, seek peer circles, and give yourself permission to let go of perfection.

7 **Cultivate a Circle Habit of Mind**

Circle becomes a way of seeing the world: a lens for listening, a tool for learning, and a practice of hope. Over time, anything and everything can become a prompt.

5

FORMING CIRCLE PROMPTS: THE FACILITATOR'S ART

ONCE YOU HAVE ACQUIRED the habit, every experience or bit of information becomes raw material for circle. Once, I received a shipment of the floor-sitting chairs for my classes. Each had to be assembled, and it is a tricky process. So, before our circle, I gave each student a box with the parts and the accompanying vaguely written instructions for assembly. It seemed simple enough, just three parts and the seat and backing material to be slipped over a frame, but the actual process filled the room with expressions of frustration and took up nearly three-quarters of our circle time. When all the chairs were finally assembled, we brought the circle together. Because we only had about 15 minutes left, I offered the simple prompt: *Tell about your experience building the chair.*

Students spoke of wishing they had had better guidance, and some made it clear that they expected that guidance to come from me! (Several students came to me, only to find that I too was struggling.) A few students found the task easy. Either they found the instructions clear or the process obvious. Some finished quickly and enjoyed watching others in their struggles. Others finished and announced their willingness to help those who were challenged. Some kept working in silent desperation, not wanting to ask anyone for help. Others knew immediately that this was not their area of strength and asked for help right away.

After a quick round of these stories, I called for a web-style round with a soft talking piece to be tossed to those who wished to speak. The follow-up prompt was: "Given the stories we just heard, what can we say about the ways we dealt with this task?" Replies included the following:

"Some of us always look to the adult to have the answers. We don't think about our peers as knowing how to do something. Teachers don't know everything!"

"Some people ask for help, and others prefer to do things by themselves no matter how difficult and frustrating it is."

"If you have to ask for help, doing something is less satisfying. Clear instructions are important!"

"It is easier to do something when you see someone else do it first."

Of course, each of these could function as thesis statements for some potentially very interesting essays on effective pedagogy! If we had more time, we might have moved more deeply into the profound issues inherent in these statements by using *them* to form additional prompts:

Tell about a time when:

- *you discovered that someone you thought had the answer in fact did not.*
- *you asked someone for help and that person was or was not able to help you.*
- *someone asked you for help and you were or were not able to give it.*
- *you needed help and did or did not ask for it.*
- *you accomplished something challenging all by yourself.*
- *you accomplished something challenging with the help of others.*

As you can see, the possibilities for prompts from even the simplest activity can lead to profound dialogue around weighty issues such as giving and receiving assistance and how we learn best.

Guidelines for Forming Circle Prompts

When I was training to become a teacher and learning how to frame an engaging question, my supervisor, Dr. Helen Lodge, would regularly remind me, "Increase your *wait time.*" Wait time is the pause we take *after* asking a question—before we either call on the first student to raise a hand, reframe the question, or answer it ourselves. We were told to let the question linger, allowing students to consider it and their responses. In circle, the form itself compels us to wait. The singular difference between teaching and facilitating is that once you put out the prompt, that's it; you're done! Once you pass the talking piece, you shift out of guiding the circle and move into *holding the container*, listening deeply, allowing for the unfolding of what will be. When we are in teacher mode and we ask a question, if we don't get the answer we want, we can reframe the question, frame it yet again, and then ask a student to shape it in a way the other students can understand. In circle, you basically get one shot, and then you let it go.

I identify four types of prompts: reflective, present moment, speculative, and imaginative. A *reflective* prompt elicits stories of past experiences. A *present moment* prompt focuses on what is happening in the circle now. A *speculative* prompt elicits thoughts about what might happen in the future based on what has already occurred. *Imaginative* prompts allow for wild unplanned expressions of novelty. Physicist David Bohm tells us that scientific breakthroughs are generally a product of the latter.[1]

Crafting effective prompts is an art cultivated through practice, and a few guidelines can be helpful. A well-wrought prompt will ...

- Be of interest to or in service of the whole group, not just the facilitator.
- Enable each participant to access and share from experience.
- Elicit story rather than opinion.
- Be stated in the clearest possible terms.
- Be developmentally appropriate.
- Not require the sharing of "feelings."
- Allow for the whole spectrum of human response.
- Not be a veiled statement.
- Not promote a hidden agenda.

Prompts in Service of the Whole Group

When you are considering a prompt, ask yourself whether the topic will engage the group or serve a need expressed by the group. This is a bit of a shift for us as teachers, especially when our classes are driven by a pre-determined curriculum that purports to know the needs of our students. It is always a good practice to gauge the level of interest in a prompt by offering it to the group *before* you begin the circle. Say explicitly: "So here is what I'm thinking about for a prompt today." Then after naming the prompt, ask the group whether they would like to take it up *and* whether everyone might have a story to tell on the topic.

Before the circle, you might offer your reasons for bringing this topic and get consensus agreement to go forward. This is transparent leadership. It is a rookie mistake to begin the circle, to call for dedications for example, and then to say: "Today's prompt is ... " If you do this, you haven't yet established a reason to begin, and the students haven't yet acknowledged a willingness to move into deep listening and heart speech.

Better to have a bit of discussion around the topic and the prompt and to ask the group if it works for them and whether they are ready to begin, than to begin just because it is circle time. Students might tell you, in all kinds of ways, that they are not willing to be in council. Learn to notice this and provide an alternative.

If the group is agendaless and not tied to a curricular goal, then you are usually offering some form of check-in to determine where the group needs to go, and then you are transparently shaping a prompt from your witnessing of what the students have shared. You will say something like: *This is what I heard in your check-in, and it seems like a good prompt for us would be* ... With older groups, you might turn over the whole process to the students: "Given what we just heard in our check-in, what might be a good prompt to take us deeper?"

If you are taking up a predetermined curricular goal or a topic for social-emotional growth, like developing decision-making skills, be sure to make this explicit and find a way to connect the topic to student felt needs. A *reflective* prompt might be: *Tell about a time when you had to make a decision.* Then, possibly in a second round: *Tell about why you made that decision, and how did it work out?* For a *speculative* prompt you might ask them to state a decision they are going to have to make soon and then ask for their reasons for deciding one way or another. A *present moment* prompt might ask students to tell of the decisions they are making right now, in the circle: how they chose to sit; by whom they have chosen to sit; whether to listen or pursue an inner dialogue; thoughts other than the circle that they choose to entertain, etc. Although all decision-making is speculative, as we are holding out hope for a positive outcome, an *imaginative* prompt might be: Imagine yourself in the future having to make a tough decision. Like choosing a job, a cause, where to live, or whether to be close to someone. How do you think you will make that decision? What factors or values will you bring to your consideration?

As language arts teachers, we might choose to offer a curricular goal such as having students understand the concept of a *theme* in literature and how to derive a theme from textual evidence. We ask ourselves, however, as facilitators, what our students' felt needs are around this concept. So, we must dig a bit deeper. A theme is really a statement made about a topic. It is an opinion based on evidence, a generalization based on specifics, a hypothesis based on observation. Why would a student, or anyone, need to practice and understand such formulations? Well, we might simply say we all have a need for order and autonomy, a need to sense our own capacity to interpret our experience of the world, to know that we can observe and make sense of things. Some prompts that might serve these needs are the following:

- *Name something you know to be true.* (This could be an opening speed round.) *Then, tell how you know that it is true.* (I call this an *epistemological inquiry circle* because it leads to a discussion of how we know what we know.)
- *Name one thing you have learned. Then, tell how you learned it.*
- A speculative prompt could ask students to predict something that they expect will happen. For example: *What do you think will happen at the end of this story? What do you predict will happen if we grow one plant in natural light and one in artificial light?*

Simply asking yourself, "Who does this prompt serve?" will often help you avoid foisting a prompt on the students that is only of interest to you. If, for example you are having some strong feelings about a current event, it is best to check with the students about whether they too are concerned with this. If they are not, then this might not be the best circle topic for today. You can still give them the information you feel they should have, just do so outside of the circle.

Prompts that Enable Each Participant to Access and Share from Experience

It may seem obvious, but keep in mind that a good prompt will be one that elicits stories about which students *can and will* speak. First, check with yourself, even if you have to pause in the middle of a circle to do so. Do *you* have an authentic, age- and context-appropriate story to tell about this topic? If the answer is yes, then ask yourself whether every student will have a story about at least some aspect of this topic? Then, if you feel the prompt is in service to the group, go for it.

Sometimes a topic comes up that is only in the experience of a few students. If that is the case, you can choose to have a fishbowl (described in Chapter 8) with those students in the center, or you can broaden the topic so everyone can share something. For example, a topic concerning financial literacy might be about the value of saving money. A few students might have the experience of saving up. A few might even have bank accounts. Others might not have any source of money to save. If this is the case, *broaden the concept* of "saving" to include more than money. You can begin with a discussion or a brainstorm about the kinds of things we save—objects, living things, memories, plans, ideas, clothes that are too small, etc. List or cluster these on the board or screen, and then ask whether everyone has saved one or more of these things. The prompt then simply becomes: *Tell about something you save or have saved.* This can be followed by a round on why we chose to save these things, ultimately leading to a harvesting of *things we find valuable.*

Sometimes, no one in the circle has had a direct experience of the topic and yet there is great interest in discussing it. Perhaps, for example students want to explore *what makes a person an "adult."* They have not yet experienced what it is to be old, yet they are trying regularly to understand the adults they deal with daily (just as we try to figure them out!). So, how to have a circle about being old when you never have been? Given that one of the guidelines for forming prompts is that participants must be able to speak from direct experience, the topic of the *being an adult or elder* would indeed be a tricky one, and yet it is of deep interest to them as they would like to figure out how to manage that life passage. A *speed round* prompt for this might be: *Name someone you know is an* adult, or When you hear the word "adult," what comes to mind? The circle, then, is about times we have witnessed someone being an adult or someone who embodies one or more of the qualities we just listed. As a follow-up, depending upon the age of the students, you might offer something from Erik Erickson's Stages of Development or literature that demonstrates qualities of adulthood that perhaps students have not yet considered.

Prompts That Elicit Story Rather Than Opinion

Opinions are stories robbed of their narratives. When someone says "I hate pizza," there is guaranteed to be an untold story about a bad experience with a particular slice sometime in the speaker's dining history. When I hear people share their opinions or even share their "feelings," I am often overtaken by a sudden drowsiness. Even a highly charged opinion like "The system is rigged, and the leaders are corrupt!" leaves me flat, unless it is quickly followed by a story direct from the speaker's experience. When someone names a deep feeling like "I am desperately sad and lonely," I am moved to empathy but even that compassionate reaction remains thin until I hear *the story behind this feeling*. With respect to differences of opinion, hearing another person's story, their direct experience, generally does not raise our ire in the way that an ungrounded opinion does. This notion underlies the statement "An enemy is one whose story has not yet been heard," variously attributed to Thích Nhất Hạnh and Gene Knudsen Hoffman.

Perhaps we are so opinionated because we feel we don't have *time* to tell our stories. We are in such a hurry to "get to the point" that we omit what led us to it. In the circle we are always inviting story, whether it is a story from the past, the story of the present moment, or the new story as it unfolds in our imagination. This is why we rely so heavily on the stem "tell about a time when ... " Other prompt stems that can elicit story include the following:

For past experience (reflective):

- *Share a story about a time when ...*
- *Tell about a specific moment when ...*
- *How many of you have ever had an experience of ...? Tell us about one of those times.*
- *Recall a time when ...*

For the present moment:

- *What are you noticing now?*
- *What do you see going on in the room at this moment?*
- *Tell the story of what you are experiencing right now.*

For speculation:

- *Given the stories we have heard and the information we have received, what do you see happening next?*
- *Using evidence from texts and primary sources (including stories shared in the circle) what do you predict?*

For an imagined future:

- *What do you imagine will happen?*
- *Looking toward the future, what do you see?*
- *Tell the story of what you think might happen.*
- Here are some prompt stems that will usually lead to the sharing of opinions, and thus I recommend avoiding them:
- *What do you think about ... ?*
- *How does that make you feel?*
- *What should be done about ... ?*
- *Why?*

Using these opinion-eliciting prompts is not necessarily a facilitator faux pas, particularly when you make it clear that statements elicited by them should be supported, perhaps in a subsequent round, with the personal stories and evidence that led the participants to hold these opinions. Behind every opinion, there is a story.

Often in the telling of our stories, we begin to question our opinions. To paraphrase poet Jorge Monterrosa, "When we speak, our ignorance reveals itself to us." This is a good thing! As I talk about a particular instance of a negative interaction with a colleague, for example, I might begin to see that I am engaging in the fallacy of arguing from the particular to the general, that I am judging this person based on a sample of one experience. This self-reflection is one of the great benefits of speaking in circle. Speaking into the listening of others helps us to reflect on what we are saying. In this regard, you might consider a speed or opening round that calls for an opinion and then follow this with a prompt that leads to stories. For example, an opening round of "What did you think about the President's State of the Union speech last night?" can be followed with: *Tell a* story about an experience you have had that is in some way connected with one of the topics the President discussed.

Prompts Stated in the Clearest Possible Terms

A game to play when you practice forming prompts is to imagine that you are speaking to a group of five-year-olds. Use the fewest possible words and the simplest, most direct vocabulary, so the little ones are excited to burst into story. *Tell about a time when you played with another person* will get more traction than *Tell about a time when you were included in cooperative play with another person.* If, for example, you want to get at the complicated, salient, and appropriate-for-all-ages topic of *inclusion and exclusion,* you can say: *Tell about a time when a person or group invited you to play* (or work or plan or go somewhere), and: *Tell about a time a person or group did not let you play*, or even more simply: *Tell about a time when someone asked you to play* or *a time when someone said you could not play*. For older students, you can expand the prompt: *Tell about a time when you were included or not included in a group.* Once the stories are told, you can introduce the vocabulary of inclusion and exclusion, and the stories will serve as immediate tangible examples. Including distinguishing modifiers in your prompt such as Tell about a time when you played *well* with another person will limit the scope of possible stories. Tell about a time you learned something will yield more than Tell about a time you learned something important. A rule of thumb is to try to limit modifiers, especially when they are "leading" or implying a predetermined moral directive or a hidden agenda (an idea we will take up shortly). Tell about a time when you were stressed out is better than Tell about a time you were stressed out, and you handled it well. It is better to allow for the full spectrum of responses and then afterwards look at what might be useful, healthy, compassionate, or adaptive.

Even terms we assume students understand might need to be defined or unpacked. A good example of this is the word "justice." *Tell about an experience of justice* might be a simple enough prompt, but it is not entirely clear. To begin a clarifying process, *before* going into circle, take some time to brainstorm or develop with the group a working definition of the term. You might ask students what comes to mind when they hear the word "justice." You will get answers that include fairness, law, judges, police, courts, prison, payback, equality, an eye for an eye, etc. List these and then ask students whether they have *ever* had an experience *with any one of these*. The prompt is simply: *Tell about a time when you had an experience with one of these things.* After the stories are told, call for a harvesting round such as *Given the stories we have just heard, what can we say about this thing we call "justice"?* After closing the circle, the group comes up with a working definition. At this point, you can bring in various quotes about and definitions of justice, describe types of justice—distributive, retributive, restorative, transformative—and share stories from history and literature. Then, start the process again and watch the stories and the definition deepen.

There are several strategies to help you clarify prompts:

- *Before* going into circle, check with the students to see whether they understand the prompt. Ask them to help you shape it.
- Use group brainstorming to clarify and define terms in the prompt.
- With the group, create a list of related terms for a key term within the prompt. Then, ask the group whether they have had an experience with at least one of the things listed.
- Eliminate limiting or leading modifiers.

Prompts That Are Developmentally Appropriate

When you form a prompt, consider the range of experience of those in your group. According to the National Association for the Education of Young Children (NAEYC), there are three core considerations in determining "developmentally appropriate practice:" knowledge of developmental stages (age appropriateness); a child's individual interests, abilities, and needs; and social and cultural appropriateness.[2]

The developmental stages articulated by Jean Piaget, Erik Erickson, and many others are well known to educators and can provide guidance when we consider age-appropriate prompts and topics for discussion. For example, a child in Piaget's "pre-operational" stage will be challenged to think in terms of multiple perspectives. Hence, a prompt that asks a five-year-old to consider a situation from another person's point of view could fall flat. Similarly, a prompt that asks early teens about experiences of "intimacy" will likely have to be reframed, as Erickson suggests that our capacity to understand intimacy doesn't begin until early adulthood. To reframe the topic, we unpack what we mean by "intimacy" and take a broader view. We might say that intimacy is the capacity to see beyond personal needs and thus to be in deep relationship. For young teens, we can approach the core of this by exploring friendship. A prompt like *Name someone who is a true friend (speed round) and then tell about a time when you first realized this* will elicit stories that convey the inherent values of friendship. The same prompt can be used for younger children, except the second clause would shift to something like simply *Tell a story about this friend.* Prompts such as *Name someone who* really listens to you (or cares about you, "has your back," etc.), and tell about a time you knew this to be true, will also get at these qualities of relationship.

To understand your students' individual interests, abilities, and needs, will require direct observation. When you take notice of these things and feed them back in the form of a prompt, you are likely to get full participation in the circle. Asking about them in circle will give you a lot to go on. For example, use a prompt like *Tell about something you enjoy doing* or *Tell about something you know how to do*. The "mysteries" question process, which will be described in Chapter 10, will give you a year's worth of age- appropriate prompts based on what the students themselves want to know.

Cultural and social appropriateness requires an awareness of your students' linguistic and cultural backgrounds, traditions, and family structure. This can be a sticky wicket when assumptions and stereotypes cloud our ability to see our students as individuals. Still, knowledge of your students' ethnic affiliations and cultural identities will serve you well as a facilitator of circle. You can access some of this information through prompts such as these:

- *Tell about a holiday your family celebrates.*
- *Tell a story about a favorite meal with your family.*
- *How do you celebrate special occasions, like birthdays, with your family? Tell a story of one such occasion.*
- *Do you have any special objects in your house, books or other treasures, that you know have special meaning for your family? Tell about one of them.*
- *If your parents or other family members have told you stories about when they were young, what is one that you remember?*
- *Name an ancestor—a grandparent, a great-grandparent, or older—and tell a story you have heard about this person.*

Prompts That Do Not Require the Sharing of "Feelings"

I hear many students and adults refer to circle as a place where we "share our feelings." By saying this, I believe, they are indicating that something is happening in circle that is deeper and more honest than what we usually express around others. These statements can also be dismissals of circle as a fluffy, touchy-feely process lacking the rigors of rational thought. I'm puzzled by the whole idea of "sharing" one's "feelings."

I'm not sure how such an expression is done, but I imagine that the true expression of feeling is mostly *wordless*: open weeping, ecstatic dancing, tense frustration, angry gesticulations, loving embrace.

As facilitators of circles, we avoid forming prompts that *require* the sharing of feeling primarily because such verbal expressions are necessarily abstractions. To say "I am sad" does not convey sadness unless it is accompanied by non-verbal elements of posture, facial expression, and tone. Prompts, once again, should elicit *story*, and the stories will convey feeling without our asking for it explicitly.

Some examples of prompts that "require" the sharing of feelings and so should be avoided:

- *How did that make you feel?* (An extremely challenging prompt in that it requires the participant to *label* the feeling, which is a rational process that creates an abstraction of what is actually felt.)
- *Tell about a time when you were lost and how that felt.* (Just leave off the last part.)
- *How do you feel when you accomplish something that was a challenge?* (This prompt is likely to yield one-word responses, usually some variation on "good.")
- *Tell about how it made you feel when* (something happened).

Circle, however, can be an excellent place for developing a vocabulary of feeling (the academic value of which we will take up in Chapters 7 and 8). In circle, we can come to understand the full spectrum of human emotion through concrete experience from the stories we share. Circles that ask students to tell about *a time when* they felt sad, mad, glad, or scared, will help us all understand the subtleties and expressive range of these feelings, giving them a depth and nuance far beyond what a dictionary can provide. Again, these prompts do not ask students to label a feeling but to recall a time when they experienced a feeling.

Prompts That Allow for the Whole Spectrum of Human Response

There is a trend in schools called "character education." The first such program I became aware of was Josephson Institute's "Character Counts," which promotes activities to strengthen what they call the "six pillars of character:" trustworthiness, respect, responsibility, fairness, caring, and citizenship.[3] Activities to develop these traits are in wide use in schools. Christopher Peterson and Martin Seligman take a more expansive view in their extraordinary book, *Character Strengths and Virtues*. The authors classify 24 character strengths that remain consistent throughout known history and within all cultures. These strengths are categorized under six broad virtues: wisdom, courage, humanity, justice, temperance, and transcendence.[4] Called by its authors "a manual of the sanities" to distinguish it from the American Psychiatric Association's *Diagnostic and Statistical Manual of Mental Disorders* (DSM), a kind of manual of pathologies, *Character Strengths and Virtues* combines deep research, statistics, and methodologies to teach, develop, and reinforce these apparently universal values. The outline from this book can provide a wealth of topics for circles!

Circles, however, embrace the whole spectrum of human response—adaptive and maladaptive—the good, the bad, and the ugly. While collaboration, cooperation, honesty, and respect are implicit in circle practice, we do not explicitly promote these values, especially if doing so will limit the participation of those in the circle who are attempting to reflect on the times when they have *not* embodied these virtues. We create a space where students can speak of experiences of cooperation, for example, and *at the same time* they can tell stories of when they did *not* cooperate, when they did *not* go along with the crowd. Circle is a practice wherein we can *discover* how values are formed. Can we learn as much from stories of dishonesty as from talking about a time when we told the truth? I believe so. A wonderful circle prompt is *Tell about a time you told a lie.* This is followed by a round using the question: *Why do you think you did?* When we feel safe to tell such stories, we begin to develop the capacity to reflect on our actions. In restorative, healing circles (which we will take up in Chapter 10) we also benefit from the stories of those who have been affected by our actions, and this strengthens our capacity to reflect.

In *Sand and Foam,* Kahlil Gibran says, "I have learned silence from the talkative, tolerance from the intolerant, and kindness from the unkind; yet, strange, I am ungrateful to those teachers."[5] So, how do we fashion a prompt that allows for the full spectrum of human response? Sometimes this requires a two-part prompt: *Tell about a time when you cooperated with others or chose not to cooperate.* Occasionally, we split the prompt into two rounds: *Tell about a time when you cooperated with others.* Then, in a second round, *Tell about a time when you chose not to cooperate.* In some cases, we catch ourselves forming prompts that are "leading;" that is, the structure of the prompt *leads* participants in a predetermined direction. For example, if the topic is "frustration," a *leading* prompt would be: *Talk about a time when you were frustrated and you handled it well.* It is better to simply say: *Talk about a time when you were frustrated.* If it is not apparent from the stories, you can call for a second round that examines the question of how they dealt with, handled, or responded to the experience of frustration. Use simple questions, such as *What did you do when you first had this feeling of frustration?* or *What happened after you realized you were frustrated?* These will allow for the full spectrum of responses—from what we might consider "adaptive" (calling a friend, writing in your journal, taking a walk, etc.) to "maladaptive," harmful, or violent (getting drunk, punching a wall, hurting someone else, etc.). After such a circle, if we simply brainstorm the various ways participants deal with inevitable frustrations, we have in front of us *the raw material of choice,* and, according to Marshall Rosenberg, a basic need—the autonomy of choice. At this point, we are also able to bring in materials and information from experts about ways to manage frustration, and the group will be well primed to receive it!

Prompts That Are Not Veiled Statements

When we offer gender circles to middle-school students, we invariably get a question that students who identify as girls would like to pose to those who identify as boys: "Why are boys so crazy?" While we understand the desire here, the question is really a statement: "Boys are crazy. Why?"

Answering such a question is to validate its assertion, as in the old conundrum, "When did you stop being a thief?" As facilitators, we must look underneath what instigates such a statement posing as a question. What do the girls really want to know?

In a case like this, we work with them to get at what they really want to understand. Obviously, the girls have seen some behaviors they consider "crazy." We encourage them to share stories of behaviors they actually *observed.* Ultimately, a prompt might look something like this: We have noticed that some boys do some crazy things, maybe to get attention or to impress someone. This is probably true for girls as well, but would you be willing to tell a story about something you did to try to get attention or to impress? I have seen this prompt put even more simply: What is the craziest thing you have ever done to impress someone?

Of course, such a prompt does not rest with the experience with just boys or just girls. What we really want to know has to do with a more fundamental, more universal, question of why people do outrageous things. In its first formulation, "Why are boys so crazy?" responses are likely to be defensive or dismissive and will not ultimately provide what the questioner is looking for. Just imagine, however, how rich the sharing could be around stories of the lengths to which we go to impress, to get attention, or to challenge and impress ourselves!

Prompts That Do Not Promote a Hidden Agenda

A simple guideline for handling hidden agendas when you facilitate circle: reveal them! When I first started teaching in the early '80s, I was influenced, woken up really, by a book by Casey Miller and Kate

Swift titled *Words and Women.*[6] This book revealed to me how the language I used every day reinforced harmful gender stereotypes. I hadn't even thought about the ubiquitous use of the pronoun "he" to refer to an unspecified person, the "man" on the street or "mankind" in general, the rarity of words such as "chairwoman" or the neutral "chairperson," the attachment of diminutive suffixes such as "-ess," and "ette," meaning "little," making an "actress" a "little actor," etc. I learned that the word "girl" is derived from the Middle English "gurle," "girle," or "gerle," meaning a "child" or "young person." So originally, *all* young children were called "girls." The females remained "girls" as they grew into adolescence. The "girls" who were males became "boys." This was just another example how language reinforced male dominance. I found this all quite shocking.

With this new awareness, I began teaching reading and writing, literature, and grammar. Although I was not aware of it, I had a hidden agenda: not only did I want my students to question and revise inherently sexist vocabulary and usage, but I also wanted the boys and young men in my classes to grapple with this realization alongside me. And I wanted the girls and young women to see that I was an enlightened male!

Do we as teachers ever have a "hidden" agenda? Every time we ask a rhetorical question, what is hidden is the fact that we know the answer we are looking for. I have a deep habit of asking rhetorical questions when I am teaching or leading workshops, and I imagine it becomes a bit annoying for those listening to me. Is a rhetorical question really a question, or is it a statement in a question form? Why not just make the statement?

What are some hidden agendas we might bring to our facilitation of circle? We might want to have everyone follow the "rules" of circle. We want people to listen and speak from the heart. I recall a hidden agenda that often popped up in my facilitation. It was around taking the patriarchy, of which I am a representative, down a notch. In effect, I wanted my students to work out my own discomfort with the part of myself that denigrates and diminishes the power of women.

To do this, I would teach lessons around sexism and have students examine the sexist notions they held. This unconscious hidden agenda often affected the gender circles I facilitated.

So, what is a prompt that reveals a hidden agenda? How can we fashion prompts that are free from such manipulations? It is not so much the shape of the prompt that is manipulative; it is about the intention behind it and the expectations we carry about the kinds of stories we *want* the children to share, and those we are hoping they won't share.

A simple test to determine whether your prompt contains a hidden agenda: *Ask yourself what you are hoping for.* If you are hoping, for example, that the students will be kinder to one another, just state this openly. A hidden agenda that comes out of hiding ceases to be a manipulation.

Turn, Turn, Turn: Embracing Polarity in the Forming of Prompts

There is a song, originally from Ecclesiastes, which through the hands of Pete Seeger and finally the Byrds became our familiar *Turn, Turn, Turn.* The song itself turns on a series of polarities: life-death, love-hate, reap-sow. A wonderful text for circle, the song touches on many seeming opposites in the human condition. It also gives us some guidance in the art of the prompt.

A *useful* circle prompt embraces not only the whole spectrum of human response, as noted above, but the *totality* of human experience, the dark and the light, foul and fair, good and bad. So, for example, when we are trying to understand topics such as *health and hope,* it is better to ask for stories of hurt *and* of healing, of desolation *as well as* consolation. In public life, we often avoid the negative side of the polarity. We also tend to limit the spectrum of human emotion in public life. At a certain point it becomes uncool to be too happy or too upset. When I was growing up, to be "cool" meant to be completely unruffled. For some of us, particularly for men, it remains permanently uncool to display emotion (except for anger), and we thus limit our capacity to feel. This shutting down of feeling usually begins in adolescence as we try on various masks to see which will help us fit in. Ask a middle-school student about a "time they were really happy," and they will probably tell you it was when you hadn't asked this question! And to really speak about our grief, loss, sadness, isolation, and loneliness at this age is equally, if not more, challenging. Sadly, this might also be true of younger students as well and is likely true for most of us.

Just as our emotional lives traverse a spectrum, it seems as well that all "academic" pursuits also turn on fundamental polarities. Literature turns on expressions of "love and loss," social studies on "collaboration or creation and destruction," the sciences on "particle and wave, stasis and action," math on "order and chaos." As you will see in the chapters on using circles to deepen understanding of academic curriculum, what appears at first as an intangible abstraction can become meaningful and relevant through reflection.

This verse from Ecclesiastes is perhaps the clearest, most concise articulation of archetypal polarities relating to the human condition and so serves as excellent source material for the shaping of prompts:

> To everything there is a season, and a time for every matter under heaven:
> a time to be born, and a time to die;
> a time to plant, and a time to pluck up what is planted;
> a time to kill, and a time to heal;
> a time to break down, and a time to build up;
> a time to weep, and a time to laugh;
> a time to mourn, and a time to dance;
> a time to cast away stones, and a time to gather stones together;
> a time to embrace, and a time to refrain from embracing;
> a time to seek, and a time to lose;
> a time to keep, and a time to cast away;
> a time to rend, and a time to sew;
> a time to keep silence, and a time to speak;

a time to love, and a time to hate;
a time for war, and a time for peace.
—Ecclesiastes 3:1–8[7]

Exercise: Before moving on, take some time to form prompts from the polarities in each line. Consider how you might form a prompt that is age appropriate for the students you teach. Also look at how you might phrase a prompt if you were facilitating a group of adults. Finally, for each prompt you shape, see if you can access an age-appropriate, context-appropriate, "facilitating" story from your own experience. Note how you might change this story or present it differently if you were in a circle of peers.

Now, let's use the prompt-forming process with the first four lines from this passage. We begin by asking what the inherent topics are in each statement and then we consider a few of many possible prompts:

> To everything there is a season, and a time to every purpose under the heaven:

Inherent topics: change and purpose
Prompts:

- *Tell about a time when you changed.*
- *Tell about a time when you noticed that someone or something changed.*
- To get to the question of purpose: *Tell about what led to this change.*

> A time to be born, and a time to die; a time to plant, and a time to pluck up that which is planted:

Topics: birth (origination), death (termination, loss), planting (investing time, energy, and resources to bring something about), and harvesting (the result of that investment)

Prompts:

- Birth: *Tell about a time you did or realized (became aware of) something for the very first time.*
- Death: *Tell about a time you lost something or had to let something go (such as the death of an idea or belief).*
- Planting: *Recall a time when you started something that took a long time to complete.*
- Harvesting: *Recall a time when you accomplished something or learned something that took a long time complete or to know.*

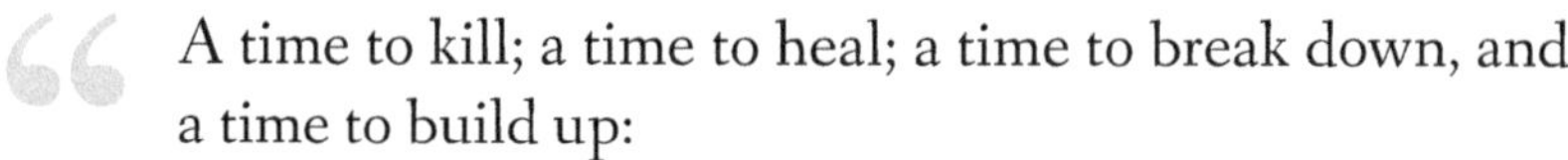

> A time to kill; a time to heal; a time to break down, and a time to build up:

Topics: termination/destruction, healing/repair
Prompts:

- *A time when you had to end something or had to take something apart.*
- *A time when you had to put something back together after it had been broken (an object, situation, or relationship).*

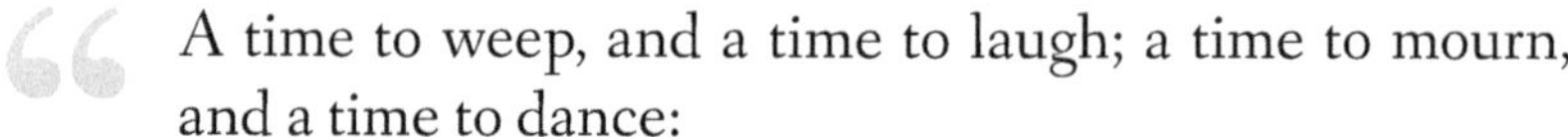

> A time to weep, and a time to laugh; a time to mourn, and a time to dance:

Topics: grief and celebration
Prompts:

- *A time you cried or wanted to.*
- *A time you laughed out loud.*
- *A time you said to yourself, "Wow, this is wonderful!"*

A Last Word on Forming Prompts

A circle prompt is not like the prompt for an essay. A circle prompt is formed to elicit lived experience. Since we rarely have the attention of listeners for as long as it takes to tell our stories, and we are conditioned to value immediate response and repartee, we often don't take the needed time to pause and reflect long enough to access memories. In the classroom (and elsewhere), we must unlearn the anxiety and pressure of time if we are ever to bring forward memories and deeply considered responses.

Although time's winged chariot always seems to be at our backs, in circle we attempt to promote a sense of timeless time. Therefore, encourage each participant to *pause* when they receive the talking piece. When you have it, model for them *how* to pause: Take a moment to let go of awareness of others in the group and the environment. Hear the prompt again internally. If you thought of an experience, story, or response *before* receiving the piece, ask yourself whether that is what you want to offer to the circle *now*. Pause long enough to make room for something new. It is within this pause, that circle magic happens.

For Reflection and Imagination

1. Circle prompts should be "authentic, age- and context-appropriate, and facilitating."

- Use the exercise on p. 127. Form prompts from each topic polarity in "Turn, Turn, Turn."
- Then, consider the stories your might tell for each side, given the age of the students you teach.

2. Consider some points, virtues, or values you would like you would like to convey to your students.

- How would you make these points explicit, rather than part of a hidden agenda?
- What lived experiences have you had that support each point or value? What stories would you tell?

Chapter 5:
Forming Circle Prompts: The Facilitator's Art

1. **Turn Everyday Moments Into Prompts**
   Anything can become a prompt, from a science experiment to assembling chairs. Look for themes like struggle, collaboration, or surprise, and invite students to tell stories.

2. **Craft Prompts That Invite Story, Not Opinion**
   Start with Tell about a time when ... to draw out lived experience. Opinions often mask stories: go to the source to build connection, empathy, and reflection.

3. **Name and Clarify Your Intention**
   A great prompt serves the group, not the facilitator's hidden agenda. Be transparent, developmentally appropriate, and willing to adapt based on the group's readiness.

4. **Use Polarity to Deepen Reflection**
   Design prompts that embrace the full range of human experience—joy and grief, failure and triumph, isolation and belonging—to unlock richer conversations.

5. **Test for Access and Inclusion**
   Check whether each student can respond to the prompt. Broaden when needed. For example, shift from "saving money" to "saving anything meaningful."

6. **Wait for the Magic**
   Pause is part of the practice. Circle teaches patience. Let prompts land and give students time to reflect before they respond.

7. **Practice Prompt-Making as a Creative Art**
   Use reflective, present-moment, speculative, or imaginative prompts. Try exercises like transforming Ecclesiastes 3:1–8's polarities into circle-ready questions.

6

CIRCLE MODES AND FORMS

Not Just Sitting Around Talking

WHAT WE CALL the arts must have originated in circles: storytelling, dance, drumming, music, ritual enactments of myth, the fashioning of tools, the preparation of foods, the education of children.

Even the "solitary" arts, like writing and painting, have an aspect of collaboration. For example, as I write this sentence, I am in a sense in dialogue with you, and I try to consider what might be of service and how to say it in a way that can be heard and understood, to speak into your listening. Even if no one else is present physically, the poet has an inner listener; the painter, an inner viewer; and the musician, an inner audience.

Later in this chapter, we will look at circle forms. We will first explore circle *modes*, ways of bringing a heightened awareness of self and other that don't necessarily involve talking. Mostly, we will look at ways to bring *multimodality* to your circles, combining language expression with fine arts, spatial awareness, music, and movement, as well as the "imaginal" or intrapersonal—the capacity to look within.

The value of Howard Gardner's work on multiple intelligences (MI) in education is largely focused on expanding the capacity of educators to vary the strategies through which they convey information. Gardner emphasizes that everyone has multiple intelligences, but that we "single out as a strong intelligence the area where the person has considerable computational power." We might say that this power is inherent and naturally accessed by a person, but it can be further developed. Gardner also makes clear that MI is not the same as "learning styles" or information processing "styles" (visual, tactile, auditory). The intelligences have to do with how the mind "acts upon sensory information, once picked up." His advice for educators is to "individualize," to teach in ways that are effective and comfortable for each student, and to "pluralize," using various ways to convey the same information.[1] This pluralization or varying of modalities is also critical for the practice of circles. Circle is not *just* sitting around talking.

To review, here is a list of the intelligences provided by Gardner's official website, the MI Oasis:

- **Spatial:** "The ability to conceptualize and manipulate large-scale spatial arrays (e.g. airplane pilot, sailor), or more local forms of space (e.g. architect, chess player)."
- **Bodily-Kinesthetic:** "The ability to use one's whole body, or parts of the body (like the hands or the mouth), to solve problems or create products (e.g. dancer)."
- **Musical:** "Sensitivity to rhythm, pitch, meter, tone, melody and timbre. May entail the ability to sing, play musical instruments, and/or compose music (e.g. musical conductor)."
- **Linguistic:** "Sensitivity to the meaning of words, the order among words, and the sound, rhythms, inflections, and meter of words (e.g. poet). (Sometimes called language intelligence.)"
- **Logical-mathematical:** "The capacity to conceptualize the logical relations among actions or symbols (e.g. mathematicians, scientists)."

- **Interpersonal:** "The ability to interact effectively with others. Sensitivity to others' moods, feelings, temperaments, and motivations (e.g. negotiator). (Sometimes called social intelligence.)"
- **Intrapersonal:** "Sensitivity to one's own feelings, goals, and anxieties, and the capacity to plan and act in light of one's own traits. Intrapersonal intelligence is not particular to specific careers; rather, it is a goal for every individual in a complex modern society, where one has to make consequential decisions for oneself. (Sometimes called self- intelligence.)"
- **Naturalistic:** "The ability to make consequential distinctions in the world of nature as, for example, between one plant and another, or one cloud formation and another (e.g. taxonomist). (Sometimes called nature intelligence.)"[2]

The naturalistic intelligence might also include what we call "street smarts," the capacity to *read* environments and to act accordingly. In addition, there has recently been serious investigation of "spiritual intelligence," a possible combination of intrapersonal, interpersonal, and naturalistic intelligences. Gardner does not use the term "spiritual," but is open to the possibility of a category called "existential intelligence," which he describes as "concern with ultimate life issues."[3] I am aware of a doctoral dissertation that measured the impact of circle training on emotional and spiritual intelligences.[4]

When you facilitate circle with young people, it is critically important to vary topics, forms, and modes. This is where the so-called "morning meeting" can lose its effectiveness. I have seen even the most engaged groups sour to the process if the form is always *basic*, with the talking piece going around the whole circle, and if the mode is always *linguistic*. Hence, I consider the label "talking circles" a very limited view.

There is also value in helping students to become aware of which of the intelligences come naturally to them and which provide challenges. And this is particularly true when they are subjected so relentlessly to testing strictly in the cognitive domain—the linguistic and mathematical intelligences.

Intrapersonal

One of the most persistent misunderstandings about the practice of circles is that one needs a group to engage in it. How do we develop our capacity to know ourselves? How do we attempt to fulfill the Delphic injunction, "Know thyself"? For the most part, we come to know ourselves through the reflection we receive from others, particularly those who are willing to tell us the truth and to hold up a clear mirror with which we can witness our own image. Such witnessing, mirroring, and reflecting happen regularly in the practice of circle. There are, however, ways to deepen self-awareness in the absence of others, ways to have a *circle of one.*

Here are some activities that can be done in a circle with others or alone. *The focus is on the self.*

Inner Dialogue and Inner Circles

In Chapter 3, I recommended some practices for prospective facilitators to engage in a "circle of one." All mindfulness practices, such as the simple noticing of breath and forms of yoga and body movement, belong in this category of the *intrapersonal.*

It is also possible to create the conditions to speak honestly to yourself and to listen deeply, suspending judgment and the need to act. We are always in some form of dialogue with ourselves. It is the basis of reflection and self-awareness. There are many ways to help students *externalize* the process of inner dialogue.

As teachers of writing, we often encourage students to keep a journal or to respond to journal prompts. When they do so, they are engaged in a dialogue. If they know that we will be reading what they write, then it is a dialogue with us. For English Language Learners, I found the "dialogue journal" an effective tool. This is a practice where students write in a journal and the teacher responds. We would even begin just by drawing pictures and then adding very simple questions and answers. If the journals are private, and we, the teachers, only serve an accountability and encouragement function, then the journal is an inner dialogue. What makes this writing more explicitly an inner dialogue is when we introduce the idea of imagining another character with whom you are in conversation. For example, when I was teaching persuasive writing in my English classes, I would ask students to think of a point they would like to make or something they would like another person or group to understand or do. With younger students, the focus was often on something they wanted, like an item or a freedom that, thus far, the parent or caretaker was not willing to grant. Then, they would identify their "audience," the person or persons they wanted to persuade. I would ask them to write out a dialogue, in the form of a little play wherein they try to persuade that audience and offer room for the other to respond. From this writing, we would begin to look at arguments and counterarguments. After the writing, to expand the process, students would work in pairs to role-play the dialogue, and I would recommend that the persuader take the role of the one they wish to persuade, as a way of teasing out counterarguments.

Younger students can playfully engage in such dialogues:

- Imagine that your pet could speak. Begin by writing, "What's it like to be my dog?" And they write what their dog might say.
- Find a natural object, like a plant, a rock, a leaf, or a pill bug. Then, imagine a conversation you might have with it.
- Find a partner. Have the partner pretend to be you and you pretend to be your dog or a tree and have a conversation. Then, write down what you remember.
- Draw a cartoon that shows you and someone else having a conversation. Use dialogue bubbles to show what a person is saying or thinking.

Older students can engage in such dialogue at a more sophisticated level:

- Question historical figures or characters from literature and engage in a back and forth about motivation for various choices and actions.
- Prepare for a job interview by anticipating questions and responses.
- Dialogue internally with a person you find yourself, for whatever reason, unable to speak with directly.
- Dialogue with someone who has passed away.
- Dialogue with the elements or the seasons: What would fire have to say about your question? What would the perspective of autumn bring to your intention?
- Dialogue with features of the natural world—a landscape, mountain, stream, the ocean, the sky, animals, birds, insects, plants, etc.
- Dialogue with figures that appear in your dreams.

Any of these intrapersonal activities can be shared in an interpersonal circle. Doing so exposes students to the insights gleaned by their peers. Imagine the richness of sharing in a circle where students convey what occurred when they were in dialogue with, for example, Black Elk after a reading of *Bury My Heart at Wounded Knee*! Imagine the value of having students share the kinds of questions and responses that might occur in an interview with a prospective employer and the harvest of strategies that might come from this. Imagine the wealth of insight that would come from sharing the ways we hold in our hearts those who have passed on.

The inner dialogue can also expand to become a multilogue—*an inner circle*. There is a therapeutic practice called Internal Family Systems (IFS) developed by Dr. Richard Schwartz that invites the client into such dialogues.

According to The Center for Self-Leadership website, Schwartz developed IFS "in response to clients' descriptions of experiencing various parts—many extreme—within themselves. He noticed that when these parts felt safe and had their concerns addressed, they were less disruptive and would accede to the wise leadership of what Schwartz came to call the 'Self.'"[5] Essentially, this practice, pioneered by C. G. Jung, invites a person to enter into circle with various aspects of the psyche. Although it might seem strange, this kind of talking to yourself, no one would fault Shakespeare for doing so! All playwriting and fiction writing involve interaction with inner figures. Here are a few ways to do this in a school setting:

- In thinking about a time you got into trouble, was there a part of you that was tempted while there was a part of you that knew better? Write the dialogue between those two parts.
- Recall a time you had the chance to try something new: was there a part of you that was excited and another that was fearful? Write that dialogue.
- Imagine that your whole family meets in a circle, and you get to suggest the prompt! In writing, begin with yourself, and then pass the talking piece around the circle to imagine what each person might say. (Such an activity can remain completely private—as some sensitive material might emerge.)
- In a history class, imagine you can interview various historical figures about a particular event, for example John F. Kennedy, Nikita Khrushchev, and Fidel Castro about what they were thinking on the eve of October 14, 1962. From your study of the various points of view of these national leaders, how might each respond to your questions about this event?
- In a science class, you can host a conversation (or circle) across ages between Ptolemy, Copernicus, Galileo, and Newton.
- Using various cyclical elements from nature—the seasons, the times of day (daybreak, noon, sunset, midnight), the four directions, the four basic elements, the stages of life (birth, youth, young adulthood,

elderhood), etc.—conduct a dialogue inviting the "voices" of these quaternities to give their opinions on a question you have or a matter you are considering.

Dreaming

Children love to bring dreams to circle, both the kind we have in the night and the visions we have of possibilities. Dream circles connect participants in a very deep way. Learning to recall one's dreams, at least initially without the filter of interpretation, is a practice of listening "from the heart." Students can simply share dreams in circle. Or, in a process called the "Dreamstar," students lie on their backs with their heads in the center, forming a "star." An alternative, when there is no carpeting or inclination to lie down, is to have chairs turned out, away from the center. This creates a more private space and allows one to become more introspective in the recalling and telling of the dream. Without a talking piece, in popcorn fashion, students share dreams recalled from any time in the past. Once all those who wish to share have done so, begin a "dream weaving" where students state the images and phrases that they recall from the dreams shared by others. What begins to happen is a kind of weaving together of dream elements from all the students. With this, an awareness of connections and common thematic elements emerges that is often quite significant. After the weaving, students turn around (or over, if they are lying on the ground) and for the first time look at their fellow dreamers.

Dream circles are also important because in our image-saturated environment, putting into words the unique scenes that arrive in dreams stimulates imagination. Imagination deserves care and encouragement. It is our innate ability to create novelty—stories, inventions, solutions to complex problems. Wars and all conflicts, as is said, are tragic failures of imagination.

Bodily-Kinesthetic Circles: Traditional Physical Education and Movement Education

Circles can be integrated into traditional physical education curriculum. In fact, they often naturally are—in team huddles, pre-game motivation, and post-game processing. In my personal experience as a student and in my witnessing of how physical education was delivered, this essential aspect of the curriculum was mostly focused on military style conditioning and competitive sports. Pushups, sit ups, pull ups, jumping jacks, and running laps. We were tested on how many, how fast, how long, and how far. I remember being *told* to stretch but not *how* to stretch. I was told to run but not *how* to run. While I was a decent player, I was not "good at sports," and completely lost touch with group physical activity in high school.

A Vocabulary of the Body

Just as acquiring a vocabulary of feelings and needs serves our ability to feel more, to understand ourselves, to express ourselves and work through conflict, and to characterize the behavior of others, so developing *a vocabulary of the body* and its systems will heighten body awareness.

Beginning with preverbal infants, we begin identifying body parts. We play, "Where's your nose?" "Where's daddy's nose?" touching and naming parts. The Total Physical Response (TPR) method developed by James J. Asher for second language learning begins with students touching and naming body parts, then doing various movements and actions, all leading to complex and deep, lasting learning of vocabulary and syntactic structures.[6] This method, applicable to first language learning as well, locks vocabulary and syntax into "muscle memory" or "motor learning," making actions, structures, and vocabulary "second nature."

Beginning with the most basic parts of the body, Asher has teachers use simple commands, at the same time modeling the movement. "Touch your nose." "Touch your knee." Then, he suggests novel commands: "Touch your knee with your nose!"

The delight that comes from such novelty is a sign that the "affective filter" is down and the student, now emotionally receptive, is acquiring language. In the example above, the preposition "with" is *experienced physically* rather than merely observed. TPR can involve pairs of students and groups. To build a vocabulary of the body, combining the words with actions—and especially with novel actions—makes them unforgettable.

Actively teaching a vocabulary of the body begins very early and can progress to the finest details of anatomy. Imagine trying to do a proper sit up if you don't know where your abdominal muscles are! And how much more accurate and efficient your exercise will be when you know *from the inside* where the transverse and rectus abdominis and the internal and external oblique muscles are.

Mirroring and Polyvagal Theory

There is a wonderful clip from the "I Love Lucy" television show that features Lucy and Harpo Marx. To his surprise, Harpo catches a glimpse of Lucy dressed exactly as he is. He tries to trick his doppelgänger into revealing herself by moving in ways and showing facial expressions that are unique to him. Again, to Harpo's surprise, Lucy mirrors his movements and expressions precisely until he prepares to drop his hat, and as they appear to drop their hats simultaneously, Harpo's hat springs back into his hand because it has an elastic band tied to it. They burst into laughter and hug. This routine has become a well-known classic.

I believe its appeal derives not just from the humorous situation but because it demonstrates positive social engagement, two people fully concentrating on mirroring each other's movement and affect. We might even say that this is a *circle* where each person is listening with their full body, including all the tiny expressive muscles of the face. This activity of *tuning in* and *mirroring* another person's expression is the basis of what we call "attachment," the connection between child and caregiver. When this attachment is neglected in a child's development, all kinds of challenges ensue. The good news is that attachment can be repaired *through play* and through circle practice.

According to the latest research on the healing of trauma, feelings of safety emerge when people feel seen and heard, when they are *mirrored.* Polyvagal theory suggests that face-to-face interactions that involve the expression and reception of facial expressions, gestures, prosodic vocalizations (rhythm, tone, and pitch of voice) enhance the capacity of nerve cells to communicate more efficiently from the brain to the organs and other parts of the body, increasing both physical and emotional well-being.[7]

When the world was experiencing the COVID-19 pandemic, schooling took place largely online. So many physical and tonal social cues are absent when we are connecting online via screens. I have found that a few simple activities that can be played with all ages engage the polyvagal system through sound and movement. Here are a few examples:

- **Imaginary ball toss:** One student holds an imaginary ball, calls the name of another student, and "throws" the ball to that student who in turn catches it and "throws" it to another. I learned from a teacher in the UK who used this game to throw an imaginary talking piece because students could not pass an actual item in the class. Simple as this activity sounds online, it requires seeing another student when your name is called and moving in a way that shows you are receiving something. This promotes concentration, attention, and spontaneity.

- **Funny faces:** One student makes a funny face, and either the whole group mirrors it, or it is "passed" to another student by saying their name. After the receiver mirrors the expression, they create a new face and choose another student to mirror it. Besides being hilarious, the activity encourages spontaneity, and it gets students to look closely at one another to try to pick up subtleties.

- **Gestures:** One student makes a gesture, and it is copied by all or is passed from one to another as above. In a "sound and movement check-in," a student shows how they are feeling through body movement and sound. The circle mirrors.

- **Prosody play:** This game of copying vocal intonation and rhythm can take many forms. On its simplest level, a student makes a sound, and another tries to copy it exactly. A classic improv game invites players to say one word, like "yes," and just through intonation and rhythm have it mean different things. For example, saying "yes" to mean "tell me more" or as a question indicating doubt. The same can be done with phrases where the same words can indicate excitement, boredom, indifference, curiosity, anger, etc. Try it with the phrase, "How are you?" We also like to *mimic* each other. Have one student after another mimic something said by the student before. Again, this builds skill with tuning in to the emotion underlying the simple content of words. Another variation is playing with saying one thing and meaning another.

- **Oh, what a lovely ...** : To engage movement mirroring, imagination, and creative expression, this variation on Viola Spolin's "space substance" games begins with one person pantomiming an object and its use.[8] For example, I might pretend to have a fishing rod and I am reeling in a fish. Without naming the object myself, I would say, "I want to give this gift to Tameka." Tameka receives it and uses it in the same way and says, "Oh, Joe, thank you for this lovely fishing rod." It is OK if she doesn't realize what the gift is, but she has to say what she thinks it is. Then, Tameka says, "But did you know that it is also a," and she fashions the space substance into something else, which she in turn gives as a "gift" to someone else.

Proprioception

Helping our students expand their capacity to perceive what is happening in their own bodies, proprioception, serves many essential functions including physical health, resilience, and intuition. Becoming aware of the intensity and duration of sensations informs our ability to moderate exercise so that we don't harm ourselves. My years of running long distance on sidewalks and not paying attention to what my knees were telling me, resulted in my having to give up running. When a doctor asks, "Where does it hurt?" or "How does it feel?" it is nice to be able to respond with some specificity. In terms of resilience, most modern approaches to trauma therapy, such as "somatic experiencing," involve noticing the location and intensity of sensations. And intuition, the way the body "knows," can be developed through skill-building exercises.

The ancient meditation practice called Vipassana involves careful scanning of body sensations and noting them internally or aloud. Just have students close their eyes and notice where they feel sensation and how sensations travel through the body, as well as their intensity and duration. Or simply have them place hands on their diaphragm to notice the cycles of their breath. This is intrapersonal-kinesthetic skill-building.[9]

A game like "Head, Shoulders, Knees, and Toes," which requires students to touch various body parts in patterns and vocalizing the names of these parts, will increase students' body awareness in a playful way. This game and others like the classic "Simon Says" are perfect for play in circles because they involve *kinesthetic* as well as *interpersonal* and *intrapersonal* modalities.

Here are a few other exercises that develop proprioceptive awareness:

- Walk a line, putting one foot in front of the other.

- Stand on one leg, then the other.

- **Finding your center:** Have students stand straight with feet together and eyes closed (if they are willing). Ask them to keep their feet together and gently lean forward, not so far that they fall (and they always will the first time) but just to the edge of feeling off balance. Then, ask them to return to "center." Do the same with leaning back and then side to side, always returning to the center. So many intrapersonal activities ask us to "find our center" or to "get centered." With this exercise students get a palpable sense of what that means. A talking circle can follow where students tell about times of feeling centered and off-centered.

- **Rooted like a tree:** Students stand with feet slightly apart and with eyes closed. Ask them to feel how their feet contact their shoes, how the shoes contact the ground below, and then to imagine roots growing from the bottom of their feet deep into the earth. If you like, you can also ask them to imagine strings that connect their head and upper body to the stars above. From this place of being "rooted," you can ask them to sway in the breeze.

- **The human yurt:** Students form a circle as close to one another as possible holding hands on both sides. Count them off: one, two, one, two. On your signal, the "ones" lean forward, and the "twos" lean back. After a few seconds they switch, with twos leaning forward and the ones back. Inherent in the game is the idea that when we are connected to others, we can all be off balance and still stay strong. A talking circle on the topic of times you helped or were helped by another person offers a glimpse into what support really means.

- **Trust falls:** In pairs, students stand one behind the other. The one in front gently falls back and is supported. A circle follows with the prompt: *Tell about a time when someone kept you from falling, literally or figuratively.*

- **Wind in the willows:** A circle of eight with one student standing in the center with eyes closed and arms folded across the chest. The circle, standing close together, puts arms forward, palms facing the center. The one in the center goes limp and falls into and is gently passed around by the extended arms. Sometimes, we have the circle lift the one in the center up over their heads! Circle stories ensue about a time when you were supported or a time when you were down, and someone lifted you up.

Expanding the Boundaries of Physical Character

Author, critic, director, theorist Augusto Boal suggests that actors as well as individuals get locked into physical character patterns that keep them from developing empathy and from becoming more than they are, from transforming their lives. Anything we can do to break through habits of posture and movement, he contends, will help us relate more fully to others and to extend our view of what we consider our limitations. He recommends that we begin to break these "masks of behavior" by undoing "the muscular structure of the participants."[10] Here are a few of the activities:

- **The slow-motion race:** Students run with the "aim of losing: the last one is the winner." They must always stay in motion, take the longest strides possible, and raise their feet above knee level with every step.

- **The three-legged race**, tying or intertwining legs.
- **The wheelbarrow race,** with racers holding each other's ankles.
- **"Hypnosis":** One member of a pair puts his or her hand a few inches from the partner's face, and then moves the hand around, as the partner maintains the distance between the "hypnotist's" hand and his or her nose. This can also be done with three, the hypnotist using both hands.
- **Slow motion boxing**, without touching.
- **Animal partners:** Prepare slips of paper with the names of animals, two of each type. Students draw the slips from a hat. They are to become the animal, to show it physically, without making any noises of using any words. The object is for each animal to find their fellow among all those in the room.

Gesture Story Circle

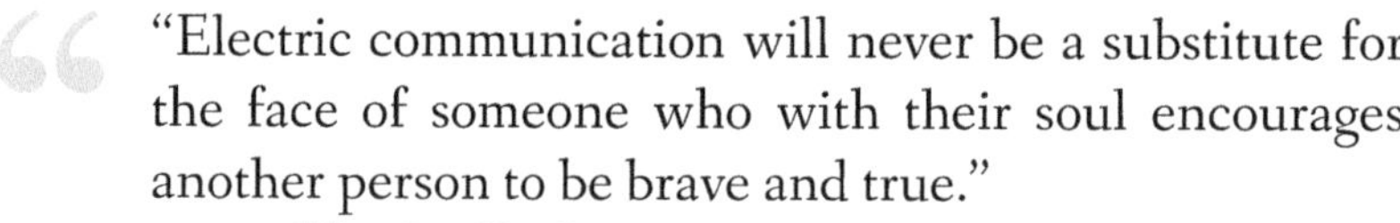

> "Electric communication will never be a substitute for the face of someone who with their soul encourages another person to be brave and true."
>
> —Charles Dickens

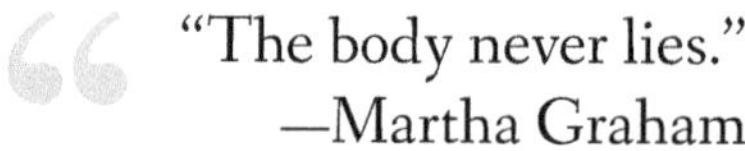

> "The body never lies."
>
> —Martha Graham

> "When the eyes say one thing, and the tongue another, a practiced man relies on the language of the first."
>
> —Ralph Waldo Emerson

Circle facilitator and butoh dancer Roxanne Oguiri Steinberg created this movement- based circle series. As it provides an opportunity to check in, it also develops empathy among group members as they embody the stories of others. At the same time, it promotes deep listening by generating curiosity.

Begin in a standing circle. Ask participants to silently think over the events of the last week and see which, experiences, feelings, or conversations come to their awareness. Check to see that everyone can recall at least one memorable moment from the last week.

Ask participants to think about a gesture, a movement that might represent the experience that they had. For example, if someone had a revelation, a new understanding, or a great idea during the week, that person might touch their forehead with both hands and then raise both arms in a victorious skyward gesture.

The facilitator can begin by modeling a gesture. The whole group is instructed to mirror any movements, facial expressions, and sounds that the sharer conveys. The next sharer then performs their gesture, and the circle tries to imitate as fully as possible. Then, the next person shares their representational gesture, and the process continues until everyone has done so.

After all have shared movements and all have mirrored each, the first person repeats the gesture and then *tells the story* of what actually occurred. After telling the story, the group again mirrors the movement—this time with a deeper understanding of the experience of the sharer.

Then the next person repeats their movement and tells their story, and the process continues around the circle. If there is time or the group is small, a "dance" can be conducted at the end by having the group do all the movements in sequence. When they do this, there is a powerful recollection of all the stories and a powerful experience of group connection.

They gesture-story circle

In a simplified form, participants can just "show" in a movement or gesture how they are feeling in this moment. All others mirror. Without words, this can give all a powerful read of the group's emotional field in the present moment. While the Gesture Story Circle is a complete process, many circles can follow on: What are some "memorable moments" in your life? Tell about a time you had an experience you know you will never forget.

Earth Run

The "Earth Run" or "Planetary Dance" is a score from dancer/choreographer Anna Halprin. It requires a central person or persons playing drums or clapping in unison. One by one, students enter the large space, running *counterclockwise* in a wide circle around the drummers. When they choose, they can turn and move *clockwise* at a slower pace in an inner concentric circle.

They can then shift into a third inner circle moving counterclockwise again, this time walking. From this third circle, when and if they choose to do so, they can stop to drum or clap with those in the center. The same patterns operate with students moving from the center out to the walk, slow run, and fast run circles. With the opportunity to slow down and to rest, the Earth Run can go on for hours!

With older students and adults, the Earth Run has a preliminary phase where each participant formulates an intention, something they "stand for." Then, as they enter the outer circle, they announce these, saying things like, "I run for equity and justice," "I run for Black lives," "I run for more circles in schools!" We suggest that participants keep this intention in mind as they are moving like planets around the central sun. More circles can follow this activity: Tell about a time you had to stand up for someone or something. Tell about a time you wanted to help someone or take an action but you didn't.

Spatial Circles

The spatial modality for circles offers students the opportunity to manipulate materials, organize spaces, draw, and work *collaboratively* with any kind of visual artmaking. When the youngest students work together on a block sculpture, sandbox play, sorting or placing items in by order or category, done with a partner or group—all of these are *spatial circles*. So too are cooking, garden work, science experiments, anything involving measurement and procedures. The activities themselves are circles if students are working together, and they can also lead to talking circles. Students reflect on the process, on the quality of the collaboration, on what made the activity easier or more difficult, as well as on feelings of satisfaction or frustration.

Here are a few more ideas for working in the spatial mode:

Self-Image: This exercise can spark awareness in students that how they see themselves may be different from the image they project to others. It can be done privately or, if trust has developed in the group, it can be shared. On a sheet of paper ask students to draw a self-portrait, the way they see themselves. Ask them to show their personality, their abilities, what they like and don't like. It can be done with symbols. They can also do this in writing, simply a list of qualities and traits. On the back of the paper, ask students to draw (or write about) themselves the way *others* may see them. Depending on the group, this activity can lead to reflection or open discussion of the differences between the two images, how we are perceived and how we really are.

Personal Bag or Box: Students collect images and words from magazines, or they can draw or write them on the outside of a lunch bag or shoebox. These images and words show something about what most people who meet them can easily see about who they are and what they like. On the inside of the bag or box, ask students to place images and/or words that show aspects of themselves that few people might know. In our groups, as a bonding exercise, we sometimes ask students to *tell the group one thing about yourself that you think no one would know just from looking at you.* An exercise such as this can help students see that in circle and elsewhere, they choose which aspects of themselves they wish to reveal to others.

Mask-Making: Sometimes the best place to speak from the heart is behind a mask. From simple paper plate versions to elaborate papier-mâché decorated with found, natural objects, masks can allow students to tell stories and express themselves in ways they might not otherwise. After creating a mask, students wear it and tell the story of who they are. They respond to a question *from behind the mask.* An example of this is from Joanna Macy and John Seed's "Council of All Beings," a version of which has participants make masks representing other life forms on earth—animals, birds, insects, fish—or forms of nature such as trees, rocks, oceans, air. These "beings" then respond to the question: "How are you affected by humans' presence on the planet, and what is to be done?"[11]

Imagination as Listening: Learning to pay attention to the play of one's imagination, what comes to our awareness when we aren't trying to *create* anything, is the art of listening to the internal world. Imagination is not the same as "guided imagery" or "visualization." In guided imagery, the facilitator/teacher suggests a direction or context for the imagination, for example giving an instruction like, "Let yourself imagine a place where you feel safe." In contrast, free imagination is not directed. The facilitator only creates the opportunity and sends the invitation, as you can see from the following types of activities:

Mandalas: These are spontaneous drawings usually set inside the template of a circle, a symbol of wholeness. The main instruction for students doing mandala drawings is *"Don't think. Draw!"* Distribute paper with a circle template or use a paper plate. Have colors available. Tell students to take the colors that appeal to them without thinking about why. Invite them to let their hands and the colors guide the drawings rather than their minds. This activity can be done as a warm-up for centering. The mandalas can be shared or not. Sometimes to check in, once the drawings are done, we sit in a circle and simply pass the images silently from person to person. The drawings can then be placed on the floor, forming an inner circle, and we can reflect on commonalities and contrasts. (Fun fact:

"mandala" is a Sanskrit word meaning both "circle" and "community.")

Personal Shields: Personal shield activities are slightly more directed than mandala drawing, which emphasizes spontaneity and intuition. Shields can use any shape as a template, but they are often formed like medieval heraldic shields, divided into four or six sections. Each section is labeled and then students draw and/or use words and symbols that occur to them as they are thinking about that section. Examples for the sections include strengths, interests, family, favorite place, wishes (for self, others, the world), future, fears, people I admire, etc. The results are shared in circle, or this exercise can be used to get students prepared to listen to themselves when they are in circle and are sharing about any aspect of experience.

Musical

Consider the difference between the music produced by highly trained musicians who play each note and rest as written but are focused only on playing their part and the music from a less skilled but competent group who really listen to one another. Without the listening, there is no jazz, no soul. Of course, music and dance expressed in circles date back to the beginnings of humanity. Using the musical modality in circles trains and encourages deeper "listening" in all contexts. Here are a few ideas:

Echo drumming: This activity can be done with drums, desktops, handclaps, or body percussion (tapping on chest, legs, etc.). One student taps out a brief rhythm. Others echo back, and the process continues around the circle. This can be done spontaneously or as a check-in with an instruction like *tap out a rhythm that shows something of how you are feeling.* Like *witnessing* in a talking circle, listening to produce an echo promotes attention, concentration, and connection.

Rhythm Council: This activity can be done with or without instruments. First, I ask students about the different ways we can produce sound: body tapping, lip smacking, whistling, singing, making animal noises, clapping hands, tapping on the table, rapping, repeating spoken phrases, etc. (Of course, they will mention burping and farting, but whatever sound they choose it must be something that repeats in a brief rhythmic pattern and can be sustained for 5–10 minutes. There might be some who will take up the challenge!) One (steady) leader begins a repeated rhythm. The student to the leader's left listens and then makes it a duet by adding their own "voice," one that *fits* into the rhythmic pattern set up by the leader. Then, one by one slowly students create the trio, the quartet, and so on until it becomes the orchestra as the last person joins in. I ask them to listen for a while to this symphony. Then, the leader will signal the student to their left with a look, and that student stops, passes the look on to the third, and so on until all drop out leaving the leader to conclude. It is hilariously funny, unique every time, and tends to be noted by the teacher in the next room! Sometimes, to demonstrate the difference between "noise" and "music," before they do the rhythm council, ask everyone just to start producing sound any way they want (also a favorite of the teacher next door), and then I give them a signal to stop.

After we do the rhythm council, which requires everyone to listen deeply and to express themselves uniquely, the difference between noise and music—and by extension casual chat and council —is palpable.

Music and Imagination: Play a piece of unfamiliar instrumental music. I like to use a short portion of Stephen Scott's *Vikings of the Sunrise: Fantasy on the Polynesian Star Navigators.*[12] This composition is especially unusual as it is played by ten musicians on one grand piano by bowing and tapping the strings and other parts of the instrument. As students listen to the piece, I ask them to write (or draw) any images that come to mind. Closing eyes usually helps. Then, in small groups or a full circle, we share what came to our imaginations as we listened to the piece. Inevitably, there are correlations between what each student imagined during the listening. With the Vikings piece, images of journeys by sea or in space occur. If you wish, you can follow this sharing with a council on personal experiences that in some way relate to the images that occurred: a time you took a long journey, a time to visited a place you had never been, an adventure you would like to have, etc. Then, listen to the piece again!

Logical-Mathematical

One might not imagine the correlation between mathematics and circles, but every concept in mathematics has an analog in human relations. For example, when I use the word "correlation," the same notion found in quantum physics, economics, and statistics also applies to the connections found between unrelated people, commonalities we might find when we sit in circle and get to know each other. In Chapter 8, we will look at ways to explore the ideas of validity and logical fallacies in circles. Anything, however, that involves a process, an order of operations, a procedure, or a plan can be considered a topic in the *logical-mathematical mode*.

Here are a few examples:

Epistemological inquiries: How do we know what we know? This circle-based activity can be used at almost any level, including adults. We simply begin with a request that everyone "name one thing you know to be true." You might give a few examples like: "I'm sitting on a chair." "The earth is round." "My mother loves me." Then, the circle continues with the question, "*How* do you know?" I recall one session where a student gave the flip answer, "The sky is blue," and having heard a few students before him take the question seriously, said, "Come to think of it, sometimes the sky is gray, or completely black, and there are sometimes even white dots in it." Although we didn't get into how the eye and brain perceive color, perhaps this young man was subsequently more inclined to think about how he knows what he knows. Further, the exercise moves students toward specificity. For example, the one who says, "I know my mother loves me," will sometimes offer a particular moment, a time when he felt that love.

Decision-making and action plans: Decision-making, when it is done in circle, has a higher likelihood of being carefully considered with manageable, time-limited steps which can be supported by the group. Simple circles on *a time you had to make a* *decision* are useful on many levels. Even the youngest students will derive value from reflecting on choices they have made: the clothes they wear, the games they play, the friends they play with, places to go, etc. When we ask older students to reflect, "What led you to make that decision?" they are obliged to think through the process. Was it impulsive or carefully thought through? What was the outcome? Would you have made a different decision if you had more information or had not acted so impulsively?

The same applies to decisions made now, in the circle. Again, I want to emphasize that when we state a decision or agreement in the context of the circle, we are more likely to give it careful consideration simply because *others are now aware of it*. When we must articulate the decision to others, we have to shape it in a way that can be understood, and that will likely provoke understanding it more fully ourselves. Once a decision is stated, it is *held* in the awareness of the group, and that alone is likely to encourage follow through on the part of the decision maker. Further, the circle community calls on the decision maker to detail the incremental steps they will take to complete their stated intention. If there is safety in the circle, students will feel free to communicate both advances and missteps and course corrections along the path.

Naturalistic

Naturalistic intelligence involves keen observation and intuition about the environment. This is equally true in nature as it is in the chaos of a fast-paced inner city. In fact, as a matter of survival, people will develop this sense when they are exposed to situations where physical and emotional safety could be threatened. The idea of "street smarts" is connected to the naturalistic way of knowing as are the skills of tracking, bushcraft, and all aspects of wilderness survival.

Anything you do that involves closer observation of the environment feeds naturalistic intelligence. The "Noticing Journey" described in Chapter 7 is a good example. Students are asked to move through an environment and to tune in to *one sense at a time* (including "thought"), and then they circle up and share what they noticed. Sometimes limiting the field of perception heightens the ability to pay attention to its constituent parts. The point is to try to respect the environment, to see it anew. A wonderful essay to offer older students is Annie's Dillard's "Seeing," in her collection *Pilgrim at Tinker Creek.*[13] In this beautiful personal narrative, Dillard compares the way she looks at the natural world to the experiences of the first patients, who, blind from birth due to cataracts, underwent surgeries in the early 1900s and thereby experienced sight for the first time.

There are many ways to have council in *and with* nature. Is it possible to listen to the environment the same way we listen to each other in the circles? Students go out into nature with a carefully considered question and *listen* for what the plants, animals, insects, wind, and water might say, questions like: *What is most important for me to be doing with my life at this time? What is mine to do? How can I better serve the people and the planet?*

Students return after a period of time alone and report what they heard to the circle. Even if they didn't manage to *hear* anything, the act of going out with a question and listening can bring about a shift in how the question is considered. For students who can't access wild nature, a park will do. Even giving them instructions to find natural objects in the environment can suffice.

Another exercise in the naturalistic mode is one I learned in 1982 from the poet Robert Bly, and I have used it with great results many times with middle-school students. Students are instructed to find a natural object, one that perhaps "calls" to them saying, "Pick me!" It should be small enough to be held in one hand. They bring the object to the circle and then go through a series of steps before the circle begins.

The first step is to hold the object in one hand and describe it in writing *without looking at it.* They note its texture, weight, and size, often comparing it to something else. The next step is to look at the object and describe it so that *another person* who not looking at it could get a strong mental image of it. At this point, I have students look over what they have written and underline or list the *descriptive terms* they used such as: brittle, sharp, light, spiraling, mottled, fragile, etc. Then, I ask them to *think of a person who has some of these same qualities.* (This is a great lesson on the purpose and use of metaphors.). There might then be some writing on how the person and the object share these qualities. In the circle, I might ask them to simply share any thoughts about the process, anything they discovered or that surprised then. They might share the object's life story or the message it has for the world. With older students and adults, I might ask: *What could you do to get a better understanding of or a better relationship with the person who came to mind?* Extensions to this activity can include writing *a story from the point of view of the object* or *a poem that uses metaphors based on the object to say something about the person.*

Circle Forms

We have already looked at the *basic* circle form, where the talking piece goes around the circle. But just as we vary topics and modes, other circle forms accommodate various purposes and conditions, and they can also be varied just to keep things fresh. The basic form can get boring even with changes of topic and mode.

The Web

For the *web* form, we place the talking piece in the center of the circle. Whoever wishes to speak goes to the center, takes talking piece, and returns to their seat. Afterwards, the talking piece is returned to the center for the next speaker. The form is called a *web* because, although the form is irregular, and allows for each person to get the piece more than once, the pattern becomes a weaving that shows, if we could see it, the lines of interaction. Sometimes we use a ball of yarn so we can literally see the pattern. We often use a *soft talking piece* that can be tossed from student to student, particularly if students are sitting at desks or tables where getting to the center would be challenging.

Often, the web is used *after* a round of basic form. This provides an opportunity for those who wish to add to what they shared in the first round. It also gives those who chose to pass in the first round another chance to speak. Occasionally, with the web, a kind of dialogue ensues between two or more people. Unlike the repartee of usual conversation, however, having to retrieve the piece slows the interaction and makes it somewhat more deliberate.

In some groups, especially with very young children, a few *guidelines* might have to be imparted about the web format. We have found that some overeager group members will dive headlong into the center and then tussle over the talking piece. The group leader can intervene directly or develop group sensitivity and etiquette by suggesting the following:

- Before you leave your seat, look around to see if anyone else also wants to get the talking piece. Silently decide who will go first.
- If you have already had the piece once, make sure that those who have not had a chance can get it before you get it again.
- Instead of returning the piece to the center, when you are finished, look around the group and see who wants to speak, and then slowly walk the piece over to that person.

Popcorn

Just as kernels pop randomly when we make popcorn, this form allows participants to speak in a kind of respectful randomness, sometimes *without* a talking piece. This form is used usually after a basic or other form where people have had time to reflect and to speak fully or when time is limited. Guidelines for the popcorn form can include the following:

- If you are *not* using a talking piece, find a way to have only one person speaking at a time. If you start to speak at the same time as another person, stop and let that person finish. Then, pop in.

- If you are using a talking piece, make sure it is a soft one that can be tossed from person to person. Like the web format, the speaker holding the soft piece should look around the circle to see who wishes to speak, and then gently toss the piece to someone who has not yet had a chance.
- Popcorn comments are very brief, often just a word, a phrase, or a single thought.

Response Council

A *response council* is really a variation on any of the forms and can be used at any time. There are times when a member of the circle needs an immediate response to a question. As the talking piece goes around in the usual way, this member can call for a *response council* and then pose a question to members of the group. They can ask the whole group for a response or a particular individual or individuals. In effect, the person holding the talking piece, empowers others to respond directly to them without having to retrieve the piece. Often, questions are posed as requests, such as: "Would you be willing to tell me why you feel that way?" As with all requests, we have to be content with the answer being "no." Sometimes the group will use an *answer piece* that is passed among those who wish to respond. Response councils can include the following:

- **A call for advice:** *In eighth grade, I've been having trouble getting all my work done and still finding time to see my friends. I'd like some advice on how others deal with that.*
- **A call for witnessing:** *Someone told me I was "annoying." I'd like some witnessing from the group on this. Do you see me that way?*
- **A direct inquiry of the group:** *I'd like to know what people think about the new "no hat" rule.*
- **A direct inquiry of one individual:** Addressing the teacher/facilitator, *Could we change the topic?*

> Addressing a group member, *I want to know what you, Rina, will be wearing for Halloween. Would you be willing to tell me?* Just as with questions to the whole group, Rina has the option to choose not to answer.

As people are learning to be with one another in circle, it is best *not* to introduce the response option too early. When overused it can reinforce familiar, default patterns of dialogue. Much of our time in circle involves developing patience and listening for answers that come indirectly and collectively.

Spiral

The *spiral form* is excellent for large groups, and it brings in some physical movement that can energize a group. This form is called the *spiral* because participants move into and out of an inner circle from various points of an outer circle. To create the spiral form, some chairs or cushions, usually four to eight, are set to fashion a smaller circle inside a larger one.

In the inner circle, to begin, person A picks up the talking piece, speaks, and then passes to the person on their left, person B. Person B then speaks, and, when finished, hands the piece to person C. *Before* person C begins, person A gets up and moves toward the outer circle, *leaving a seat open in the inner circle.* Whoever wishes to occupy that seat moves to it from the outer circle. Then, person C begins to share. The process continues until participants *spiraling in* from the outer circle are no longer filling the inner circle seats. If the time allotted is running short, the facilitator looks at the number of participants yet to speak and designates the last in as the final speaker. With very large groups, you can form several concentric circles set up with three or four aisles leading to the inner circle, so anyone, from anywhere, can access the inner circle.

The reason for waiting for the person *after* you to conclude before you leave the circle is to avoid the all too familiar pattern of *shoot and run*: I get the talking piece, I speak, and I split. The fact that even after entering the inner circle one has to wait for several others to speak is a valuable way to decrease emotional reactivity. One can't just jump in and respond instantly to what another has said. The waiting and the listening often affect the content and tone of what one had expected to contribute. A simple direction for the spiral is *speak, listen, leave.*

Fishbowl

Circles within circles, called *fishbowls,* have many uses in the classroom. Basically, several seats are set in the center of a larger circle. This inner circle may represent a particular group, for example all those who identify as female in the class, or participants with a particular view, or simply a group invested in speaking to a particular issue. The outer circle may provide witnessing for the inner or might rotate in to provide an alternative view.

One example of the use of the fishbowl is in the *gender councils* described more fully in Chapter 10. In this process, one group identified with a particular gender will sit in the inner circle and conduct a council as others witness from the outer. Then, the groups switch.

The fishbowl is also useful when space is limited and numbers are large. It may be difficult to fit all the desks in a classroom in one large circle, so creating a fishbowl will bring the students in closer to one another and will make listening easier. The only drawback to this form is that students in the outer circle see only the backs of a few in the inner circle, and those in the inner circle can't see a few in the outer at all. In cases where there are a very large number of participants, multiple concentric circles can be formed.

Dyadic Council

Once circle practice has been established in a group, the skills are easily transferred for use in smaller groups, including dyads. In a *dyadic council,* two participants face one another, signal the beginning, and pass the talking piece until time is up or the council ends of its own. The entire class can be split into dyadic groupings, and this can be done as a brief portion of a regular class period.

Also, the dyad can be used as a fishbowl, with the outer circle serving a witnessing function. In that case, two people, possibly in conflict or representing two identified viewpoints, pass the talking piece as many times as necessary and then hand it out to the outer circle, whose members speak to what they noticed in the dyadic exchange.

There is another practice called *listening for "the third" or "the voice of the relationship"* that can also be used in dyadic councils. A third chair or cushion is provided to the pair. After both participants feel that they have exhausted what they have to say as individuals, the talking piece is placed on this third space, and the participants are instructed to *listen for the third*. One way of accessing the voice of the relationship is to ask: *What does this relationship need from us to be stronger, more trusting, or satisfying?* After some silence, whoever in the pair has a sense of what this *voice* might say will offer that to the other by picking up the talking piece and speaking this consensus or third position. The other can then take up the piece to give an alternate take or provide agreement. Although the *third* can be thought of as the position that presents the areas of consensus in the viewpoints of the participants, this process often yields surprising and novel results. Even in larger groups, pausing to hear the voice of the circle is powerful and productive. For example, with a school staff, asking them to *listen for what the children are needing or calling for* (rather than what we as adults want). *If the students had a voice in the circle, what would they be saying?*

Multiple Circles and "The Grand Council"

At the beginning of this chapter, you were asked to imagine. Now imagine a circle of 400! Imagine a culminating class engaging in a collective rite of passage as they get ready to move on to new schools, new friends, and new possibilities. It *can* be done.

From the classroom to the entire school community, multiple simultaneous circles can bring intimacy and connection to a large group. The *Grand Council* form was inspired by the Longhouse practice of the Haudenosaunee (Iroquois League). Each of the five and then later six of the Native American nations that formed the League individually held its own council. Then, male representatives chosen by the women of each nation would meet in the Longhouse to speak the "breath of their people." In an outer circle, women and children of each tribe would witness the transactions.

They were the auditory scribes, the institutional memory of each nation. Scholars have proposed that when the writers of the Constitution of the United States observed this process among the native peoples, they were inspired to create the tri-cameral form of our government.[14]

In the classroom, groups as small as four students can take up a question, an issue, or an activity. At the end of their time in this small group they elect a representative to *witness* their process, conclusions, and recommendations to the whole class. These representatives meet in the inner circle of a fishbowl. The rest of the class forms the outer circle. After the representatives have spoken, the talking piece can be passed to the outer circle for any additions.

To work with a very large group, like the whole culminating class, multiple circles, each one a full class or homeroom, meet in a large open area. They take up a prompt like *If a younger schoolmate asked you, "What advice could you give me from your experience so that I too can successfully culminate?" What would you say?* or *Imagine getting together with a group of students that you think you will never forget. You might begin by saying "I think I'll never forget when ...* " At the conclusion of the time allotted for the multiple circles, each elects a representative. The representatives from each circle form an inner circle surrounded by many closely gathered outer circles. If the inner circle representatives rise to address the group, all can, under favorable conditions, hear them. A microphone can also serve as a talking piece.

A Few More Circle Styles

While each of the above forms is particularly well suited for particular functions, it is also important to vary the forms if for no other reason than to avoid ruts in which the form itself becomes a cause of boredom. So, mix things up. As with all the guidelines presented here, allow the group to evolve its own forms. Here are a few styles to try to keep things lively:

- **Virtual** – Create an overhead projection or poster with students' names in a circle. Without having to move chairs or create a center, with a moment's notice you can call for a virtual council. Just give a prompt, ring a bell, and ask, "Who would like to begin?" The invisible talking piece travels around the circle as students are aware of the order of speakers from the projection or poster. There is a critical caveat, however: *Do not use the virtual style until students have significant experience in actual circles.*

Student names for a virtual circle

- **The Flower** – Another great time-saving style, named by teacher Susan Fisher, *the flower* involves placing a marker of some kind (flower, bead, the usual centerpiece) in the center of the room and asking students simply to turn their chairs or their bodies to face it. The talking piece wends its way up and down the rows like the petals of a flower in an irregular pattern. The same caveat as above applies.

- **Iroquois Style** – Conducted in a circle but *without a talking piece*. No particular order is followed. Whoever is moved to speak *rises*. The rest observe a profound silence. When the speaker finishes, they sit down. In the Iroquois way, the circle waits 5–6 minutes so that if the speaker wishes to add something, they may rise again to do so.

- **Quaker Style** – This form can be used in rooms that will not allow for circular seating. Like the Iroquois style, there is no talking piece and whoever is moved to speak rises.

- **Drop-In Style** – There are occasions when people will need to enter or exit the circle as it proceeds. While this rarely happens in the classroom, students have led lunchtime, drop-in circles; counselors have conducted day-long drop-ins; and there are weekly faculty drop-ins. For this style, if the group is small, set up as usual and pass the talking piece web-style. The only rule here is that people entering after the council has begun must listen to at least one speaker before they take the piece, and those who need to leave must remain to listen to at least one speaker before going. If the group is large, use a spiral format. Latecomers enter the outer circle and enter the inner circle when a space becomes available. Those who need to leave must do so from the outer circle whether they have entered the spiral to speak or not.

- **Internet, Web-Based Style** – Using the web, students can have inter-classroom, inter- school, and international councils. Using either the simple *chat room* process or services like Zoom, Facetime, Google Hangouts, or other video or audio-conferencing platforms, students publish in advance an image of the circle, then meet at a designated time, and use the usual council protocols.

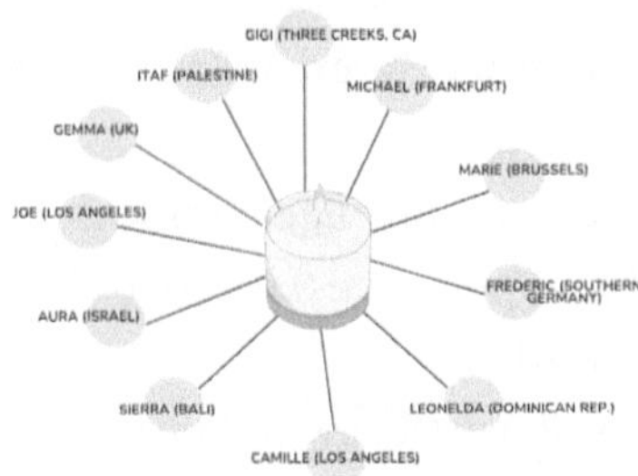

A graphic establishing the order for an online circle

- **The People's Microphone** – Developed during the Occupy Movement, when there is a large crowd outdoors, the designated speaker speaks in phrase chunks, and the crowd repeats each phrase, so it carries through the whole group. Speaker order is usually pre-determined, and all speakers gather in one spot. How to employ a talking piece to allow for unscheduled others to speak from wherever they are is still to be explored.

I hope this chapter will spark your own creative ideas for ways to engage students in *relational fields*, ways that don't involve only talking. Students will engage with the circles if you *vary the topic, form, and mode*, just as our ancestors did when they danced, sang, and enacted myths and cultural stories around the children's fire.

For Reflection and Imagination

1. Modes:

- Create your own personal bag or box (spatial/linguistic).
- Use a circle template to create a don't-think-draw mandala (spatial).
- Listen to an unfamiliar piece of music and note or draw the images (or experiences) it evokes in you (musical/spatial).
- Name one thing you know to be true. What experiences have led you to this conclusion? (logical/mathematical).
- Select a person you know or a figure that came in a dream. Conduct a dialogue with this person or figure (intrapersonal).
- Choose a natural object and imagine a dialogue with it (naturalistic/intrapersonal/linguistic).

2. Forms:

- Consider some controversial topics that might arise with your students. How would you frame a prompt and divide the group to use the "fishbowl" form.
- Imagine a prompt you would like to use with a large group (e.g. Congress, a graduating class) and then consider the instructions you would give to conduct a "Grand Council."

Chapter 6:
Circle Modes and Forms

1. **Vary the Mode and Topic**
   Keep circles engaging by mixing forms, prompts, and types of expression.

2. **Draw on Multiple Intelligences (Howard Gardner)**
   Use spatial, musical, kinesthetic, interpersonal, intrapersonal, logical-mathematical, and naturalistic activities.

3. **Encourage Intrapersonal Practice**
   Begin with journaling, inner dialogues, and "circles of one."

4. **Include Movement and Mirroring**
   Build trust and regulation through kinesthetic games and gesture work.

5. **Use Sound and Rhythm**
   Echo drumming and rhythm councils cultivate group attunement.

6. **Incorporate Symbolic and Spatial Tasks**
   Artmaking, mask work, and object-based storytelling deepen reflection.

7. **Match Form to Purpose**
   Choose from forms like spiral, web, dyadic, or fishbowl to suit your context.

7

CIRCLES IN GENERAL CLASSROOM USE

THIS CHAPTER APPLIES a circle-based pedagogy to common classroom issues. Feel free to take the topics out of order:

- Marking and celebrating beginnings
- Marking birthdays, holidays, and other special moments
- Unearthing expectations
- Fostering attention, concentration, and focus
- Collaboration, perseverance, and integrity
- Developing classroom norms
- Accessing prior knowledge and attitudes
- Developing study skills
- Motivating students to engage subject matter
- Checking for acquired knowledge
- Setting intentions, engage accountability, and make course corrections
- Celebrating accomplishments and transitions

Marking and Celebrating Beginnings

In my middle-school classes, I would often start the year with a solemn reading of the class roster and the creation of a seating chart, followed by a recitation of my class rules, procedures, expectations, and grading policy. Any questions? I remember having been told *not* to smile until Christmas and to immediately establish authority by having students do *something, anything,* on my command—open a window, take out supplies, bring something to me, even if there was no actual need to do so. As a new teacher, I followed this routine perhaps because it gave me some sense of control at the threshold of a new year. The truth is that *every year* I restlessly anticipated the first day of class. Who would show up? How many troublemakers this year? How many with learning deficits and challenges I could not hope to reach? I wondered also about my own capacity to sustain the energy it takes to teach English to 150+ students, commenting on their writing, grading their papers, and at the same time trying to make a personal connection with each student beginning with remembering their names!

Consider also what it means for a *student* to cross the threshold into a new class. Can you remember what it was like to go to school on the first day; to move from grade to grade; to be the big kid in fifth grade and then to become little again in sixth; to meet these adults for the first time, knowing that they will spend more waking hours with you than your own parents; to wonder whether a teacher will be *mean* or *nice*; to find, perhaps, some friends in the class with you, and some people you would be content never to see again, all the time wondering whether this class will be *easy* or *hard, interesting* or *boring?* And all of this would be hard enough if you weren't also mourning the loss of summer and dealing with whatever personal and relational problems you and your family might be experiencing at the time.

At Palms Middle School, Principal Hugh Gottfried used circles to welcome new students a few days before the beginning of the new year. Groups sat in the Sean Duncan Memorial Council Circle, pictured below. The prompts were usually something like: *When you think about coming to Palms, what do you hope will happen? What if anything worries you about coming to Palms? What stories have you heard about Palms?* In addition to marking the usual hopes and fears at this major threshold, students learned that they were not alone in what they were anticipating. We even had the opportunity to do some myth busting.

Students gathered in the Sean Duncan Memorial Council Circle.

If we hold all of this in mind, we realize just how momentous the threshold moments of entering a new school or class can be! We might even consider these events as *rites of passage,* rites of *entry* and *exit.* The traditional rite of passage has three phases: *separation, transition, and incorporation.*[1] There will be more on this in Chapter 11, but for now we can think about these phases as follows. *Separation* is looking back, telling stories of the time *before* the present moment; in this case, for example, giving students the opportunity to tell stories of the prior year. *Transition* is a time of clearing the plate, letting go of the past through direct involvement in the present moment. One example of a threshold experience is *play.* If you involve your students in some form of play, they will begin to let go of old stories, fears, and concerns, and they will bond with each other in what I like to call *collective mastery,* an experience where everyone wins. Finally, *incorporation* is the setting of intentions in the context of community. For example, students will set goals for themselves for the class or for study in general, and when this is done in the circle, in community, it results in support and accountability for the actualizing of those intentions.

Separation Activities: Here are a few ideas for ways to welcome students to circle at the start of a new year:

- Decorate the door as a threshold and welcome students across it as they enter.
- Prepare a circle with students' names placed on their chairs or cushions. This will let them know that you have thought about them beforehand and that they each have a coequal place in the circle.
- Place items in the center that are beautiful and welcoming such as fresh flowers and items from nature.
- Include items that represent the content and experiences students will encounter during the year such as books to be read; photos of places and people they will study; symbolic representations of social-emotional and content outcomes you are hoping for such as sprouted seedlings, a photo of hands clasped in friendship, a trophy, a bridge, a double rainbow.

Your first circle with kindergarten students (or any age) can be a simple *silent council.* Have students pass an object around the circle and tell them to simply *watch it go around.* Even this can have an educative effect. Students see that they have the object, that when they pass it, another person has it, and that eventually *it comes around again*! Depending on the maturity of the group, you can send the object around a second time and ask students to hold it for a moment as other students *look at the person who has it.* If students are sitting on the floor, they can roll a ball from one to another.

Older students can toss a football or play the ball toss game or name games:

The Stuffed Animal-Plushie (ball, sock) Toss begins with the teacher saying their name and the name of another participant, like this, "Mrs. Flores, Clarence." Then, the teacher tosses the soft object to that participant. That participant says their name and the name of another participant: "Clarence, Amanda." They throw the object to that participant. This continues until every participant has received the object, and it is returned to the facilitator.

Then, use *the same pattern* as the object is tossed silently. As this gets going, slowly add the second, third, and fourth item. At first, participants will probably be distracted by all the activity in the room and the flying plushies. Let this go on for a short while, and then say, "After the next toss, whoever has the plushie, hold it."

Ask the group, "What can we do to make this work better, so that fewer plushies are dropped?" Typical responses include: "Don't throw the it too hard," "Make sure the person is looking at you before you throw it," "Look only at the person who is throwing to you. Then, focus on the person you are throwing to. Don't be distracted by all the activity in the room."

Encourage participants to take each other's advice and then start the exercise again. It should run more smoothly. If not, stop again.

Tell the participants: "Tossing a ball is like communicating a message. If I throw the ball gently, while you are looking at me, ready to receive it, we will probably be successful. If I throw a fastball at you, what kind of message would that be?"

Possible answer: "Like someone yelling at you."

"What do you do when someone tries to bean you with a fastball?"

"I duck, block it, or get out of the way."

"What do you do when someone screams at you?"

"I don't listen."

"What would it mean to say that someone 'throws you a curve'?"

"That person is trying to confuse me."

Ask students what the elements of successful communication are. What are the responsibilities of the speaker? What are the responsibilities of the listener? List participant answers on the board. This can lead directly into the four intentions of Council.

Possible follow-up circle topics:

Tell a story about a time when:

1. *you tried to tell someone something important, and that person didn't listen to you.*
2. *you told someone something important and you really felt that person heard you.*
3. *you "threw a fastball" or a "curve."*
4. *someone yelled at you or tried to confuse you. Tell how you responded.*

Once you have introduced the circle and the talking piece, you can offer some prompts that allow students to reflect on the past as well as speak about what they have anticipated:

- *Looking back on your last year's class, what is one story that comes to mind?*
- *When you think about this class, what are you hoping will happen, and what are you concerned about or afraid might happen?* (Teachers, be sure to speak of your own hopes and fears. You are one among many in this circle.)
- *What stories have you heard from others about this class? About me?*

If a new student enters the class any time after the first week, ask the circle to convey class procedures, requirements, expectations, and the content covered so far. Coming from the students, rather than you, this information is received differently, as what the students themselves have come to understand. At the same time, it's a good review.

Transition Activities: Think about *transition* in terms of the things *you* do to clear the plate, get off the wheel, quiet the monkey mind, connect with your body, or restore yourself. Consider when you get your best ideas: taking a shower, going for a walk, cooking a meal, taking a power nap, meditating, engaging in a sport or physical activity. The Sufis say: "There is no learning without laughter, no learning without leisure."

Transition activities are those that bring students fully into the present moment, including non-competitive games, movement and dance, singing and playing instruments, collaborative art activities, and improvisation. Simple meditation techniques like following the breath or sensations in the body are excellent transition options and can be employed any time you are wanting to make a clean shift from one activity to another.

Incorporation Activities: Setting intentions and acting upon them are aspects of *incorporation*. You might simply ask students to reflect on something they would like to be able to do or to do better. When they speak these intentions in the circle, others become aware, and that creates an opportunity for accountability. Most people need some support with breaking down broad or general goals into manageable, short-term objectives. "I want to get better grades," for example, must begin somewhere. So, we can coach students to say *one thing they know they can do this week* to be one step closer to their goal and then to craft that into an *I will* ... statement. "Tonight, I will clear off a table in my room where I can study." The value of sharing these statements in circle, is that once others are aware of your intentions, you can receive support and encouragement, and you have created a context for accountability, especially when students have a chance to check in about their progress in the next circle. The prompt for such a check-in might be, *Tell how you were able to accomplish your goal for the week, and if you couldn't, say what you think kept you from it.* This, then, is an opportunity for re-setting intentions for the coming week.

Marking Birthdays, Holidays, and Other Special Moments

While the first day is always a threshold experience, there are many special moments throughout the year that can be honored in circle:

A birthday council

We all know how one birthday in the room can affect the entire day. Conducting a brief birthday council can wrap it up with a bow, and it beats singing the birthday dirge! You don't even need to form a circle. Just ring a bell and have students, randomly, one by one, offer wishes for the child celebrating a birthday. Once the wishes wane, the recipient says *thank you*, and you ring the bell to conclude.

Holidays

- *Tell about a non-material gift you would like to give someone.*
- *Tell about what you and your family do to celebrate a certain holiday.*
- Use a particular holiday theme to construct a related prompt:
    - Thanksgiving: In a speed round, *Name one thing you are glad is in the world.* Then in a story round, *Tell about a time when you were glad for this thing.*
    - Dia de Muertos: *Tell a story of you have heard about a relative or ancestor who has passed on.*
    - New Year's: *If you could change one thing about yourself—to stop doing something, to start doing something, to be better at something—what would it be?* For a closing round ask everyone to tell the circle *one thing* they can do today to begin to fulfill that intention.
    - Spring break: Spring is a time for new birth. *What is new in you?*

Personal, special moments

Anytime you become aware of meaningful occurrences in the lives of your students, you can mark these events with brief *popcorn* style circles:

- An honor received or an accomplishment
- The birth of a sibling
- A random act of kindness

Unearthing Expectations

Everyone arrives in a new class with expectations, hopes, and fears. We want some things to happen, and we hope other things won't. We have expectations of ourselves, of the instructor, of what we might learn about the subject, of what might be difficult or easy, etc. If we take the time to *name* these expectations, they can serve rather than impede our growth, the quality of our experience, and the quality of our relationships.

For *kindergarten*, when students might not have had a previous school experience and they are not yet ready for questions that ask them to reflect on experience, here are a few activities and circles to get them naming what they hope for and what they fear:

- Standing in a circle, have students *show* one thing they like to do by making a gesture or pantomime to suggest it. Give examples: play baseball, swim, draw, dance, make friends. Once a student demonstrates a gesture, others in the circle imitate it. Then, ask: *What does Alex like to do?* Students answer aloud. Continue around the circle. To close the circle, have the students do the *I-know-how-to dance*, a round where each gesture is done in order, with the *expert* prompting the others to remind them, and the whole group mirroring each gesture progressively. It is a celebration of capabilities! You will find that sometimes the group remembers all the gestures without prompting.

- Repeat the above process with one thing that students find *hard to do*. Doing this, in addition to the above circle on capabilities, sets the stage for students to share what they find difficult. Students discover that everyone has challenges, and perhaps more importantly, it is okay to talk about these difficulties in the classroom community.
- Have students draw pictures of one thing they know how to do. Do the same for one thing that is hard to do or that they don't like to do. In circle, share the pictures. If the students want to talk about these things, they can describe what they have drawn. If they don't, it is enough to have them share.
- Use the above procedures to access and share one thing students *want to be able to do*.

In upper elementary, students can begin to reflect on experience in previous classes to clarify expectations in a new class:

- Use a prompt such as *Tell about a time in class last year when you said to yourself, "Wow, I didn't know that before, and now I do!"*
- *Tell about a time last year when you thought to yourself, "This is too hard," "I don't know how to do this," "I don't understand," or "Get me out of here!"*
- *Tell about a time last year in class when something was hard at first but then it became easy.*

In middle and high school classes, when classes tend to be divided by subject, you can access student expectations more directly:

- Begin with a discussion of the term "expectations," noting that the word contains the root *spect* (*to look*) and the prefix *ex-* (*out*) so it really denotes what you are looking for or looking out for; what you hope to see, and what you fear you might!

- *What do you hope to learn or discover in this class?*
- *Based on your previous experience, what do you expect of yourself in this classroom? How do you imagine you will do? What do you foresee to be difficult or easy?*
- *What do you expect of other students?*
- *What do you expect of the teacher?*

In post-secondary classes, it is good to explore students' prior experience, as we will take up below, but also to look at their reasons for taking the class, including the possibility of hearing "Because it's a requirement."

Fostering Attention, Concentration, and Focus

For as often as we ask students to "pay attention," we so rarely teach them *how to attend.* As I noted above, being in circle and using a talking piece *is* always an exercise in concentration and attention. We notice that our attention is on one person and then it moves to the next. In circle, students begin to value their classmates' perceptions and experience. When a student values something or someone, they tend to find it easier to pay attention.

Whether it is a *talk-based* circle, sound and movement, or other group sensitivity and trust exercises, the formality of circle practice itself encourages students to concentrate and attend. The talking piece is a *focusing agent*, a helpful reminder of where to rest one's attention. When a student holds the talking piece, they learn to gather their thoughts and attend to what is coming up for them. And when they see another student holding the piece, they know where to rest their attention.

In kindergarten and the lower grades, any exercise that involves *mirroring*—watching closely another person's movements, speech patterns, and energy—will build attention and concentration as well as empathy. Here are a few other exercises to try:

One thing you noticed

To help students begin to recognize that they do already pay attention to many things (perhaps too many), play some games that have them notice what calls their attention in different environments. For example, take a walk through the school and then standing in a circle, have them say *one thing they noticed*. Project a painting or picture, and have students simply say what draws their eyes. Have them close their eyes and silently note what they hear and then share what they noticed afterward.

The *Change Three* game

Students form two lines facing a partner. Those in line "A" study their partner's appearance carefully for a brief period. When students in line "A" turn their backs, those in line "B" make three changes in their appearance (change their hair, rearrange clothes, untie a shoe, etc.). Line "A" turns back around and tries to guess what is different. Repeat the process. The same game can be played in the environment. For example, before students arrive, change three things in the classroom or in a familiar outdoor setting. Both activities can lead to circles on:

- *A time when you changed.*
- *A time when someone you know changed.*
- *A time when a familiar place changed.*

Demonstrate and play with focus and concentration

Ask students to watch you and notice what is happening as you toss a beanbag into the air with one hand and catch it, showing how your head and eyes follow the bag. Then, do the same *but don't watch the bag*. You will very soon not be able to catch the bag. Then give out bags to every fourth student in the circle and ask them to see how many times they can catch the bag with one hand. If they drop it, they pass the bag to the student on their left, and the process continues. Afterward, discuss the most successful strategies for catching the bag, and ask them what they noticed happening when they dropped it and whether the cause was external or internal, outside themselves or inside. Sometimes it's something that happened in the environment, such as a student laughing or making a noise. Sometimes students are distracted by their own thoughts.

Mindfulness

The best way to train focus, attention, and concentration is to teach *mindfulness*. In practice, meditation often *limits* the field of awareness by having a person focus on one thing, such as the breath, a sound (mantra), a sensation, or an image. Here is an activity to help students bring awareness to the breath, again by having them observe you: sit in a stable posture. Either close your eyes or gaze softly toward the floor a few feet before you. Inhale. When you exhale, softly say the number *one*. Continue counting each exhale aloud up to 10, and then repeat the sequence. Then, have the students tell you what they noticed, and then ask them to try it on their own, counting silently. Tell them that if they lose track of the count, just notice that, and return to *one*. Just a few minutes of this can make students more attentive to whatever the lesson is. A discussion or circle might ensue on how this felt to do as well as what kinds of things distracted their focus.

In middle and high school, we hope that students have learned mindfulness practices in the lower grades. If not, there should be a class where these and other *life skills* are practiced and developed. In addition, students can begin to reflect on the following in circle. (While they can certainly respond in writing, the value of sharing in circle lies in the opportunity to learn from one another.)

- *What are some things that distract you and keep you from doing your work, even when you want to get it done?* (It is good to give a few examples: phone calls, television, siblings, noise, clutter, etc.).

- *Tell a story about a time when you focused on something even though there were many distractions. How do you stay focused on something you want to do even when there are distractions?*

- *How do you imagine you can eliminate some of the distractions in your life?*

- Students often blame their inability or unwillingness to do work on their "laziness." They readily admit to being "lazy" when it serves a purpose. This concept can be challenged in circle, however, by asking: *What gets you charged up, activated, and focused, so that nothing can take away your attention? Tell a story about a time when you really worked hard, and nothing could stop you.* If they come up with anything at all, even "playing video games," it will become clear that it isn't quite fair to call yourself "lazy." Some things *do* get you going!

At the post-secondary level, we tend to expect that students have developed these capacities. And we might be wrong! With very few exceptions, college classes do not consider the social-emotional growth of students a priority. If you offer circles in these classes, however, you will simultaneously deepen content knowledge as well as intra- and interpersonal skills.

Collaboration, Perseverance, and Integrity: Developing Class Norms

To this day, in most secondary schools, teachers still give students marks for *work habits* and *cooperation.* At the elementary level, there are grades for *effort* in each academic area and separate grades for *work and study habits* and for *learning and social skills.* I find it fascinating that the assessment variable *works independently*, both at the elementary level and as one of seven "college and career ready" standards, is enshrined in the Common Core in the United States. At the elementary level there is a variable for *cooperates well in a group situation*, but nowhere do we find a standard for *collaboration.*

Is there a difference between cooperation and collaboration? I think so. If you recall what cooperation meant when you were in school, it was likely the teacher's assessment of how well you followed orders, not talking out of turn, not challenging the teacher's perspective, and things like coming to class on time. It was and still is a measure of a student's *compliance.* Collaboration, on the other hand, is actively working with others for the benefit of all. Collaboration is what we do in a community. Cooperation is what we do when we comply with a social or power hierarchy.

The notion of work *habits* suggests fixed patterns in the ways we approach a task. In my experience, this category of assessment usually has to do with whether students turn in assignments and whether they do so on time—again a matter of *compliance* rather than the development of *perseverance.* The measure of *effort* is similarly a completely subjective judgment by the teacher. Helping students to develop their capacity to persevere in challenging situations and to determine when to quit, when discretion *is* the better part of valor, is of greater value than simply telling them to work harder.

Circle is by its nature a collaborative activity. The value of such collaboration becomes apparent as the group gets a sense of its own wisdom emerging from the honest exchange of experiences. Here are some prompts for exploring the notion of collaboration:

- *To* co-labor-ate *is to work together toward a common goal. Tell of an experience where you successfully collaborated with others on a project or activity. In a second round, try to say what contributed to that success.*

- *Tell a story about a project or class where people didn't seem to get along, did not work well together. What do you think kept the group from being successful?*

- *We speak of class "work habits." What is a "habit"? Tell a story of a habit you developed that has helped you.*

- *Tell a story of a habit you developed that you have broken or would like to break. If you ever successfully broke a habit, how did you do it?*

- *What are some habits you would like to develop in this class? What might help you develop this habit? What might stand in your way?*

- *To persevere is to keep going even when something is difficult. Tell of a time when even though something was difficult or you thought you couldn't do it, you kept working at it and you did it. What do you think kept you going?*

- *Tell about a time you tried to persevere in something, but you felt you just had to quit. What do you think made you choose to give up?* (Emphasize that giving up, surrendering, is not in itself a bad thing. Knowing when to quit is called "discretion").

- William Blake says, "The fool who persists in his folly will become wise." After discussing what this means—allowing yourself to be foolish and to make every mistake—have students *tell about a time when you kept making mistakes over and over and then discovered what to do.*

- Albert Einstein said that definition of insanity is "doing the same thing over and over again and expecting a different outcome." *Tell of a time when you were, in effect, banging your head against a brick wall, and then you discovered that you* had *to do something different.*

To be in "integrity" is to integrate all of who you are, and in so doing to align thought, word, and deed. When we are truthful, acknowledging our fears, our grief, and our longing as well as our hopes and visions, we learn to trust ourselves and others learn to trust us. If we are to be in integrity in a classroom or school community, we must be able to speak the *whole* truth.

From "the dog ate my homework" to "I didn't copy!" teachers are regularly lied to. When this happens, we learn not to trust. But what would happen if we created a space for students to speak openly about the *fears and concerns that bring about the choice to lie*? And what if we told our stories of transgression? In the Hawaiian practice of Ho'oponopono, when a member of the community violates a community norm, there is a call for a storytelling gathering. Rather than pointing the finger at the transgressor, each person tells a story of a time when *they* crossed a similar line or wanted to do so. The telling of these stories does not, as one might think, make the transgression acceptable.

Rather, it creates the conditions for the transgressor to reflect on their actions. When dealing with errors in judgment or actions we regret, it is important that the teacher lead by example. *Young people need to see exemplars of reflection on past behavior*. Consider how rare it is to hear a public official acknowledge a poor decision. If we don't have models of reflection, honesty, regret, remorse, and acknowledgment of wrongdoing, we can't begin a process of redemption, responsibility, and reintegration.

Here are a few prompts that can begin to open this territory:

- *Tell of a time when you knew you could trust someone.*
- *Tell of a time when someone trusted you.*
- *Tell of a time that someone broke your trust.* (Use no names or obvious references.)
- *Tell of a time when you broke someone's trust.*
- *Tell of a time that you pretended to be something you weren't or to know something that you really didn't know.*
- *Tell of a time that you knew someone else was trying to be something they weren't.*
- A circle on lies: *When the talking piece comes, try to recall the tallest tale you ever told.* (This can be great fun, and it can open dialogue regarding the importance of honesty about what we know and don't know.)

Asking such questions does not, as some teachers feel, wrest authority from the teacher. To the contrary, sometimes students will cede more power to the teacher than one would expect. Some think that the circle by its egalitarian nature obviates hierarchy, when in fact quite the opposite is often true. When everyone speaks of their talents and their needs, there often emerges a recognition of what we want from and expect of each other, and our mutual "roles" are acknowledged and supported. Students might acknowledge their *need* for a teacher.

Once issues of collaboration, perseverance, and integrity are explored and there is some collective understanding of their value in the class community, a *set of classroom agreements* are developed in a *norm-setting circle*:

- *What should the agreements be in this classroom about the way we treat each other, what we expect of each other, how we resolve problems, how we handle assignments and homework, etc.?* Be clear that this is a living document, subject to revision as necessary.

And remember, teachers, that you too have a voice in the circle! You can help guide and shape these agreements. And there are certain non-negotiables. When the students are co-creators, however, they are likely to not see the *rules* as arbitrary and imposed because they are derived from consensus.

Community Norms Circle

We have found that circles will naturally develop agreements that mirror the four intentions of council. Students will suggest variations of speaking and listening from the heart if we simply ask: *How would you like to feel in this circle? What do you need from me and from the other students? What can you do to make sure others feel this way?*

Chart their answers. This is a good time to discuss these norms and to present *your* non- negotiable requirements. The value of collaboratively setting norms is that the whole community has a voice and buy-in, and when the norms are stretched or violated, the circle can discuss how to return to these agreements. Norms are to be revisited regularly.

Accessing Prior Knowledge and Attitudes

When students walk into a new classroom, they carry with them a cargo of previous experiences—with subject matter content, with their views of themselves in relation to the subject area, and with teachers they associate with the subject. Some might carry the story of "hating" or "loving" the subject. Some will carry the mythology of defining moments with teachers—moments of encouragement and success or of shame and failure. Some will come with a preconception about the subject being *hard* or *easy* or even *useless*. Some will come with a family myth, that the whole clan lineage contains either good or bad historians, scientists, athletes, mathematicians, readers, and speakers.

The teacher also carries stories about their relationship to the discipline, both personal and professional. For one, the subject might come easily, might be part of their *natural intelligence*, and for another it might have been a struggle to learn.

In circle, there is an opportunity to hear these stories. When one tells a tale, especially in the heightened attention and focus of a listening group, rather than on a piece of paper, one can hear one's own story as it is being told and see its effect on listeners. This feedback develops *reflective consciousness*, and initiates attitude revisions on the spot. The mythology of one's relationship to a subject area constantly evolves.

A good circle prompt is framed in such a way that each participant can address the topic directly from personal experience. You will notice that there is always an emphasis on *story*. All class members, including the teacher and any classroom aides can speak from experience about these issues. I use a hypothetical math class in the framing of these questions. If you teach in another discipline, substitute that for the questions phrased here in terms of math. Some circle topics and questions for an early middle or high school math class might include:

- *When you hear the word* math, *what comes to mind?*
- *You have had many experiences with math, experiences with teachers, projects, classes, and working with numbers in your life. When the talking piece comes, tell about any one of these experiences that you can remember here in the moment.* (If everyone practices the intention of *spontaneity* with this, much can be learned.)
- *Do you consider yourself* good *in math? If so, tell of a time when you knew this to be true. If not, what happened that made you feel this way?*
- *Do you consider math an* easy *subject or a* hard *one? Recall an experience when you felt this to be true.*
- *Have you ever had an experience with a math teacher who really helped you to learn? Recall and share one such experience.*
- *Have you ever had an experience with a math teacher who seemed to make the learning too difficult for you (perhaps the same one who at another time helped you)? Recall a particular moment when you felt this to be so.* (With respect to the intention of not commenting negatively about people who are not present in the council to respond, we ask that no names be used in recalling an experience of this type.)
- *Do you imagine that you will do well in this class? What gives you this feeling?*
- *Do you imagine you might have difficulty in this class? What do you imagine might cause these difficulties? What do you imagine you will do when something becomes too difficult? Would you ask for help, tough it out, etc.?*
- *What qualities do you look for in a good math teacher? What do you expect of me as your teacher?* (Teachers can also express their expectations of themselves, of their

students, and can recall stories of *good* math teachers they have had and the qualities these teachers displayed.)

Good teachers often solicit such information from students. However, this is usually done in one-to-one correspondence, in writing or in dialogue. Rarely are these discussions given the respectful formality, spaciousness, and attentive listening engendered by circle practice. Such circles provide a teacher with a wealth of information about student attitudes and expectations and about classroom dynamics. For students, such circles not only allow them to see themselves in commonality with the community of learners, but also to view the *teacher as a student* of the discipline as well.

Developing Study Skills

The word "study" means many things. For some, it is synonymous with memorizing. For others, it means *looking over* material. For yet others, it is something merely to avoid. Students have often challenged me to explain what I mean when I ask them to "study" for a test.

Traditional study skills, especially those involving note-taking, test-taking strategies, organization of effort, and time management, are rarely taught before college, if at all. Perhaps the best text available, with materials and concepts that can easily be adapted for secondary (even elementary!) school, is Walter Pauk's *How to Study in College.*[2] Significant study skills topics include: creating an environment for study and dealing with chaos and interruptions, time management, prioritizing, organization, paraphrasing and note-taking, test-taking, textbook and study-type reading, studying with a partner or group, preparing for standardized tests, dealing with stress and test anxiety, and improving memory and recall.

These issues make for very rich circle topics. Once again, the value of such circles, even prior to the teacher's delivery of specific information and strategies, is twofold: students feel safe to acknowledge both their successes and failures, their strengths and weaknesses regarding learning. In addition, students experience an *internal locus of control* when they *discover* adaptive strategies in themselves, in the stories of others, in the teacher's personal stories about their development of these skills, and in the information provided by the teacher and in textbooks. This sense of ownership of the process is crucial to the development of new study *habits*.

While students in kindergarten and the lower grades are rarely asked to *study* something, the idea of *looking again* can lead to an understanding of what it means to *review* and ultimately to *study*.

- A game like *Change Three*, mentioned above, can help students to look again at each other and at the environment.

- Project a picture that has many things going on simultaneously, such as *Where's Waldo.* Ask students to notice as many things as they can but only show the picture for 15 seconds. Popcorn what they remembered. Show the picture again, this time for 30 seconds, and see how many more things they remember. The point is that *when we look again*, when we spend more time looking, *we see and remember more.*

- A similar process can be done with a book or story. Read it through one time and then ask students to say what they remember. Read it through again and ask them if they heard anything the second time that they did not hear at first.

One of the great challenges in the upper grades is to get students to read something again or to look again at a formula—especially if the first time around they did not understand it. So, playing with the concept in the lower grades of looking again, looking deeper, looking for more will make the *close reading* and analysis required in the upper grades much more second nature.

For secondary students, I believe that there should be direct instruction in study skills. As with anything else, students will only adopt strategies that seem relevant. In circles we can create a linkage between the strategies and students' lived experiences:

Initial topics:

- *When you hear the word "study," what comes to mind?*
- *What do* you *do when you study?* (The class can derive a working definition.)
- *Tell a story about a time you studied for something, and your effort paid off. Tell of a time when you studied, and it really didn't help.*
- *Tell a story of a time you didn't study, and you still did well.* (Students love this one, and it is important to acknowledge that sometimes we do well in spite of the prevailing wisdom.)
- *Tell of a time when you didn't study, and you wished you had.*
- *Tell of a time when you cheated rather than putting in the time to study. In a second round, reflect on your reasons for choosing to cheat.*
- *Which subjects do you find easy to study for and which do you find difficult?*
- *Which topics or subjects do you find so interesting that you would study or practice them willingly?*

Creating an Environment for Study

It is a sad fact that many students do not have access to quiet places where they can reflect, consider, and develop understanding of information they receive. This reality is further complicated by the speed at which we can access information on our phones and computers and using AI. The result is that, in the *information age*, we have little of what we might call *knowledge*, let alone *wisdom*. Circles provide a time for us to *reflect* on our own experiences and those of others, a time to slow down and consider and perhaps even become more *considerate* in the process.

- *Describe the place where you feel most able to be yourself. If you don't have such a place, what do you imagine it would look like?*
- *Do you have a place you can go where you feel best able to concentrate, stay alert, and not be interrupted? If so, please tell us about that place. If not, try to say what you think keeps you from having such a place.*
- *How could you change your study place to make it better?*
- *Tell a story about a time when someone interrupted you as you were trying to do something. How did you deal with it?*
- External challenges: *What distracts you and keeps you from doing your work? Tell a story about a specific time when this happened.*
- Cell phones have the capacity to entice us to be continually occupied with messages, games, information, movies, etc. They diminish our capacity to reflect and consider. *Recall a time when you lost or had to put away one of your devices. What happened? What thoughts and feelings did you have? How long did those feelings last? What did you do after the loss?*
- Internal challenges: *What do you do to distract yourself or put off your work? If you can, tell an actual story of when you did this.*
- Play games and use activities that develop concentration and attention: the ball/sock toss, movement mirroring, clap pass, find the leader, change three, etc. Then, share strategies that worked and didn't work to stay focused during these activities.

Time Management

Not having enough time is one of the reasons teachers give for *not* offering circles. The pressure to get through the curriculum can be overwhelming. How we *find* or *make* and *lose* or *waste* time are worthwhile topics for consideration as these concerns seem to plague us through life. Just how do we make time for the things we love and waste time doing things that are of no benefit? And what is it, this thing called *time*?

- *Tell a story about a time when you were having so much fun or were so involved in something that you completely lost track of time.*
- *Tell about a time you were so bored, you thought you were going to die.*
- *Tell a story of a time when you made time for something you really wanted to do.*
- *Talk about a typical day. How do you actually spend your time from morning to night?*
- *What do you wish you had more time for?*
- *What do you do in a typical day that you consider a waste of time?*
- Have students create a weekly schedule of what they would *like* to be able to do, including what they *must* do —sleep, eat, travel, work, study, play, etc. Then have them keep a log of what they *actually* do in a week. Talk in circle about what they discover from the comparison.

Prioritizing

Deeply connected with time management is developing the skill of finding your priorities. This is never easy as it often involves letting go of something we want to do but just don't have *time* for. It is fruitful to consider how we make choices about what is most important to us or most necessary in each situation.

- *Tell a story about a time when you had to decide between a few options. In a second round, tell how you made that decision.*
- *What to you are the most important things in life?*
- *What are the most important things you do every day?*

Organization

Anytime you have students clean up after a project or put things in their right places, you help them build organizational skills. Circle is a good time to consider *how* we make choices that make things easier to access or do.

- *Tell a story about something you organized: a project, a party, a room, a drawer, your notebook, etc.*
- *Tell a story about a time you lost something because you couldn't remember where you put it.*
- *Tell a story about a time you tried to organize something, and your plan didn't work.*

Paraphrasing and Note-Taking

Walter Pauk recommends, and many schools teach, the Cornell Note-taking Method. In simple terms, the system is about distinguishing general from specific, examples from assertions, and the using key words as mnemonics. Generalizations and assertions are written closest to the left margin line (which is sometimes expanded). Examples are indented. Then the note-taker decides, usually after a lecture or reading portion, on *a key word that will serve as a trigger* to remember each group of generalizations and examples, and writes that word (phrase, date, name, formula, etc.) to the right of the extended margin line. When it comes time to study, one looks first at the trigger words. If you remember what is written to the right of that word, you go on to the next one. If you don't remember, you look again at the generalizations and the examples. If you study these key words every day, you will be fully prepared to recall the related details.

In the circles, when we ask students in a *witnessing round* to recall a word, phrase, or image from what they heard another person say, we are exercising the "paraphrase muscle." We are practicing moving information into long-term memory. Further, stories have a way of staying with us longer than ideas. There is truth to the saying: "Tell me a fact, and I'll remember. Tell me the truth, and I'll believe. But tell me a story, and it will live in my heart forever."

- Use dyadic or whole group circle to practice *witnessing*, recalling the essence of another's story.
- *When the talking piece comes, name something someone said or something you read a long time ago that you still remember. Why do you think this stayed with you?*

Test-Taking

By the time I left daily classroom teaching, I calculated that 32 of the typical 168 yearly "instructional hours" allotted in a secondary school class were dedicated to mandated tests. We were either preparing for, taking, or reviewing state- or district- required tests. Succeeding on so-called "high-stakes tests" was a primary and continual concern of students, staff, administrators, and many parents. Parents seek schools that demonstrate the capacity to produce high test scores. Teacher and administrator evaluations and compensation have been tied to test scores, and many have been busted for faking or changing scores. Students develop elaborate schemes for cheating. Being in school, sadly, becomes synonymous with being tested. Is this what education is about?

We will never get away from evaluating competence, performance, and growth in schools. We can, however, do something about diminishing the *anxiety* that accompanies these exercises.

- *Recall a test or a challenge that you looked forward to or that you dreaded. What do you think caused you to feel one way or the other?*
- *Recall a time when you prepared for a test or a challenge. If your preparation helped, what did you do that created that success? If your preparation or strategy didn't help, why do you think this was so?*

One of the keys to retaining information from textbooks and other sources is to approach the information *inquisitively*, even if what you are about to read or hear holds little interest for you. When the latter is the case, I like to employ what I call "artificial motivation" by forming questions about what I might read or hear. In circle, to prepare ourselves for active listening we might silently ask: *What will I learn from this person who now has the talking piece?* Or simply: *What will Susanna say now?* If we are exploring the topic of discrimination, we might ask: *What will Susanna have to say about her experience of discrimination?* Remind students, and yourself, to keep this questioning mind throughout the circle. The same approach is recommended in the classic SQ3R close reading process: skim, *question*, read, recite (internal witnessing or paraphrase), and review.

Developing an inquisitive, curious attitude in circles is then easily transferred to textbook reading (*What is a differential equation?*), lectures (*What will this person say about African art?*), and other communications that require our attention and retention. Here are some practices and prompts to develop this inquisitive mind, this *spirit of inquiry*:

- After a *witnessing* round, students learn to form a circle prompt from the theme that emerges. The group then uses this prompt for a subsequent round, giving participants an experience of how a good prompt provokes a "deepening" and focusing of the group.
- In dyads, students first listen to each other's stories. Then, each forms one prompt (one that enables the speaker to recall an actual experience), and they use these questions in a second round.
- Every circle can benefit from a *harvesting* process. The prompt stem for harvesting is: *Given what others have shared in this circle, what can we now say about ...?* Harvesting statements are like *thesis statements* or

generalizations based on the stories and information shared. Playing with this again and again in circle develops students' paraphrase muscles as well as their capacity to get to the point and then support that point with textual or primary data and examples.

Peer-Editing and Studying with a Partner or Group

Students who succeed in school naturally seek support from fellow students, if only to remind each other of what must be done. Daniel Goleman has shown statistically that students who learn to work cooperatively, those who develop a high *emotional and social intelligence,* will perform better in school and in life.[3] Students also seek confirmation from others about how much and what kind of effort is required for a task. "Did you do the homework?" and "What did you write for number 17?" are questions teachers often overhear. We should also acknowledge that *working together* can be viewed in some contexts as *cheating*. We often send students double messages about the value of collaboration and consensus versus competition in learning and about knowledge as a private possession.

Exploring questions of partnering and cooperation can prepare students for these crucial study skills:

- *Tell about a time when you successfully worked with another student or a group to study or on a project. In a second round, say what you feel this group did to be successful.*
- *Recall a time when a group effort ended in frustration. What do you think made working together so difficult?*
- *Tell about a time you tried to do something alone and you wished you had help.*

In a fashion similar to the classroom agreements process, you can develop a list of study strategies and post this in the classroom.

Circles also provide for strongly focused discussion in a limited time, especially when students understand the process well from less outcome-oriented sessions. For example, my middle-school students met in groups of four to provide feedback to each other on poems they were writing. These were the instructions given on a handout:

Today you will sit in a small circle. Each student will recite one original poem. (If there is time, after everyone has read, you can read a second poem.) One student begins the process by reciting a poem. Don't "explain" the poem; just recite it. The person sitting to the speaker's left will begin the circle process. Just like in circle, the focus passes from person to person clockwise. There is no "crosstalk" in the first two rounds. The third round only will be a "discussion."

Round 1:

- Where did you "enter" the poem? What part caught your interest? What have you experienced in your own life that feels connected to what the poet is expressing?
- Where, if anywhere, did you "exit" the poem? Where did you lose interest or stop following the images? What, if anything, confused you?
- After each student responds to these questions, the speaker recites the poem a second time.

Round 2:

- How do you think the poem can be improved? Some possibilities to consider:
- Which images can be clearer?
- Are there any places where "showing" would be better than "telling"?
- Are there places where the poem feels too short or too long?
- How can the theme or the feeling come through with more power or clarity?
- Are there any words that are vague and need to be more precise?

Round 3:

- The poet "witnesses" what has been said by the others. The poet recalls what others have said.
- All members contribute to an open discussion of the poem. Begin the same process for the next student.

The effect of such a process for small group work is profound. Students are better focused, more considered in their responses, and "listening from the heart," they do so with respect and heightened attention. Any teacher who has used "cooperative learning" in the classroom knows that these activities must be carefully structured. The relaxed formality of the circle process provides such structure.

Motivating Students to Engage Subject Matter

A new unit of learning is a threshold experience. Beginning a new novel, a project, formula, or concept is a crossing over into uncharted territory, sometimes one filled with excitement and anticipation, sometimes with indifference, and sometimes with dread. In any case, this journey into the new should be honored. Certainly, before any actual travel, we would study maps, ask others who have walked the same path to share their experiences, and we would determine what and how much we need to pack into our carry-on.

As teachers, we often find ourselves charged with *motivating* our students toward the new unit. We try to motivate our students through pre-reading, pre-writing, and other pre-instructional activities. Circles serve exceptionally well in this regard. A few examples:

Preliminary: This is an exploration to gain deeper understanding of what it is to engage in something "new:"

- *Tell of a time when you tried something new, and you succeeded!*
- *Tell of a time you tried something new, and you wished you hadn't!*

- *Tell of a time you were afraid to try something new, and you found out it wasn't so bad after all.*
- *Tell of a time you were afraid to try something new, and you were right to be afraid.*
- *Tell of a time someone helped you try something new.*

Pre-reading: The teacher chooses a theme that will be explored in a work of fiction and then asks students to connect it with a personal experience. A few examples for works of fiction:

- Before reading the tale of *Hansel and Gretel*: *Tell about a time when you were lost or alone.*
- Before reading *Where the Wild Things Are*: *Tell about a time you got caught doing something you were not supposed to.* Or, *tell about or draw an imaginary place.*
- Before reading the myth of Phaethon: *Tell about a time when you tried to do something, but it turned out you weren't quite able to handle it.*
- Before reading *Huckleberry Finn*: *Tell about a time you befriended someone who was very different from you.*
- Before reading Langston Hughes's "A Dream Deferred:" *Tell about a dream you had that you have already had to put off or let go of.*
- Before reading *To Kill a Mockingbird*: *Tell about a time you were treated differently just because you are young, your gender, tall or short, able or unable to do something, rich or poor, identified with an ethnic group, or because you believe in something that others don't.*

For works of nonfiction or informational text, the teacher chooses a topic and asks students to connect it with a personal experience:

- Before reading a biography of Dr. Martin Luther King Jr., Dolores Huerta, Sojourner Truth, Henry McNeal Turner, Abraham Lincoln, or any other recognized great leader: *Tell of a time when you had to be a leader. Tell of a time when it was important for you to have and follow a leader. Name some great leaders you know. These could be family members, friends, and characters from history or fiction. What are the qualities you find in these leaders? Which of these qualities do you find in yourself? In others in this class?*

- *Epistemological inquiry circle:* Before a chapter in a science textbook that describes the scientific method: *Name one thing you know to be true, from "The sky is blue" to "My mother loves me" to "My neighborhood is a scary place." In a second round, say* ***how*** *you know this thing to be true. What is your experience?* (In one such session, a student offered, "The sky is blue," as a flip response. During the second round, however, he shifted his assertion to include the times when the sky is gray or black, or bright orange and purple, or filled with twinkling lights!)
- Before a chapter introducing students to the American Revolution: *Tell of a time you were fed up and felt that something had to change!*
- Before an article on ecology: *What is one thing you do that helps the environment? What is one thing you do that you think might be harmful to the environment?*
- Before text about health: *What is one thing you do to stay healthy? What is one thing you do that you think might not be good for your health?*
- Before a piece on social justice: *Describe a time when you had a problem that was resolved fairly. Describe a time you were involved in a problem that ended in a way that you felt was unfair.*

Some will say that the sharing of personal experience in the classroom is an invasion of privacy. We are reminded, first, however, that in circle *no one is required to speak, ever*, and second, that *all history was once personal experience.*

One might also ask why we would want to submit these questions to a circle rather than having a normal classroom discussion. There are a few reasons. Generally, classroom discussion tends to be unidirectional; the teacher asks a question, and the student responds to the teacher. In circle, the form encourages all participants to speak to the whole group. Also, in teacher-directed discussion, students who respond instantaneously, sometimes without careful consideration, often eclipse those whom we might call *considerate,* those who need time to *consider* a question. The use of a talking piece allows students the time to *see what comes*. Students also have the benefit of hearing the teacher's story, as one among many, about the same issues and experiences.

Pre-writing:
To write, one must feel that one has a story to tell. When I have asked students to tell a story, I have often heard something like this in response: "*I don't have any stories. Stories are in books and movies.*" This breaks my heart. Somehow, children have come to devalue their lived experience. Either they have learned that the experiences of daily life are not "stories," or they have received a message that they don't have the maturity to understand what they are experiencing.

Circle practice encourages students to recognize the value in their own personal experience, and to see the value in the experiences of others. Without this sense of the value of one's own story, responses to teachers' questions will tend to be a best guess at what the teacher is looking for, or no response at all. Here are few examples of prompts based on common rhetorical modes for writing:

- **Before a *personal narrative*:** *Tell a story about a time when you felt you changed—from thinking or believing something to thinking or believing something else, from being unable to do something to being able, etc.* (These *turning points* or *moments of truth* make for wonderful stories.)

- **Before a *cause/effect* paragraph or essay:** *When the talking piece comes, name something that you witnessed—a car crash, an argument, a celebration, etc. In a second round, say* ***why*** *you think this event occurred.*
- **Before a *comparison/contrast* paragraph or essay:** *In a first round, name two items, places, or people you know to be very different (e.g. a basket and a Bengal tiger). In a second round, try to come up with at least one similarity these two items share.* (This leads to discussion about areas of differentiation for compare/ contrast forms.)
- **Before a *problem/solution* paragraph or essay:** *Tell about a problem or difficulty you had that you were able to solve. What were the steps you took in working it out? Tell about a problem or difficulty that you couldn't fix even though you tried. Why do you think your attempts were unsuccessful?*
- **Before a *persuasive* paragraph or essay:** *Tell about a time you convinced someone, or someone convinced you, to do something. What did you or this other person have to do or say to make this happen?*
- **Before a *practical/informative, process*, or *how-to* paragraph or essay:** *Tell a story about something you did or made, from running a marathon to making a peanut butter and jelly sandwich. What steps did you take to achieve this goal?*
- **Before a *descriptive* paragraph or essay:** *Tell a story about something or someone you saw that was amazing or unusual!*
- **Before an *analytical* paragraph or essay:**
  - For *character analysis or* looking at "round" and "flat" characters in literature: *Tell about two different parts of your personality. Tell a story about a person you know who has at least two different parts to their personality.*

- For *plot analysis*: *Tell a story of a conflict you had with another person. In a second round, say what led to the conflict, what happened in the middle of it, and how it did or did not work out.*
- For *analysis of theme*: Brainstorm or give students a list of themes: unrequited love, greed, joy, foolishness, etc. Have them choose one that appeals to them and then tell a story from their own experience that shows an aspect of the theme.

- **Before a paragraph or essay that develops a *figure of speech*:**
  - For *metaphor*: *Name two unlike things that share some similarities.*
  - For *personification*: *Tell of an experience you had with a nonhuman thing—an animal, or something in nature—the wind, a tree, a stone that seemed to have human qualities.*
  - For *hyperbole*: *Tell an actual story of something you accomplished but exaggerate what you did. For example, if you went swimming in the ocean, exaggerate how far you went, how long you stayed in the water, or how big the waves were.*
- **Before writing *fiction*:** *When the talking piece comes, see what imaginary place, person, or situation comes to mind.*
- **Before writing a *poem*:** *Tell a story of a moment of powerful feeling or new understanding. This moment could involve any flavor or intensity in the range of human emotions: mad, glad, sad, or scared. For example: "when I stood at the rim of the Grand Canyon for the first time;" "when my grandmother died;" "when I stayed home alone for the first time;" "when I realized I had a true friend," etc. In a second round, tell the story as leanly as possible.*

In addition to acknowledging the value of their own experiences, through circles of this type students get a sense of the value of these rhetorical modes, rather than simply a conceptual understanding of their structural form.

Checking for Acquired Knowledge

How do we know that we know something? Without getting into the deeper epistemological questions, perhaps it is enough to say that we know something when we can express this knowledge in some form, either to ourselves or to others. We show that we "understand" a "give-and-go" play in basketball by doing it, that we understand balancing chemical equations by balancing them, that we understand an arpeggio by playing one, etc. Odd as it might seem, we can give tests in circle. Even traditional tests.

Students can dedicate, sending out a wish that all will do well, and then the class can shift into the respectful silence of circle as they work with paper and pencil. This simple act just might create a "field" that promotes concentration and reduces anxiety.

The beauty of reviewing material in circle is that the atmosphere creates what linguist Stephen Krashen calls a "low affective filter" necessary for the deep acquisition of language and information, there is *collaborative reinforcement,* and it can all be done *very quickly.* It is a tried-and-true practice for teachers at the conclusion of a class or lesson to ask the group to say something they "learned." This is usually done with just the raising of hands. The circle twist on this is to focus attention by marking a beginning (ring a bell), and then to ask students to recall *one thing that stayed* with them from the hour, from the day, from the unit, from the reading, from the lab, from an activity, etc.

There is much lower cognitive demand when a student is asked to *remember* one thing rather than to say one thing that was *learned.* You can also ask them to share any questions still with them. In this way, within five minutes or less students are *reminding each other* of the information, which is a form of *study,* and simultaneously the teacher gets a very quick read on what has been retained and what needs to be reinforced. After any experience—a soccer game, a museum trip, a science lab, a wander in nature—ask students to recall *one thing they noticed* that made an impression. The fantastic thing here, in addition to the review, is that the same experience is viewed from multiple perspectives, expanding the awareness of that experience for the whole group.

Setting Intentions, Accountability, and Making Course Corrections

We often talk about accountability in education: superintendents and directors are accountable to the board, legislators, and national policymakers; principals to their directors; teachers to their school administrators; students to their teachers, etc.

Accountability, however, is most powerful when it is to a circle or community. It is so easy, for example for a teacher to dismiss critical feedback from a single administrator, but when feedback comes from a circle of peers, it is much more difficult to write off! The same is true in the classroom. If a student *only* feels accountable to the teacher, it will be easy at challenging moments for the student to think, for example, *Oh, Mr. Provisor just doesn't like me,* or to think that he is just *unfair*. When students state their intentions to one another, however, and these intentions are held (lovingly) by the group, the process serves to provide motivation, support, and accountability. This story will serve to illustrate:

Math teacher Lisa McDannold asked me to conduct a circle with her new algebra class. Put together for the spring semester, the class consisted of students who had failed in the fall, and many had failed with Lisa as their teacher. Lisa recognized, however, that this was a chance for them, and for her, to start fresh, and she wanted to find a way to acknowledge that.

As you might imagine, this was a rather defeated and defensive bunch. All circles, even "remedial" ones, should begin with some celebration of commonality. So, after dedicating to success in this class in the coming semester, we began with the question, "What was one good thing that you learned or that happened in this class last semester?" Answers ranged from "the day we got to watch a video because we all did our homework" to "when I got an A on the unit test." Even the passing of the talking piece and the answer of "nothing" had a context. Lisa even recalled a time when, after her shifting some seats around, the class was able to concentrate and pay attention. I acknowledged that even though students did not do well the first semester, I heard the sharing of some positive experiences. I mentioned that a failure is only a failure when we fail to learn from it.

The second round began with this question: "What do you see as some of the difficulties you had last semester that seemed to keep you from doing well?" Students spoke of the difficulty of learning algebra, of getting homework done, of dealing with personal issues at home, at school, and in the classroom. They spoke what was on their minds: not being "good" in math. Being too tired to work when they got home. Having responsibilities with younger siblings. Being scared or intimidated about carrying books home. Feeling unable to concentrate because of the behavior of certain others in the class. Feeling that the teacher *just doesn't like me*. Not caring. Lisa also spoke of the difficulty of teaching algebra to eighth graders who just might not be ready developmentally and about teaching certain individuals in particular. It is not important to challenge the language used to describe these experiences or to attempt to refute them, so I simply witnessed, "It seems that there are lots of things that can get in the way of doing well."

When we reconvened the circle the following week, after reconnecting with the work we already accomplished, I asked, "*Without blaming the class, the teacher, your situation, or anyone else, how do you think you contributed to your difficulties last semester?*" Students admitted to slacking off, to watching too much television, playing too many video games, being "addicted to the net," to making friends more important, to not giving the teacher a chance, and to not caring.

Of course, Lisa had to answer this question as well. She admitted to frustration, focusing more attention on students who were doing their work, and at times to being sarcastic and dismissive of students she had "given up" on. I think everyone in the class was surprised at the level of honesty, and I can only attribute that to Lisa's authenticity and the respectful, non-threatening, nonhierarchical atmosphere generated by the process.

Our third meeting had to do with *intention setting*. We talked about the difference between a long-term goal, like "getting an A," and a short-term goal, like "doing my math homework tonight" or "taking my book home tonight." I asked the students to take some private time to write out on index cards one long-term goal and a few related short-term goals regarding the class. Once they had done so, we opened the circle. As the talking piece went around, the students and Lisa spoke their intentions. Cynthia said, "I'm going to sit somewhere else in the class because Felicia is my friend, and when I sit next her, I just have to talk with her." Jorge volunteered, "I'm going to walk home a different way so the guys who tease me won't see me carrying my math book." Jason promised, "I'll do my homework tonight, as soon as I get home, after I get a snack, and maybe I'll try to do that every night." A few students stated no intention at all, and a few showed that they hadn't really understood the distinction between a short and a long-term goal ("I'm going to do better"). Each, however, got to hear some strong intentions stated publicly and perhaps more importantly saw that it was okay to own challenges and to take steps to meet them. Even Lisa stated her intention "to help each of you succeed in fulfilling your intentions." Also, a long-term goal.

I suggested that Lisa hold periodic circles to check in on the intentions. All intentions must be re-evaluated, extended, reduced, dropped altogether, or re-affirmed from time to time. Lisa collected the index cards the students used to write their intentions, and she placed them in a manila folder marked ***PERIOD 2 INTENTIONS***. She posted it above the chalkboard and said that whenever attention starts to drift in the class, she points to the folder!

This story illustrates what we call *turning into the skid*. This class had already skidded off the algebra tracks. Loading this group with guilt, haranguing them with stories of what happens to dropouts, or tightening up requirements and oversight would have been like attempting to steer the vehicle straight on an icy road. When things aren't working, we teachers should open and turn toward the difficulties, acknowledging, as poet Benjamin Saltman once said, "All are guilty, no one is to blame."

A few other mid-term or periodic course correction circle prompts:

- *So far in this class, what have you found most interesting, helpful, or useful? Tell a story if you can. So far in this class, what have you found most challenging, boring, or useless?*
- *Give me some reflection as your teacher. When you think about me, the way I am, the way I teach, what comes to mind?*
- *Give some reflection to your classmates. How do you feel about the way we are together as a class?*

Some teachers might be terrified to hear this kind of "truth." My experience has been that hard as it is to hear, I become a better teacher when I can allow myself to be open to this feedback.

As a teacher I have made many assumptions about the value of what I teach. Sometimes I even try to motivate students by assigning value to things I don't consider all that important or useful! The student refrain "We are never going to use this stuff" can be obviated by submitting the following questions to a circle:

- *Now that you have learned this information, what do you imagine you might do with it? How do you think you might use it in the future?*
- *State one short-term, attainable goal you could set for yourself now that you know this information.*

Celebrating Accomplishments and Transitions

Just as the beginning of a new school year, a new class, a new unit, or a new project is a *rite of entry* so the completion of any of these is a *rite of passage*. As noted above, traditional rites of passage in many cultures occur in three phases: "separation," "transition," and "incorporation." Roughly speaking, *separation* involves bringing consciousness to what was, looking with clear eyes at past experiences, knowledge, relationships, and attitudes, and an acknowledging of the need to move on. *Transition* is being with what is—the feelings, hopes, questions and fears that arise from being on the verge of something new. *Incorporation* involves conscious intention setting and commitments made both to oneself and to the community, in this case the school, one's classmates, teachers, parents, and other involved adults. Circle is an invaluable tool for marking these three phases of change. More particulars about rites of passage will be provided in Chapter 10, but for now we will look at a few ways we can acknowledge accomplishments and transitions in the classroom

With the fast pace of curriculum requirements, it seems a challenge to even find a moment to take a breath before moving on. Once the papers are turned in and the project done, we just start the next one. Taking the time to mark completion, ceremonially, in circle, however, brings meaning to what we have done:

After students complete a project, paper, or unit, it is a good time to reflect on the process:

- *Now that you have completed the project, what is one thing you might have done differently?*
- *What is one thing you wished you had known or that could have been clearer in the instructions?*
- *What is one thing you think you will always remember?*

Once students have come to know each other well, *appreciation circles* deepen their bonds and create an atmosphere of acknowledgment:

- **A shout-out:** At any time, offer a virtual or actual circle for students to speak their appreciations of others.

- ***One thing you notice*****:** Students may need some guidance in how to speak an appreciation. It is often much easier to say what we don't like about a person than to find words for admiration. We can start simply: students say one thing they notice and like about the person sitting across the circle from them. It might be something they remember that person doing, something that person said, even their choice of shoes or hairstyle.

- **Appreciation cards:** Students receive 5 x 8 index cards upon which they write their name. Cards are passed around the circle with the following instruction: *Write one thing you notice and like about this person. It might be just one adjective that describes a positive quality.* When the cards circulate around the whole circle and return to their owners, the group uses a prompt such as: *Read over what others have written on your card. What seem to be some of the qualities that other people appreciate about you? Is there anything there that surprises or puzzles you? Is there something there you have never heard before? Are there any things that you have heard others say at other times?"* Many facilitators have used *The Story of Mark Eklund*, written by Franciscan nun Sister Helen Mrosla, Mark's third grade teacher, to emphasize the value of an exercise such as this. The true story goes that an appreciation card such as this was found among the few possessions Mark carried with him when he served in Vietnam, a fact revealed by the family at his funeral.

- **Yarn appreciation, a web of compliments:** This form of appreciation is often done at the end of a year because students are able to take away a souvenir. Using a ball of yarn, instruct students to hold the end of the yarn and toss the ball to someone else at random, trying not to pre-plan what will be said. The student who tosses the ball compliments the receiver and so on until everyone in the circle has received it once. Other colors of yarn can be added. Eventually, a multicolored interconnecting web is visible to the whole circle. Students then cut the strands and wrap the pieces around their wrists to form bracelets commemorating the experience.

- **Water appreciation:** Facilitator Dan Brumer developed this beautiful ceremony. Items needed are one large bowl/container, two smaller bowls, and a utility pitcher with water, flowers, etc.

Phase 1—*COLLECTING OUR WISDOM*:

1. Place a large empty bowl, decorated and surrounded by beauty, in the center of the circle. Place two smaller bowls nearby. Someone pours water (from a utility pitcher) into one of the smaller bowls, which will be used as a talking piece. Dan points out that using a partially filled bowl of water, which is itself alive, as a talking piece engenders great care in its handling—as it should be when we acknowledge ourselves and each other.

2. Ask each person in turn to walk to the center, say something they learned *about themselves or others* in this last year and pour a small amount of water into the larger bowl. The small bowl/talking piece is then passed, and each person does the same. Finally, the last person empties the small bowl into the larger one and places it in the center. The effect is that the larger bowl is symbolically filled with all the experiences/lessons from the circle.

PHASE 2—*APPRECIATIONS*:

3. One person takes an empty small bowl and the person sitting directly across the circle is asked to pick up the other. They stand and meet on either side of the larger bowl and the person beginning scoops some water from the larger bowl, tells the other person something they appreciate about them and pours their water into the other person's bowl.

The first person goes back to their chair and sits down, handing their small, empty bowl to the person on their left. This next person walks to the center and receives an appreciation from the last person, who then sits and passes the now empty bowl to the person on their left, and so on around the circle.

PHASE 3—*NEW PAIRS AND SPONTANEOUS ADDITIONAL APPRECIATIONS*:

4. At the end of the first cycle, begin a second round which can either start with another pair (so we appreciate and are appreciated by a second person) and/or leave it open to spontaneous appreciations, done in the same way but not in any order. Each person may appreciate someone they choose. This can continue as long as time allows.

- **Random Appreciation, Final Words:** With some groups it is enough to suggest that there will be an appreciation council, and it can be conducted in the basic form with students randomly appreciating others in the circle. To add a bit of *present moment, only moment* awareness to this, the leader can suggest, *Not knowing what can happen in the future or whether we will ever be together again in this way, what would you like to say to people in this group?*

- **The Three Phases of Change:** We often use this three-step process to mark the closing of a year, but it can be used whenever something is ending and something new is beginning:

- **Phase 1—severance:** Students consider the following prYompt: *Looking over the past year (or the project or phase just completed), what memories come to mind?* What emerges from such a sharing in circle is a kind of verbal scrapbook, which, in its totality, is a ceremonial acknowledging of what has occurred, what we have passed through together. This often takes a full hour.

- **Phase 2—transition:** This phase, conducted after severance, can be as simple as being together or playing a game that brings everyone into the moment. It can be a group meditation. *Alone time* walks, where students just notice their breath, movement, what occurs inside and outside, are also aligned with this phase. This may also be a time for private reflection or the writing of questions about the future. It is, in effect, a time for consciously clearing the plate. This is also a good time for statements of gratitude or apology.

- **Phase 3—incorporation:** Students speak of their visions, hopes, and dreams for the near and distant future. They then set intentions and make commitments, again moving from the visions to short-term, manageable goals. If this is an end-of-the-year circle, students can set intentions for the summer, for the coming school year, for maintaining connections with friends, for learning something new, for taking the time to just hang out, etc. When these commitments are shared, the group can energize and strengthen the speaker by saying something like "Go for it!"

And so, we come full circle from the first tender moments of anticipation and welcome into a new school, a new grade, a new class, to the farewell that must be marked as we take our leave. While it would be impossible in the general classroom, especially at the secondary level, to conduct *all* the circles suggested in this chapter, my hope is that you will consider these examples and then co-create, with your students, your own applications to bring meaning to the collaborative enterprise of learning.

For Reflection and Imagination

1. Consider the idea that beginning a new school year and the end of a year are rites of passage:

- Recall a moment from your own school experience: a first day in a new school, a first day in a new grade.
- Try to recall your hopes and fears about that day.
- What actually happened? Was it what you expected.
- Recall experiences of the end of a year, especially matriculation to a new level of school.
- Did the experience feel meaningful? Pro forma?
- Imagine how you would have liked to mark these moments of transition.

2. Recall a teacher with whom or a class where you felt seen and heard, curious, and free to make mistakes. What contributed to your feeling that way?

3. Recall a teacher with whom or a class where you felt unseen, alienated, shamed, or inadequate. What contributed to your feeling that way?

4. Consider your own "study skills." When you were the age of the students you teach ...

- which environments contributed to your being able to concentrate?
- which environments were distracting?
- what systems did you use to manage your time and to prioritize tasks?

Chapter 7: Circles in General Classroom Use

1. **Mark Threshold Moments with Intention**
   Use circle to honor beginnings, endings, and transitions. For example, ritualizing entry into a new school year, unit, or classroom dynamic with shared stories and reflection.

2. **Build Community Through Shared Rituals**
   Celebrate birthdays, holidays, and personal milestones in circle. These practices cultivate belonging, joy, and emotional safety.

3. **Unearth Expectations Early**
   Invite students to name their hopes, fears, and expectations: of the subject matter, the teacher, themselves, and each other. This fosters clarity and collective responsibility.

4. **Teach Attention as a Skill**
   Circle rituals like silent councils, mindfulness, mirroring, and talking piece practice help students develop focus, self-awareness, and concentration.

5. **Explore Collaboration, Perseverance, and Integrity**
   Use circle to distinguish collaboration from compliance, build habits of perseverance, and create classroom norms rooted in honesty and trust.

6. **Connect to Prior Knowledge and Personal Experience**
   Before starting new topics, use circle prompts to surface students' lived associations, transforming curriculum into meaningful inquiry.

7. **Use Circle to Deepen Study Skills and Motivation**
   Embed circle throughout academic routines to teach note-taking, study strategies, time management, and goal-setting. Let students learn from one another's lived wisdom.

8

CIRCLES AND TRADITIONAL ACADEMIC DISCIPLINES: LANGUAGE ARTS, SOCIAL STUDIES, MATHEMATICS, AND SCIENCE

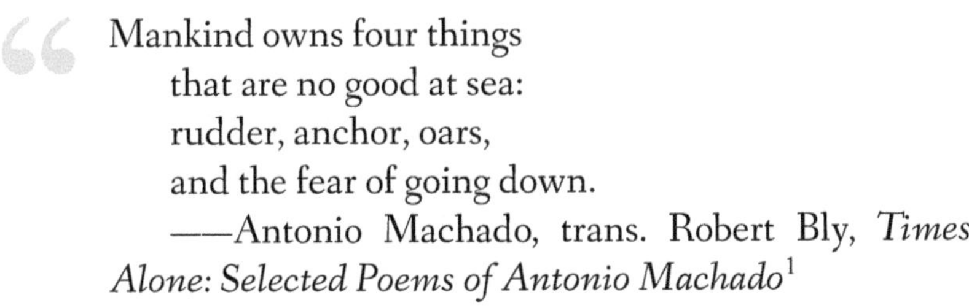

> Mankind owns four things
> that are no good at sea:
> rudder, anchor, oars,
> and the fear of going down.
> —Antonio Machado, trans. Robert Bly, *Times Alone: Selected Poems of Antonio Machado*[1]

Circle and Curriculum

This chapter explores the connections between circle practice and traditional academic disciplines: language arts, history/social studies, math, and science. For most of human history, we learned in circles, sharing the wisdom of our lived experiences, cultural values, and mythology.

More than anything, a circle-based pedagogy serves the students. It keeps our focus on their needs—not our own, nor those of the state, textbook writers, or test designers. In this spirit, this book does not aim to offer step-by-step, grade-level-specific curriculum. Instead, this chapter offers a way of seeing curricular terrain through a circular lens. The "map" is not fixed: it reflects the organic unity of the students in front of you, the content you are expected to teach, and the changing circumstances of the present moment.

When I began researching learning standards beyond my field of language arts, I came across one that I absolutely fell in love with! It is a California History-Social Studies standard from 2000 that encapsulates the learning proposed in that discipline for an entire year. As you read it, see if you can guess the *grade level* of students for whom it is intended:

> "Students are introduced to basic spatial, temporal, and causal relationships, emphasizing the geographic and historical connections between the world today and the world long ago. The stories of ordinary and extraordinary people help describe the range and continuity of human experience and introduce the concepts of courage, self-control, justice, heroism, leadership, deliberation, and individual responsibility. Historical empathy for how people lived and worked long ago reinforces the concept of civic behavior: how we interact respectfully with each other, following rules, and respecting the rights of others."[2]

When students have mastered these skills, they are ready to enter ... *first grade*! Yes, this was the introductory Social Studies standard for students enrolled in kindergarten in California public schools. I like to imagine the writers celebrating when they arrived at this formulation: "Eureka!" as it neatly summarizes universal human values. In fact, if anyone asks you what you are doing with the circles in your classes, you might reply, "I am *remediating* the California kindergarten social studies standard!"

At the other end of the spectrum, we now have "graduate profiles:" lists of competencies students should demonstrate by the time they graduate from high school. According to the Common Core State Standards, students who are "college and career ready" will ...

1. Demonstrate independence.
2. Build strong content knowledge.
3. Respond to the varying demands of audience, task, purpose, and discipline.
4. Comprehend as well as critique.
5. Value evidence.
6. Use technology and digital media strategically and capably.
7. Understand other perspectives and cultures.

Each of these proficiencies is cultivated in circle practice. Students learn that their voices matter—they are independent, autonomous beings whose experiences are valued. At the same time, they come to appreciate collaboration and interdependence.

In curriculum-based circles, students build strong content knowledge by exploring how course materials connect with their lives. Responding to the varying demands of audience requires awareness of who is listening and how their experiences differ—something circle makes vividly real.

Comprehension—literally the ability to "hold" or "grasp" what is before us—is a prerequisite for critique. In circle, we practice this kind of deep, receptive attention: listening from the heart. Circles also prioritize story over opinion and lived experience over assumption. This teaches students to value evidence and question unexamined tradition. And while circle is low-tech (it even works when the power goes out!), students can apply it in digital spaces too, developing awareness of how to share meaningfully on social platforms across cultures. The best way to understand other perspectives and cultures? Be with people from different backgrounds, in a space that invites heartful sharing. That's what circle offers.

Integrating Circle with Learning Standards in All Disciplines

Since learning standards provide the scaffolding that supports students' progress toward proficiencies, we now consider how circle practice can work with what states, districts, and schools require. I view all standards as artifacts of an ongoing dialogue among educators. But without input from students about *what they need,* we will forever be behind the curve. Still, I take some comfort in recognizing that, although the organization and emphasis of standards shift—usually every seven years—the directive verbs they rely on remain largely unchanged since Benjamin Bloom's taxonomies.[3] Terms like "describe," "communicate," "understand," "connect," "represent," "apply," "visualize," "formulate," "respect," "advocate," "analyze," "synthesize," "evaluate," "compare," and "contrast" appear regularly. Many of these imply *a quality of relationship*—to concepts, to techniques, to the environment, to the self, to text, and to others. Take "communicate"—*to share, to carry across.* It suggests respect: for the concept itself, for ourselves as communicators, and for those we hope to reach. "Understand" literally means *to stand among.* "Comprehend" means to grasp or *catch a hold* of. These are not solitary acts—they are relational.

I recall students practicing circle at the Marlton School for the Deaf and Hard of Hearing in Los Angeles. When asked to "witness" what others had shared in circle, instead of signing the phrase "I *heard* someone say," they used the sign for "I *caught* ... " I love that phrasing. It suggests active, intentional receiving—a readiness to grasp what's offered.

Every directive verb in education implies a relationship. As I noted in Chapter 1, reading is a form of listening; writing, a form of speaking. Where better to cultivate this relational awareness than in circle, where we remember we are not separate from one another, or from the world?

World as Text

Let's expand our concept of what it means to be "literate." True literacy may involve not only reading and writing in the conventional sense, but also the ability to *read* ourselves, others, and the world around us. Circle facilitators often speak of *reading* the field: being attuned to what is happening (or not happening) in the group at any given moment.

What if our students came to see the world as *text*? What if reading extended beyond moving our eyes across printed words? After all, we often say things like "reading a situation," "what's your read?" or "that person is hard to read." The word *text* from the Latin root *tex*, meaning "a weaving"—a pattern, a structure. It is related to *textile, tactile, tangible,* and *tact.* To read, then, might mean to touch or connect with something in a way that brings about right action. Isn't that the ultimate goal of reading? To better understand ourselves and others—and to act in the world more efficiently, more creatively, more compassionately? For a deeper exploration of this idea, see Joanna Macy's *World as Lover, World as Self.*[4]

I am not a proponent of standardized testing. The notion that all children must learn the same content at the same time feels dystopian: a system designed for machines. Still, in the U.S., Common Core assessments attempt to measure students' ability to interpret various forms of text. These assessments typically present clusters of materials: a poem, an informational piece, and a piece of fiction, sometimes paired with a photograph, video, painting or sculpture. Students are asked to identify connections within and across these texts, including visual and spatial ones.

Why stop there?

Let's consider even more ways that meaning is conveyed and "text" can be read:

- **Environmental text**: Interpreting cues from the natural world or built environment
- **Non-linguistic auditory text**: Reading sound itself —rhythm, music, silence
- **Tactile text**: Attuning to texture and touch
- **Proprioceptive/intuitive text**: Listening to one's body
- **Empathic text**: Sensing another's experience—human, animal, or natural object
- **Relational text**: Perceiving meaning through proximity and awareness of others

By limiting reading to the words on a page, we constrict our awareness, and with it, our capacity to see, feel, connect, and truly understand. Circle practice expands that field. It deepens our ability to read the world—and to respond with empathy, insight, and presence.

Communication (Language) Arts

When I run into former students, they inevitably remember two things from their year with me in middle school: circles and the I-Search. The latter was a yearlong investigation into a topic of their choosing, using both primary and secondary sources. For some, mostly those who did not choose carefully, it was hell. For others, it was transformative. One student, facing an upcoming brain surgery, chose to research brain surgery itself. That project helped her prepare for what lay ahead. Today, she's a pediatrician.

What made the project so memorable was the opportunity it gave students to deeply explore something *they* cared about—a process rarely offered before graduate school, if at all. When I reflect on my own public-school education, only a handful of moments stand out. One was in Mr. Swartz's tenth-grade English class. It was late in the year. I hadn't read more than a few pages of *Moby Dick*, and little else from the course stuck—except one day when we entered to see the classroom walls covered in abstract original oil paintings. I assumed that Mr. Swartz was the artist. He gave us a simple instruction: "I'm going to play some music, and I want you to write whatever comes to mind." No grading, no assignment to turn in. I didn't know it at the time, but the music he played was John Coltrane's *Transitions*. I had never heard anything like it. The artwork, the sound, and the invitation to write freely transformed the space. I wrote—nonstop —for the whole 50 minutes!

In the 1970s, Paulo Freire and his team developed what became the most successful literacy program of our age, designed to teach indigenous adults in Brazil to read and write Portuguese. Freire used what he called "culture" or "investigative" circles.[5,6] Participants sat in a circle surrounded by images depicting daily village life. Using the images as prompts, they told stories: a myth about the village well, a memory of someone who built it, a story of healing, of scarcity, or of an encounter. These stories did more than build literacy: they affirmed each person as a "subject" in the world, capable of making, shaping, and transforming their environment.

As stories accumulated, so did shared understanding. It is what we might call the "wisdom of the circle." Participants realized that while they knew much, they also *didn't know everything*—that others in different places might have stories as well. This sparked curiosity, and with it, the desire to read, to access new stories, new perspectives, beyond their village and culture.

In the same spirit, circle honors each student's lived experience as a valid source of insight. That experience becomes the starting point, the touchstone, for new learning. Educators often talk about bringing "relevance" to curriculum. Circle helps us activate it. When students connect new information to their own lives, learning becomes meaningful. Of course, circle is not a substitute for direct instruction. We are still tasked with delivering specific content. But circle is a powerful tool for helping students discover why that content matters. The examples in this chapter are not prescriptive. They're offered to help you see how any standard, topic, or process—no matter how abstract—can be approached through circle. Doing so invites students to engage more deeply, and often, more joyfully.

Four Domains and Three Skill Areas in Language Arts

Language arts instruction generally centers on four domains—narrative and descriptive, expository, persuasive, and analysis of text—and three skill areas—vocabulary, grammar and usage, and style. Each of these domains offers rich opportunities to integrate circle practice with curricular goals:

Narrative and Descriptive

At its heart, the narrative domain is about telling and receiving stories. Circle-based pedagogy begins with the premise that everyone has a story to tell, and that listening to these stories with an open mind can expand our knowledge, awareness, and humanity. Many students today have had little exposure to live storytelling, despite its historic role in cultural transmission. In circle, we work to revive both the art of storytelling and the joy of listening. As students grow in appreciation for their own stories and those of their peers, they also develop the foundations for literary analysis. Importantly, circle practice nurtures not just literacy but oracy—the ability to express oneself confidently and clearly in speech. When students learn that their stories matter and will be received with compassion, they begin to find their voice. And having a voice—truly owning one's perspective—is essential for self-advocacy and social participation.

The witness cycle: Inferring themes from everyday experience and in literature

Many of the same critical and analytical skills we teach through literature can also be developed using students' own stories, as shared in circle. One such skill, introduced around third grade, is inferring a theme or central idea from a story. While in some cultures "getting to the point" may be considered impolite, the ability to form a generalization based on particulars, to formulate a take-away, is fundamental to learning. Supporting those insights with details is a mark of growing mastery.

Circle offers a simple, powerful structure for developing this skill: the witness cycle:

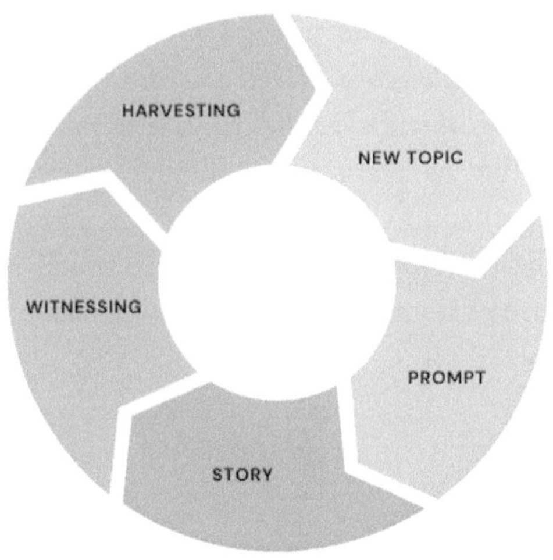

The witness cycle

This structure works equally well for interpreting personal experience and for deepening understanding of literature. It also functions as a meaningful check-in.

For younger students, a topic like "fun" might begin with the **prompt**: *Tell about a time when you said to yourself, "Wow, this is really fun!"* Then, conduct a **witnessing** round, where students say what they remember of the fun things shared by others. The **harvesting** prompt would be: *Now that we have heard everyone's stories about having fun, what can we say about the ways people in our group like to have fun?* You might help them craft a statement like: "People in our group have fun with friends, in nature, and doing things that are a little scary."

This is a *thesis statement*, which could then be supported, in the circle or in writing, with examples from the stories shared. The harvesting statement can then be recycled in prompts for new circles on fun with friends, fun in nature, or fun doing scary things.

For older students, a topic like "discrimination" can be approached similarly. **Prompt**: *Tell about a time when you or someone you know was treated unequally simply because of some perceived external difference—such as age, race, gender, appearance, status, etc.* Then conduct a **story** round. In a **witnessing** round, students say what stayed with them (or what they remember) that others in the circle said. The prompt for **harvesting** in this case would be something like this: *Given the stories we just heard, what can we say about this thing we call "discrimination?"* The statements generated from the harvesting are themes, points, takeaways, or supportable generalizations about the topic of discrimination in the lives of the students. This process can stand on its own, or you can link it to literature or an event in history, which might then broaden or shift the theme.

Literature-based circles

Every circle is a story circle, and every time students *witness* one another, they're practicing paraphrasing, summary, and interpretation. In literature-based circles, students tell stories from their own lives that echo events or emotions in a text. You might begin by asking one student to share a personal story that related to reading, then pass the talking piece for others to offer their related stories.

These circles offer endless possibilities. Any story, poem, or passage becomes a springboard to deeper reflection. Mythologist Michael Meade taught me to pay attention to where we "enter" or "exit" a text—what sparks our interest, and where we tune out. These are rich clues for personal resonance and learning.

For younger students: Use picture books like *Where the Wild Things Are*. After reading, pass the book as a talking piece. Students can show their favorite picture and might say something about it. If time allows, a second round might invite stories about being wild, missing home, or imagining another world.

For upper elementary and middle-school students: Myths, folktales, and fairy tales have powerful resonance. I recall ninth-grade remedial reading students, many disenchanted with school, requesting I read them a myth or fairy tale each week. One favorite was the Greek myth of Phaethon. After reading it twice, I'd prompt: *Say the moment in the story that caught your interest.* With the older groups, you can add the idea of *exiting* the story, noting the moment they *lost interest* or blanked out. Arrange students chronologically around the circle according to their chosen moment. Then, pass the talking piece: each student retells the moment and explains why it spoke to them. A final round invites them to share a story connected to that moment. This gives students a deep, experiential entry into the archetypes and motifs of the story.

You can pair such readings with other media: for example, the myth of Icarus and Daedalus with Brueghel's painting *Landscape with the Fall of Icarus* and William Carlos Williams's poem of the same title.

Poetry circles

Poems and songs are excellent springboards for circle at any level. Begin by reading the poem twice, without asking students to analyze or try to understand the poem. Simply invite them to listen.

In the first round, students share a word, phrase, or image that stayed with them. Then, the narrative prompt is: *Tell about an experience you had that in some way is related to the word, phrase, or image you remembered.* The first time we do this, I like to say: *If there is a "sea" in the poem, you might tell about an experience you had at the ocean; if you recalled the phrase "concerned with itself," tell a story about a time when you or someone you knew was concerned about something; if the word "unnoticed" stayed with you, tell about a time you either felt unnoticed or a time you noticed something you hadn't noticed before.*

After these rounds, read the poem *a third time*. You'll notice students listen more deeply now, attuned to the lived experiences their classmates connected to the text. This does not replace guided literary analysis—but enhances it. Circles make the poem feel alive and relevant and often yield original insights.

"Show, don't tell"

To help students develop specificity in writing, use the "show, don't tell" strategy in circle. I first encountered this strategy in Rebekah Caplan's remarkable book *Writers in Training.*[7] Begin with a statement like, "It was a scary monster," "It was a beautiful day," or "I was frustrated." Rather than stating the feeling, students use the talking piece to *show* in detail: what the monster looked like, what was beautiful about the day, or what was frustrating about the situation. Caplan also applies the process to the "undoing" of clichés. Present a phrase such as "a chill ran down my spine," and challenge students to describe a time when they actually felt such a sensation.

The method works well for exploring *cause and effect* or *compare and contrast.* Try a prompt such as: *The landscape was devastated: show, don't tell,* or *Cats and dogs behave very differently: show, don't tell.* Students' stories become rich with concrete detail and structure.

Use the same process to introduce the concept of themes in literature. Use a theme you know they will see in a text, such as "We often fear things we don't understand" or "In dreams begin responsibilities." Then, use a prompt to elicit stories: *Tell about a time you were scared of something or someone because you didn't understand it or who that person was.* Or, *tell about a time you dreamed about doing something, then you found out how hard it was to do.* When students then read the text, they are prepared to see how that theme emerges.

You can also reverse the process: begin with students speaking about an experience, then ask them to generate a single "telling" statement—a theme, thesis, or main idea—based on their own story or on what they heard from others.

Expository

Expository writing explains. Whether in third grade or graduate school, the purpose of research is to explore multiple perspectives on a topic and draw conclusions based on them. Students summarize, compare, and sequence ideas. They consult "primary" (people and firsthand observation) and "secondary" (written) sources.

At the heart of expository writing is paraphrase: restating information concisely in one's own words, with quotes or details as needed. Although students paraphrase frequently, they're often unaware they're doing it. This is where witnessing in circle becomes fundamental. No matter the topic, a witnessing round encourages students to recall and restate what they heard others share. Followed by a harvesting round, students form generalizations—what we might call a topic sentence or a thesis statement. This lived process helps students reflect on how they learn and develop metacognitive awareness.

Circle also teaches students how to move personal stories to broader themes, and from there to action. Before we can write an expository essay—or act on an issue—we must first hear a range of perspectives. Drawing inferences from shared experience is an essential intermediary step.

When students engage in project-based learning, circle can be a space to explore and refine topic choices. A project without curiosity becomes a burden. In circle, students can explore their interests (what they want to know), hobbies (what they enjoy doing), concerns (what they want to change), and passions (what they feel deeply about).

My eighth- and ninth-grade students conducted a yearlong *I-Search* project using these four categories to refine their topic choices. We brainstormed using mind maps, noted overlapping topics, and then held a circle. Prompts included: *Given the topics that occurred in more than one of your brainstorm categories, which topics are you considering for your project?* Then, *tell a story about the moment you knew you were "hooked" on this topic or activity.* A final round let students voice any questions or concerns they had about their chosen topic. If there are no questions, if there is no curiosity, there is no need to search (and re-search) for answers. The same process can be used to aid students when they must choose from a prescribed list of topics provided by the instructor, the goal of course being student *engagement* rather than mere acceptance.

Analogy

To describe something unfamiliar, we often compare it to something known. After reading a tale of dragons, prompt: *Tell about a time when you felt like you were fighting a dragon.* Responses might include: confronting a bully; overcoming a fear of heights; playing a drum. My son's djembe teacher, Ayo Adeyemi, once told him, "When you fight the dragon, you must use both hands with equal skill. You would never fight the dragon with only one hand."

Once students have told their stories, use sentence completion: _______ *is like fighting a dragon.* Then introduce the term *analogy.* This process makes abstract academic concepts feel relevant and lived.

Analogies apply across disciplines. How is calculating the radius of a circle like honoring every person in a circle? How are Sun Tzu's recommendations in *The Art of War* connected to the tactics used in the French Revolution? How is the balancing of a chemical equation like the art of mediation and conflict resolution?

Comparison

Circle offers a visceral understanding of similarities and differences. For younger students, use a light topic, such as people who like dogs and those who like cats. Create a fishbowl format: dog lovers tell a story and explain why they prefer dogs, while cat lovers listen, and then reverse. Afterward, list the reasons in a Venn diagram and use it as the basis for compare-contrast writing. With older students, this can extend into pro-con debates, but unlike traditional debate, circle encourages mutual listening and personal reflection, not "winning" the argument.

Cause and Effect

Something happened. How did it happen? This is the basis of so much academic inquiry—from witnessing a chemical reaction in the laboratory and tracing its causes to the fall of the Roman Empire. To explore causality, try a simple prompt: *Say something that you know actually happened*, followed by, *Why do you think that happened?* Or pick a shared outcome (e.g., We won the soccer game) and explore contributing factors.

From here, bridge to literature or history. Prompt: *Tell about a time you felt excluded or different. What made you feel this way?* Then connect to Holden Caulfield's sense of alienation in *Catcher in the Rye*.

You can also explore speculative causes: *What is one thing you would like to change (in your life, the school, the city, the world ...)? What would have to happen to bring that change about? What steps would need to be undertaken?*

In Chapter 9, we will look at the place of circle in restorative processes in schools, where cause and effect are central. Students learn to examine harm, trace its roots, and consider how healing might occur. Circles like these support both academic reasoning and social-emotional growth.

Process

It is often easier to do something than to describe how it's done. Having students reflect in circle after completing a task deepens their awareness of steps and decision-making. For example, have students make a sandwich in small groups, then describe the process. After writing instructions, students read them aloud while the teacher follows them. Inevitable mishaps spark laughter and revision. Students begin to see the gap between doing and explaining.

Circles can also reflect on group processes. After a class decision (e.g., where to go on a field trip), hold a witnessing round: *What did you notice about how we made our decision? What steps did the group take to get there?* Students gain insight into collaborative thinking, and circle becomes a tool for reflecting on process itself.

Analysis of Text

Text analysis is a form of expository writing we can introduce to very young students and develop later into literary and textual criticism. Many literary terms can be explored experientially in circle, providing a foundation for later academic application. A few examples:

- **Irony:** *Tell a story about a time when you expected something to happen, and it turned out in a completely different way. For example, you thought something was going to be fun, and it turned out to be awful, or you thought someone was going to be mean and they turned out to be nice.*
- **Mood:** Begin by brainstorming mood words on the board: *happy, sad, generous, suspicious, angry, lonely*, etc. Have students choose one silently and tell a story about a time when they felt that way without explicitly stating the mood. Others guess in popcorn fashion what the mood was. To deepen this, students can embody moods through expression, gestures, or movement for classmates to guess. These embodied practices prepare students to identify moods in texts, even when it's abstract or implied.
- **Tone:** Like mood, text tone can be elusive. Play with tone by having students say the same phrase (like "Good morning") with different tonal inflections. Follow this with a circle of stories about when you experienced in someone's tone of voice something other than or beyond what their words signified.
- **Setting:** Guide students to remember a favorite place and have them recall it with complete "sense memory." In the circle, students describe a place as fully as possible using sense detail "so that listeners can really see the place in their imaginations."
- **Climax:** Have students recall a "turning point" in some conflict or difficulty they have experienced, the moment

when they realized that a problem was turning in a completely new direction.

- **Personification:** Tell of an experience you had with a nonhuman thing, an animal, or something in nature—the wind, a tree, a stone—that seemed to have human qualities.
- **Hyperbole:** A circle on exaggerations about yourself or an event you witnessed. These could be exaggerations you told to others, those you told yourself, those you got away with, and those for which you got caught. (Great fun!)

Persuasive

In the persuasive domain, students learn to identify the strength and validity of an argument. They identify logical fallacies, counterarguments, rhetorical strategies, and they develop their own coherent essays using proposal/support patterns.

They also build a critical consciousness of how persuasion operates across media—newspapers, magazines, social media, ads, packaging, and entertainment. They evaluate what advertisers and authors want us to believe and the methods they employ to persuade us. In addition, students learn about multiple points of view on a single issue, and how to frame arguments that demonstrate this awareness.

Circle provides a natural environment for exploring beliefs, values, and opinions. When we began the project at Palms, one aim was to create space for students to share cultural stories, building cross-cultural understanding and reducing prejudice. In speaking about their own experiences, students *hear,* sometimes for the first time aloud, the stories they tell themselves. The attentive listening that circles evoke encourages reflection, metacognition, and, sometimes, revision. Many students ask to speak again, to clarify or build on what they've said.

In listening to others, students hear how their classmates formulate and support ideas, and how deeply or tentatively they hold their positions. If we want to teach students to persuade others, we must first give them the chance to explore and articulate what they—and their peers—believe and value.

Circles in the persuasive domain

Convincing others: *Tell about a time you convinced someone, or someone convinced you, to do something.* In the second round, explore what made the argument persuasive: *What did you or this other person have to do or say to be convincing?* Remember that force, intimidation, and threats can also motivate others. With this awareness, students can engage in circles about the difference between persuasion and coercion—*a time when someone got you to do something you didn't want to do*—and the ethical implications that follow.

Point of view: Use the story of "The Blind Men and the Elephant" to introduce the idea that everyone may have a different perspective on the same issue. Have students engage in a common activity (e.g., art, movement, rhythm), then tell what it was like for them. A witnessing round reveals how diverse the accounts of a single event can be.

Controversial issues and points of view: Generate a list of hot-button topics. Choose one and prompt: *Where do you stand on this issue, and what experiences, beliefs, or values brought you to this viewpoint?* A final round witnesses the range of opinions expressed. For topics with clear divides, the fishbowl format allows each side to speak while others listen. This fosters appreciation of counterarguments as well as a clarification of assertions.

Products and advertising: *Name something that you want to buy or own. How did you come to know about it, and what convinced you that you had to have it?* This prompt alone brings out a harvesting of effective persuasive methods in advertising and might make students more aware of how these methods affect their choices.

Logical fallacies in circle (with playful examples):

- **Ad hominem:** *Tell about a time you dismissed someone's ideas because you thought that person was* *foolish, naive, crazy, ignorant, unethical, or any other such judgment.* Discuss why we stop listening to certain people, and what we might miss.

- **Non sequitur:** *Tell about a time you said or did something unrelated to what came before.* Or, play the "cut-off continuation stories" game: one student starts a story; the next picks up mid-sentence and takes it in a wildly different direction. It's absurd and helps students recognize illogical leaps in arguments.
- **Begging the question:** *Tell about a time you thought something was true and then you found out that it was not.*
- **Bandwagon:** *Tell about a time you did something because you thought everyone else was doing it—even though you didn't want to or knew it was wrong.* We have all heard the rhetorical admonition, "If everyone were jumping off a cliff, would you jump, too?" *Tell about a time you went along with the crowd.*
- **Post hoc ergo prompter hoc:** *Name a time you experienced or saw something happen and ever since you have been afraid that it will happen again.* This prompt leads to an examination of superstitions.
- **Poor sampling or argument from particular to general:** Giving too few examples to prove a point. Using the same process as the one described in the beginning of this section—*name something you know to be true*—explore whether the examples given are *enough* to prove the assertion.

Vocabulary, Grammar, and Style

It should be quite clear now that circle is an effective means for vocabulary development—especially with abstract concepts like *freedom, responsibility, love, justice*, etc. We've also discussed the importance of teaching a vocabulary of feelings and needs. Likewise, in circle, we can shape prompts that get at grammatical structures. Here are a few simple examples:

- **Third person singular:** *Name one thing your mother does every day*. In a witnessing round, students say what they heard another student say: "Nelson's mother *drives* to work."
- **Present progressive:** *Using a complete sentence beginning with "I," name one thing you are doing right now, such as "I am thinking about lunch" or "I am sitting on the floor."* In the witnessing round, students use the past progressive: "Sabine said that she was thinking about lunch."
- **Subordinating conjunctions:** *Provide a sample sentence using a subordinating conjunction such as "I do pushups because I want to be strong." Then show a cloze form of the same sentence with blanks: I _____ because I* ____. Use this as the prompt for the circle. Note that they have a choice, a style choice, to switch the clauses: "Because I want to be strong, I do pushups." This can extend to a circle about cause and effect and the reasons we do things. Another example: *If tomorrow is a sunny day, then I will go to the park. Use the cloze: If , then I will* . This can extend into a circle on conditions: *Tell about a time when you were told you could do something if you did something else first.*

The language arts provide rich opportunities for connecting circle and learning standards, from the most basic to the most complex analytical and critical skills. More importantly, though, is that through circles students see that they are active agents in the creation of language, that language evolves, that they are carriers of story, and that stories are alive. The quote from Antonio Machado at the beginning of this chapter serves as a reminder. While it is important that we follow a curriculum, that we learn to use the tools of language, that we take sail, rudder, and oars into its depths, we must also be prepared to surrender these tools when a new story emerges from those depths.

History/Social Studies: A Pedagogy of Relevance

For most of my education in Los Angeles public schools, I struggled to find relevance in what I was learning. Few teachers attempted to relate the curriculum to what we students were living. I do, however, distinctly remember my first day in Mr. Lee Simon's tenth-grade World History class. Mr. Simon stood out: long hair, sandals, vegetarian lunches, and the way he would sit in a high-backed chair at the front of our U-shaped student desk arrangement waiting silently for the class to get quiet. He rarely had to wait long. On the first day, he gave us an assignment: to become careful observers of our world and our daily habits, rituals, and routines. We were to notice what we ate and how our food was purchased, kept, and prepared; how we moved from place to place; how we bathed, slept, and spent our free time; how we connected with others, how we got information; how we interacted with devices like the telephone, the television, and the toaster.

This invitation was a revelation. No one had ever asked me to be mindful and aware in this way. It was a movement towards personal agency: a message that my perceptions, my experience, had value. I didn't have the language for it then, but I felt engaged! This was an assignment I *wanted* to do.

As we charted and compared our responses, patterns emerged. We began to see our assumptions, our shared habits, the unexamined ways we lived. Just how *did* we get those Apple Pan hamburgers and fries we were all so fond of? Where did our gasoline come from? Were there other ways of acquiring the necessities of life? What unconscious patterns governed our choices?

Mr. Simon used this inquiry as a foundation. As we studied ancient civilizations, their quandaries and quests, their creation and dissolution, the history of ideas and inventions, up to the present day, he related each to our lived experiences in the present. The evolution from hunter-gatherers to an agrarian society suddenly became palpable and meaningful. The history of cultural and religious practices had resonance with our personal traditions and beliefs. Concern for the environment, the use of resources, and the consequences of our actions became palpable, touching our lived experience, and something we could choose to change. This assignment and this class brought about, at least for me, an evolution of consciousness.

What was Mr. Simon's secret? A pedagogy of relevance.

Social Studies

What are the social studies? We think of history, geography, economics, psychology, sociology, anthropology, and civics (engaged citizenship). We might say that the field of social studies is primarily concerned with *relationships*—person-to-self, person-to-person, person-to-group, group-to-group, person/group-to-environment, and the environment to itself (as in geography and geology).

Social studies are also deeply concerned with *values*—honesty, integrity, justice, and compassion—all of which can only be understood in the context of relationship.

While there are implicit values in circle practice, we do not explicitly teach values through circles. Rather, *circles engage participants in the process whereby values are formed and discovered.* Bloom tells us that value formation begins with the capacity to receive and then to respond. The development of these capacities requires relationship.

A Thematic Focus

This section uses a thematic, concept-based approach to highlight the endless ways circles can bring relevance and meaning to the study of all things *social.* Among various frameworks, the following ten themes from the National Council for the Social Studies (NCSS) offer a broad and inclusive overview:[8]

1. Culture
2. Time, Continuity, and Change
3. People, Places, and Environments
4. Individual Development and Identity
5. Individuals, Groups, and Institutions
6. Power, Authority, and Governance
7. Production, Distribution, and Consumption
8. Science, Technology, and Society
9. Global Connections
10. Civic Ideals and Practices

Culture

This entire book is about the dynamics of culture. Council is a practice that shifts school culture in real time. The circle itself is a cultural form, carrying inherent values like respect, honesty, collaboration, and shared leadership.

At the outset of the Council Project at Palms Middle School, Jack Zimmerman suggested that its greatest offering might be to give students a space to "share cultural stories." Until we *speak* values aloud—and listen to others do the same—those values remain largely unconscious. When we articulate our beliefs, traditions, and assumptions in the presence of attentive listeners, we begin to see them from the outside as others would. As John Dewey remarked in *Education and Democracy* (1916): "Try the experiment of communicating, with fullness and accuracy, some experience to another, especially if it be somewhat complicated, and you will find your own attitude toward your experience changing."[9]

Circle makes space for this reflective transformation. Here are a few ideas for exploring culture in circle:

- **Stories of family traditions, values, and beliefs:** The term "tradition" must be unpacked, especially for very young children. It is the idea of something you do regularly with your family.

- **Stories of the ancestors:** *Tell a story you have heard about one of your ancestors.*
- **Food:** In a speed round, *Name your favorite food that someone in your family cooks.* In a story round, *Tell about a time you remember when you ate that food. What foods does your family serve on special occasions?*
- **Holidays:** *What holidays does your family celebrate? Tell a story about one holiday experience you remember well.*
- **Leisure:** *Tell a story about something your family likes to do when they get together.*
- **Passages/life events:** Families often have special ways of celebrating life events such as the birth of a child, entering the adult community (quinceañera; bar and bat mitzvah), reunions, marriage, death, etc. *Recall a time when your family celebrated one such event. Describe it so others can really get a sense of what happened.* In a witnessing round, students can share what they see as the commonalities and differences in the details of these events.
- **Language:** It is always fun to explore favorite sayings that are particular to a family or a group. For example, in my family the most oft uttered phrase was the Yiddish *oy vey ist mir*, "Oh, woe is me." But it was even used to express joy such as in the sentence "Oy vey ist mir, look how tall you are!" A circle prompt such as *What is one thing someone in your family says over and over whenever you see him or her?* often elicits wild examples.
- **Dress:** *Tell about some kind of clothing that family members wear for special occasions.*
- **Music, dance, and art:** *Tell about music or songs that are special to your family, dances your family does, or ways of making art.*
- **Stories of belief:** The root of *belief* is "lief," meaning "wish." *Tell about something you or your family believes to be true.*

- **Stories of value and virtue:** *From your experience in your family, what are the most important things in life? Examples might include education, self-reliance, helping others, etc. Tell a story about someone in your family who has done something to show that value or virtue.* Note: at the Pressman Jewish Day School in Los Angeles, educators use circle to explore eight Jewish values, the eight "middot:" respect, support and healing, attentiveness, honesty, self-care, gratitude, openness, and trust.

Time, Continuity, and Change

Over time, some things change, and others remain the same. In Chapter 1, I noted that the practice of circle may seem new, but it is ancient—forgotten, perhaps, for just a few centuries. Young people refer to "ancient history" as something that happened last week. We talk about eons and eras, but time is slippery. The Hindu concept of a "kalpa"—measured by a celestial being brushing her wing against the top of Mount Meru once every thousand years until it completely wears down—is one such image of vast, cyclical time. Modern science complicates things further: atomic clocks show that even the "constant" of time is subject to fluctuation.

When we adopt a *historical perspective*, informed by the experiences of others, we begin to see patterns and shifts in human behavior over time with greater clarity. But for young students—and those of us lucky enough to live fully in the present—time and history do not exist. This is one reason play is so vital. In play, we aren't constrained by what has come before. We are free to imagine what could be.

Here are a few circle practices to explore time and change:

With younger students:

- *Tell about something you did yesterday.*
- *Say something you did today that you also did yesterday.*
- *Say something you did yesterday and today and will probably do tomorrow.*

These prompts build a sense of continuity. Students can also *show* the thing they did with a gesture. You can follow up with: *Tell about something you used to do but probably won't do again—and why.*

With older students:

- *Tell of a time when something that took a short time seemed to go on forever.*
- *Tell about something that took a long time but seemed to pass very quickly.*

Harvesting rounds explore what made time expand or contract in those moments.

Exploring change (all ages):

- *Tell about something you used to believe or enjoy, but don't anymore.*
- *Recall a shift in attitude, ambition, or perception—what changed, and why?*

These activities link students' personal experiences to larger historical processes. Simultaneously, they create the conditions for reflective consciousness, the development of conscience, and personal growth.

People, Places, and Environments

Histories tell stories of other people in other places and other times, to help us better understand our responsibilities in this precious present. But unless we make meaningful links to *now*, history risks becoming a collection of meaningless facts. We use circle both before and after introducing new material (through reading, lectures, movies, etc.). Circle helps anchor historical knowledge in personal relevance. It links backward, by helping us interpret the past through personal experience, and forward, by clarifying how historical lessons inform future choices.

With our youngest students, just getting them to tell stories about other people and other places expand their world. Circle prompts like these help:

- *Tell a story of a person you met for the first time.*
- *Tell about meeting someone who was very different from other people you know.*
- *Tell about going to a new place for the first time.*

For older students, we can explore interactions between people and places: Environments dictate how we act within them. Prompt: *Tell about a place where you had to behave differently than usual.* This might be at grandmother's house, at church, or a natural environment such as a place you were able to run free or had to be very careful. Students reflect on how place affects actions, beliefs, and perceptions, laying the groundwork for understanding human-environment interaction.

Natural forms and human experience

Nature often mirrors inner experience. Prompts might include:

- *Tell about a time when you felt "on top of the world."* (linked to stories of mountains)
- *A time you took a big leap.* (waterfalls)
- *A time you transformed an old belief.* (composting)
- *A moment of sudden clarity or new awareness.* (dawn)

These metaphors make environmental and emotional learning deeply personal.

Individual Development and Identity

In 2003, my colleague Betsy Perluss invited me to introduce circle into her university-level Lifespan Development course at CSULA. Over the next 10 years, I visited her class twice annually. The course served students preparing to become teachers, counselors, and therapists. Betsy's insight was this: beyond textbooks and lectures, her students themselves were sources of rich developmental data. After exploring a stage of human development (e.g., Erikson's "young adulthood"), students formed circles to share personal experiences. A prompt might be: *Tell a story about a time when you really questioned your life direction and purpose. How did you resolve this dilemma?* After the circle, students reflected on challenges or obstacles they faced or are currently facing to realize their dreams. For later stages, *Tell about a memorable time you spent with someone you considered to be an elder.* For individual reflection after the circle, students received this prompt: *Imagine that you are facing the final years of your life. With this awareness what would you do differently in your current life situation?*

As John Dewey tells us, "We do not learn from experience but from reflection upon experience." Through these reflective circles, students didn't just learn developmental theory: they *lived* it, and they learned from each other. That's education at its best.

Identifiers

To explore identity and bias, I introduced the following activity with middle-school students before reading *To Kill a Mockingbird.*

We often judge, and are judged, by "identifiers." These include:

1. Age
2. Distinguishing characteristics (e.g., short, tall, skinny, bald)
3. Race
4. Ethnicity
5. Religion (including agnostic, atheist, or syncretic)

6. Gender identity and expression
7. Interests
8. Annoyances

Here is an example of an identifying statement: "I am a 14-year-old, tall, muscular Latino, Jewish-Buddhist cis male who enjoys breakdancing and is annoyed by people who drive too fast." Students create such an identifying statement and share this in circle. Then, they share a story of an experience of discrimination based on one of the identifiers. They also share a story of when it was to their benefit to be identified in one of these ways.

Individuals, Groups, and Institutions

My wife, Abbe, teaches preschool music and movement. At that age, group dynamics are in flux: students are just learning how to join, leave, and rejoin group activity. As students grow, group identity becomes even more pronounced, especially in middle and high school. We all remember how closely our sense of self was tied to who we did or didn't associate with.

Trainer Camille Ameen offers a wonderful circle warm-up called "Cultural Mapping" (or "Take a Stand"). Students begin in a line. Camille offers simple choices:

- *If you are a night person, take one step to the right. If you are a morning person, step to the left. Not sure? Stay where you are.*

After each move, students observe who shares their position. This simple sorting becomes the foundation for deeper discussions—about likes/dislikes, identity, or even historical viewpoints:

- *Based on the primary source documents we have studied, would you stand with the Whigs or the Democrats on Manifest Destiny? Or neither?*

Students form small caucus circles to discuss their positions, and then take turns in a fishbowl format with one group sharing while others witness.

Another variation uses four corners of the room. For example:

- Birth order: youngest (north), middle (east), oldest (south), only child (west).

Students then share stories about how their birth order shaped their experience. Camille adds a playful touch: each group creates a physical tableau in a gesture.

Here is a group of teachers in their birth order tableaux:

The oldest child → The youngest child

The middle child → The only child

Even a simple brainstorm on group membership can lead to powerful insights:

1. Speed round: *Name groups you belong to.*
2. Story round: *Choose one group and tell a story about your experience in it.*
3. Reflect: *Why do you identify with this group? What are its benefits and challenges?*

Then flip the lens: *What groups do you not identify with—and why?*

Finally, introduce the distinction between groups and institutions. Where groups may be informal, institutions have structure—governance, traditions, rules, expectations. Once this difference is clear, you can revisit the same prompt with institutions in mind.

Exploring Power, Authority, and Governance

Adolescence—what many traditions call the "goes-within-place" of the West—is a time for questioning all of the stories we've been told and those we tell ourselves.[10] It's no wonder teens often feel powerless, push back against authority, and challenge institutions. Rather than resisting this questioning, we as educators can support it as a vital part of values development—where the inherited becomes examined and chosen.

Let's begin with power. What is it? Who has it? How is it used—and what happens once it's gained? Few willingly give it up. To explore these dynamics viscerally, we often turn to embodied games.

Boal's Colombian Hypnosis[11]

In this activity, one student stands at the center with both palms extended. Two others follow, keeping their noses near the leader's palms. As the leader moves slowly, the followers must follow, keeping their noses near the leader's palms. Then, the two followers extend their open palms, and four more participants enter. The process continues until the whole group is involved. Then, ask everyone to freeze, observe, and debrief in circle:

- How was it to lead? To follow?
- What was it like to do both?
- What real-life experiences echo what you felt?

This exercise often evokes topics like control, responsibility, conformity, bureaucracy, and resistance. Write the topics students see inherent in the game on the board, and then use them as a springboard for a circle prompt: *Tell about a time when you experienced one of these things.* The harvesting prompt is something like this: *Given the stories we have heard, what can we say about people and power and authority?*

You might then connect these dynamics to historical examples. Boal's reference to a period when there were repressive regimes in Colombia offers one frame, but the game's relevance spans governments, classrooms, corporations, and families.

Circle prompts on power

- *Tell about a time when you felt you had the power, strength, knowledge, or understanding to attempt something difficult.*
- *Tell a story of someone you know who you feel is powerful.*
- *If you could have superpowers, what would they be, and how would you use them?*
- *Tell a story about someone who had power and used it in a way that was helpful—or harmful.*

On perseverance and surrender

Circle can also explore inner power and discernment. Prompts include:

- *Tell about a time you gave up and it was the right thing to do.*
- *Tell about a time you kept going even though something was difficult.*

These lead to a nuanced understanding of power—not just as control over others, but as wisdom, will, and restraint.

Exploring authority

Unpack the word authority (from *auctor*, to create or originate) and discuss what makes someone an authority. Then try these prompts:

- *Tell of an experience with someone you consider an authority.*
- *Name a situation where you have been an authority—the person to whom others look to be in charge.*
- *Tell of a time when you or someone else used their authority well; that is, in a way that helped people or made a situation better.*
- *Tell of a time when you or someone else (including characters from history and literature) abused authority.*

Exploring governance

From the Greek, *kubernan,* "to steer," governance includes not only political structures but also self-regulation. Prompts might include:

- *Tell about a time when you did or did not govern or control yourself.*
- *Tell about a time you were or felt governed by another person or group.*

- *Tell of a time when you had to or felt you had to govern the actions of others.*
- *What does it mean to have a "government of the people, by the people, and for the people?" Tell about a time when you participated in some aspect of government.*
- *Discuss this quote from Thoreau: "That government is best which governs least"* (Civil Disobedience). *Tell of a time when it would have been best for you to have less external control of your actions. Then tell why you think that would have been best.*
- *Tell of a time when it was helpful to have someone* (*or a group*) *tell you what to do or how to do it. Or tell of a time when it was or might have been helpful to have someone provide more control of your actions. How would this have been helpful?*

Production, Distribution, and Consumption

To make, to give, and to use—simple actions are at the root of economic systems and offer rich material for exploration at every grade level. In early grades, circles can focus on *something you made*, as well as how and why you made it; then expand to *something you made for someone else*. These stories often surface students' own creativity and generosity.

From Use to Usefulness, From Want to Need

Our students are the inventors and entrepreneurs of the future. Circle prompts like *name something you use every day and why* lead naturally to conversations about usefulness. A witnessing round—What's the most necessary or important item mentioned so far?—can spark reflection on value: survival, well-being, joy, ease, growth, etc. From here, students might imagine *something useful you would like to invent or make*. Such exercises deepen their understanding of technological change, and may even plant seeds for future innovations.

Like most parents, I'm sure that I am not alone in attempting to help my children distinguish *want* from *need*. Our needs are few; our wants, inexhaustible. In circle, this lesson becomes real. Students reflect:

- Name something you want. Why do you want it?
- What do you want but don't need? What do you need but don't want?

You might introduce Maslow's hierarchy of needs: physiological (air, food, water, shelter), safety, love and belonging, esteem (being seen and appreciated for who you are as well as self-respect and integrity), "self-actualization" (becoming fully who you are), and ultimately "self-transcendence" (being in service; engaging in altruism and spirituality). Keep in mind that the order of these needs can be somewhat culturally influenced. Let students notice how their stories align or don't. The contrast between individualistic and collectivist cultures can enrich the discussion without moralizing.

A Non-Material Gift You Would Give

Giving and receiving gifts can also be a basic human need. Circles about *gifts given* or *received*, especially non-material ones—kindness, attention, help—can reveal profound meaning. Variations might include:

- *A gift you didn't want*
- *The silliest gift you have ever given*
- *A gift that wasn't well received*
- *A non-material gift you would like to give someone*
- *A non-material gift you would like to receive*
- *A gift you would like to give to the world, etc.*

Such prompts are especially welcome around holidays, offering inclusive, cost-free ways to reflect on generosity and appreciation.

The Giveaway

Inspired by the Native American potlatch, the "giveaway" ceremony is a meaningful classroom practice. Students bring in an item they value, wrapped and anonymous—that they're willing to give away. (It is important for the teacher to get a probable count and to consider bringing something for those who are unable to contribute.) These may be possessions, drawings, poems, or other personal creations.

During the circle, one student selects a wrapped gift from the center and opens it. Then, the giver shares the story behind the item: how they came to have it, its meaning, and how they came to choose it for the give-away. The process continues until all gifts have been shared. A final round allows students to reflect on the experience of giving and receiving. This ceremony not only honors cultural traditions but also gives students a lived understanding of generosity, gratitude, and community—without requiring material wealth.

Science, Technology, and Society

In social studies, we often examine how technologies and scientific discoveries shape human interaction. Circle itself is a decidedly low-tech, yet enduring, technology. Likely older than agriculture, circle practice probably originated in nomadic societies, and may have been most fully developed by women. As caregivers, women often remained near the hearth, preparing foods, tending children, and—face-to-face—developing language and cultural wisdom. Interestingly, studies show that the corpus callosum (which connects the brain's hemispheres) is more developed in women, linking the capacity to feel with the capacity to express feelings through language.[12] This may explain why, even today, more women than men tend to engage in the circles!

To call circle a "technology" is to view its structure and purpose as a tool. Why a circle? Why do we have a center? What is the purpose of the talking piece? Why have dedications or other openings and closings? What role do the four (or more) intentions play in the function of this technology? These are design questions, worthy of exploration. Rather than *telling* students what it means to *speak from the heart,* ask them: What might that mean? Why might it matter—or even feel risky! As students gain experience, their understanding of circle deepens, and the structure evolves. Like all living systems, circle adapts. I'm sure the "spiral" as a form did not exist in those proto-circles of the village women. Students will evolve innovations of form, mode, intention, and purpose.

Circle is one of many dialogic technologies. For instance, "Open Space Technology," developed by Harrison Owen,[13] invites large groups to self-organize around shared questions. The book *Mapping Dialogue* surveys 23 such practices and a includes a chart for choosing the best model based on context and group dynamics.[14]

Of course, we can also explore material technologies. Invite students to consider the machines they use every day. Which ones do they "love?" Which do they rely on? Which frustrate them? Which could they do without? In many Waldorf schools, for example, all parent-teacher communication must be face-to-face—no email. How does this affect relationships? Contrast this with the digital images schools use to market themselves, often showcasing students behind screens. What would happen if internet and cell phone service went down? Could we still connect meaningfully? Circle reminds us: when the power goes out, this technology still works.

And, yes, circles can be digital. Students at the International Studies Learning Center in Los Angeles hold videoconference circles with their sister school in China. Soliya, a non-profit, uses a circle-based video streaming platform to connect Arab and Jewish students around the world. Even a group text can function as circle, if it's guided by presence. When the text arrives, just take it in; let it settle in you. *The object is not to respond but to receive.* Then, listen for what needs to be said, if anything, in response. If there is nothing but grateful silence, linger there, knowing that those in the virtual circle are with you.

Global Connections

Whatever your view about the practical effectiveness of the United Nations, its 1945 Charter, drafted in 1941 and signed by 193 nations, remains a visionary statement. The Preamble outlines goals that closely align with the values at the center of circle practice: ending war; affirming human rights and equality for all people and nations; upholding justice and international law; advancing social and economic progress; and fostering tolerance and peace. To end violence, we must learn to talk through our differences. To affirm equal rights, we must listen to one another—across lines of race, gender, creed, or identity. We can only practice compassion, acceptance, and peace in the presence of others.

Many schools, including those affiliated with the Asia Society as well as International Baccalaureate schools, now include "global competencies" in their graduate profiles. These often include the ability to investigate the world, recognize perspectives, communicate ideas, and take action. Circle fosters each of these.

By inviting students to share their observations and experiences, circle practice helps them become more active, reflective participants in the world. Even young children begin to understand the value of multiple perspectives. Consider the story of "The Blind Men and the Elephant:" everyone feels a different part of the animal and declares their perception to be the correct one. Imagine if the story ended with the men sitting in a circle—discovering together the full truth.

In circle, students learn to communicate ideas with confidence because they are met with respect. And meaningful action—whether internal or external—grows from that foundation.

Without reflection, action is impulsive. When we set intentions and voice them within a group, we invite both support and accountability. We are heard—and we are held.

Civic Ideals and Practices

Let's return to that lovely kindergarten social studies standard we saw earlier. It captures, in simple terms, the essence of civic life:

> Students are introduced to basic spatial, temporal, and causal relationships, emphasizing the geographic and historical connections between the world today and the world long ago. The stories of ordinary and extraordinary people help describe the range and continuity of human experience and introduce the concepts of courage, self-control, justice, heroism, leadership, deliberation, and individual responsibility. Historical empathy for how people lived and worked long ago reinforces the concept of civic behavior: how we interact respectfully with each other, following rules, and respecting the rights of others.

As you see, all *social studies* begin with stories, those of the ordinary-extraordinary people sitting with us in the circle now. Once we learn to express and receive the stories of those around us, we become able to reach outside the circle and take in the stories of other peoples in other times and places. Doing so develops empathy, the capacity to see and feel things as other beings do. And it is such empathy that brings about respectful interaction.

Mathematics

A bit of self-disclosure: despite more than 10 years of school math, I remember next to nothing. I never grasped the simplicity, beauty, elegance, and utility of math. My only memory, besides struggling with ninth-grade algebra, is failing tenth-grade geometry! I had to retake the class the following year, but this time I had a different teacher: a young woman, probably about 25, and new to teaching. For some reason, I wanted to get it right for her.

The content may not have changed much, but the presenter made all the difference. As it turned out, I began to enjoy these proofs. After a few months, I was tutoring classmates. I used to tell myself it was because I had already taken the class, but the reality was that I wanted to please this young woman.

So, what did she offer that the previous teacher didn't? Looking back, I'd say my first teacher brought the weariness of repetition—having seen all the behaviors, heard all the questions. There was nothing vital about the air in this class. My new teacher, on the other hand, was fully engaged. She wanted us learn to succeed, and it mattered to her that we did. It was not just another year of teaching the same old thing—it was a relationship.

Linking Lived Experience with Analogous Formulas

"When will we ever use this stuff?" "What is math?"

We usually give a few answers. "You need it to manage money and finances." And "Algebra is the great leveler, the gateway to the sciences." Another is, "Math puzzles strengthen your thinking skills"

These are all true, but what's the deeper impulse? I believe every equation has a parallel in human relationships and behavior. If we can discover those analogies, we can create circles that deepen conceptual understanding and make even the most abstract operations relevant to students' lived experience.

One More, One Less

Children develop their capacity to move from concrete operations to abstract reasoning, from tangible objects to symbolic representations. Even the pronoun "one" is a symbol: it stands in for a specific item. A very young child might say, "Cookie!" to express desire. Later, they might say, "I want one!" which combines three symbolic concepts: "I," "want," and "one" as a representation of the object of desire. We parents know that our children will incessantly employ this symbolic expression well beyond their early years.

The foundational math operation—addition—begins with the concept of "one more." In circle, we make this concept concrete. Begin by having students count off (e.g., 1–20). Invite one student to come and sit in the center, and ask the class, "How many students are in the center?" Then, ask a few more to join. Ask, "If we want to have seven in the circle, how many *more* would we have to add?" This "fishbowl" form introduces both math and circle vocabulary. You can follow this with additional questions:

- How many students *were* in the inner circle the first time, when only Alex was there?
- How many students did we *add* to the inner circle when Sylvia, Michael, and Louisa came in? Then how many students were in the center?
- How many students were in the center *before* Alex came in?
- How many students were in the *outer circle before* Alex came in?
- How many students were in the outer circle *after* Alex came in?
- How many students were in the outer circle *after* Sylvia, Michael, and Louisa joined Alex in the fishbowl?
- How many students *will be* in the outer circle when the four students in the fishbowl return to the outer circle?

This can lead to personal storytelling circles that deepen understanding of the "one more" concept and each other. Prompts might include:

- Tell about a time when you wanted (or needed) one more of something. Did you get it?
- Tell about a time when you didn't want one more of something.
- *Name an activity that you wish you could do one more time, or many more times.*

The concept of subtraction, or "one less" or "one fewer," is a bit more challenging. And it really is the basis of a circle topic with relevance for all ages—the topic of *loss.* What isn't here? Where did it go?

Algebra

Algebra introduces another level of abstraction, where letters now stand for unknown or variable quantities. Algebra offers rules for manipulating symbols. To enter this abstract space, circle prompts can ground students in lived experience:

- Tell about a time when you experienced something you couldn't explain.
- Tell about a time you thought something was mysterious and then you found out why it happened.

Circle concepts themselves can illustrate algebraic thinking. Nathan Brewer, a math teacher and circle facilitator, posed this problem:

If X number of people are sitting in a circle, and each person occupies two feet of space, what is the radius to the exact center of the circle?

We sometimes speak of a "strong circle," one where everyone is equidistant from the center and occupies the same amount of space along the perimeter. If we are to create such a circle using chairs or floor mats, what formula do we need to apply?

Here is Nathan's formula:

Each person needs 2 feet of space, so for *X* people, we would need 2*X* feet of space.

That gives us a **circumference** of 2*X* feet:

$$c = 2X$$

We also know that circumference is equal to $\mathbf{2 \times \pi \times r}$, so we have:

$$2X = 2 \times \pi \times r$$

Dividing both sides by 2:

$$X = \pi \times r$$

Dividing both sides by π:

$$r = X / \pi$$

Using 3.14 as an approximation for π, we get:

$$r \approx X / 3.14$$

You might follow this collaborative calculation with a **circle prompt**, such as:

Tell about a time when you sat equally with others or felt a sense of fairness—and tell about a time when you experienced inequality or unfairness.

If we return to Kurt Lewin's formula, **B = f(p + e)** (behavior is a function of the person and the environment), we can see the importance of setting up our circle with intentionality.

Geometry

The practical study of lengths, areas, and volumes, geometry is also concerned with shapes, sizes, relative positioning, and the properties of space. Consider classroom layout: a triangle with teacher at the apex implies hierarchy. A circle, by contrast, redistributes focus. Yet even in a circle, if all eyes are on the facilitator, the interaction remains triangular.

Adding kinesthetic experience—students embodying shapes—can deepen understanding. Prompts might include:

- **The line:** *Tell a story about a time you stood in a line.*
- **Parallel lines:** *Parallel lines go in the same direction, but they never touch. Tell about a time when you walked side by side with another person.*
- **An angle:** *An angle begins going in one direction and then it takes another. Tell about a time when you were going in one direction and then you changed your mind and went in another.*
- **The triangle:** *The triangle has one point at the top. When were you ever at the top of something? When were you the leader? An equilateral triangle has three sides of equal length. Tell a story about a time you did something with two other friends.*
- **The square:** *The square has four sides of equal distance. Tell a story about a game you played that had a square surface.*

- **The polygon:** *The polygon has many sides. Tell about a time when although you had the same experience, everyone saw it in a different way. It was the same experience but everyone saw it from a different point of view.*

Using tape or a string, students can explore what it feels like to form and transform these shapes. This segues into deeper relational questions:

- *Tell about a time when you felt you had a "direct line" to another person.*
- *Tell about a relationship where you felt that the direct line traveled equally in both directions.*
- *Tell about a relationship where the direct line had a kink or a knot in it.*
- *Tell a story of an experience with three people ...*

Science

> "All science is observations and conversation."—Niels Bohr

> "Science is rooted in conversations."—Werner Heisenberg

> "We cannot create observers by saying 'observe,' but by giving them the power and the means for this observation and these means are procured through education of the senses."
>
> —Maria Montessori

Sciences begin with observation, inquiry, theory, and experimentation—almost always in that order, followed by a recursive progression toward deeper understanding. Although circle practice can be applied to complex scientific topics, as physicist David Bohm demonstrates in his book *On Dialogue*, it is best to begin with the basics.[15] How do we give our students the power and means for observation? How do we "educate the senses?" I love to ask teachers, "What are you doing to expand your students' capacity to perceive?"

Sometimes science arises from necessity. At Palms Middle School, we facilitators often had to escort groups of students across campus to a dedicated circle space. On many of these walks, the admonition to "respect other classrooms" by staying quiet just didn't hold up. One day, it occurred to me to brief the students before our walk. My speech went something like this:

"Today we are going to go on a 'noticing journey.' As we walk to the council room, I want you to really use all your senses. Notice what you see with your eyes, listen to what strikes your ears. Notice any smells or tastes, even if they come from your imagination. Feel what you feel, like the sun on your face, your feet in your shoes, the touch of your clothes. And try to notice what you think, the thoughts and images that come into your mind. To notice much more of what is going on around you and inside you, *remain silent for the whole journey*. That way you will be able to use all your senses. Let's see how much more we can notice."

"To begin, I'll ring this bell, and we will go into council, into silence. When we get to the council room, we will continue in silence because we are still in council. We will stand in a circle and each person can share a few things they noticed on the journey."

What began as a ploy became an adventure. In circle, students shared what they had perceived on their journey from the sixth-grade bungalows to the Lana A. Brody Council Room:

- That electrical thing on the side of the auditorium, humming.
- My nose itching.
- Through the fence, I saw a man taking out the trash.
- There's a palm tree by the corner of the auditorium. I never saw it before. And it has yellow dates near the top.

- Lots of gum on the ground, red and blue but mostly black because it has been there a long time.
- Thinking that other people looking at us must think we are stupid looking around smelling things.
- Leaves moving on that bush outside the library and feeling that same breeze on my arms and face.
- David's shoes shuffling in front of me.
- Mr. Gottfried on his walkie-talkie, looking at us on the quad.
- The security guard eating an orange by the doors near the stairs.
- Loud stomping in the stairwell.
- Jessica looking at me as I passed Mrs. Chi's class.

When we sat down, I asked, "How many of you noticed something you never noticed before?" Most raised a hand. "How many of you heard someone share something that you also noticed?" Again, most. "How many of you heard someone say something you *didn't notice?*" Again, most raised hands. We then began a council using the prompts:

- *Tell about* a *time you noticed something for the first time.*
- *Tell about a time you realized you hadn't noticed something that was always there.*

The harvesting question was, *What can we say about what it takes to notice things and why sometimes we don't?*

My suspicion is that these students, at least for a while, left this circle with a heightened awareness of the world around them. We have used the noticing journey with the youngest students as well as with adults. Jane Raphael reads *The Listening Walk* by Paul Showers with illustrations by Aliki Brandenberg to her kindergarten students before their journey. The book includes the line:

"On a listening walk I do not talk. I listen to all the different sounds.

I hear many different sounds when I do not talk."[16]

Sometimes we focus on one sense at a time in these noticing journeys. This mirrors meditation practices in which practitioners focus on a single sensation, like breath at the tip of the nose, letting all else fall into the background. Such attention sharpens concentration and deepens awareness. In science, this process of isolating variables, analyzing a system's parts, can bring about a fuller understanding of its operation as a whole.

There are many extensions of the noticing journey for the science classroom as well as for other academic disciplines:

- For the elementary grades, begin a noticing journey in the classroom. Simply have students wander around the room noticing what they notice and then bring them together in a circle to recall what stayed with them. Try the same activity after reminding students of the six sense gates: sight, smell, taste, sound, touch, and thought. You might send them on separate journeys focusing on each sense gate, one at a time.
- Follow the classroom journey with one that takes them around the school. Then, take one around the neighborhood.
- Once students are sensitized to deep observation, you can add a particular focus to the journey. A few examples:
    - Notice things that are beautiful.
    - Notice things that need attention or fixing.
    - Notice things that make you feel glad, sad, mad, or scared.
    - Notice things that are natural, living things.
    - Notice things that are made by people.
    - Notice things made of wood, metal, plastic, or cloth.
    - Notice things that are made of or contain earth, air, fire (electrical), or water.
    - Notice natural things that people have cared for.
    - Notice things that you would like to do something about.

- Have students conduct a noticing journey in their own homes or neighborhoods and report back in a circle.

Expand students' capacity for observation by teaching a vocabulary of the senses.

For older students, the noticing journey becomes a bridge to formal scientific inquiry. You might reframe it as "heightened awareness using all the senses" or "deep observation." Encourage them to approach the world as scientific investigators, curious and open. Again, you might emphasize that while scientific inquiry is meant to be "objective," all data, even mathematical formulas, are filtered through our subjectivity, and that this subjectivity alters what we observe. A discussion with the class of the "observer effect" in physics will remind them that science itself is *an interaction* between people and the world around them. (This includes noting your own thoughts and feeling states as you conduct the observation.) Science is a relationship between the observer and the observed. We might say that the scientist must be "in council" with the observed. This will make a lot of sense to students who have grown up with council!

The Water Cycle: A Tale of the Sands

I learned the Sufi "Tale of the Sands" from council trainer Leon Berg. We have used a version of it as a basis for council with all ages, including adults.

This tale involves the journey of a stream as it begins in the high mountains, gathering itself into a broader expanse, traversing alpine meadows, tumbling over cataracts, pooling in mountain lakes, and eventually finding itself at the sands of the desert. There it throws itself against the sands attempting to flow as it had always done. After many fruitless attempts, it hears the voice of the sands that tells it to surrender into the arms of the wind. The stream objects, saying that it does not know how to fly, that it is more like a snake that moves across the ground. The sands answer that while this surrender does not sound like the reasonable thing to do, it is what must be done. When the stream does surrender, it is taken up in the arms of the wind to begin the cycle again.

Clearly, this tale is about more than just the water cycle. It is about life itself. As with any story that contains archetypal elements, in circle we can simply listen for words and phrases that catch our attention and then tell stories about experiences that we have had of *meandering, becoming part of something larger, turning back upon ourselves in a quagmire, tumbling over a precipice, feeling as if we were dashed on the rocks, the futility of doing the same thing over and over and expecting a different outcome, and experiences of complete surrender*.

Younger students can simply tell stories of their experiences with water, all of which provide a foundation of relevance for learning about the water cycle.

Finally, public-school science standards typically ask students to observe, experience, interact with, and understand these aspects of our world:

- Objects, liquids, solids, and gases
- Plants
- Animals
- Mountains, rivers, oceans, valleys, deserts
- Weather
- Motion
- Life cycles
- Resources
- Energy and matter
- Light
- Objects in the sky
- Electricity and magnetism
- Respiration, digestion, waste disposal, and transport of materials

Circle pedagogy can be integrated into the investigation of each of these aspects. Prompt students to tell stories about experiences with each. Their personal experiences can then be compared to what they learn through presentations, reading, and experiments. Again, it is best to create relevance before introducing a new concept.

Circles are also useful to review and check understanding at the end of a unit. A simple prompt like *Share what comes to mind now when you think about the solar system* can reinforce learning and tell us what stuck and what didn't. After a lab experiment, you can offer a brief virtual circle (or popcorn) with the prompt: *Say one thing you noticed during our lab today*. What is shared will be a review of the process, deepening recollection and retention.

For Reflection and Imagination

1. Choose any standard, concept, or curricular goal—especially one students find challenging—from the discipline you teach.

   - Look back over the samples given in this chapter for your subject area.
   - Craft a prompt that in some way will elicit students' lived experience in relation to it.
   - See that it checks off the eight features of an effective prompt described in Chapter 5.
   - Consider the story you would tell to model the connection between concept and experience.

2. Pages 267–270 describe a "noticing journey."

   - Go to a familiar place: your home, classroom, yard, a path your often take.
   - Attempt to notice, at separate times or sequentially, everything you see, hear, feel (both tactile and emotional), smell, and think.
   - After the journey, write down what you remember. Did you notice anything different than you normally do in this "familiar" environment?

3. Using "The Tale of the Sands" (p. 270), recall, as fully as you can, times when you were ...

- meandering
- becoming part of something larger
- turning back upon yourself in a quagmire
- tumbling over a precipice
- feeling as if you were dashed on the rocks
- doing the same thing repeatedly and expecting a different outcome
- surrendering completely
- feeling transformed by an experience

Chapter 8:
Integrating Circle with Academic Disciplines

1. **Align with Standards**
   Use circle to meet key curriculum goals: analysis, synthesis, communication, and critical thinking.

2. **Start with Lived Experience**
   Build relevance by using students' personal stories to explore academic content.

3. **Develop Literacy through Oracy**
   Strengthen reading and writing by first cultivating speaking and listening in circle.

4. **Make Social Studies Relevant**
   Use thematic prompts to explore culture, power, and civic life through personal reflection.

5. **Connect Math and Science to Life**
   Ground abstract concepts in metaphor, movement, and story to enhance understanding.

6. **Encourage Observation and Inquiry**
   Use noticing journeys and sensory prompts to develop scientific and critical thinking.

7. **View Circle as a Learning Technology**
   Treat circle not just as a practice, but as a tool for deeper, relational learning.

9

CIRCLES IN THE RELATIONAL ARTS

Social-Emotional Learning, Counseling, and Restorative Justice: The Interactive Field

Now that we have considered ways to apply circles in academic contexts, we address the ever-changing tapestry of relationships in the classroom and school community. This chapter concerns what we might call the relational arts: social-emotional learning (SEL), school-based counseling, and restorative justice or restorative processes. When we view relationship as an art, we understand that through a combination of direct instruction (learning the craft), modeling, and practice we develop proficiency and originality in our interactions with others, responding appropriately and in a life-affirming way. These relational arts require skill-building to "read" what we referred to in Chapter 4 as the "interactive field."

Much depends on our ability to "read" and respond to this interactive or relational field. It is both a somatic and a cognitive experience. We *feel* the field. We *sense* the energy in the room. We know when our students are bursting with excitement, when they are engaged in a task, and when they have had enough and need a break! The field begins with our own inward awareness of our physical and emotional states and extends into the immediate environment, the whole school, the community, and beyond. The field includes the *physical structures* present—the shape of the room, the arrangement of seats, the presence of artificial or natural light, and the sounds, scents, and textures of our surroundings. The field is also affected by the *emotional and psychological* realities, the dynamics of those who inhabit it—whether they feel safe and connected or fearful and alienated.

The field also includes what is present in the school, its history, current conditions, and anticipated future. For example, at Palms there was that pedestrian tunnel under the street that connected the two halves of the school. Its mythology as a dark underworld brought fear to generations of new students. Likewise, holiday times bring their own set of influences. If there has been a loss, a conflict between individuals, or fear for security—these are *felt*, however subtly, by everyone on the campus. And when there are dramatic events in the local community or in the world, these also powerfully affect the field in the classroom. As teachers we are often faced with a choice of whether to turn towards or away from consciousness of these influences, to note them or ignore them.

Field theory looks at the interaction between individuals and environments. As we have already seen, simply rearranging the chairs will radically shift the way people perceive themselves and others, as well as the ways they behave within that space. Note what happens when you bring a group of children to the park or wilderness, to a museum, or to a sports event. Environment affects behavior. I have had the sad experience of working at campuses where buildings and grounds are in such a state of disrepair, even what remains of plant life appears choked for nutrients. What effect does this environment have on the children and adults who spend most of their waking hours there?

In this chapter we look at how to expand our ability to read this field and thereby to know what is needed in our circles. The greater our capacity to stay aware, the greater our responsibility to attend and respond. As council trainer Marlow Hotchkiss says, "The one with the greatest consciousness has the greatest responsibility."

So why would we want to have any *more* responsibility? Why would we want to feel and know more than we already do about the inner lives of those around us? The myth of Prometheus tells us that stealing fire from the gods, expanding our light and knowledge, brings inevitable suffering. Certainly, when we offer circle to our students and staff, we learn more about each other than if we did not. Do we really want to eat the fruit of that tree of knowledge? This question is one that asks us to look at our emotional bandwidth and how we might expand it and still care for ourselves. By turning the chairs toward a common center, you have already shifted the relational field towards one that encourages heightened awareness of self and other. It is a first step in social-emotional skill-building.

Relational Arts and Sciences

I want to propose that serious consideration be given to the field of relational arts. We might well call this field "relational arts *and sciences*" since it includes psychology, sociology, organizational management, and systems theory in general. There is of course a basic premise in all these fields, and it is that we exist and function because *we are all related*. When the Lakota people say "Metakwe Oyashin!" (all my relations!), they are proclaiming this most fundamental truth.

When we view relationships as an art, we understand that through a combination of skill-building and practice we develop proficiency and originality in our interactions with others, responding appropriately and in a life-affirming way.

Science requires a minimum of a dyadic relationship—a council, if you will—between observer and the observed. Good science requires multiple observers of the same phenomenon, who confer with each other to derive general principles. David Bohm, whose mathematical formulations contributed to the development of the atomic bomb, devoted the last 30 years of his life to groups of scientists committed to engage in dialogue to generate novel ideas and new directions for research.[1]

Social-Emotional Competencies

According to the Collaborative for Academic, Social, and Emotional Learning (casel.org), there are five social-emotional competencies that can be taught:

- **Self-awareness:** The ability to accurately recognize one's emotions and thoughts and their influence on behavior. This includes accurately assessing one's strengths and limitations and possessing a well-grounded sense of confidence and optimism.
- **Self-management:** The ability to regulate one's emotions, thoughts, and behaviors effectively in different situations. This includes managing stress, controlling impulses, motivating oneself, and setting and working toward achieving personal and academic goals.
- **Social awareness:** The ability to take the perspective of and empathize with others from diverse backgrounds and cultures, to understand social and ethical norms for behavior, and to recognize family, school, and community resources and supports.
- **Relationship skills:** The ability to establish and maintain healthy and rewarding relationships with diverse individuals and groups. This includes communicating clearly, listening actively, cooperating, resisting inappropriate social pressure, negotiating conflict constructively, and seeking and offering help when needed.
- **Responsible decision-making:** The ability to make constructive and respectful choices about personal behavior and social interactions based on consideration of ethical standards, safety concerns, social norms, the realistic evaluation of consequences of various actions, and the well-being of self and others.[2]

Circle practice promotes *all* the above. *Self-awareness* follows from participating in a context where you are aware that others see you and value you. When you speak into the compassionate listening of others, you tend to *self-reflect* on what you say, choosing appropriately what and how you say it. All moral judgment depends on our ability to self- reflect. When no one is listening, people will feel free to say whatever they want without any awareness of its effect on others, as often is the case on social media. This of course can also happen in circle, but as the group begins to value itself, it will generally send messages to indicate that the content, the tone, or the manner of expression is or is not being well received.

Self-awareness also comes about in what Zimmerman and Coyle call "a circle of mirrors." Others in the circle reflect our behaviors back to us, giving us the opportunity to self-reflect. It is the old desert island question: if there is no one else there, how will we be able to perceive ourselves?

In the same way, awareness of the group facilitates individual *self-management*. When we feel ourselves connected to others, and we see the effect our words and actions have, we are more likely to manage our behavior and the way we express ourselves. It is the sense of isolation, of not fitting in, that makes us act egregiously, attempting to get attention by any means necessary. When we speak of self-management it is always in the context of awareness of others, of the group. Otherwise, there is no one for whom we manage ourselves. Accountability is always to the group.

In terms of *social awareness*, circles expand one's capacity to hold *multiple perspectives* and to empathize with others whose experiences may be very distinct from ours. You cannot have empathy for another if you are not exposed to another's experience. As Thích Nhất Hạnh and Gene Knudsen Hoffman say, "An enemy is one whose story has not *yet* been heard." *Responsible decision-making* is the result of self-awareness and awareness of others. Circles facilitate the possibility that we consider the greater good, something we cannot do without awareness of the stories of others. The notion that *we must make all our decisions with awareness of their effect on the children for seven generations* is wisdom aligned with this understanding. Here are several circle-based activities to bring about skill-building in social-emotional competencies.

Developing a Vocabulary of Feelings and Needs: Self- and Social Awareness (Primary Grades +)

As a teacher of English, I find the language of feelings one of the most important of the *academic* vocabularies, superior in many respects to the language of literary "devices" and rhetorical forms, which get so much emphasis in traditional language arts classes. As students develop proficiency with words that describe the subtleties of human emotion and interaction, they become more precise in their capacity to understand and critique literature of any kind.

I begin by telling students and teachers that there are four main categories of feeling, and the words for these categories all end in "d:" mad, sad, glad, and scared. There is a spectrum of intensity for each of these categories. For example, on the "mad" spectrum one can feel the low- level intensity of being mildly "irritated" or "peeved," building to the high-level intensity of "psychotic rage." On the "glad" spectrum, one can feel at one end "satisfied" and at the other "ecstatic."

A person can also feel more than one feeling simultaneously. For example, one can be both mad and scared when confronted with a threatening situation, and, if one recognizes the suffering of the person who is threatening us, one might even feel glad to not be experiencing similar suffering. Other feelings are themselves a combination of categories. "Lonely," for example, might be a combination of sad, mad, and scared.

We can *play* with the language of feeling as we learn the subtle shadings of feeling words along the four spectra. With the lower grades, I like to use a circle I call "Show with your Body and Face." Students stand in a circle. I offer a prompt like: *Who can show with your body and face what you look like when you feel "scared?"* As a volunteer makes a gesture, such as tensing the body and putting hands over their face with eyes just peeking out through the fingers, I ask the group to mirror *exactly* the way the volunteer is expressing the look and feeling of "scared."

The whole group mirrors. Then, I ask for another volunteer to show what "scared" looks like. Another expression of the same feeling is then mirrored by the group. By doing this, we see that *different people can express the same feeling in different ways.*

Many teachers use a feelings chart to help students learn and identify these terms. When we engage the body in language acquisition, the words go into muscle memory, and this is especially important when we are learning to recognize feeling states. Acquiring this vocabulary of feeling can be a lifelong pursuit as there are thousands of words for describing the subtleties and complexity of human experience. Show with your body and your face what is feels like to be surly, appreciative, unrepentant, contrite, perplexed. As students play this game in circle, there is inevitable laughter and that indicates a much deeper form of acquisition. You can then follow these activities with circles about a time when you felt one of these ways.

Social Cues: Relationship Skills (Multi-grade)

A useful variation on this activity is to *play with social cues.* For example, tell the group to imagine that they are walking into a group of people they don't know well but they want to convey non-verbally the idea: *I am a friendly, open person. You can talk to me.* Then, ask a volunteer to show what this might look like, for example, feet planted confidently, forearms turned forward to reveal vulnerability (as in many Greek statues), and head lifted with a bright smile. The group then mirrors this gesture. Another student can then show the same cue in another way. Here are a few more social cues to play with:

- I want to be left alone.
- I have something for you.
- I appreciate what you are doing.
- I respect you.
- I want to go now.
- I'm surprised to see you.

- I'm happy to see you.
- You frighten me.
- I'm angry with you.
- I have missed you.
- I'm proud of you.
- I want you to stop what you are doing.

As students express and mirror these social cues, they are becoming more aware and mindful of their own non-verbal messages and more sensitive and attuned to the messages conveyed by the body language and energy of others. They literally learn to *inhabit* the feeling states of others and to recognize their own. As Atticus Finch says in *To Kill a Mockingbird*, "You never really understand a person until you consider things from his point of view, until you climb into his skin and walk around in it." Note that any of these cues can lead to stories shared in circle.

Needs: Self-Management and Relationship Skills (Multi-grade)

We are all familiar with Abraham Maslow's Hierarchy of Human Needs in order of primacy: physiological, safety, love and belonging, esteem, and self-actualization. To these five he later added a sixth—self-transcendence. To transcend the self is to embrace interdependence, an implicit value derived from participation in circles. Psychologist Marshall Rosenberg, author of *Nonviolent Communication: A Language of Life*, suggests the following list of human needs (without regard to an order or hierarchy): physical well-being, connection, honesty, play, peace, autonomy, and meaning.[3] A recent, circle-based, dynamic model has been proposed by Deborah Heifetz. She suggests four "hungers" (survival/staying alive, power/impact, meaning/values, and love/connection) and their "associated needs pairs," physical aliveness and safety (for survival), autonomy and fairness (for power), identity and esteem (for meaning), and recognition and belonging (for love).[4] It is of great value to learn the meaning of these terms and to explore the experiences of them through telling stories in circle. All behavior is the expression of an underlying need. When our needs are met, we experience well-being, and when they are not, we experience dis-ease. As Rosenberg says, "Violence is *a tragic expression* of an unmet need."

Although the following prompts are crafted for the lower grades, with minor variations they can be used for any grade to develop this vocabulary, its deep meaning and application:

- *Tell about a time or a place where you felt completely safe (physiological, physical well- being, safety, love, peace).*
- *Name someone you trust or who trusts you. Then, tell about a time you felt this trust with the person you named (belonging, honesty, esteem).*
- *Recall a recent moment of joy, happiness, or play (safety, love and belonging, physical well-being, peace).*
- *Name someone you feel is a true friend. Then, tell about a time when you knew this to be true (connection, love and belonging).*
- *Name a person, place, activity, or thing that is important in your life. Then, tell about a time when you were sure of this (meaning).*
- *Name someone you helped, or something you helped another person do. Then, tell the story of that time (self-transcendence, meaning, connection, esteem).*
- *Tell about a time you had to make a choice. It could have been the "right" choice or the "wrong" choice (autonomy, esteem, meaning).*

After a storytelling circle elicited by such prompts, through *witnessing* (of what others said) and *harvesting* (of what was resonant in the circle), we develop a deeper understanding of what these needs mean individually and collectively. Each of these prompts can also be fruitfully formed using its contrary; for example, *tell about a time when you felt unsafe, untrusting, unhappy*, etc., and the yield will be equally valuable. As poet Kahlil Gibran says, "I have learned silence from the talkative, tolerance from the intolerant, and kindness from the unkind; yet, strange, I am ungrateful to those teachers."

When we look over the panoply of history and literature, we find these needs in all human endeavors, and our ability to name, describe, analyze, evaluate, and predict depends on how deeply we comprehend these needs and their associated terms. Again, we see the connection between social-emotional and academic learning.

The Images We Carry: Self- and Social Awareness (Secondary)

In my middle-school English classes, when we were studying *To Kill a Mockingbird,* I introduced students to the idea of *projection*. When we don't really know someone, and even when we do, we tend to create stories about that person that tell us more about ourselves than about the other person. In the novel, the children make up stories about Arthur (Boo) Radley, whom they have never met. They see him as a monster.

In the same way, many people in the novel's town of Macomb see Tom Robinson, the Black man falsely accused of rape, as subhuman. The entire book is about the painful process of how we learn to undo our stereotypes and withdraw our projections. This is what happens when we get to know each other, when we listen to each other's stories.

Middle school is a very sensitive time when it comes to self-image. As youth at this age are actively forming their identities, there is an increased tendency to type, categorize, and box-in everyone else. The process never stops as we get older and is the product of the fact that we don't have the opportunity to sit in circle with everyone who comes into our lives. We no longer live in the village where we see the same people day in and day out. Except, of course, in school. Even in a large school, the classroom is a small community. When we practice circle, we quickly become aware of our natural tendency to project positive and negative qualities onto others.

One exercise that boosts awareness of our tendency to project is what I call "The Images We Carry." For this activity, I recruited about eight students in each of my five classes to allow me to take a digital photo of them individually. I compiled these images into a slideshow. At the bottom of each slide, I provided the following sentence starters beginning with the clause "this is a person who ... ":

- This is a person who likes to ...
- This is a person who always ...
- This is a person who never ...
- This is a person who cares about ...
- This is a person who believes ...

With each image, as the sentence starter appeared beneath, the students would complete the sentence in writing. As these were students who knew each other, I told them that what they might say can be based on already knowing things about this person or what they might imagine. I asked them to take it seriously, to be honest, but not to say things that might hurt the person.

Students who volunteered to have their pictures taken understood beforehand what we were going to do, so they were somewhat prepared.

After the lists were compiled, I invited the volunteer to come up in front of the class. For each statement, students who wanted to test their observation against reality raised hands to speak. The volunteer either confirmed, refuted, or clarified the observation. We were then able to discuss what gave the observer the impression that they noted.

The same process can be done, a bit less impactfully perhaps, with *photographs* of people the students do *not* know. After the impressions are shared, you can reveal a brief bio on each person.- Follow this activity with circles using prompts like these:

Tell about a time:

- *you got a first impression of someone, and it turned out to be either true or false.*
- *you were treated differently, either better or worse, because of your appearance (age, race, gender expression, clothing, etc.).*
- *you were judged wrongly, or you wrongly judged someone else.*

- *you became a friend to someone you thought you would never be friends with.*
- *when someone turned out to be other than what you expected.*

A Circle of Mirrors: Relationship Skills (Secondary)

> "Pay close attention when someone in the circle says something or behaves in a way that irritates you, particularly if your reaction is stronger than the behavior warrants. The individual may be reflecting an aspect of your shadow side in the form of a disowned or disparaged quality. This is one of the main ways council acts as a circle of mirrors."
>
> —Jack Zimmerman and Virginia Coyle, *The Way of Council*

How do we tell others what we think of them? How do we learn to receive the reflection of others? In all meaningful relationships, we must be able to tell one another how we see each other, what we notice, what we hear, and how it affects us. We must, in effect, become accurate *mirrors* for one another.

In the Hawaiian practice of Ho'oponopono, there is an assumption that the community is 100% responsible for every individual's behavior. If someone steals from another, then a circle convenes where everyone explores the issue of our inclination to take things that don't belong to us and what it is to have things taken from us without our consent. This is not about shaming. The whole enterprise is designed to bring about *reflection* on the issue to prevent a repeat of the transgression.[5]

When circles are a regular part of school culture, where students really get to know one another as well as the subject matter, each student becomes a mirror for every other. First, when we speak into compassionate listening, we hear our own words. That is often enough to get us to reflect deeply on our experience and sometimes to reassess our conclusions. When we get to the point that we can accurately describe what we see a person doing and what we hear them saying, without judgment, we are able to give an extraordinary gift to each other, the gift of *mirroring*.

The following circle protocol should only be offered after trust and safety are established.

The first part of this is a reflection on how we imagine others see us. A good preparatory activity is the *me-bag* where students decorate a paper bag, putting images and symbols that represent how they believe others see them *on the outside* and then place items inside that represent how they see themselves *inside*. The same can be achieved through mask-making. The point is that students begin to understand that they convey a certain image to others, that they have public *personae* that might be different in different contexts—at school, at home, with close friends.

The protocol goes like this:

- Begin circle as usual. Perhaps do a "clearing round" (whatever you need to do or say to become fully present).
- In *basic* form or *web*-style, use a prompt like: *When the talking piece comes, consider the self-image or persona you imagine you bring to this circle. How do you imagine others see you? Share only what you trust can be heard.*
- Using a *response* council form, a volunteer who *wishes* to receive reflection from the group, takes a talking piece and asks the question, "How do you see me?" Others in the group speak only to the volunteer.
- In *popcorn or web style*, students offer some form of *mirroring*. This may come in the form of a list of characteristics or qualities: "When I see you sitting before me now ... " Or, one might recall a story or vignette about this person, a memory of something said or something seen that you carry with you when you think of this person: "When I think of you, I recall ... "
- The volunteer responds at the end, beginning with a "thank you" and then can affirm, refute, or clarify what

> they heard from others. *What did you notice in yourself and in the group as you participated in this process?*

I have used this protocol very successfully with 14- and 15-year-olds at the end of a school year. I also volunteer myself to hear their reflections. It is important that *only those who wish* to have this mirroring receive it and that not everyone feel compelled to offer observations. What is offered must be observations, not evaluations.

Making Decisions, Setting Intentions, and Taking Action (Multi-grade with an Example from Primary)

Like forms of meditation, circle is an "intentional practice." To "intend" is to "aim at." We distinguish an "intention" from a "goal." Inherent in the concept of a "goal" is that one either reaches it or does not. The same word is used for the scoring of a point in soccer, football, and hockey. If one doesn't reach the goal, one has, in effect, failed. An "intention," on the other hand, is something we aim to achieve. We speak of four "intentions" of council because we recognize that speaking and listening "from the heart," speaking spontaneously, and speaking leanly can only be done relatively well as we continue the practice.

Similarly, "decisions" must be seen as a matter of process, something to be acted upon and then re-evaluated. To emphasize the process aspect of actions, dancer, choreographer Anna Halprin distinguishes between evaluations and what she calls "value actions." The idea of an evaluation carries with it a connotation of absolute and static value, while a value action eliminates judgment of whether the action was good or bad, right or wrong, and instead emphasizes *what is to be done* given the results of a particular action.[6] Similarly, in the circle we are not looking to moralize about past actions but to reflect on how we made our decisions, what resulted from them, and what we might consider doing the next time a similar situation arises. Once again, we do not use the circles to instill values, but we use them to create the conditions wherein values *can* be formed.

The American School Counselor Association (ASCA) developed the counseling standards for American schools. According to their website at www.schoolcounselor.org, the organization, founded in 1952, "supports school counselors' efforts to help students focus on academic, personal/social and career development so they not only achieve success in school but are prepared to lead fulfilling lives as responsible members of society."[7] One of the core standards set by the ASCA is: "Students will make decisions, set goals, and take necessary action to achieve goals."

A basic circle on the topic of decision-making would be simply to ask students to speak about a time they *had* to decide. To create the possibility to see that decisions have consequences, follow this story round with one that asks students to reflect on what happened *after* the decision was made. To go even further, we might ask them to consider *who was affected by their decision*. We will return to this critical step when we explore "restorative" justice.

To achieve the standard above, however, four steps are necessary. First is *a reflection on the past* to describe a current situation. Next is developing *an awareness of available options*, and, we might add, *engaging imagination in the service of creative options that are not at first easily apparent*. Then come *clear intention setting* and *the articulation of action plans*. Finally, there must be *an opportunity to return to the circle* to reflect on progress and results and to restart the cycle.

Let's look at an example of how this sequence might work in an elementary classroom where *teasing* has become an issue:

- Begin by asking students to define the term "teasing." If there is time you might have students improvise a teasing situation or draw. This can be done in or out of formal council. Combine their ideas and yours to create a working definition.
- Then, move to the circle, and use a prompt such as the following: *We have all decided what "teasing" means. When the talking piece comes, try to remember a time when something like this happened to you or maybe when you teased someone else.*

Follow with second round: *What did you do, feel, or say after the teasing?* This encourages students to look beyond the drama of the incident and toward the aftermath, the effect of the teasing.

- A harvesting round is next: *From all that has been shared, what can you say about when, why, and how teasing happens?*
- Finally, ask students to set intentions regarding teasing: *What do you imagine you might do the next time someone teases you or someone you know or you want to tease someone?* Generally, students will come up with adaptive solutions. If one says "Punch 'em in the mouth," consider letting that go. If the circle has become safe enough for such an expression, it might also be safe enough for students to develop caring connections, and as the talking piece goes around, the outlier will be able to hear other possibilities.
- Have students write down their intentions and create a display board or a packet that can be posted with the words "Teasing Intentions."
- In a subsequent circle, ask students to "check in" about how it's going with the keeping of their intentions. Depending on what comes up, intentions can be modified and reset.

As always in circle, don't exclude yourself from the question. We adults are always learning how not to tease, to put down, to ridicule, to disempower. Let the students see that you too struggle with the desire to one-up others, to define a self by comparing it favorably with the foibles of others.

Circle and Counseling

In traditional counseling groups, participants look to the facilitator to guide the process. To do this, they must see the facilitator as a wise, competent healer. In psychoanalytic terms this is called a "transference," where the therapist is seen as the one who will mitigate the suffering of the clients. We might say that in a traditional counseling group, there is an *assumption of dis-ease;* that is, the participants are there to solve a problem, resolve a trauma, heal, or become well, and the therapist is seen as the one capable of bringing that about. In a group that practices circle, in contrast, there is an *assumption of health;* that is, everyone sees themselves and others as complete, healthy human beings, who occasionally face some kind of crisis. The *transference,* we might say, is on the circle, not on any individual.

When a counselor leads a circle (and when a restorative justice facilitator leads a "harm" circle), the task is to move the transference toward the center of the circle. *The outcomes and agreements are determined by the circle.* The facilitator cannot be attached to having a "good circle," or to resolving a conflict, or indeed to where the circle needs to go. The circle is the healer, not any one individual. It is quite natural for young people participating in a circle to tell their stories to the adult, and this is why, whenever possible, it is best to have two adults in every circle, sitting directly across from one another. As facilitators, we must turn the attention away from us and back onto the center or the circle as a whole. One way to do this nonverbally is when a student looks only at you while speaking, after indicating that you are indeed listening, slowly turn your gaze to the center or to a broad view of the whole circle, and whenever possible *remind the students that they are addressing the whole circle, not just you.*

If circle practice is systemic in the school, it means something when a counselor or teacher says to a student, "Would you be willing to sit in circle about this?" This is to say, "Are you willing to do some deep listening here?" and "I will listen from the heart as you speak the truth of your experience." If a student says, "No," we can revert to another counseling paradigm. We can also ask two or more students in conflict if they are "willing" to sit in council.

Here are a few activities that address how circles can be effectively used to approach the big questions of love and loss as well as a few very common concerns that typically arise in a school.

Managing a Counseling Caseload

I am told that at the Plum Village Monastery, in southern France, once yearly the community of monks invite two individuals suffering from severe mental illness to have an extended retreat there. Thích Nhất Hạnh, founder of the monastery, suggests that bringing such individuals into a community of 40 mindfully living monks will bring about healing of their afflictions. *It is a therapy of no therapy.* The individuals are simply integrated into the life of the community. They are handed brooms. They work in the kitchen. They attend meditation sessions. There are no specific interventions. They are immersed in a mindful community, 40- strong, with every member presumably aware of each inbreath and outbreath at any given moment. The ratio of two afflicted individuals to 40 monks, however, is crucial. When there is such a ratio, the afflicted individuals get better. If there are more than two, the monks run the risk of becoming ill!

When we think about this model, we realize that our model of mental health treatment (and schooling!) is upside down. We employ *one* healer to *a caseload* of the afflicted. Our model of individual or group counseling involves one therapist (whom we hope lives mindfully) and either one "patient" or "client" or a group of such. Individual therapy is a hugely impractical model simply because the number of individuals in need far exceeds the number of trained professionals. In the group therapy model, there is often just one healer for a group of those seeking help.

Returning to the mission of the ASCA, it is daunting to attempt to fulfill the academic and personal guidance suggested there with caseloads of 600:1 in the secondary schools. What typically happens is that counselors will program all students and then personally see only those who are struggling. Ultimately, with the circles, students are working with each other to explore relationships, challenges, visions of the future, etc. The group engenders an opportunity for students to set manageable, behavioral objectives, personal intentions, and it provides the community necessary to bring about *adher-*

ence to those goals and *accountability*. Circles enable counselors to meet with vastly more students than in the typical one-on-one format. And in a school where students have learned to lead their own councils (as we will see in Chapter 10), counselors can simply provide a prompt and perhaps some background information on a topic, and the students will engage each other to reap a harvest of insight and understanding.

Inner Resources

Counselors know that the best outcome is one that activates the client's capacity for self- healing. Many schools today are becoming "trauma sensitive," and circles serve this purpose in a profound way for both students and staff.

For many years, the treatment of trauma depended on an individual's bonding with a compassionate therapist to whom they could tell the story of their trauma and therefore gain mastery over it. The problem was that in many cases detailed recollection of a traumatic event can cause one to be *re-traumatized*. Recent treatment advances emphasize a very different approach. Peter Levine, in his book *Waking the Tiger,* offers a process called Somatic Experiencing.[8] Levine suggests that just as a post-traumatic trigger can send an individual into what he calls a "trauma vortex," so it is also possible to activate a person's "healing vortex." This healing vortex is a product of "grounding" through awareness of body sensations along with the recall of what Levine calls "resources." The circle-based process I present here does not replace professional treatment, but the circle is an excellent way to acquaint people with and to deeply ground their "inner resources."

An inner resource is anything the mere thought of which brings you back to a degree of calm, a degree of centeredness. Resources include, but are in no way limited to, the following categories:

- **People:** These can be people we know or have known or someone we simply know about. For example, when I think of my grandmother, Mary, I'm reminded of someone who I know loved me unconditionally. She has, of course, passed on, but she still lives in my heart. People in this category can include historical figures or even characters in fiction.

- **Places:** These are places where you felt safe and free to be who you are. It could be a place you visited many years ago, but it lives in your memory because being there felt so good.
- **Events:** These are experiences of accomplishment, like winning a race or overcoming an obstacle; of wonder and awe, like seeing the fullness of the Milky Way for the first time or the birth of a child; but they can also be "small" (but significant) events like witnessing a hummingbird in your backyard or finding a lucky penny.
- **Words to live by:** These are sayings, song lyrics, a passage from a sacred book, something you heard from a wise person, a line from a play, movie, or poem, or something you tell yourself to re-center.
- **Personal qualities** (that you recognize in yourself but don't often think about): You might note that you are a generous person, patient, persistent, reasonable, imaginative, etc.

You carry many of these resources inside you wherever you go. When they are "grounded," making what Levine calls a "healing vortex," they can be accessed at will, even unconsciously, ultimately providing a counter-valent force to mitigate the power of a "trauma vortex" (the spinning out that occurs when traumas are triggered).

I have staff and students make lists of items in each category. Sometimes we draw symbols or pictures that remind us of our resources. Sometimes we even dance or act them out.

After the lists are done privately, in a circle, conduct a *speed round*, where participants simply name *one* of their resources without saying anything more about it. This alone generally lifts the mood of a group as we witness each person recalling something they value personally. In a *story round,* the prompt is something like: *Tell us about one of these resources so we can better understand why it is important to you.* If the group is large, the story round can use the *spiral* form.

What happens in this circle, with people of any age, is truly extraordinary. First, when a speaker tells the circle about one of their resources, they are *lingering* in the memory much longer than they did when simply recalling an item on their list. The speaker is, in effect, *meditating upon their own resource*; that is, they bring extended, focused awareness on this one thing. Doing this, the speaker is "grounding" the resource, deepening their contact with the memory. This, of course, could be done in writing or in just speaking to one person. In a circle, however, participants are immersed in each other's stories. They begin to see others in the circle as carriers of resources. They learn what sustains others in the circle, and each person broadens their understanding of what resources can be, consequently becoming more sensitive to such people, places, and experiences when they occur in life.

Any time students tell stories, draw pictures, express a resource in a "gesture story circle" (see Chapter 6), they are strengthening their capacity for equanimity. One session of simply making the five lists of resources can generate a wealth of circle prompts.

Students' resource reminder wall

Discussing Drugs, Sex, Sticks, and Stones

In circles we often become profoundly aware of what is missing or misunderstood in the lives of our students. It is natural to have the desire to "do something about" these issues, to enlighten our students, or to share how we have overcome these losses and missteps. *The circles, however, are not the place for giving advice; they are for telling stories.*

When a child in circle reports drug use, non-consensual sexual experiences, or potential or ongoing violence, we must report this to school counselors or administrators, and students must know that we will do so. When we do this, we fear students will no longer trust the circles. Further, they may feel that there is nothing else to talk about if these topics are taboo! As we will see, the issues are not drugs, sex, and violence per se, but *risk and relationship, cruelty and kindness*—topics that can inspire many fruitful circles.

Not being certified drug counselors, sex educators, or anger managers, and not being hired for these purposes, we need resources, protocols, and procedures for dealing with these issues when they come up in circle. Because of the limits placed on us by law in the public education setting, we take great care with what we say, noting the weight with which children weigh our comments. Again, our stories must be *age- and context-appropriate, facilitating* students' ability to tell their stories.

Drugs and Risks

The following few paragraphs are based on my experiences of leading mandatory groups for students who had been caught under the influence, in possession of drugs or alcohol on campus, and those who had self-referred. Parents gave their consent for these groups. Although these situations would not likely be evoked in classroom circles, I provide this as context for what we *can* do in the circles to get at some of the underlying causes and needs that lead to substance use. A typical conversation overheard in one of these mandatory groups would go something like this:

"Aw, man, one time we were over at Jimmy's place, and we got so bombed we were falling down."

"Yeah, what were you doing?"

"We had 40s in this beer bong, and big old blunts were going around." Laughter.

"Yeah, and Jimmy's mom came home."

"Really, what happened?"

"We jumped out the window. I nearly killed myself on his rose bushes!" Laughter.

"Yeah, well, *I* remember a time when ... "

In drug counseling sessions, these are called "war stories," the inevitable tales told when people are called upon to relate their drug experiences. The atmosphere in the room is pure excitement as heroic yarns are spun and each participant seeks to outdo the other in this contest of recalling who went the furthest, who took the greatest risks.

War stories may form a part of early group bonding. But, if they are the *only* stories, they do nothing but raise the desire of kids to continue their substance use. The real impetus, the energy behind these stories and behind the reactions of the listeners, is a developmental issue having to do with the formation of an autonomous self, one that feels capable of surviving the most extreme risks. Keep this in mind because the risks involved in being authentic in circle are a healthy way for students to develop not only a sense of an autonomous self but also to see how that self is interrelated with those of other group members and with the circle as a slightly larger self.

I don't believe that young people really enjoy being completely out of control. In my conversations with them, they would ultimately express how scared they were, how they thought they would never come down, how they would damage themselves or be busted. But something happens when they do come down. What was an experience of fear becomes an heroic feat!

A child's sense of self at 13 years is very permeable. It changes from moment to moment. There is a period, sometimes prolonged, *after* an experience of danger and loss of control, when the child has a sense of the solidity of the self. This sense of self is the thing that they have "come down" to. It is the home to which they return. And when this sense of a home base is so fleeting, as it is naturally in adolescence, the desire increases to have experiences that bring this return about. Taking greater and greater risks provides the opportunity to repeat this sense of homecoming. Although there may be despair that sets in before the next round of drug use, what kids talk about are their accumulated heroics.

Even the legitimate shamanic and initiatory uses of plants from the dawn of human culture have as their goal an informing or reshaping of the self. On some level, kids know the value of these initiatory experiences. When the culture does not provide meaningful rites of passage, youth will attempt to self-initiate. War stories are all about an "experience" of peril. The word "experience" literally means "coming out of" (ex) "peril" (peri). What are the perils we expose ourselves to *so that we can come out of them*? Is there such a thing as a *healthy peril*?

The above, as I said, is a conversation that would probably take place in a public-school drug and alcohol counseling session, not in a public-school circle. For one thing, imagine the affect the "war stories" might have on the students in the group who are not using. Second, there are two issues underlying the use of drugs, use being symptomatic of these two: *risk taking* and *the need to change one's mood or perspective*. I am purposefully not including the issues surrounding a child's need for acceptance (peer pressure and peer bonding) and rebellion since drug taking is just one of many ways these issues manifest. These latter two issues are also ripe for circles, though.

Risk taking is how we learn the boundaries of the self and its ever-growing orbits. Drug taking is a rather *emotionally* safe form of risk. It doesn't require much more than a certain foolhardiness and a strong stomach. Potentially much more frightening are *emotional risks* such as telling the truth in the moment, speaking from the heart, *physical risks* such as learning a new dance step, and *intellectual risks* such as opening to a world view that seems vastly different from our own.

If students want to talk about taking drugs, refer them to their counselor, where they can speak confidentially about it. In circle, try to move the discussion toward the larger issues of *risk taking* and the desire to change moods or perspective. Remember that it is our task to create prompts that enable *all* students to share from their experience.

Here are some possibilities:

Tell a story about a time when you took a risk to try to learn something new, something that seemed impossible at first, or you did something you thought you couldn't do. This can be anything from learning to ride a bike, playing an instrument, staying home alone, or speaking in front of a group, to completing a semester of algebra.

A circle topic like this can be broken into two cycles. In the first, just ask students to talk about something new they learned *that seemed difficult at first.* This puts the different challenges into the circle. Then, the second time around, ask students to tell how they managed to deal with taking on this new experience. Allow for the complete range of human response, from diving headlong into the new experience to being dragged in forcefully. Through your example, make it okay for students to say that they resisted, ran away, refused. Make it clear that we may respond differently to each challenge we face, that we may show heroic courage in a new gymnastic routine and then shrink from telling someone that we admire them. What students learn from a circle like this is that we do, in fact, learn new things, and that there is a range of human response to the attempt to learn these things. *Tell about a time you...*

- *thought you couldn't do something and then you did it!*
- *took an emotional risk: speaking to someone you were really afraid to talk to; daring to have a different opinion; sticking up for a friend; talking out a conflict with someone rather than resorting to violence or gossip.*
- *tried something new and were successful.*
- *tried something new and failed.*
- *worried because someone you know took a risk.*
- *felt proud to see someone you know take a risk.*

Another impulse underlying the desire to use drugs is the very human wish to *change a mood or a perspective*. We live in a culture that advertises that every pain has its product, that one need not feel anything, physical or emotional. We learn in many ways that moods can be manipulated, altered, delayed, sustained.

There is a pill for everything. Kids know this, so much so that they see the hypocrisy of our telling them to live "drug free." Drug taking is a process of learning how to affect a mood swing, seeking the mood swing, and then ultimately using to feel normal. Perhaps we need to *acknowledge the desire to shift how we feel* and find a middle ground between heroic stoicism and primal scream. And in the process, perhaps, to give ourselves permission to feel.

Help students to see that they are always feeling something. They, and we, often suffer from alexithymia (a=not, lex=word, thym=feeling), *the condition of not having words for our feelings*. As noted above in the section on developing a vocabulary of feeling, a good place to start is with the big four: mad, sad, glad, and scared. Most other feelings are shades of these. You can use these as part of a "check-in." Here are some possibilities for circles around the issue of the need to change the way we feel: *Tell about ...*

- *a time when you were sad, worried, or upset. In the first round just say what you were sad, worried, or upset about. In the second round, say what you did, if anything, with the feeling or about the situation that may have caused it.* (Again, facilitators should model and allow for a complete range of responses.)
- *the different ways people distract themselves. What do you do to try to change the way you feel?* In a second round, discuss how successful these strategies were.
- *a time when you were so bored you thought you would die.* This often leads to a very lively circle! Then, in a second round, *tell how you dealt with the boredom.* (The experience of boredom, and long summer breaks, often provide ripe ground for first time drug use.)

- *a time you were scared. How did you deal with the fear?* (It is best to take these questions in two rounds since the students might resist the idea of sharing how they "deal" with a feeling. Once they are in, however, by having told about a fear, and by hearing others do the same, they may be more willing to take the next step.)
- *a time you were so angry you could have exploded. How did you deal with the anger?*
- *a time when you were truly sad. What, if anything, did you do with that feeling?*
- *the happiest moment you can remember. What caused your happiness*? You can deepen this circle by making it a witness circle that, after listening to rounds of sharing, can tackle the question, "What kinds of things seem to make people happy?"

Having these types of circles may not satisfy our need or our students' desire to speak freely about drugs. If so, we can make the proper referrals. What these circles can do is help students to see that everyone has feelings, that there is a range of coping strategies, and that there are many challenging and rewarding ways to take risks. These are the *healthy* perils.

Sex, Relationship, and Love

Once again, as circle facilitators we don't have a mandate to serve as sex educators. Students must have signed parent consent forms for discussion about sexual practices, and the notice to parents must include a detailed curriculum of topics to be covered. If students start to talk about their sexual experiences or have specific questions about practices, we generally refer them to their counselors, and they must know we will do this. Counselors can speak with them confidentially on these topics, but they, too, must observe the limits of confidentiality.

While it is inappropriate for us as facilitators to share our sexual histories, we are certainly free to model and give words to our feelings, especially when they are feelings we had as adolescents. Remember developmental appropriateness. A large part of the learning we experience as circle facilitators, working with young people in the affective domain, comes from our willingness to return, mentally and somatically, to the affective states of childhood. For example, before we ask *them* to share a time when they felt betrayed by a friend, it is incumbent upon *us* to fully revisit our own such story from childhood.

What is the value of having an adult present in a circle of young people? From their perspective, certainly not to have us preach to them about what they should or shouldn't do, feel, or tolerate. *The value of having an adult in children's circles is that we may, after long introspection, be able to put words to what we were feeling when we were children.* This modeling, in turn, shows young people that it is possible to put language to our feelings. For example, a child who is rebuffed in a first relationship risk may feel lonely, angry, inadequate, hurt, but it is rare that they can express these feelings in the moment. We, as facilitators, can model the possibility of putting words to these feelings.

In gender circles (to be described fully in Chapter 10), what young people most often want to know is "How can I get someone to like me?" "How will I know if someone likes me?" "How do I show someone that I like that person?" "What do others find attractive or off- putting?"

Young people, and apparently mainstream media—all of us, in fact—love a bit of titillation. But do we want our circles to be about the same topics that young people already spend a great deal of time with, out of our presence? Perhaps we have an opportunity, a rare and unusual one, to talk about *the real mystery: relationship*. As circle facilitators we are always looking to find the broader umbrella category under which a subtopic can reside. We have already looked at how the umbrella category for "death" is "loss." Likewise, we can say that for "sex," it is "relationship." Relationships range from anonymous to casual to committed and enduring, but there can be no sex without some form of relationship. Circles on the dynamics of relationships—how they form, evolve, endure conflict, heal, or dissolve—are of the greatest value.

Circles About Love

All literature is about love and loss, what binds us each to each and what separates us. We all long for deep connection, but while attempts to describe this thing we call "love" have filled many libraries, we still struggle to understand it. The Greeks called it "eros," and they gave us six categories to consider, with each offering many fruitful possibilities for circles.

I have used the following prompts with children as young as seven, regularly with adults, and most edifyingly in intergenerational groups. To warm up, I like to ask the group: *How many* of you have ever felt this thing we call "love?" How many have felt love for someone or something? How many have felt someone's or something's love for you? Now, think about a when you felt this thing called "love." Think of a place or an occasion when you felt it. (Perhaps give some examples.)

After opening the circle, use a speed round, perhaps several, to brainstorm and hear all voices. Use a prompt like, *Just say the name of the person or thing (object from the natural world, item, place, or activity) you associate with "love." Or just say the place or occasion where or when you felt it.* Follow with a story round that elicits a vignette, a particular time, using a prompt such as, *Tell about a time you* ***knew*** *you felt this thing called love, either for someone (or something) or from someone toward you (or even a time of self-love).* Once all the stories are shared, offer an echo or witnessing round: *Say something you heard another person say in the story round.* (A deeper witnessing would be to also say what it was that resonated for you in the story of another.) Finally, after closing, use a harvesting round: *Given the stories we just heard, what can we say about this thing we call "love?"*

It is at this point that you can offer a Shakespeare sonnet, a love song, or love story, and then compare what it says with the lived experience and collective understanding of the group.

With older students or adults, you might want to use the same process to explore the subtle differences between and within the six types suggested by the Greeks: *eros* (sexual love), *philia* (deep friendship), *ludus* (playful love), *agape* (love for all beings), *pragma* (long-standing love), and *philautia* (love of self). For a game option, after hearing each story of an experience of any form of love, the group can *guess* the type. Here are a few prompts for exploring some aspects of relationship: *Talk about ...*

- *a time when you knew you had a real friend. Describe the moment or experience when you were sure.* Try to keep this focused on that moment of awareness that something had shifted in the relationship. This provides for richer storytelling. Once the stories are all told, you can ask the circle to witness what they have heard about the qualities of friendship.
- *a time when you disliked someone and you found, after a while, that you liked that person.*
- *someone you really admired or were attracted to, but who you later discovered wasn't what you imagined.*
- *a time when you discovered that you really cared about another person.*
- *a time when you discovered that someone really cared about you.*
- For older students, you can use this show-don't tell prompt: *In that moment, the relationship changed.*

Sticks and Stones

When we are told, in circle, that students have witnessed or participated in some form of violence, we must make a quick assessment of the ongoing risk to that student or to others. If we find that there is a risk, or that we are unsure about the degree of risk, as mandated reporters we must take this outside of the circle. Students must know that we are required to do this.

You need only spend a short time on a school campus to see the excitement that erupts over conflict. A verbal or physical confrontation will draw waves of students around the campus in pursuit of ringside seats. It is no surprise that boxing is a major sport, with pay-per-view and multimillion-dollar purses. The reality is that life is full of conflict. Without conflict, there is no story. So, in general, it is fruitful to explore experiences of conflict that have passed. As with the circle on cruelty and kindness described above in Chapter 4, engaging in circles on the topic of conflict has the potential for raising consciousness so that decisions made in moments of conflict in the future might evoke a more thoughtful response. When there is enough distance in time from a conflict, in a circle we can examine adaptive and maladaptive strategies for dealing with it, thus providing a range of options other than simple or habitual, reactive responses. *Tell about a time you ...*

- *had a conflict, problem, disagreement, or fight with someone.* In a second round, *talk about how you dealt with the conflict or what happened afterwards.* Again, allow for a complete range of responses, and suggest that range with examples. In a follow-up to the circle, ask students to make a list of things they heard in these stories that seemed to make conflicts worse (maladaptive) and another of things that made them better or resolved them completely (adaptive).
- *had a conflict with someone, and you were able to work it out successfully.*
- *had a conflict with someone, and you were unable to work it out.*

After a circle about conflict, harvest *adaptive strategies* (actions that make a situation better) and *maladaptive strategies* (actions that make a situation worse).

We cannot legislate behavior. We can, however, provide opportunities for people to reflect on their behavior and perhaps take a beat before engaging in it repeatedly or automatically and so to make a *different* choice. Acknowledging the ever-growing normalization of profanity, insults, and put-downs used in public, in the media, and even in political discourse, the following circle protocol allows for exploration and reflection on words that hurt and words that heal.

Pre-circle activities:

The old saying "sticks and stones will break my bones, but words will never hurt me" is not always true. Words can hurt and words can heal. Ask students to say words they have heard that might hurt someone. List these on the board. Don't censor. In this context, it is appropriate to write whatever words the students say. After taking the first words that come, begin side coaching, gathering words that could hurt women, men, people who don't identify with a particular gender, Black people, white people, brown people, Mexican, Arab, Jewish, Christian, Muslim, people who are poor, immigrants, etc. This list will be long as there tend to be many more words that insult or demean than those that uplift and encourage.

Then, ask students for words that heal, words of appreciation and acknowledgment, words that give people strength to endure and to carry on, to raise them up when they are down, etc. Go through the categories again.

With the words still visible, ask: *How many of you have ever used any of the words that hurt? How many of you have ever been hurt by one or more of these words? How many have heard someone say any of the words that heal to you? How many of you have ever used one or more of these words to encourage, strengthen, heal, or just make someone feel better.*

Noting the likely unanimity of response, initiate the circle. To begin with a speed round, you can simply ask students to *say a hurtful word you remember someone directing at you or one that you used to hurt or insult another person.* Then, use a prompt like: *Share a story of hearing or using a word that hurts, an actual experience of having used or been the target of these words.* Use basic form with a web for additions followed by simple echo witnessing. For the second round: *Share a story of a time someone said something to you that made you feel better, or gave you strength and encouragement, or of a time that you said something to someone that helped that person feel better.* Follow with a witnessing round. Conclude with a harvest round, with participants noting what they are taking away from what they heard. If it seems appropriate, ask students to say one thing that could make the situation regarding words on campus better for all.

These circles provide students an opportunity to reflect on how words affect relationships. They will get a feeling of the life-affirming qualities of words that heal as well as a sense of the impact of words that hurt. If you notice a barrage of insults in your own class, and you are actively offering circles, when you convene, express as objectively as possible what you are noticing and the sadness and fear you have when you do. In the circle, you are seeking their input about how to make this situation better. If it becomes clear that there is ubiquitous use of words that hurt on a campus, an administrator, for example, can write a letter from the heart expressing their feelings when they notice this. A place is set for the administrator in the circle, and someone reads the letter. The questions to the group are something like: *What have you noticed about this issue on campus?* How have you been affected, and how have you participated? And what can we do to make it better (in this case, better would be a lessening of insults and other words that hurt).

Responding to School Crises: Loss and Death

When I was in the third grade at Cowillia Elementary School in Palm Springs, as we arrived one day we discovered that a student from our class was not present. Right next to me, Ricky's desk was empty. The teacher told the class matter-of-factly that there had been a fire at his house and that his whole family died. She seemed sad and uncertain of what to do next, and I recall that she just carried on with the lesson. I'm sure that I didn't understand what she meant, but I do remember being haunted by the image of the house burning and my friend inside feeling the flames.

My only experience with death up to that point was that of a pet hamster that we left too long in a hot laundry room. We buried him in the garden with some ceremony.

But what is to be done with the inevitable losses that occur in a school community: students, staff, and parents? And it is not only death that profoundly affects the relational field in a school. All losses are felt: staff leaving or transferring, classmates who move away, divorces, illnesses that affect the participation of various members of the school community, changes in employment, housing, and immigration status. Here in Los Angeles, fire took the homes and schools of many.

Wisdom Circles About Loss

As circle practice is meant to be proactive, it is never too early or too late to offer councils that explore the nature of loss and the range of human reactions associated with it. Everyone has lost something. Even the youngest children can tell stories about something they lost, and while it may not get any easier to cope with loss, at least we can begin to understand some adaptive strategies for dealing with it. We begin by simply asking students in the circle: *Name something you have lost,* and we might even add, perhaps as they get older, *something precious or meaningful.* You can give a few examples, but we don't usually offer death in the prompt. The range of examples can go from a favorite toy to the loss of a home, from an article of clothing to a best friend. After a *speed round* simply naming these things, begin a *story round* where students can talk about what they lost. In a third round, ask them to include how they reacted *after* the loss and what they did to cope with it. After round of *witnessing* the stories, close the council for a *harvesting* of "adaptive" and "maladaptive" coping strategies, or *things* you did that made the feeling of loss worse or that made things better. This kind of circle can be offered many times as the topic of loss is with us always but is rarely taken up in the school context. Let's consider a few specific losses and how circle might be useful and appropriate.

Accidental Death or As the Result of Illness or Natural Causes

When my mother passed, we had an intergenerational gathering. Some people brought photos and placed them in the center. The first round for those who wished was to tell *a story that comes to mind of an experience you had with Barbara*. The second round: *If Barbara were here to hear you (and perhaps she is), what would you like to say to her?* (Even the youngest were able to participate in this.) And finally, *in her honor, what if anything would you like to say to another person present in the circle?* The latter evoked expressions of gratitude, acknowledgments of wrongs done, and even brought about some healing of relationships that experienced harm long ago.

While there are considerable developmental considerations around the topic of death, doing nothing—or, as is often done, the school only finding out who has been affected and offering a support group—are hardly adequate responses. With the youngest children, K-2 for example, while they may not have a concept of death, they certainly experience absence and loss. It is honest to say, for example, that "Ricky has gone away, and I don't know where, but he will not be in our school anymore." You might even say that Ricky died, and that means he won't be with us anymore. It is crossing a line to say that he has gone to God or to heaven or is between worlds waiting to come into a new body—unless this is the common understanding in a parochial setting. Even in the latter circumstance, saying such a thing is *more likely to limit expression than to evoke it*. Such announcements are explanations meant to settle the issue and move on rather than offering the possibility to explore the loss and to grieve. They can temporarily relieve us of discomfort but rarely bring healing. If there are facts about the cause of the death, these can be offered by the teacher or by anyone who has this knowledge.

No matter the explanation, we are left with the reality of loss. The person we knew is no longer with us. To honor this loss is to engage in some form of the phases of a rite of passage: severance, threshold, and incorporation. Simply, these are opportunities *to reflect* and tell stories, *to clear* the plate and become fully present in the moment, and *to act* in a way that heals physically, mentally, emotionally, and spiritually.

Doing what is suggested here may very well evoke tears. The general suggestion when someone in the circle has a strong emotion is to have the circle pause and offer a "virtual hug," by placing full attention on the one grieving, who, when ready, will give a nod to indicate when it is time to move on. This response should be practiced *proactively* any time a strong emotion, such as an upwelling of anger or fear, occurs in the circles, so that it does not feel strange when this pause is offered in the grieving process. The same process is used when many begin to cry. The circle pauses until it is clear that we can continue.

Using the example of Ricky, the phases of reflecting, clearing, and acting can take a form something like this:

At the *severance* phase, you might offer the following:

- *When you think of Ricky, what is one word that comes to mind?*
- *Tell a story of a time you remember with Ricky.*
- *When you hear that Ricky is not going to be with us anymore, what would you like to say?*

At the *threshold* phase, you might do the following:

- *If Ricky were here with us right now, what would you want to say to him?*
- Offer art supplies for students to draw or sculpt whatever they wish and then to share these with the circle. At this point, avoid tying this to the loss as this is just an opportunity for individual students to get clear and present.
- Sing a song together.
- Play drums or make music in another way.
- Dance.

- Offer silent time or a mindfulness activity.
- With slightly older students you might offer a "medicine walk" or "silent walk" where they go out on the yard without engaging with other students doing the activity and notice whatever they notice and then return to the circle and recall what stayed with them.

For the *incorporation* phase, the group explores what they would like to do to remember or honor Ricky. A circle with the prompt: *What would you like to do or what do you think the class might do to remember Ricky?* is helpful. Record their answers. Some possibilities might include the following:

- A group art project or individual drawings put together in a book and presented to the family.
- A remembrance book that records class memories of Ricky.
- A remembrance board or space in the classroom where items related to Ricky can be gathered and assembled.
- A community service project done in Ricky's honor.

Suicide

When suicide occurs, the living are often plagued by guilt, wishing that they had known enough to act to prevent it. In schools, there is also the risk of contagion or "copycat" effects. Those of us who offer circles in the schools maintain, however, that the connection that ensues from regular circle practice will ultimately minimize the chances of students (and teachers) feeling unseen or suffering in isolation. As noted earlier, if anyone expresses that they are contemplating suicide or any form of self-harm, this is information that must be taken outside of the circle, and the students should be reminded of that fact. Our hope is that in the safety of the circle, we will hear about it before there is any attempt.

Given that a suicide often evokes guilt in those close to the person, we must make space for its expression in the circle. Noting that it is natural to feel like we could have done more, in addition to the steps suggested above, we might include a prompt such as: *What, if anything, did you notice that might have been a sign indicating that the person had been suffering to such an extent?* You can also call upon the *wisdom of the circle* as to what might be done should someone else exhibit these signs. And it is always appropriate to remind students of where and to whom they can go for help when they are suffering.

A school that embraces circle practice, where students feel safe to speak their truths, is likely to be privy to their inner lives, their joys and longings, their losses and suffering, as well as expressions of the desire to harm self or others. The fear of this happening is often something that will stop implementation of a circle program. While it will challenge our emotional capacity to embrace it all, the option of staying silent to keep a lid on things has proven to be disastrous.

Such a practice will test the resources of a school, and so we recommend that every school compile a resource guide of mental health services in the community, make sure that all stakeholders are aware of these, and where they are missing advocate for their presence. Most cities have Social Service Resource Guides. Schools must develop their own and make direct, personal contact with these groups and organizations. The US Department of Health and Human Services maintains a guide to federal resources, and the National Association of Social Workers (NASW) updates guides in each state.

Circle practice will inevitably both lift and break your heart. Hearts in isolation are limited in their capacity, and must, for their own protection, close. Open hearts together grow larger. If your school offers circles, be sure that the adults who facilitate them have a circle of their own.

A Tiered Approach to "Restorative" Practices

What we now call "restorative justice" comes to us from people who lived close to the earth and close to each other. It is a gift from people who knew something that perhaps we have forgotten—*we belong to each other; no one is expendable.* It has its roots in a worldview unfamiliar to most of us in the Western world, a view wherein *exile is seen as a fate worse than death.* It is a worldview wherein every child, every person, is precious and cannot be excluded even when that person has brought about grievous harm. As Howard Zehr, the foremost exponent of the modern iteration of restorative processes in the criminal justice system, puts it, "If crime implies hurt, then justice must involve healing." Or as Beverly Title states, "Restorative Justice is *accountability in a context of care.*" Where a "retributive" form of justice looks at what happened, who is to blame, and who should be punished, a "restorative" approach is one that looks at what happened, who was affected, what obligations the incident evokes, and how we *heal* from the harm done so that all parties not only repair the harm, but the relationships are restored.

While many schools are embracing restorative justice, much about the worldview described above is not appreciated. Put simply, *where there is no relationship, there is nothing to restore.* A culture that embraces circle ways must precede any "restorative" process. That is, we must build relationships and community before we can attempt to *restore* these things. Circles are the foundation upon which restorative processes operate. Without that foundation, restorative justice becomes a mere conflict mediation protocol rather than a process that brings healing and health to relationships and communities. True efforts to build relationships where every voice is valued, where there is a true "context of care," often appear too daunting, and school RJ programs fall away or are entrusted to an outside agency of a staff member who acts more like a discipline dean than a healer of relationships.

When we at Circle Ways offer systemic programs to schools, we only offer the workshop on restorative practices after staff has had a full year of circle practice. We understand that before attempting to restore relationships, there must first be creative, mutually enriching, joyful relationships among all school stakeholders. Then, when there is an inevitable bump in the road, all will be willing to do the hard work of taking individual responsibility for their actions when that bump occurs. To put it simply, if I don't care about you, why would I engage the effort to acknowledge and understand how my actions may have harmed you? The challenge is not with "accountability" but with creating a context of care.

The approach outlined here is tiered, with one level of intervention resting upon another. The foundation consists of systemic circle practice, nonviolent (or compassionate) communication, and mindfulness/wellness training and support. The second tier involves what we call "wisdom" or "issue" circles. The third is Peace Talks, training students to work though conflicts with peers and others. Fourth-tier interventions involve processes mediated by trained students and staff. And last is what is called a Formal Restorative Conference, reserved for issues of great harm that affect many in the school community.

Tier 1: The Foundation

Restorative justice is not a program. It is not a protocol. It is not mediation or conflict "resolution." It is a complete shift of consciousness, a circle-based worldview, and it is not "new." It is embodied in the Zulu term "ubuntu," meaning "I am because you are"; in the Seneca greeting "niyawen," meaning "thank you for being;" in the Sanskrit "namaste," meaning "what is divine in me bows to what is divine in you;" and in the authentic practice of circles. Also, in the foundation, we suggest training in Marshall Rosenberg's Nonviolent Communication (NVC), and we include a few of its elements in Circle Ways' trainings. NVC is *how* we can deepen our ability to speak and listen "from the heart." That is, to speak in a way that can be heard, that does not foist blame on the listener but fully communicates how we feel and what we need from others. And NVC is to listen with empathy, to understand how another person is feeling and what they are needing. NVC requires progressive skill-building, distinguishing observations from evaluations, recognizing our feelings and the basic needs that underly them, and making effective requests and apologies. Finally, a restorative culture must actively promote *mindfulness and wellness practices*: meditation, yoga, intuitive eating, nutrition education, exercise, dance, play, and journaling are among the many possibilities. In addition, we learn how to rely on the classroom and school community to support adherence to our healthy lifestyle choices. More on this in Chapter 12.

Tier 2: Wisdom and Issue Circles

Tapping the wisdom of the circle is something that happens naturally. When we listen deeply in a circle, insights and new directions of thought will emerge. Wisdom comes from cumulative experience, and in the circle, we are privy not only to our own but the to the experiences of many. One kind of *wisdom circle* is a conflict *"exploration."*

Conflict "resolution" is a myth, particularly when solutions are imposed from the outside. In circle, our aim is understanding—what happened, why it happened, and what is to be done. Although the term "conflict" generally has a negative connotation, viewed in terms of narrative it is the essential driving force of a plot. Conflict is what creates interest. When we remove it artificially, deus ex machina, the audience complains ruefully. In effect, life and literature would be quite boring without conflict. Through conflict exploration in circle, we can reframe the term so that it returns to its roots as a necessary catalyst for change. Children in conflict—with each other, with us, with the world—must learn to view themselves not as "bad" but as participants in the necessary polarity, the necessary divisions, the drama, the unfolding story that proceeds creative new possibilities for relationship and action.

We begin this reframing by looking at conflict in general and then, when it is viewed as something human and universal, we can begin to explore interpersonal conflicts in the circle and celebrate them as opportunities for understanding and change.

Begin with a discussion of the term "conflict." You might ask: *When you hear the word "conflict," what comes to mind?* Students might share out some synonyms, like *problems, fights, arguments*, and *wars*; more personal associations like *my little sister, homework, curfews, getting money*; or more broadly, concerns like racism, poverty, health care, and the justice system.

Acknowledge that conflict takes many forms and that everyone alive experiences some form of it every day. Begin circle as usual. Prompt the circle: *Think about the words and ideas that we just shared related to conflict. When the talking piece comes, recall a time when you experienced a conflict in your life. Just tell the story of what happened.* After a round of such stories, suggest a witnessing round by asking: *Recalling what you just heard in the stories shared, what kinds of conflicts have students in the circle experienced?* Once the stories are in the circle, prompt a second round: *Now tell what happened after the conflict. Was it resolved? Forgotten about? Is it still going on? If it was resolved, how did that happen? If it wasn't, why do you think that is so?* Such a round provides information about the many ways we manage or mismanage conflict, the dark and the light, the adaptive and maladaptive strategies. In a final round, ask students to reflect on what they have heard about what causes conflicts, what seems to perpetuate them, and from what they have heard, what are some ways of dealing with them?

This is considered a conflict "exploration" because we are reflecting on past incidents of conflict rather than those that may be happening in the moment. All participants have an opportunity for reflection in a safe and nonreactive state. Harmful strategies, like having punched a wall, are allowed to stand along with helpful strategies. In the circle, we are investigators, curious about the very human experience of being in conflict.

Another iteration of conflict exploration is the *Socratic dialogue in spiral form:* this form can be applied to interpersonal conflict, but here I present it as a practice with issues that may be important to students but are not urgent in the moment. As we know, Socrates would debate topics such as the meaning of "truth" and "beauty," but for the sake of relevance, here students begin by creating a list of topics about which people clearly have contrasting views. The greater the pro-con polarity, the better: the death penalty, gun control, affirmative action, etc.[9] You can also create polarities based on situations in the literature they are reading or an event in history. You can even explore a decision that the class is facing.

Place four seats in the middle of the circle and designate two facing one another as Advocates for Position A and the other two Advocates for Position B. As with any circle using the spiral form, one person speaks (in this case an Advocate for A), then listens to the next person (an Advocate for B), and then opens the space to be filled by another advocate of that position. After the spiral winds down, it is valuable to have the outer circle witness what they have heard from both sides. Another twist for this activity is to ask students to advocate for a position *other* than their own.

An *issue circle* is one where the group takes up a particular problem that has been identified either by the students, like pushing on the playground, or by the teacher, like students not coming prepared for class. Before the issue circle happens, the group must agree that the issue is indeed a problem and that they want to understand what it is about, why it is happening, and what they can do about it. The issue circle is not about blame. It is about understanding what happened and what can be done about it.

Sometimes an issue is something that affects the whole school. In one such instance at Palms Middle School, principal Hugh Gottfried noticed that during passing periods students were running out a set of double doors leading to the quad. Between the doors was a vertical post, and principal Gottfried was concerned that someone was going to be injured. As might have been expected, he could have simply gone on the PA and announced that students *must* stop running in the hall and that there would be consequences, such as closing the student store for a week, if the behavior did not stop. Instead, because we had a systemic circle program, principal Gottfried wrote a *personal* message, speaking from the heart about his *fear* that someone could be gravely hurt by slamming or being pushed into that post in a crush of students. His message included an appeal for students to help *him* find solutions to the problem. In each of our classroom circles that week, a seat was held for principal Gottfried, but because our school of 2,000 students had nearly 100 circles every week, in lieu of his presence his statement was read as if he were a member of the circle. The talking piece was then passed for students to offer their stories, their observations, about the issue. Finally, there was a request for possible actions we could take to prevent accidents in the hallway. These suggestions were recorded and submitted to school leadership. The simple fact that time was taken to consider the issue raised the consciousness of the school community. That the principal offered his observation in such a heartful way, emphasizing his fear and concern, rather than as a threat, gave students agency to be part of the solution.

Tier 3: Peace or Restorative Talks

In all cases, our aim as educators is to give students the tools and experience to solve their own conflicts. Before this tier three intervention can be effective, students must have practice with the sequence of restorative questions:

1. What happened?
2. What were you thinking and feeling at the time?
3. What needs to happen to make things better?
4. What can you do to make things better?

Responding to each of these questions requires significant skill-building opportunities for students of all ages. None of them can be answered effectively without the foundation of community. The first question—"What happened?"—assumes that students feel capable of describing an event as objectively as possible. This is where the experience of storytelling they get with regular circle practice is most valuable. The second question assumes students can name their feelings, and so exercises in developing such a vocabulary become vital as noted earlier in this chapter. The third question requires experience with what in this chapter we are calling "adaptive strategies," and this is acquired through practice in the wisdom and issue circles. For the fourth question, to state a commitment to a restorative action, students must have practice stating intentions with clear, short-term behavioral objectives. Doing this is also a product of the intention-setting circles described above. And finally, students in a peace or restorative talk learn to check with each other as to whether the stated intentions are acceptable. Simply asking, "What do you think? Would that work for you?" is one way to initiate this check.

In many classes there is a peace or restorative talk corner where students can go when they have an issue to work through. On a table, there is a bell to begin, some talking pieces, and a printout of the restorative questions. Once the council (often dyadic) has begun, students take up one question at a time, passing the talking piece back and forth. Sometimes students will witness or repeat what they heard the other say and then check to see whether they got it right.

Whether the peace or restorative talk is dyadic or a group, what is crucial with the peace or restorative talks is that *all participants agree to conduct it.* If even one student is not willing to participate, we move toward the next tier: the mediated restorative circle.

Tier 4: Mediated Restorative Circles

In Chapter 10, I will take up youth circle leadership and youth-led restorative mediation. I'd like to simply note here again that the aim is for students to lead these processes and so to take these valuable skills with them as they go through life. If there is reluctance on the part of any person involved to engage in a leaderless restorative talk, then we offer a *mediated talk.*

Essentially, the mediator keeps participants on track with the restorative questions and checks for understanding by calling for mutual witnessing so that all parties feel heard and understood. In addition, the mediator will often record the agreements determined by those involved and call for signatures to affirm them.

In some instances, a conflict between two individuals in a class affects the whole class. In this case, the mediator is the circle itself. The following is an instance of such a conflict. The process involves inviting the two in conflict to each designate a personal witness to sit with them in a fishbowl inner circle. The function of these personal witnesses, or "coaches" in the story below, is to diminish emotional reactivity, slow the process of exchange, and rephrase the statements of the two in conflict. The process can use the restorative questions noted above, or, as in the story to come, a freer form can be offered.

An experience I had one Valentine's Day at the middle school will illustrate a mediated intervention. As I was escorting a group of sixth grade boys to a room for a gender-separate circle, two boys, Andres and Daniel, squared off to fight. I told them that I would allow them to "fight" when we got to the room. Both expressed disbelief, but I assured them that I was serious. Once we arrived, I asked them to each choose a "coach," and I instructed the rest of the students to form a "ring." I told the whole group that it's easy to fight with fists, much more difficult to fight with words. Andres, picking up on my ruse, ran out the door. I followed him and managed to convince him to come back and give the circle a try.

Four boys sat in a center circle, Andres and Daniel, and their two "coaches," Byron and Manuel. Once we opened the circle, one student took the talking piece to say what happened that caused the conflict. After his opening statement, Andres passed the piece to Byron (his coach), who paraphrased what Andres had said. He checked with Andres to see if he got it right.

This paraphrase by the "coach" is intended to decrease emotional reactivity. Then the talking piece passed to Daniel, and the process was repeated for several exchanges. In the process, it emerged that Andres didn't like Daniel calling him "Horse."

There seemed to be little movement, just more threats, with one small exception. The outer circle picked up the fact that this seemed to be going nowhere, and many began to slump in their chairs and pull their attention away from the exchange. Sensing this shift in energy, Andres ventured, "I could go for a truce if you could promise to stop looking at me all the time." Daniel did not pick up on this opening, and he issued a new threat. At this point, I asked that the talking piece go around the outer circle for witnessing. Witnesses shared what they remembered of what they saw and heard. Something seemed to shift. There was an echo that could only happen in circle. Many students picked up on the offer of a truce.

The talking piece returned to the inner circle, and the process continued, but there seemed to be some softening between the combatants. At one point, Daniel revealed that he started calling Andres "Horse" in the fourth grade because he thought a horse is a strong animal. Andres was not quite ready to hear or accept this explanation. As our time was ending, I asked, "What can each of you do to make this situation better?" They both agreed not to fight ... for now. I asked them to keep that promise until we came back to the circle the following week. They agreed.

The next morning as I was walking to my class, I saw Daniel sitting with friends. He greeted me with, "Are we going to have circle with just the boys again next Friday?" I assured him that we would, and I again congratulated him for making the effort. After the nutrition break, Andres found me as I was returning to my room. This was completely out of the ordinary since before this time he would not have looked at me on campus. He began with, "That was pretty good yesterday. Can we fight again in circle next Friday?"

"How is the truce going so far?" I asked.

"Fine. He didn't look at me in class today, and I didn't call him 'Horse.'"

Will the truce hold? Was the conflict "resolved?" Perhaps not. As far as I knew, though, and from their teacher Diane's report, the boys had no further incidents the rest of the semester. Rather, we might say, the conflict was "explored," as it often is in this form of circle, and the whole group had the experience of broadening the meaning and potential in the term "fight."

Another incident shows how the circle can have a restorative effect on the student-teacher relationship. I had particularly challenging eighth-grade class. After eight or so circles, I was ready to deem this group "not ready for council." One day, they walked particularly slowly to the council room, and I had to prod them on. When we got to the room, some stood by the walls, others sat on tables, but only a few came to sit in the circle.

All sense of compassion vanished. I was an angry, isolated leader in a group of uncaring, stupid, cynical teenagers. "What is going on here? I'm trying to get you guys to our council space, and you're all lagging and lolling, hanging back, taking your time. This is a part of our class! Council is a part of English class. We're trying to learn how to talk and listen to each other in a new way. And you guys don't get it. You don't see what a *great opportunity* you have here. People don't know how to tell the truth to each other. Nobody listens. And we have a chance to do it here, and you guys are blowing it!"

They were all looking at me now. The talking had stopped. "Look, if you have something you want to tell me, go ahead. Let's start the council and say whatever you want, and I'll listen to you, and I won't interrupt you, and I won't kick you out. I had a plan. I had something interesting for us to talk about. I thought about it very carefully, but now I don't think there's enough time. So, if you've got the guts, go ahead and say whatever it is you have to say! I'll put the talking piece in the center. Anyone who wants to start can take it."

I was fuming. Why do I even try? These kids don't care. I don't care. What a waste of everyone's time.

Elisio, sitting just to my left, took the stick, decorated with some initials, tag names, and a Band-Aid. He settled onto his mat and began. "Provisor, you think you're such a hard ass." He looked to see if I was going to keep my promise. I gave him an expressionless, unchanging gaze.

He continued, "You're always on my case. 'Where's your homework? Get in your seat. Quit talking.'" He then passed the piece. With a few exceptions, each student spoke and basically echoed Elisio's sentiment, although one student said, "I think Provisor is OK" before passing the piece.

When it was my turn, I told them how hard it was for me to try to teach them, to prepare lessons and not have them bring materials or do what I was asking of them. Then, I passed again to Elisio, and the critique of my teaching continued.

There was still time for another round. It was Elisio's turn again. He began, "You want to know what I'm really afraid of? *I'm afraid I won't live to be 18*. You come to my neighborhood and see how people die. You keep telling me I have to do this and that so I can get a job when I grow up. I'm afraid I'll be dead before I grow up!"

He passed the talking piece to Mario, dropping it hard into Mario's upturned palm. Mario spoke for the first time. "I'm afraid everybody in my family is going to die. My brother's in jail, and sometimes my sister doesn't come home." The talking piece continued around the circle.

"I'm afraid my parents are going to split. They fight all the time. It seems like they never talk to each other anymore. They're always yelling."

"There are lots of drugs in my neighborhood. I know where these guys are that sell them. I have to walk the long way through the alley if I want to stay away from them. And I don't like walking in the alley."

And so it went, each student, unprompted, sharing what was probably the thing that makes school a place to let go of the fear and to be their goofy, innocent, selfish, loving selves, perhaps the only place where they can play and mess around. And even council, with the formality of its circle, the talking piece, one person speaking at a time, everyone required to listen, reminded them of the visceral tightness of the neighborhood outside.

I felt waves of sensation, sinuses and tear ducts activated, my heart breaking open. There was a minute or so left. I got the talking piece. "Thank you. Thank you for helping me understand who you are. You all spoke from the heart. I'm honored to sit in council with you. If it's OK, I'd like to come back next week."

A few smiles. A few nods. I knew we would be back next week. Did I change my expectations? Did I lighten up on the work? No. If anything, I found that what these young people were capable of, what they had inside them, was beyond the confines of my expectations.

Council changed, too. The last seven sessions began promptly, no visitors were allowed, and the lingering, the lolling, and the lagging now occurred *after* the dismissal bell had rung.

Tier 5: Formal Restorative Conferencing

This level of restorative process must be facilitated by a trained person who is neutral and does not have a stake in the outcome. It poses a challenge in schools because conferences are usually conducted by counselors or administrators. Some school districts employ restorative mediators who travel from school to school when such high-level incidents occur. Vandalism, theft, harassment, and extreme defiance are some of the high-level harms that call for restorative conferencing. It is beyond the scope of this book to detail all the steps in this process. It is part of our second-year training at Circle Ways, and there are many reputable agencies who can offer this relatively standardized course for educators.[10]

Essentially, the restorative conference process involves three stages: pre-conferencing, the conference itself, and follow-up. In schools, incidents that rise to this level are usually handled by suspension. Students are removed from the environment for a time or until a conference with parents can be arranged. This may still be the case in a restorative process as it allows for an opportunity to assess who was involved and who was affected.

In the *pre-conferencing* phase, those directly involved in the incident are contacted first to explain what the restorative conference is and to get an agreement to participate. We begin with the individual or individuals who appear to be the "perpetrators" (sometimes called the "respondents," and so-called "victims" are called "claimants"). They are told that they will have an opportunity to meet with the person or persons who claim to have been harmed and that the aim of the meeting will be to find ways to make things right between them. If these people are not willing to participate, that is the end of the process, and traditional (retributive) discipline measures are used. Sometimes saying this can help sway those involved to participate. We also explain that to participate, you must be willing to take responsibility, to tell the truth about what happened and your part in it. As we are having these pre-conferences, we are discovering any others who might have been affected by the incident. For example, an act of vandalism in the school not only affects the building itself, but also those who may be inconvenienced, such as the students and teacher of a class that has been disrupted. So, too, the administrators, parents, and even facilities people who must be involved with clean-up.

This aspect of determining *who has been affected* can be challenging as we tend not to see the extent of the impact an incident has on others not directly involved. So, to prepare students we use the conflict exploration process explained above to see how a conflict between two people can sometimes affect the whole community.

Formal conferencing is not per se a circle or council. It does use circular seating, but the dynamic is more "triangular" in that the meeting is heavily directed by the facilitator.

In the formal conferencing phase, a particular seating arrangement is used, with the respondent and claimant sitting next to the facilitator and supporters of each as well as others affected by the incident following on from them. The facilitator then guides the group through the restorative questions sequence, essentially: What happened? What were you thinking and feeling at the time? What do you need or what can you do to make things right? And what actions will you commit to? The facilitator then draws up an agreement for all to sign and designates someone, usually an administrator or counselor, to oversee the completion of the agreements.

The *follow-up* involves both monitoring accountability for the actions agreed to and *reintegrating* the respondent back into the community. The latter involves some real creativity depending on the offense and the developmental level of the students involved. If reparations are made, a message that these steps have been taken must be conveyed to the community, to let everyone know that the agreements have been carried out, and that all parties are satisfied. Sometimes this is done by a letter to all members of the school community, and other times, for example if only one class has been affected, there may just be a statement to that effect by the teacher.

A Final Word on Restorative Justice

As I have noted above, this fifth tier of restorative practice rests upon a foundation of deep and joyful circle practice. This restorative paradigm shift is no less than a shift of culture and worldview. No amount of "training" will create this shift and putting the burden on a few restorative justice counselors will not change the culture in schools. If restorative justice is seen as just something we do with students who misbehave, rather than a way of being, it will not be successful. When a teacher suggests that students "listen and speak from the heart" and that is not a practice the teacher lives, students will smell a rat and not trust the process.

For anyone wanting to get a deeper understanding of the worldview, the cultural shift, that engenders a restorative mindset, I refer you to Rupert Ross's extraordinary account presented in his book, *Returning to the Teachings: Exploring Aboriginal Justice* (1996).[11] Ross was a district attorney in Manitoba, Canada who was tasked with determining why there was such disproportionate incidents, compared to the general Canadian public, of domestic abuse, sexual violence, and suicide among the indigenous population in the province. It is an account of Ross's 10-year awakening to the meaning of a circle-based worldview. At first, his Western mind was completely bewildered by what he was hearing from the first nation's peoples. After a long period of confusion, he comes to understand how different this worldview is from the one to which he has been acculturated. One of many insights he has is that English is a *noun-based* language so especially well-suited to classifying things, while the language originally spoken by the indigenous people is verb-based. That is, things (and people) are seen as processes, rather than rigid fixed entities. The word for a "table" conveys awareness of where it came from, what it is now, and what it will become. Applied to people, this means that when we categorize each other, when we put each other in boxes, it is very difficult to see that a person can be more or other than the label we put on them. Restorative processes require us to see that people can change and that relationships can be restored.

When restorative justice is seen as a "program" or a "protocol" and is hastily rolled out (in 50-minute "training" sessions) by people who have no understanding of its roots and foundation, teachers will naturally reject the process. They too smell a rat. Sadly, this lack of understanding has devastating effects beyond a distrust of the program. It causes a distrust of the circle itself, a lack of confidence in our ever being able to live harmoniously with others and the natural world. And if we as teachers carry a conviction that the world *cannot* become a better place, our students will rightfully reject whatever it is we attempt to teach. A thoughtless roll-out of a beautiful practice poisons the well of possibility.

For restorative justice to work, the adults in the school community must practice what they preach. This means parents and teachers, teachers and administrators, staff and parents with local elders, merchants, and service providers—all sitting down together to walk the talk of mutual respect. And this must *not* be done only when there is conflict or a breach of relational norms. This "field" of positive adult interaction creates an atmosphere wherein we can begin to honestly offer circle practice to the students. We cannot hold our students to a higher standard than that to which we hold ourselves and our culture. They know when we are again asking them to do something we don't do.

The eye-for-an-eye, tooth-for-a-tooth retributive mindset is so ingrained in our culture that most people can't even imagine what it takes to heal relationships that have been harmed. The first step is to return to practices that develop empathy and relationship. For "restorative" justice to be viable, we must first establish connection and community. Without this sense of connection, no one will do the hard work of restoration and healing of relationships.

For Reflection and Imagination

1. Look back at the five "inner resource" categories (p. 293).

- Makes lists for yourself from each category.
- Take one of your listed resources and recall as fully as you can what happened with that person, at that place, during that event, what those words mean to you and at time you called upon them for comfort, or what you do that is an expression of one of your core qualities.
- Now "ground" that resource more fully by drawing or crafting something or write about it in such a way that if a person were to read what you wrote, they would gain a good understanding of why and how that is a resource for you.
- Dance in a way that expresses how you feel when you think about that resource.
- Consider the topic at the heart of that experience, and craft a prompt that would elicit stories from others related to that topic.

2. Reflect on an interpersonal issue that you have noticed in your classroom, with your colleagues, in your counseling caseload, or in your experience as a parent, then ...

- Craft a prompt that would evoke stories, recollections of lived experience (rather than opinions or judgments), for those involved in that issue.
- Think about the story you might tell related to your experience with that issue.

3. Make a list of people with whom you can recall having significant conflict, the write about ...

- What happened?
- What were you thinking and feeling at the time?

- What outcome were you hoping for?
- What would you ask of the other that, if agreed to, would restore the relationship?
- What did you or could you have offered that, if accepted by the other, would have brought some healing to the relationship?

Chapter 9:
Circles in the Relational Arts

1. **Use Restorative Circles to Address Harm**
   Circle can be a powerful tool to restore trust and repair relationships after incidents of harm, including emotional outbursts, physical aggression, or community-wide disruption.

2. **Respond to Trauma with Structure and Compassion**
   In times of crisis or loss, such as the death of a student or experiences of violence, circle offers a structured space for students to grieve, process, and support one another.

3. **Create Safe Spaces for Gender Identity and Expression**
   Circle allows students to share experiences related to gender, sexuality, and identity. Prompts that invite personal storytelling can foster understanding, safety, and belonging.

4. **Navigate Sensitive Topics with Care and Intentionality**
   Facilitators must remain attuned to the emotional temperature of the group. Use pre-circle check-ins and post-circle processing to support vulnerable students.

5. **Include but Don't Center the Facilitator**
   In emotionally charged circles, the educator's role is to create a container—not to dominate. Speak as one among many, and let students' voices lead the healing.

6. **Use Circle to Break Silence Around Taboo Topics**
   Difficult conversations about suicide, bullying, or sexual harassment can be initiated in circle using carefully crafted, story-based prompts that make space without forcing disclosure.

7. **Embrace Circle as a Tool for Justice and Inclusion**
   When designed with intention, circle practice can challenge systemic inequities, affirm marginalized identities, and foster an inclusive classroom culture rooted in shared humanity.

10

FOLLOWING THEIR LEAD: WHAT STUDENTS WANT TO KNOW AND THE ROLE OF CIRCLES IN RITES OF PASSAGE

WITH THE INCREASING rate of technological, cultural, and environmental change, any curriculum we design is immediately obsolete. If we are not listening to the needs of our students and are unable to remain flexible and adapt, we will not be able to serve them. This chapter will provide some guidance for handing off leadership to students and further deepening their sense of agency and ownership in circle processes.

Circle-based learning is as old as time, so taking the long view, we return to one of the root meanings of the word "educate:" to "bring out" what is within a person rather than to "put in" our pre-determined curriculum and standards. This is not the tabula rasa view of children. It is more akin to seeing each child as a gift from the universe waiting for some assistance in unwrapping itself. Each child is a unique and necessary offering to the community. According to Bonnie Bernard, in her study of resilience, the single most significant factor contributing to the success of a student is a relationship with one stable adult who "sees and expects" the best in and from the child.[1] The challenge in this equation for resiliency is not about having high expectations, it is in *seeing* the gift a particular child brings to the world.

This chapter will explore how we access what is alive in each child, offer ways for them to turn towards those things, and then ultimately how we turn over circle leadership to our students. It will also cover how we create space for youth to turn towards their and our deepest fears about the future and the global crises we now face.

We begin by looking at student "mysteries," what is alive in their heart/minds at this moment, their deepest longings and their fears, and how to structure circle experiences for them to deepen their awareness, understanding, resiliency, and resolve. Then, we turn to youth council and restorative practice leadership. Finally, we return to the critical role of meaningful rites of passage in the lives of young people.

Student Mysteries

I can't remember a time in grade school when I was asked what *I* wanted to learn, what I cared or wondered about. I also don't recall the issue of what students *want to know* coming up in my teacher training. As a teacher, I developed the lesson plans and assignments, and students were to learn what I had to teach them. I was enacting what Paulo Freire calls the "banking model" of education with my predetermined deposit of what I, *and the state,* wanted them to know. Yes, I allowed students from time to time to choose which books they wanted to read independently. I would even ask students to fill out an "attitude/interest survey" on the first day of class—mostly so I could relate *what I was teaching* to their interests.

In the mid '80s, I discovered a book by Rebekah Caplan called *Writers in Training* in which she suggests a project called "The I-Search."[2] I-Search rather than Re-Search. For this project, students search for information on *a topic of importance to them,* rather than "searching again" what others had deemed important. The emphasis is on primary sources. For about 15 years, the I-Search was a yearlong standard assignment in my eighth- or ninth-grade classes.

It was at this time that I came upon a process called "mysteries," which was being used at Crossroads School in Santa Monica. I am grateful to Rachel Kessler, author of *The Soul of Education,* for introducing me to the concept of mysteries and to the teachers at the school who were practicing it.

Part of the inspiration for making mysteries a centerpiece of my classroom circles (and later circles with educators, parents, and community members as you will see in Chapter 12), came from seeing the following quote from poet Rainer Maria Rilke, which I found posted on a wall at The Ojai Foundation:

"Be patient toward all that is unsolved in your heart and try to love the questions themselves, like locked rooms and like books that are now written in a very foreign tongue. Do not now seek the answers, which cannot be given to you because you would not be able to live them. And the point is, to live everything. Live the questions now. Perhaps you will then gradually, without noticing it, live along some distant day into the answer."[3]

The quote is from Rilke's book *Letters to a Young Poet.* The young poet Rilke refers to was a soldier who had a longing to become a great poet and so he wrote to the most famous German poet of the time. His letters asked for responses from the elder poet to questions about life, love, and art. The big questions. Rilke's answer was to "try to love the questions themselves." Just how do we do that? As I describe the following process, which has become the cornerstone of our work with all school stakeholders, you will see lists of mystery questions that appear impossible to answer, and to read many of them together can be overwhelming, but we must face the reality of these concerns and create conditions where students can explore possibilities for action.

To "love the questions" is to hear them, to let them linger in awareness *without seeking an answer*. You will see that the answers come in the form of collective *understandings based on the lived experiences shared in the circles*. This collective understanding then forms the basis for further inquiry and inviting other primary (people) and secondary (books, articles) voices into the awareness of the circle.

The Mysteries Process

The mysteries process begins by having students consider the questions that most impact their lives currently. I like to say, *These are the questions that wake you up at night. They are questions that even though you may have asked trusted adults and* consulted books, it still feels like you don't quite have the whole answer. Or, I simply ask them what they *wonder* about. The questions can be the big ones of life, how things came to be, why things are the way they are, why people do what they do, or what the future will bring. And they can be very personal, questions about family and friends, relationships, and interests. If they have personal questions, I ask that they leave out the name of the person to whom they refer.

Students are then given time to reflect, sometimes in the moment or over a longer period to encourage more consideration. I then ask them to *anonymously* write three or four of these questions legibly on a card. (Younger students can dictate to a scribe.) We place the folded cards into a "wonder basket" in the center of our circle. After we open the formal circle, the basket is used as a talking piece and passed from student to student. One at a time, students pull a card randomly from the basket and read what is written there *as if the questions were your own.*

Just this one round of reading and listening to carefully considered mysteries makes the world a bit *less* mysterious. The group members often hear that they are not alone, that others have the same questions. This round of circle alone is an extraordinary experience—even if we don't follow up by trying to address the questions.

I collect the cards and type them up to be resubmitted to the circle later. In a class of 30, we might have 150 mysteries. This process is a training for students to be able to conduct circle independently throughout their lives. We begin by searching for *inherent topics* in each question. For example, *Why is it that, throughout history, nations and peoples enter into wars? Is there not a better way?* is a question about *conflict,* with *war* being a subcategory. We then start to look at the *resonances* within the list, we see topics coming up again and again with slight variations. Then, we *prioritize* the topics in order of importance.

Here is a list I gathered recently from a class of seventh graders at an inner-city school. They had experienced trauma several years earlier because of the handling of a teacher sex abuse scandal:

- Why didn't you give me a hug or tell me earlier?
- Why am I so ugly?
- Why is my dad still buying sugar at the store and hasn't come back?
- Why did my dad choose beer over my sister and me?
- Why do people even try if it is all going to fade away?
- What happens after you die?
- Why does everybody go away?
- Why did thug life choose me?
- How can you get wiser?
- Are dreams portals to another dimension?
- Why do people separate families just because they are immigrants?
- Why do we have bad people who can live with themselves?
- Why do we rob innocent people who have done only good?
- What is that "better place" everyone talks about?
- Why do we have wars against other innocent people?
- Are you going to look after me?
- Are you going to miss me?
- Why is pain always within you?
- Why does my friend always destroy my hopes?
- How is my dad feeling when so much has happened?
- Why do humans judge each other on their appearance?
- Why does ____ not stop doing what she is doing even though it hurts everyone?

One can imagine the stories behind these questions. Read in a list like this, the experience is overwhelming. To diminish the emotional charge, to gain some distance and perspective, as we move from *question to prompt,* the first question I ask is: *What is this question about; what is at the heart of it; what is its kernel or core?* For example, the questions "Why does everybody go away?" and "Are you going to miss me?" have at their core the topic of *loss.* We look for the broad, general categories in which these questions are a subset. Looking at the entire list above, we might say that the most resonant topics are the following: *loss, change, death, destiny, crime, relationship, morality, dreams, and wisdom.* As described in Chapter 4, to form an effective prompt, we begin with a topic and then shape it so everyone can access a story in some way related to the topic.

Having offered the process to my middle-school students for over 20 years, I found that the single most prevalent mystery was "*What happens after you die?*" Quite dramatic as you can see. We can gain distance from the drama by asking ourselves what is the kernel, the inherent topic, in this question? For this example, we might say "death" is the topic at its core. If we choose this topic, and we want students to access memories of direct experiences, how do we frame a prompt about death? How do we move from a recitation of beliefs and get to stories? And what are we to do with the qualifier "after," as the students have said that they want to know not only about "death" but what happens "after?"

What is really going on when we ask about "life after death?" One possibility is that this phenomenon we call death is one of many forms of *loss.* "Loss" is a category within which "death" is a subset. We certainly could have a circle on what students "believe" or have been told about life after death. Beliefs, however, are not stories—unless we examine the experiences that led to those beliefs. Also, not every student (we hope) has had a direct experience of someone close to them dying, and we would *never* use the prompt *Tell about a time someone close to you died.* Although they might *choose* to bring up such experiences, we don't want to require such disclosure.

A more common, universal experience is that of losing *something* important or meaningful. We have all experienced this. Perhaps the longing inherent in this question is to know how we carry on living *after* a profound loss. In this case, a prompt could be: Tell about a time you lost something that was important to you. To this you can add some examples: "It could be a favorite thing, an important or meaningful possession. It could be a person or other living thing. It doesn't have to be a death. It could be the loss of a pet or a friend you lost. It could be the loss of leaving a familiar place, like a home, a town, or a country." Once you have determined that everyone has lost something—by a show of hands for example—you can begin the circle. The stories give a sense of the many ways we human beings experience loss. A useful second round, especially in this case, is to ask, "What did you do after you had this loss?" Such a round usually brings out the spectrum of responses to loss—everything from forgetting about it to being completely unable to let it go—multiple iterations of Kubler-Ross's stages of grief: denial, anger, bargaining, depression, and acceptance. You might even ask students to categorize adaptive and maladaptive strategies for coping.

There are other significant considerations when you facilitate a circle on the topic of loss and death, even though everyone by school age has had many such experiences.

One is your own capacity to listen deeply to your students' stories. Consider the facilitating story *you* might tell if you are speaking in such a circle. If you have lost a loved one, and you are still actively grieving, consider whether you want the students to share your grief, to help you hold it. *If that is the case, think twice, and then don't.* Better perhaps to model speaking about the loss of a childhood friend or a treasured possession. A useful question to ask yourself before you share a story is: *Will it serve the circle?*

There are also cultural and religious considerations with a topic such as loss and death, and developmental appropriateness is crucial. You will likely get into some emotionally heavy material. My experience is that the circle, the container, will invite only as much as it can hold. Often in the circles someone who is still grieving a loss hears a story from someone else that brings a kind of balance to the emotional situation. I have also seen students time and again create a loving space for anyone who genuinely expresses the challenges they face.

With such "heavy" topics, one might ask whether we should bring them up at all!

And yet, not only are loss and death things students *want* to talk about, but they are also the subjects of nearly all great literature and the stories we call history. It is what Spanish speakers refer to as *duende,* an awareness that loss accompanies every moment. It is perhaps difficult to imagine a situation that doesn't somehow touch on loss. Consider, therefore, the curricular context. So much literature involves the topics of *love and loss.*

Science and history are filled with *creation and destruction, gain and loss.* Loss is inherent in every game we play. How do we create relevance around these foundational topics if we don't find out how our students live them? If we don't make room for the sharing of personal stories about these universal human experiences, we also miss an opportunity to foster empathy and understanding.

In addition to profound questions of life and death, you might also find in your wonder basket *nonsense questions* like, "Why do hot dogs come in packs of six and buns in packs of eight?" A circle about *things that just don't make sense* is a wonderful one!

You might also find *questions that are really statements,* like, "Why are teachers so rude?" This question has two identifiers, teachers and rudeness. There are wonderful circles to be had around, for example, people in your life who have taught you something, not including professional teachers, or a time when a teacher really helped you understand something you didn't know before. For a circle on rudeness, we might ask: Tell of a time when you saw someone being rude, someone was rude to you, or you were rude to someone. Much can be learned from such reflection.

You will also get what you might deem *inappropriate questions.* Even with these, a kernel can be found. "Why are you such a jerk?" can lead to a circle about *things that annoy you and things that you do to annoy others.* You can choose whether to feed back the questions in their original form, to amend them for clarity, or drop them altogether.

As we teachers are always searching for ways to make content relevant to students' backgrounds and lived experiences; beginning the year with mysteries will give you touchstone referents that are alive and meaningful for your classes. For example, using the question above, "How do you get wiser?" with its inherent topics, "change," "knowledge," and "wisdom," consider the many ways you can refer to these topics in the study of science, history, or literature. Chemistry, for example, is about change. And it is good to gain some knowledge and wisdom when you want to combine chemicals in a lab!

The list of mysteries above was generated from an *open prompt.* Students were asked in general what questions were most important to them at that moment. You can also focus the exercise any number of more specific ways: what are the mysteries of science? What are the mysteries of history? What are the mysteries of health and well-being? With adults, the process can focus on roles: what are the mysteries of parenting, teaching, counseling, of being an administrator, a small business owner, a job seeker, etc.? Discovering a question is the beginning of inquiry, and determined inquiry leads to learning and new discoveries as well as intrinsic motivation to seek more information.

When we lead students through the process of generating meaningful questions, determining the topics inherent in them, finding the resonances that show what is most alive and urgent in the group, and then crafting prompts that evoke recollections of lived experience, we are giving them a skill that will serve them throughout life.

Frequently Recurring Topics in Student Mysteries

While none of us can presume to know what students need now or in the future, there are some topics that appear to be constants. Here are some ideas about how to turn *towards* these great student mystery topics: relationships (friendship, family); relational harm (conflict, war, violence, injustice) and repair (restoration, healing, peacemaking); gender and sexuality; love; service (meaningful action); rites of passage (change); leadership; global challenges (climate collapse, adaptation, pandemics), and imagining the future.

Relationships, Friends, and Family

At all levels of human development, friends and family play a central role. If students have had experience with circle practice, and you have been transparent about how you facilitate and form prompts, *they* will be able to shape their own prompts. The following plans are offered as samples. Here is one that is useful at any age: Begin with a speed round where participants say the names of people whom they consider to be friends. For the story round, a useful prompt is: *Now, tell about a time you knew for certain that this (or another) person was truly a friend.* Again, we are encouraging stories that are focused vignettes, show-don't-tell moments, not a listing of the qualities we find in friends. The stories reveal moments that demonstrate true friendship: a person gave up their food so you could eat; a time when someone stood up for you; a time when you were comforted by someone; a moment of recognition that you and another person feel and share the same values, experiences, thoughts, and beliefs; etc. Follow this story round with a witnessing round, and then ask something like, *Given the stories we just heard, what can we say about what makes a true friend?*

Another way to approach this is to have participants share stories of meeting a person for the first time, a person who would later become a friend. What was it about that moment that set up a lasting relationship? Consider also having students tell stories of a time *when you were a friend*, again focusing on an actual moment in time. In the same vein, stories of the *unexpected* blossoming of a friendship are always plentiful: *Tell about a time you had a bad first impression (or preconception) of someone, with whom you later became a friend.*

Relational Harm and Healing

A sometimes-unspoken truth, and therefore perhaps more interesting to explore in circle, is that *relationships can end.* For older students, *tell about a time you knew a relationship was over* is a useful prompt to explore this reality. Telling stories about the moment a relationship came to an end also instructs us in how to be mindful of how we might want to sustain relationships we cherish. We can reflect on our own actions that may have brought about the end, as well as what others did that caused us to lose faith in the friendship.

Perhaps the single most valuable exploration is the fact that *relationships can be renewed.* From the primary grades on, ask for a show of hands, *How many of you have had a friend who became not a friend and then was a friend again?* Then have a circle that evokes these stories.

Recognizing that *harm can be done* and *harm can be healed* is the foundation for practices of restoration and transformation. We are all capable of causing harm and of contributing to healing. "Let he who has not sinned cast the first stone." Awareness of the resiliency of relationships grounds every moral code, including virtues such as *forgiveness, redemption, and love.* Love, because we come to know its capacity to endure only *as* it is tested. To guide people into looking at how harm can be healed, consider these prompts:

- For the very young: *How many of you have ever had a boo-boo? And how many saw it get better?* Boo-boo councils are very popular with the youngest! It may be in part a fascination with the *fact of healing* that they find so compelling and memorable.
- Appropriate for the very young and the rest of us: *How many of you have felt hurt (or a boo-boo) from something another person said or did?* Show of hands. *Tell about a time you felt hurt.* This is a good time to remember the agreement that we don't say the names of people who are not present, people who might be hurt by our telling those stories. And if the story of hurt is about someone in the council, we first ask that person's permission before telling it.
- Older students love to tell stories of *surviving a risky situation.*
- To expand understanding that hurt comes in many forms, physical and emotional, and that healing from both is indeed possible, after the circles above, open discussion

on *what are the different ways someone can be hurt? What are some of the ways people can heal from such hurts?*

Gender Councils

> Be still and know that dark and light,
> Be still and know that day and night are one holy circle.
> —Indigenous American chant

There comes a point—sometimes earlier, sometimes later—that gender identity and questions about the mysterious "other" become a foremost concern for young people.

Circles provide unique opportunities for students to explore stereotypes and compare experiences in a way that promotes healthy relationships and saves a lot of grief and misunderstanding for everyone. You will recall from the introduction my involvement into circles began with participation in men's groups, and later I had the good fortune to sit with women, and then with those who did not identify with these binary distinctions. At the same time, I came to reassess my cultural inheritance around issues of gender, looking at my conditioning and preconceptions. This inner work continues to this day, and I believe it is a necessary precondition for being able to create a safe space for young people to explore their own identities.

When I first started conducting gender councils in the '90s, I was stuck in what is now called "binary" thinking. That is, you were either a "boy" or a "girl," a "man" or a "woman." I did have a sense that there were young people whose identities did not fall within this simple (and simplistic) division, but I told myself that the only other possibilities were homo- or bi-sexuality, and that my students in middle school might not have yet identified with either of these, so I didn't have to be concerned. I continued to confuse anatomy, gender, and sexual orientation, and had no understanding of gender "identity" or "expression."

As teachers we are always separating boys and girls. We do so even in our casual address, "Now, boys and girls, I need your attention!" Having some degree of consciousness when there might be other or as yet unknown or unsettled categories of identity, when I divided students for gender councils, I would say, in a rather clunky way, that they should choose groups based on "having been born into a male or female body." My justification for this was that so much of what the external world would project onto them was based on how they *appeared* to others, and, of course, in middle school appearance counts for so much. With this justification, I thought we could fruitfully explore gender stereotypes. And we did! What was missing, though, was gender "identity" (the internal, felt sense of who you are), and "expression" (what you show to the world).

Even with this qualifier of "having been born into" a male or female body, I could tell that there were students still uncomfortable with the simple choice of one or the other. I have an evolving understanding of this and will have more to say soon.

Nonetheless, gender-separate councils have proven to be some of the most memorable. I often tell students about how I met my wife, Abbe. I would say something like, "You might not believe this, but I met my wife when we were in fifth grade. We now have two beautiful children." Noting their astonishment, I continued, "Well, we didn't *get married* in fifth grade! We re-met at our high school reunion, and we have been together ever since." Pause. "I tell you this story because, who knows, maybe your future husband or wife is sitting right here in this classroom!" The majority of these eighth graders would laugh and make sounds of disgust. But there were always a few who, after looking around, considered the possibilities.

This led to a discussion and consensus around the idea that almost everyone, at some time, will fall in love with someone and that many will want to take on a life partner. Then, I would bring in the statistic that divorce rates in America hover somewhere between 40 and 50 percent. Scratching my head, I would say, "I wonder how it happens that people can go from 'I will love you forever,' to 'If I ever see your face again, it will be too soon!'" We would then explore whether couples doing council with one another might help them work through some of the problems that can lead to divorce. Ultimately, we came to conclude that learning to speak honestly and to listen wholeheartedly would be of benefit to *any* relationship hoping to last.

In the gender council protocols that follow, I distinguish *binary separate*, *non- binary separate*, and *nonbinary whole* groupings. In all cases, gender councils involve recognizing gender stereotypes, introspection around personal identity, and a gathering of questions for others who *are not or do not identify as we do*. We then form the best of these questions into prompts to be explored when the circle returns as a whole.

As I recently learned myself, it is helpful to begin any gender council process by providing information about the four gender spectra:

1) **Biological/anatomical sex**: or the designation of sex assigned at birth—AFAB, assigned female at birth, AMAB, assigned male at birth, or "intersex," possessing both male and female anatomical features

2) **Gender identity**: an internal, felt sense of who you are

3) **Gender expression**: how you show that identity to the world through clothing, hairstyle, voice and body characteristics, and mannerisms varying based cultural views of masculine and feminine qualities

4) **Sexual orientation**: emotional and sexual attraction to another person based on the gender of the other person.[4]

These four designations each represent a range of possibilities, making for a multiplicity of genders along these spectra. For example, on the spectrum of anatomical possibilities, with typical male-female anatomy opposites at the extremes, there is a designation of "intersex." This is a person born possessing both male and female anatomical features. In 2016, the American Psychological Association put the ratio of intersex births at 1:1500.[5] There are limitless possibilities of hormone balance and chromosomal coding, so on a purely *physiological* level the possibilities are endless. Similarly, gender identity, gender expression, and sexual orientation all have ranges between the "binary" extremes.

When we have such a wide range of possibilities inherent in each spectrum, and when we add the possible combinations of how the four spectra interact, it's easy to see that the pronouns we use to refer to these variations will be of the greatest importance to the people upon whom they are fixed. I'm sure we have all had a moment where a child corrected us for *misgendering*. Upon seeing a child with long hair, we might say "Oh, is this your daughter?" only to be corrected with an emphatic "I'm a boy!"

Providing ourselves and our students with this information benefits all. Gender councils offer students the opportunity to ask fundamental questions about relationships and gain true empathy for others. And it is important to convey to students that the designations "boys" and "girls," "males" and "females" are far more complex than they appear. For our youngest students, it is best to refrain from binary designations, which is also challenging if facilities don't have gender-neutral bathrooms. By the time students reach upper elementary and middle school, we can actively teach about gender differences. An excellent resource is Genderbread.org.[6]

Binary Separate Gender Council

With an understanding that these two are not the only possibilities, we ask students to join a binary grouping. The designation might simply be "boys and girls," letting the children decide where they want to go. At an adolescent phase and beyond, provide information about gender spectra and continue to *let students choose* the group they identify with. One way to do this is to have the students brainstorm cultural stereotypes we carry about masculinity and femininity, list these on the board, and then invite students to go to the group with which they most identify.

When the groups separate, ideally with facilitators who represent the binary categories, we begin an exploration of the joys and challenges of having been born exactly as you are.

Prompts for the joys are variations of these:

- What are the good things about being a boy or girl (or being born into a male or female body)?
- Tell about a time when you said: "Wow, I'm so glad I am a girl!" (or boy)
- Tell about a time you felt you had an advantage because you are a girl or boy.

For the challenges we might use:

- What is difficult about being ...?
- What do you think others expect you to do or be just because you are ...?
- Tell about a time when you felt it was unfair to be ...?

In these first two councils, you may find that students respond in the negative; that is, they describe as advantages the things that they don't have to deal with, and the other group does. Statements might include: "I'm glad I don't have to deal with having a period or having babies!" or "I'm glad I don't have to like football!"

These are powerful moments to build empathy for those in the other circle who do deal with those experiences and expectations.

The third separate council uses a mysteries process: What are the things you wonder about the experiences of the people in the other circle? What questions would you ask them if you knew they would speak from the heart to answer? With upper grades, I would write down all these questions—even the ones that might seem inappropriate or in themselves sexist. Then, I would feed back the list and ask students to prioritize the most important questions with the caveat that they must be questions that the others *can and will* answer. For example, if you ask "What is it like to have a baby?" or "How many times have you had sexual intercourse?", the first is something many *can't* answer, and the second is something they probably *won't* answer. We then begin the process of narrowing down the choices depending how much time we will spend with the whole group back together. Finally, we craft the questions so they are polite and respectful because, as I remind them, we might only get one shot at getting the answers.

When we are working in the binary mode, we use terms like the "opposite sex," "boys and girls," "male and female." Given what we now know, there really are no true opposites. Nonetheless, the questions and curiosity come from *perceived* differences, and if we acknowledge the gender spectra, using these terms can bring out these perceptions. We usually begin each question with a polite: "We really want to know, so would you please tell us ... ?" Here are a few samples from a seventh-grade class:

- What do you look for in a girl (or guy) you find attractive?
- What annoys you about what the way boys (or girls) act?
- Do you change the way you act when you are around the opposite sex? If so, how?
- What kinds of things do you talk about when you are just with your male or female friends?
- What kinds of things do you do that you would only do with your male or female friends?
- What signals do you give to show a person that you are interested in them?
- What do you like about being a girl (or boy)? Tell a story about something you experienced that you might not have if you were a different sex.
- What do find difficult about being ...?
- What's the craziest thing you have ever done just to get someone's attention?
- Do you ever wish you could be the opposite sex? If so, why?

Gender councils are usually conducted in a *fishbowl* form, using an inner circle of one group and an outer circle of the other. Members of the outer circle are designated witnesses. Those in the inner circle will tell stories, speaking from their personal experience (not as representatives of a group). The inner circle opens the council and calls for one of the questions or prompts. One person in the outer circle respectfully reads one prompt or question. The inner circle conducts council as if they were meeting alone and just talking to one another. As always, *anyone can pass.* After the inner circle concludes their stories, the talking piece is handed to someone in the outer circle. With the witness round, I like to tell students to echo something they heard someone say or to say one thing—a word, a phrase, an image—that is still with them. We agree to not indicate our *affirmation or disapproval* about the things we witness, either in tone or with further explanation. It is simply something you recall hearing, something that stayed with you.

When the witness round concludes, you might suggest a ceremonial way for each circle to show gratitude for the other. Then, the circles switch, and the same process begins again. The number of prompts you use depends on how much time you have allotted for the councils. As always, the list of what proved resonant in the witnessing gives you a clue as to which issues the groups would like to turn toward more fully if there is time. Final councils with the whole group can include takeaways from the entire process and perhaps taking vows to continue deepening our understanding of others, assessing our own fixed views, and offering respect as a default as we get to know others.

Nonbinary Gender-Separate Councils

A school where all staff practice and facilitate council, there are good possibilities for bringing together facilitator teams of at least three gender categories. I say at least because just adding a third category to a binary is still quite limiting when we are dealing with a rainbow of possibilities. What we call this third grouping is critical. Designating a third group as "other" can carry a pejorative connotation. I have heard of groups designated as Sun (traditionally masculine qualities), Moon (feminine), and Stars (all that lies in between). With older students we can introduce the term "nonbinary," a person who does not identify as solely male or female. This too allows for a broadly inclusive third group. With the resources of a fully trained faculty, there is a high likelihood of finding a facilitator who identifies with the third category.

The process is the same as above with two exceptions. Each group has to develop questions and prompts for *two* other groups, and the form of the whole group council is either two (one inner and one outer) or three concentric (one inner, one between, and one outer).

Nonbinary Whole Group Gender Councils

In many instances, there are not resources—additional facilitators, spaces, and time—to separate the groups. What is lost to a degree when splitting groups is not possible is the safety of beginning the process with people who identify as you do. If groups have developed the safety that comes from having practiced council together for many years, separating may be a non-issue. Using the mysteries process (writing and placing cards in a basket), there is a degree of anonymity that can facilitate the posing of difficult questions. Unlike the separate councils, when the process is done with the whole group together reading aloud the unedited questions, this can be problematic. If you judge that to be the case, then it is best to not have them read aloud and to look them over yourself to craft the questions and prompts for each group. Except for these possible challenges, the groups proceed as above.

Finally, there is an incalculable value of holding such councils with adult staff. In addition to the continual learning that comes from having this experience yourself, doing so will bring authenticity to your facilitation of student groups. A simple prompt is: *What would you like others to know about your experience at this time being who you are?*

Deep Adaptation

Young people understand the predicament we are in. Many, like the refugee youth who taught me when I first started teaching, live with the realities of broken social systems, a lack of resources, hunger, fear, and environmental degradation. Vulnerable populations around the globe, including the inner cities of our so-called advanced societies, have known and experienced these things a great deal longer than those of us who still live in the bubble created by the destruction of indigenous peoples, colonialism, the spoils of war, and economies that thrive on the production of weapons of mass destruction.

Even the youngest feel the fear of those around them, and they are actively questioning whether there will be a future for humanity. As facilitators of circle, what are we to do with mystery questions like, "Will there be a future? What will happen in future? Will people still be able to live on the planet?"

In his analysis of current climate science and the effects on humanity that follow from the conclusions, Professor Jem Bendell puts it bluntly:

"It is a truism that we do not know what the future will be. But we can see trends. We do not know if the power of human ingenuity will help sufficiently to change the environmental trajectory we are on. Unfortunately, the recent years of innovation, investment and patenting indicate how human ingenuity has increasingly been channeled into consumerism and financial engineering. We might pray for time. But the evidence before us suggests that we are set for disruptive and uncontrollable levels of climate change, bringing starvation, destruction, migration, disease and war."[7]

There is a growing movement that does not question the science of climate collapse, that does not turn away from the fear, that actively grieves for what has been lost, but still maintains what Joanna Macy calls "active hope."[8] It is a hope beyond hope, one that empowers us to feel, to grieve, to envision, and to act. What Bendell calls "deep adaptation" is about accepting that *we cannot return to the way things were*, and that this can be a good thing considering that the "way things were" brought us to this global predicament. He points out that "the range of ancient wisdom traditions see a significant place for hopelessness and despair. Contemporary reflections on people's emotional and even spiritual growth as a result of their hopelessness and despair align with these ancient ideas."

What I am suggesting here is not *teaching* about climate and societal collapse. This chapter after all is about *following their lead*. If the children make it clear that these issues are with them, then we have a responsibility to create structure and safety so they can turn towards them.

I turn to an articulation of questions suggested by Professor Bendell. I find these questions appropriate and useful for a wide span of ages. He calls them "a conceptual map of deep adaptation." Using a framework of "resilience, relinquishment, and restoration," Bendell suggests that these are the questions we must ask:

- How do we keep what we want to keep?
- What do we need to let go of in order to not make matters worse?
- What can we bring back to help us with the coming difficulties and tragedies?

Let's look at how we might translate these questions, so they are useful and evocative when students express concerns about the future. It is always good practice for circle facilitators to shape prompts in the simplest possible terms. This is where working with the youngest children schools us. If we look closely at the heart of what is inherent in Bendell's questions, we find: what is important (precious), what is not so important, and what can help us.

Trainer Jane Raphael in collaboration with teacher Lizbeth Trello developed a series of activities for K-2 called *Maps of My Heart* to help students answer the question about what is precious to them, and, we hope, to continue to ask it throughout life.

They begin by reading Molly Bang's book *In My Heart,* a picture book that introduces the idea of holding people inside one's heart.[9] In it, a mother explains to her child that wherever she goes in the world and whatever she is doing, her child is always in her heart. And she assures the child that wherever she goes, the child will carry her mother in her heart. After starting a circle in the usual way, they use the prompt: *Who do you hold in your heart and why,* and they offer the sentence starter, *I hold in my heart because he/she/it.* They extend this idea to include other things the children love and hold in their hearts: places, activities, objects, etc., using subsequent rounds to name these things and to give the reasons why. Finally, after reading *My Map Book* by Sara Fanelli, a picture book that shows that "maps" can chart more than just places, each child, and the teacher makes a "Map of My Heart."[10] For the maps, students draw a large heart or use a heart template and then draw people, places, activities, and things that they hold dear. This drawing makes it easy for them to have a circle where each child begins their share with, "In my heart, I have ... " These maps are shared in another circle, and as time goes on these inner resources can be shared in many circles to come.

Student "heart maps" also create a springboard for Bendell's second question, about relinquishment, and can be approached through storytelling about *things we have had to give up*. Sometimes we give up things suddenly, we *must* give them up, and other times we *choose* to let go of things. Useful circle prompts are usually about *loss* and deciding to *give away, let go, or to stop doing something*. A prompt like *Tell about a time you lost something that was very important to you* leads not only to stories about lost toys, but also about lost friends and lost homes. And, perhaps more importantly, the telling of these stories allows each student to recognize that *they have indeed coped with the loss*. We have all relinquished things ... and survived! Other useful prompts connected to this topic are:

- *Tell about something you used to do but you don't do anymore.*
- *Tell about a time you had to give something away that you didn't really want to give.*
- *What was a favorite thing that you used to have, but you don't have it anymore?*

If we follow such prompts with a second round that asks students to tell *what happened after the loss*, we reinforce their resilience, even if the response to the loss was not healthy. No matter how they handled it, they have lived to tell the tale. In addition, the "Give-away" activity described in Chapter 8 provides a tangible experience of giving up something to which you might still be attached, and it has the bonus of seeing the joy of the person receiving that thing from you.

Bendell's third question is about what we can bring back that will be of help to us in the difficulties we face now. While Bendell seems to be hinting at a restoration of indigenous, earth-based wisdom traditions, ways of living in closer harmony with the natural world, we can spark students' thinking about their personal capacity to *restore* things. Some useful prompts might be:

Tell about a time:

- *you broke something and then you fixed it!*
- *you were hurt or sick and you got better!*
- *you remembered how to do something you thought you had forgotten.*

Many of these prompts are appropriate and useful for any age, but as students get older, the circles can be used for project-based learning and activism. A wonderful activity for upper elementary and middle-school students is the Council of All Beings developed by Joanna Macy and John Seed.[11] Students choose a "being:" animal, plant, element (water, air), or natural feature (ocean, mountain). They research the nature of these beings: habitats, food sources, behavior, etc. as well as any problems they might be having at this time, such as facing extinction, loss of habit or food sources, being hunted, polluted, or commodified. They also become aware of any efforts by humans to preserve them.

After this research is completed, students make costumes to *become* their being and to report their experiences in a council of all beings. When possible, a group of adults sits in an inner circle to be the "humans." The beings surround the humans in an outer circle. Guiding questions and prompts include these:

1. *What being are you?*
2. *Please tell us about your life. Where do you live? What do you eat? What are some of your habits or daily routines? Anything else you would like to share about yourself.*

3. *Are you experiencing any problems? If so, what kind of problems are your kind experiencing currently? What role do humans play in those problems? What else would you like to tell humans if they could understand your language?*
4. *What advice can you give humans?*
5. *If you could give humans one of your powers, what would it be, and how do you think it might help them?*

Ideally, after hearing from the council of beings, the humans in the center witness or recall what they heard the beings say. This experience can then move towards activism, where students explore ways to improve the lives of their beings and then commit to manageable action steps to make that improvement happen. The activity really touches on all Bendell's questions. The mere choice of a being tells what is important to a child. Advice can lead to recognition of what can be *relinquished* if it negatively impacts the quality of life of that being. The act of learning about and inhabiting their being is itself a *restoration* of the ancient practice of imagination and merging that we see in places such as the caves at Lascaux.

Rites of Passage in the Classroom

Much has been written about the disappearance of meaningful rites of passage and the devastating effects of their loss in the lives of young people. It has been shown that without conscious ceremonies, young people will find ways to initiate themselves, often in destructive ways through drug abuse, latching on to group identification with gangs, and consumerism.[12] So what, essentially, is a rite of passage and how can young people avail themselves of these experiences in the modern urban school setting?

A rite of passage is, essentially, the ceremonial marking of a significant change in one's life, usually presided over by initiated elders in a particular tradition or lineage.

Anthropologist Arnold van Gennep identifies the three phases of a rite of passage as "rites of separation, transitional rites, and rites of incorporation" or "preliminal, liminal, and postliminal rites."[13] A useful way to think about these, taught by the School of Lost Borders in Big Pine, California, and at Findhorn in Scotland, is "old story, no story, new story." That is to say that rites of passage involve a significant period of intentional reflection on what has been (old story), crossing a threshold into not knowing (no story), and finally enacting the change in the world (new story), "being the change," as Gandhi had it.

Thankfully, many organizations now offer wilderness rites of passage, and these are particularly powerful since they are conducted in natural settings where participants are free from the routines and distractions of the city and can be informed by the rhythms, forms, and life in the natural world.[14]

The reality, however, is most young people cannot for many reasons avail themselves of these wilderness experiences. The loss of and distance to wilderness areas—along with current economic choices in the "Western," global North, especially as they relate to education—prevent them from doing so.

So, can we replicate at least certain aspects of the rite of passage in our crowded inner-city classrooms on linoleum floors where the voice of nature might only be represented by a potted plant or flower we place at the center of our circle? I believe so.

What I'm about to suggest should in no way be considered a replacement or the equivalent of what these organizations offer by taking young people into the wilderness for a week or more. My wish is that schools begin to incorporate full wilderness rites of passage experiences as a cornerstone of their curriculum. In the meantime, we can offer young people a taste of these critical themes through circle-based classrooms: *How do we tell the story of our past and then let that story go? How do we clear away preconceptions so we can truly observe? What can we commit to?* And most importantly, what will be the quality of our relationships with each other and the natural world?

For many years, I conducted mini rites of passage for my eighth graders at Palms Middle School. With the end of the year, graduation, and the scattering of friends that happens as students transition to many high schools, I felt the need to mark this threshold that wasn't merely pomp and circumstance. Our process was simple: usually over three consecutive days, we held the following councils:

The first simply involved recollections from any time during their three years at Palms. Sometimes I would say as a prompt: *Imagine ten years from now. You are getting together with some old friends from Palms. Someone says, "Hey, remember that time when ...?" What stories do you think might come to mind?* Students have an opportunity to recall and reflect on their experiences and in so doing they are conducting an act of "severance," the first stage of an initiatory rite. Speaking the old stories allows us to say goodbye to them.

Activities and prompts in the second council would vary depending on the group, but they were all designed to bring students into awareness of the *present moment.*

Students have written and read their *mysteries* of going to high school, the questions they have right now, the hopes and fears about this transition. Sometimes I would have students spend some "alone time" walking the campus or finding a personal place to sit for 15 minutes, and we would hear of what came to them during that *open* time. We might just play a few games, dance or sing a song during this *no story* time. I have also offered the possibility of conducting an *appreciation council* where students speak directly to others in the circle, thanking them for some act of friendship or kindness, possibly acknowledging something they were unable to at the time it occurred, which might also be some form of apology long overdue. Each of these activities is intended to clear the plate, to not think hard about the questions and concerns they might have, to create the useful emptiness within the container and thus, perhaps, become open to perceiving possibilities that might not have occurred otherwise. It is in such "liminal" space that inspiration comes. Consider when and how you find inspiration: a shower, a walk, as you are just going to sleep or waking up.

The third session would often involve students asking themselves: *What is one thing you would like to change, let go of, strengthen, or bring into your life?* Sometimes students would write these or simply sit silently to reflect, and then share in the council, in simple terms, that one thing. Then, I might say something akin to *the journey of a thousand miles begins with a single step* or ask: *What is one thing you can do today to bring about the change you want?* I ask them to shape these thoughts into a single, manageable, time-limited, forceful commitment, a statement of "I will ...!" As these commitments were shared around the circle the other students would shout, "Go for it!"

It is even possible to truncate this entire process, to complete it within an hour, again just to give students a taste. Simply begin with students reflecting on *one thing you would like to change, let go of, strengthen, or bring into your life.* Then, *consider the story of what happened that brought you to awareness of that one thing. How did you know that you wanted to change, let go of, or bring in something?* With limited time, just a few of these stories can be shared in a *fishbowl. Even if they don't speak,* others in the circle will consider the stories they would tell. Follow this round with a period of silence or meditation. Then, ask the group to *think of one thing you can do today that will be a first step toward this change.* These commitments are shared around the circle or in *popcorn* fashion or simply held silently. In fact, the whole process can be done silently after opening the council, with the final round being a silent passing of the talking piece with an instruction like: *When a classmate receives the talking piece, silently send them a wish that they might fulfill their commitment.*

It is valuable to give students a taste of the three phases, to give them some awareness of the change process. We can hold a vision that someday, in the witnessing of elders, either their community or school provides them with a proper rite of passage experience, conducted in a place free of the usual patterns of life and where students can feel how the natural world speaks when *it has the talking piece!* The programs conducted by the School of Lost Borders usually last 11 days: four days of telling the old stories in council, refining an intention for the threshold time, as well as preparing practically for the next phase; four days alone in nature, the threshold time; and upon return to the group, three days of stories from the time alone, and then, in the incorporation phase, refining commitments to concrete actions we choose to be responsible for in the world when we return to the environments and relationships of home. As we speak those commitments in the presence of others, we are empowering them to hold us accountable for our dreams. As poet W. B. Yeats says, "In dreams begin responsibilities."

Let's hold a vision of the possibility of all young people having such an experience led by elders who have also walked and reflected upon the path. In the practical meantime, we can offer these *tastes* in the confines of our classrooms.

Youth Circle Leadership

Consider the curious request: "Take me to your leader." In his book *Returning to the Teachings*, Rupert Ross asks us to imagine a first encounter between an indigenous group and European settlers. What is the first question the settlers ask? If we think about the many film depictions of this moment, it becomes clear that the first question is a request: "Take me to your leader." The Europeans wanted to know who the leader was, who would represent the group, who could make decisions. Ross tells us that the First Nations peoples of Canada were *baffled* by this request.[15]

Contrary to the modern Western notion of a single, absolute authority, according to Ross, the native peoples view leadership within the context of present necessity. The leader of the moment *emerges* when there is a need and, perhaps most importantly, *returns* to the circle after that need has been addressed. Sometimes the leader is the oldest and wisest, the carrier of the ancestral ways. Sometimes it is the young person, the fastest runner, or the one most capable of seeing the current situation without prejudice or preconception.

This concept of leadership follows in part from cultures that practice authentic rites of passage. When the community acknowledges that a young person has become an adult, it means that they are treated as *equal* members of the circle, and when a need arises that fits their gifts, that these newly recognized adults take on full responsibility in fulfilling the service required. Critically, and contrary to leaders who try by all means to cling to power, once the service is provided, the leader takes off that mantle and returns to the circle to be *one among many*.

Handing Off

From the moment we facilitate our first circle with students, we are simultaneously *training them* to assume the facilitator's role. We model facilitation in our behavior, body language, and tone of voice, in the stories we share, in the ways we handle disruptions, how we choose and frame prompts, and the quality of our witnessing. When we are *transparent* in our leadership, students will be engaged in taking responsibility for the circles. This means sharing our process and choices of topic, mode, and prompt. It means checking with students to see how they feel about our choices.

Perhaps the group would like to reshape the prompt to make it clearer *for them.* They need to see that we are flexible enough to consider changing everything to serve their needs in the moment. If we are holding circles in our academic classes, then we might not change the topic, as it is related to the course of study, but we might find that with student input, we can present the circle experience differently.

I remember when Julia Mason Wasson, a third-grade teacher at Wonderland Elementary School, asked her students to notice how I facilitated the council one day. After I left, the class shared what they saw me do, and Julia listed these behaviors on the board and later transferred them to a poster. The list included the following:

- "He sits up straight."
- "He leans in to listen."
- "He really listens."
- "He looks at me when I'm holding the talking piece."
- "He laughs and sometimes he looks sad."
- "He holds the talking piece and waits a while before he talks."

Once students have a feel for being in circle, it is time to turn over facilitation, beginning with small responsibilities. As early as kindergarten, students rotate setting the center and preparing the space. They can call and lead an activity or game. They can decide how to open and close the circle.

When students get a feel for what a prompt is, call on the group to help you fashion one *that will allow everyone to tell a story*. Begin to train them to shape a prompt based on the guidelines in Chapter 4. At the same time, as you employ witnessing rounds, you can ask the circle, "From the stories we heard and from the things that stayed with the listeners, what did we find most important or interesting?" Teaching them to "read the field," ask them what they think the circle should do next given what was shared this time.

If you have *acquired the circle habit,* then you are always thinking about how to use the circles to deepen understanding of academic content, to address immediate interpersonal issues, and to turn toward school, community, national, and world events. As soon as possible, ask students if they would like to lead a circle. Jane Raphael has her kindergarten students make "council kits" with a cloth centerpiece, a bell, items to use as talking pieces, and a manual to take home to parents to begin a tradition of family councils. When you see that students are interested in leading, have them sign up with a partner, someone with whom they will co-plan, co-facilitate, and debrief. Have these partners come to you to discuss their plans. Sometimes students will want you to play a role. Other times you are solely one among many, a participant. And it can also be good to be a silent witness and then offer a debrief on what you noticed.

When students learn to lead the circles and feel confident in doing so, they have acquired a lifelong, portable skill that will be useful in their personal relationships as well as in any group, organization, institution, or workplace in which they find themselves.

The following two stories illustrate the joys and challenges of student leadership. The first was a situation that I nearly shut down before it started, but it turned out to be the most extraordinary 45 minutes I've had in a circle with eighth-grade students. The second story is a cautionary tale.

Your Greatest Fear or Deepest, Darkest Secret

We had all survived the much-hyped Y2K apocalypse. Aside from a few glitches with the date, the computers are still working, and we can now call our gathered survival supplies "earthquake preparedness." And the longed-for reward of natural disasters, that school would be canceled, is not realized.

As we all settle in for the first classroom council of the next millennium, amid an argument over whether this was the real millennium or whether it is a year from now, Victoria places in the middle a party mask with the center zeros of the number 2000 making the eye holes. She dedicates the council. "In the year 2000, I want us to learn to take off our masks."

Then, Maya begins, "We thought that the New Year is a good time to talk about important stuff, so the topic today is, 'What's your greatest fear or deepest, darkest secret, how did you get it, and what are you going to do about it?'"

I try to disguise the horror that spreads over my face. I try to keep the mask on. I would never suggest or encourage such a topic for council. Especially in a public school.

Even a therapist with willing participants, knowing what they're getting into, wouldn't be so blunt. But there it is, out there, and I'm not the leader today. The odd thing is, I seem to be the only one in the circle registering any dismay.

The talking piece starts around. Andrew, sitting to Maya's left, begins, "I have a fear that I'll always be short." Then, Sonia, "They say they won't, but I think my parents are talking about a divorce." Rutherford says, "I'm afraid I'll really have to work hard to do well in high school. I won't be able to get away with so much goofing off." Noah offers, "I've always had a fear of flying objects, that I'm going to be hit by something thrown at me." And so it goes on the first round, almost everyone sharing a fear. The "deepest, darkest secret" part appears to have been dropped.

Maya gets the talking piece, and, seeing that the council has only taken up the first third of her question, says, "So, for the second round, say *how* you got your fear. I'll put the talking piece in the center, and anyone who wants to start can take it." I'm thinking, "OK, this won't go anywhere. I'm going to have to help them out, perhaps rephrase the question. After all, anamnesis is a long process in psychotherapy. Some people never discover the origins of a fear." But before I have a chance to register my doubt, the piece is on its way again.

Noah takes the talking piece. He's ready to continue where he left off. "I remember being in the back yard. My dad has a bucket of different kinds of balls. I'm maybe five or six. And he's throwing them at me. They aren't hard balls, mostly wiffle balls, soft balls, and a few tennis balls. He was showing me that even if I get hit, it won't hurt that much. I know he was trying to help me out. It didn't work. He was trying to get me to not be afraid when I play baseball. I don't like to play baseball, and I think it bugs him."

Then, he passes the piece. Many students, encouraged by this opening, this relatively pain-free return to the source of a fear, also find a story. A round of recollections: being alone for the first time; remembering the doctor who said, "He's in the tenth percentile;" the loud voices of parents arguing; a first low grade on a test from elementary school.

There's still ten minutes left. Maya reminds us, "So we have time for one more quick round. If you can, say *how* you plan to get over your fear."

Even having been a witness to the last two amazing rounds, I think we have reached our limit. Time to bring in professional help. Are we outside the bounds of what we should be doing in a public school? It's out of my hands. Maya and Victoria are the leaders.

Again, Noah, on fire with discovery, begins, "I don't know if I'll ever get over my fear, but I'm going to tell my dad that I don't like what he did. He still thinks he was helping me." Andrew says, "I'm going to be a professional hockey player. Lots of them are short. And if I can't do that, I'll be a coach. I can help other people do their best because I know what it's like to have people think I'm not a good athlete just because of my size."

Others express fears that include the dark, heights, family traveling by plane, speaking in front of a group, meeting new friends, confronting someone, learning something new. Each, in the precious few moments they have, suggests often elegant courses of action, successive approximations, either approaching a fear bit by bit or diving right in. And each vocalized intention is received in an attentive silence that acknowledges this shared endeavor. In the center of the circle, a subtle awareness that fear is a human thing, it has a cause, and there is a way through.

I'm thinking, "What could have taken 10 years of therapy has been accomplished by nearly 25 young people in approximately 45 minutes!" We hold hands and pass a pulse to signal the closing.

The Story We Live

After two days at The Ojai Foundation, on our eighth-grade Youth Council Leadership retreat, we are all feeling sad about having to leave. This was clearly expressed in the final council. We have had two days of talking about great leaders: Nelson Mandela, Rosa Parks, Shirley Chisholm, our mothers, fathers, friends, and complete strangers who taught us how to bring out the best in ourselves. We have looked at ourselves as leaders, representatives chosen by our peers, trusted to speak the truth of our experience and listen fully to the truth of others. We have studied leaders of note throughout history and mythology. We have acknowledged unnamed, innumerable leaders who dared everyday acts of kindness. And we have set intentions to notice, to bring out, and to nurture the qualities of leadership in others and in ourselves.

We gather in the center of the room to close our time. Huddled in tight, arms around shoulders, one at a time, we say our names. "My name is Claudia." The whole group chants, "Your name is Claudia, Claudia, Claudia" as each of us looks into Claudia's eyes and she scans everyone in the circle. And there are tears. And there are smiles. And no one really wants to let go. We continue with the names of everyone present.

I feel compelled to say one more thing. "We're all feeling pretty good. We made new friends. We told our stories, spoke our truths. We listened to each other. As good as we are feeling now, there is a potential for feeling the opposite when we get back to LA. Others have not had this experience, and we won't be able to fully describe it.

"I heard many of you say: 'I'm really going to miss Ojai. I don't want to leave this place.' This is a wonderful, beautiful place, but I believe we have this feeling because we participated in council with one another. If you want to bring back the feeling of Ojai, I urge you to find a friend, sit down, make a center, and begin a council. It's not the place; it's what we have done here that matters. It's the quality of the way we have been with each other. You can have that at any place and at any time. Even on the street in the middle of the city. Even if you are alone. Just decide to tell yourself the truth. And listen carefully, without judging yourself right or wrong for the way you experience the world. This place is wonderful, I believe, because that's what people do here. What you are feeling right now will come back when you bring council home."

We linger a while in the room. Tears and laughter. Kids hugging kids they had never spoken to before the trip. Kids and teachers hugging. We slowly move toward the kitchen area and circle up for our last lunch. A few songs. A silence. Another thought rises in me, "You know, I have a crazy idea. I'm just going to put this out here. I have this picture of you all sitting in a council circle on the quad at lunchtime, and the whole school is witnessing. You can bring this feeling that we are having now back to Palms. I'm not asking you to do this. It's just a fantasy I'm having, a crazy idea."

There are some nods of agreement. Then, a whisper, "Let's do it." We have our lunch, and then our yellow bus arrives to take us home.

The next day, a Friday, we are all back at school. A moment after the fourth period dismissal bell rings, Matthew, Lizzy, and Joycelyn burst into my room and ask for the bell. It's the bell we use to begin our councils.

"You're doing it?" I ask. "You know it was *just* an idea."

"We're doing it. Everyone is meeting. Will you come?" they ask.

"No. I think it's best that you do this on your own." I feel some concern for them, but I can't contain my pride.

As I walk toward the teacher's cafeteria, I see their circle forming out on the grass of the quad area in the dead center of the school. I stop there, bow to them, honoring their intention and their courage, and I move off to have my lunch.

Friday is council day in my class, and so as fifth period begins, we gather in the council space.

"Did you see what happened?" Jeff asks. "They had a council on the quad today, and kids tried to mess it up. Other kids were dancing in and out of the circle, throwing food at them. I think one kid spit in the bell. Another group even formed their own council to make fun of them."

My heart sinks. What have I done? These children had to pay the price of my crazy vision. I ask what others saw, and they confirm that this happened, but they don't seem to want to talk about it. Yoon, our representative, who was chosen to go to Ojai, gives a report about the trip. In her stoic and understated way, she also downplays the lunchtime events, and we move into a council around a predetermined topic.

As sixth period is about to begin, Joycelyn, one of the organizers of the lunchtime gathering, enters in tears. She sinks into one of the Backjack chairs and tries to disappear. I notice that Mina is also in tears. She was not on the trip.

I say, "It looks like something is going on here. Can we just begin with a check-in?" There is agreement from the group.

Someone dedicates the circle, and Emily reaches for the talking piece. She too had not been on the trip. "Everybody came back from Ojai so excited," she begins, "like they had a really great time, and the rest of us started feeling really bad, especially after they had this council on the quad. I think people made fun of them because they were feeling left out. Maybe they should have come down a little bit first. Maybe they should have waited until Monday to do the council."

David, who was on the trip, receives the talking piece and says, "There were people who weren't on the trip in the circle today. Anybody could have joined. I don't know why they had to make fun of us. They could have joined us!"

Several students offer explanations for the behavior. Some think that the mock council and the attempts to disrupt were just kids being mean. Some say it was just kids being kids. "You can't expect them to accept something different." Some offer solutions. "Maybe they shouldn't meet on the quad."

Joycelyn is still in tears. Everyone anticipates what she will say when she gets the talking piece. She passes.

When the piece gets to Mina, she admits, "I was one of those in the mock council, and I'm really sorry. I didn't want to hurt anybody." She glances at Joycelyn but can't continue as her own tears come more fully. David, sitting next to her, puts his arm around her.

Ben speaks, "I was also one of those who was making fun of the council, and I'm sorry if anyone was hurt. I can see you were hurt, Joycelyn. But what do you expect? It was just so weird, so unusual to see a council in the middle of the quad. I didn't know what to do."

"We're just kids. When we see something different, we have to make fun of it," Tameka adds.

Now Joycelyn finds the words. "How can people be so cruel! We weren't trying to rub it in your face, like we had this great experience, and you didn't. We invited everyone into the circle. We wanted to share the feeling of what we had in Ojai. And you people who threw stuff at us just wrecked it."

I see a new wave of tears flow from Mina. I'm wondering about the extent of the damage wrought by this enactment of my ill-considered suggestion. Why couldn't I foresee this activation of envy, this shock of the unfamiliar, the ways this unifying practice could also create painful divisions? I want to jump in. I want to apologize to Mina, to Joycelyn, to Emily, and to anyone who was hurt by my haste. But before I can, Sonia gets the piece.

"It's like the story 'Marigolds' we read in class. Lizabeth has to tear up the old lady's beautiful flowers before she can learn compassion. It's like wrecking the council or wrecking the marigolds were 'the last crazy acts of childhood.' And that *had to happen* before Lizabeth could really understand Miss Lottie and before you, Mina, could feel what Joycelyn is going through."

"Marigolds" is about the tumultuous shock, as Eugenia Collier wrote, "of suddenly becoming more woman than child and yet being both at once."[16] There is no safe and easy way to do this. In the story, Lizabeth, who is traversing this uneasy passage, recalls a day that "marked the end of innocence" when she led a group of younger children in an attack on elderly Miss Lottie's tenderly nurtured marigolds garden. Lizabeth describes the garden as an "incongruency ... a brilliant splash of sunny yellow against the dust" of Miss Lottie's home, "a monument to decay." She recalls, "For some perverse reason, we children *hated* those marigolds. They interfered with the perfect ugliness of the place; they were too beautiful; they said too much that we could not understand; they did not make sense."

During a sleepless night, Lizabeth overhears her father weeping about his inability to provide for the family, and she hears her mother comforting him as one would a child. Not knowing where she is going, Lizabeth runs out of the house and soon finds herself at Miss Lottie's, staring at the flowers. She leaps into the mounds and, pulling madly, destroys all the marigolds. She looks up to find Miss Lottie staring down at her "and there was no rage in the face now, now that the garden was destroyed and there was nothing any longer to be protected."

Lizabeth scrambles to her feet, and staring at Miss Lottie realizes, "That was the moment when childhood faded and womanhood began. That violent, crazy act was the last act of childhood. For as I gazed at the immobile face with the sad, weary eyes, I gazed upon a kind of reality which is hidden to childhood. The witch was no longer a witch but only a broken old woman who had dared to create beauty in the midst of ugliness and sterility."

She continues, "Of course I could not express the things that I knew about Miss Lottie as I stood there awkward and ashamed. The years have put words to the things I knew in that moment, and as I look back upon it, I know that that moment marked the end of innocence. Innocence involves an unseeing acceptance of things at face value, an ignorance of the area below the surface. In that humiliating moment I looked beyond myself and into the depths of another person. This was the beginning of compassion, and one cannot have both compassion and innocence."

We had studied this story in class, looked at the plot structure, debated the theme, but until this moment, it remained an abstraction, not touching our lives. Sonia saw a connection, an archetypal resonance between the story we read and the story we just lived. The disruption and mockery of the lunchtime council was an enactment of a pattern that reveals itself again and again in adolescence. The council continues web-style with a soft stuffed rabbit tossed from one student to another to indicate a desire to speak.

When Mina receives the rabbit, she looks directly at Joycelyn. "That's it. It was just so strange to see that circle. It was beautiful, like the marigolds, and I didn't feel a part of it. I didn't understand what I was feeling, and I just wanted to do something! I had no idea what I did would hurt you and the others in the circle. When I came into class, I just didn't want to feel that feeling. I didn't want to think about what I had done. Now I see that that craziness and confusion I was feeling is not so unusual. I think Lizabeth felt the same way, and other people who disrupted the council were also feeling that way. I'm so sorry, and if you want to do another council, I will join it." Joycelyn signaled for the piece. "Thank you. I don't think I want to be in another council outside. I know people will mess it up, and I don't want to be a part of that again."

When the bell rings, we agree to end with one of the more intimate council closings—the pulse. We take hands, and, beginning with Joycelyn, gently pass a squeeze from hand to hand around the circle. At this moment, the story is real, alive and vital, enduring. No need for a test of comprehension. Story and experience blend to reveal the challenge of leadership, the pain of envy, and the seeds of compassion.

For Reflection and Imagination

1. Consider the questions of the heart you are living with today as an educator, a counselor, a parent, a community member, a family member, or simply a member of the species "human."

- Write a list of questions you would ask if you felt complete trust and confidence in the listener(s).
- Find and list the inherent topics at the core of each question.
- Craft a prompt for each topic that would evoke the recollection of lived experiences about that topic from your peers.

2. Imagine what young people at this time and place might be wondering about:

- Write a list of questions you imagine they would ask if they felt complete trust in the listener.
- Look for and list the inherent topics in each of these questions.
- Craft an age- and context-appropriate, facilitating prompt for each topic.

3. Consider how you have managed and experienced transitions or meaningful passages in your life. Reflect on how these passages were conducted, celebrated, or marked.

- The first day of class and the last day of class.
- The first day of a new job and the last day of a job or position.
- Any common marker: a birth, graduation, wedding, birthday, a death.
- Knowing what you know now about the three phases of change (p. 216), imagine how you might have

meaningfully marked and how you might mark each of these passages in the future.

Chapter 10: Circles in the Relational Arts

1. **Honor Student Curiosity**
Rather than impose a fixed curriculum, allow students to express the questions they're truly grappling with, i.e. their "mysteries." These guide deeper inquiry and meaning-making.

2. **Use the Mysteries Process**
Invite students to anonymously submit big, unresolved questions. Group and prioritize them to uncover topics like loss, identity, justice, and belonging. These inform future prompts and circles.

3. **Foster Empathy Through Story**
Shift from belief statements to personal storytelling. This invites vulnerability and connection, even on difficult topics like grief, fear, or family rupture.

4. **Explore Gender with Nuance**
Support safe, inclusive gender councils (binary and nonbinary) where students reflect on identity, stereotypes, and relationships through structured questions and respectful listening.

5. **Name and Grieve Global Crises**
Don't avoid climate anxiety or existential dread. Use developmentally appropriate prompts to explore loss, resilience, and what matters most, inspired by the concept of "deep adaptation" and "Maps of My Heart."

6. **Facilitate Classroom Rites of Passage**
Even without wilderness access, you can create meaningful transitions through three-phase councils: recalling the past, embracing the unknown, and voicing commitments for the future.

7. **Hand Off Circle Leadership**
From the start, model transparent facilitation and gradually empower students to co-lead. This develops confidence, ownership, and lifelong skills in listening and leadership.

8. **Expect Real Growth and Real Risks**
Student-led circles may bring up raw truths or provoke resistance. But these lived experiences, when held in circle, can foster transformation, insight, and compassion.

11

CIRCLES AND INSTITUTIONAL REALITIES

The Only Imperative

THERE IS ALWAYS a degree of unacknowledged anxiety that runs through a school system, or any institution charged with showing "results" and "progress." For me as a teacher it was a vague constant that I was never doing enough. Here is how the transfer of anxiety works: top administrators feel responsible to the Board, to the public (mainly the media), and to local, state, and federal officials, politicians, and agencies. Through their operations coordinators and directors, the anxiety about continual progress is shifted to the administrators at a school site. This pressure is conveyed to the teaching staff, often with the disclaimer that "these directives are coming from the central office." At this point, the source of the anxiety is already several times removed and completely depersonalized. We hear statements like:

- "The *district* is requiring every eighth grader to be proficient in algebra."
- "The *district* wants to see a 15-percentage-point increase on the Academic Performance Indicator (API) every year."

- "The *district* has deemed our school's academic progress 'inadequate.'"

Although it is sometimes associated with a particular person, a superintendent or a charter's executive director, the "district" becomes a faceless force that affects the daily lives of everyone in it. Add to this "the union," whose existence depends on distinguishing itself from "the district," and we have a Homeric clash of the Titans.

Sadly, the fear and anxiety does not stop at the level of the teaching staff. *Like gravity, it comes down to the students.* Much of this transfer happens unconsciously, but I know that I have conveyed it with statements like "You have to learn this because it will be on the state test," the passive construction, "We are *required* to teach this," and the veiled threat, "You will have to know this in high school (or college)." The students have no place to transfer this anxiety except onto each other. This results in acting out behaviors such as exclusion, violence, and vandalism. If the anxiety is internalized, we see depression, withdrawal, school and social phobias, test anxiety, and addictions. In the context of schools that are already dealing with high degrees of trauma in their population, negative impact is multiplied.

In the 2020–21 school year, when so many students received instruction online (if they had a reliable internet connection), there was an even more insidious message conveyed to them through the system: that this was a year of "learning loss." Students have *not* stopped learning, although they may not be following a prescribed curriculum. The lessons from this pandemic year were unquantifiable and beyond our capacity to evaluate: lessons of loss (family, friends, activities, dreams), perseverance, family dynamics, economy (making do with less), introspection, new skills, new ways to connect, capabilities we never knew we had, a sense of global interdependence. These are some of the many lessons we must help students to recognize and articulate. We should not send them (and parents and teachers) the message that any learning has been "lost."

Almost without exception, when the anxiety for performance, progress, results, and compliance with mandates becomes most intense, circle practice is the first thing to go. I know that many times as state testing approached, I would *not* offer a circle that week and instead devote the hour to test preparation. As Council in Schools developed programs, we regularly had our mentoring or professional development sessions postponed because a newly mandated curricular training session had to be scheduled, a test had to be prepared for, the students in a particular class did not "deserve" circle that week, or there was just simply *too much to do*.

In this chapter, I want to address all the reasons *not* to do circles, and to suggest ways to *do them anyway*! In fact, it may just be that council is exactly the thing we need to do, *the only imperative*, precisely at the moments when we feel we have no time for it! Here is a wild idea for you to consider: imagine it is the week before some kind of mandated testing. The entire faculty is gearing up for the event, and you are feeling anxious. Have you taught the students *everything* they need to know to excel on the test? Have you done enough to refresh their memories? You are then given a choice to spend another hour if you teach elementary school, ten extra minutes in each secondary class, to prepare your students, or you can "lose" an hour of "instructional time" to offer a circle to the students or to attend a faculty circle. Which would you choose?

If students are feeling any kind of fear or are not feeling connected to others, they will not be able to access the parts of the brain that store the memory needed to perform cognitively demanding tasks, such as tests. If you take the extra instructional time to prepare, and what you convey, in addition to the information or review, is your own anxiety about their performance, it may be that the only thing the students will carry into the test is that concern. On the other hand, if you offer a circle where students can connect with their "resources" (as described in Chapter 9), their own physical well-being, their own sense of joy, and with each other in some sense of "collective mastery" (as simple as the whole class doing a simultaneous hand clap)—if you offer this, how might doing so affect their ability to perform on exams? In addition, you might sit for that hour with colleagues in council, where you see each other as a community engaged in a mutual endeavor and use a prompt such as: *Talk about what comes up for you as you prepare your students for these tests.* Even though you will likely still carry the concern about not having done enough to prepare all your students, you are able to tell these stories and listen to the ways your colleagues are holding and dealing with these concerns. Could it be that doing so would decrease your anxiety, knowing that you are not alone in this?

Could it be that this decrease in your anxiety will influence the *affective field* in your classroom as you hand out the tests the next day, and thus, the students perform better? I hope you can test these hypotheses.

This chapter reflects the challenges circle lovers are likely to encounter when you engage in pedagogy in the round, especially at this time of transition as education moves in a new direction.

It's a Nice Idea, But ...

Just a partial list of reasons *not* to offer circles in the classroom:

- I don't have enough time to get through the material I'm already supposed to teach. I can't add one more thing!
- We hardly have enough room to fit all the bodies. There's no way we can make a circle in the classroom!
- With so many students, it would take forever to get around the circle!
- My students will never sit still long enough to do a council!
- My students haven't acquired the language skills to be able to tell stories in council.
- I have a few students who will just make this impossible!
- I have students who come from cultures and religious traditions that don't approve of telling personal and family stories to outsiders.
- I don't want to open a Pandora's box! When we invite students to speak from the heart, they just might do it! I'm a mandated reporter, and if I offer circles in my

classroom, my reports to Child Protective Services would multiply exponentially!
- There are certain things we just can't talk about in schools!
- I don't know if I have the capacity to hold the personal stories of my students. I don't know if I can tolerate the emotional overload.
- It seems that council requires me to tell my personal stories to the students. Is that appropriate? What happens if I am going through a personal crisis?
- If I sit in the circle with the students, and use my first name, and tell my personal stories, won't I lose my authority in the classroom?

A few reasons *not* to practice circles with colleagues in an institutional setting:

- There is a line between personal and professional, and council crosses it!
- There are already too many required meetings!
- We have a staff of 180 at our school! We will never get them all in a circle.
- What would happen if all teachers did circles in their classes? Wouldn't the students be circled-out?
- If some teachers are doing circles and others are not, there would be an imbalance of trust and connection between students and teachers.
- How can we have a true circle of equals when administrators have the responsibility to evaluate the performance of teachers?
- If I speak from the heart about my teaching, and I speak of my mistakes, my frustrations, and my despair, my administrator will hold this against me.
- As an administrator, I will lose my authority if I share my personal stories and concerns with staff.
- I'm not sitting in a circle with *those* people!

- There is no way *some people* on our staff will ever go for this touchy-feely stuff!
- Our school district operates in a very rigid, chain-of-command style. They don't collaborate; they just issue directives. It is a dominator model, not a partnership model!

I have heard some form of all these objections numerous times over the years. While I acknowledge the validity of them all, and I will address each in this chapter, I must ask, what is the alternative? What is the alternative to creating safe, trusting environments in our classrooms where the whole child—with their fears, losses, longings, and ecstasies—can feel welcomed? What is the alternative to honestly sharing our *worst practices* as well as our *best practices* with our colleagues—fellow teachers and administrators? What is the alternative to having a place where all stakeholders can share their truths without fear of reprisal?

Now that we are developing a circle habit of mind, how do we gain some distance from the drama of these valid concerns? When we look for the inherent topics within these valid concerns, I hear these resonant topics:

- Authority
- Time
- Space
- Number
- Discipline
- Resistance and emotional bandwidth
- Practicalities of setting up and sustaining a systemic circle practice
- Having to teach online

Authority

We touched on this in Chapter 4 with the idea of shifting roles from teacher to circle facilitator. It bears repeating in terms of the institutional reality of roles within a school system, what I call the *vertical axis of authority*. In my experience, from the classroom, to the school, to the district headquarters in the LAUSD, participating authentically in a circle evokes fear in those who are in a "position of authority." This is a fear that comes up in superintendents who might participate in circle with other district officials; in district officials with school-based administrators; principals and headmasters with faculty, staff, and parents; teachers with students and parents; and even students with each other in terms of their own autonomy.

In institutions, there is always a supervisory, evaluative, or responsibility "chain of command." The fear is that participating in a *horizontal axis of authority,* where each person is just *one among many*—no more or less human; no matter the age, role, or position—will diminish one's capacity to carry out the mandates of grading, evaluating, hiring and firing.

All things spherical must integrate both horizontal and vertical axes (and everything in between). It seems to me that this dance of wholeness depends on three things:

- Self-awareness, including a willingness to hear from others how they perceive you
- An understanding of how to assess and share, as trainer Marlow Hotchkiss says, "what serves self, circle, and the greater good"
- Trust in the circle—the people and the process

Circle practice can bring about deep *self-awareness*. Within the circle, we compare our own assumptions, perspectives, and values with those of others. We also see the effect our presence has on others. As honesty and trust develop, the feedback we send and receive become gifts of great value. As the poet Robert Burns puts it, "Oh, would some Power the gift give us, to see ourselves as others see us!" This, of course, requires some courage (heart). In the classroom, this feedback can take the form of students engaging in a circle-based evaluation of you! Ask them to tell you what you are doing that they find helpful, what doesn't work for them, and generally how they feel/think about you and the class. As in the story of Elisio in Chapter 9, attempt to receive this feedback without judgment or taking it personally. Take of it what you will; leave alone what you find unenlightening. As an administrator or district official, when you hear the truth of what those you serve think of/feel about you, *the worst that can happen is that you must make some changes* (unless your actions have been truly egregious). The key here is to guard against your tendency toward retaliation. This is where self-awareness comes in handy. When you are committed to deep and continuous self-reflection, doing your own work, healing your wounds, then it is possible to notice when you are out of integrity and when you get emotionally triggered by what others say or do. This is really quite an undertaking, daunting in many ways. I can only say that having been so blessed to be with so many in circles over the years, I have felt supported in doing this deeply personal work.

This leads us to the issue of how to know what will serve self, circle, and the greater good. It can be as simple as asking yourself whether what you say or do will serve the circle. If it will only serve you—to blow off steam, to get something out, to receive approval or recognition—then refrain, as this is something that needs independent, personal reflection. For us as teachers it comes back to sharing only what is authentic, age- and context-appropriate, and facilitating of student sharing. That is, what you share with students should be real and honest, with awareness of their developmental level and of what is appropriate in the school and cultural setting. And the purpose of your sharing in the circle is to model this authenticity in a way that will encourage others to do the same. For the school administrator, remember that in the same way your staff exists to serve the needs of the students, so your position is in support of the staff. Ask yourself what will serve them, pause, and listen for the answer. When we receive honest feedback on your performance as teachers, managers, and leaders, there are three baskets into which this information will fall:

1. Things you can immediately address
2. Things that will need more information or consultation (circle) to address
3. Things that are not within your power to address given current resources and circumstances

Finally, *trust the circle.* With ongoing practice in adult circles, this trust will develop and deepen. In your circles with students over time, with their inevitable ups and downs, you will see that the practice can contain all joys and sorrows. Ultimately, we do not teach circles; *circles teach us.* Trust also that when students develop their own voice and self-awareness, they will manage to see you in both your teacher *and* human forms. As your staff comes to know that their voice, perspectives, and experience are valued, they will be able to traverse engaging with you in the vertical *and* the horizontal, the complex dance of wholeness.

Time

Students have remarked that circle is a time to slow down and not be so stressed out. Many participants notice what has been called "Sabbath time" in circles, an experience of being "off the wheel." This is true even when the circle is taking up an academic topic. In addition, for group activities, circle practice increases the possibility for deep listening in a limited time, reins in the dominance of a few quick responders (the usual hand-wavers) and provides an opportunity for more "considerate" students to participate.

When I told recycler, builder, earth-artist Skip Schuckmann that I was doing council in public schools, he warned, "Council isn't something you do at 11:26 each Friday. You do it when you need to, and you do it until you're done!"

Skip had a point. There is something artificial about doing council at the same time each week for a prescribed duration. Furthermore, if there isn't a felt "need" on the part of the class to go into council, the hour can seem endless, and the teacher feels challenged to keep things moving. Conversely, when the group is really engaged, there doesn't seem to be *enough* time, or something comes up at the end of our time that energizes the group, and we are ready to continue indefinitely!

There is great value in having regularly scheduled classroom circles, first thing Monday morning or the last hour on Friday, for example. In addition to the consistent weekly time, it is also valuable to have enough flexibility for the class or the teacher to call circles when they are needed: to mark transitions, to introduce new units and set intentions, to check for understanding, to deal with interpersonal issues, to respond to school, community, national, or world matters, etc.

When I first began teaching, my lesson plans had to account for every class moment. I wrote out my questions, acceptable answers, and the "heavy cueing" I would use if I didn't get those answers. Today, teachers are dealing with ever more inclusive curriculum design packages, rigid "pacing plans," and regularly scheduled assessments. In this atmosphere, it is entirely reasonable to ask, "Where can council fit?"

This question was raised at an early staff council at the Open Magnet Charter Elementary School. It was asked *not* in relation to finding time to practice with students, but to meeting regularly in a staff council. One teacher held the talking piece and lamented, "Look, this is great, but we already have so many meetings—curriculum planning, Open School Institute meetings, regular staff meetings. This seems like just one more thing to add to an already overflowing plate." I could see that this sentiment resonated with this dedicated, high-functioning group. When the talking piece came to me, I had an inspiration: "Let's try something in silence," I suggested. "I'll hold the talking piece. When I feel everyone's attention resting on me, I'll pass it. When you get it, hold on until you sense the whole group holding you in regard, and then pass it." This whole process including all staff members took less than five minutes, and it completely shifted the mood! At its conclusion, two things were clear: council does not have to extend into the wee hours, and it is *not all about talking*. I now recommend such a "silent council" before the commencement of any agenda-driven staff meeting.

Although I have come to see circles with students and colleagues not as an *extra* but as *essential,* here are few suggestions for dealing with seemingly ever-contracting time:

- Even with no time to form a circle, you can pass an item from student to student with a simple instruction such as *notice who has the talking piece as it goes around.* This simple act of silent recognition of each person in the class can really change the energy. If there is time to get into a standing circle without moving the chairs, the same *silent council* can be even more powerful.
- After a lesson, a reading, an experience, a game, an experiment, etc., use a *popcorn* style and ask: *What's one thing you remember* (from the lesson, etc.)? Often teachers will ask students to write in a "learning log," to make a private note of one thing they *learned.* There are two limitations in doing this. One is that the information is kept private when written in a log. The other is that asking anyone for something they "learned" creates a *heavy cognitive load.* Many will say that they didn't "learn" anything. Simply asking for *one thing you remember* will bring out what has been learned because it is something that remains in awareness. If for example, you take students through a museum, and just before you leave you ask for one thing they remembered, this will result in *a nearly complete revisit of the experience* as each sharing will spark recollection in all, a review that will deepen the impression and therefore the memory of what they witnessed.
- *Saying one word, phrase, or image:* Looking back at the "resource circle" discussed in Chapter 9, a very powerful, brief circle can be simply saying a name, a place, or an event, the recollection of which brings a sense of calm or pride.
- *Five word or haiku response:* Limit the responses to a question or prompt to five word or five-seven-five.

- Brief check-ins: A word or two about how you are doing. Or use a category to indicate how you are doing: colors, animals, ice cream flavors, weather check, etc.
- Naming *favorites:* songs, historical figures, places, etc.
- *Integrate* the circle into another small group activity. Have each group conduct a circle around a topic, and then, if there is time, have each group select a representative witness to report out.
- Use the *fishbowl* format. Depending on the time available, have a few volunteers, or students engaged in a mutual endeavor or dealing with a particular issue, form an inner circle, surrounded by the rest of the class, a circle of witnesses. This inner circle takes up the question. If there is time, the outer circle can "witness" (recall) what has been shared in the inner circle. Also, depending on time, the number of rounds can be limited.
- *Link circles.* Most conversations these days take place in installments. We learn to speak in sound bites for fear that we will not have enough time to fully express ourselves. To *link* circles, at the end of a session, summarize what has gone on or have a student "witness" do so. Acknowledge any issues that have been left unfinished and any students who have not had a chance to speak. At the beginning of the next circle, remind students of where the group left off. Doing so provides continuity and connection between sessions.
- Use *virtual circles* like those described in the next section.

Space

When I first started at Palms Middle School, I taught seventh-grade English in the woodshop. Wood chips, dust, and keeping students away from the power tools were only a few of our problems. The student chairs, with half-sized desks attached, were *bolted* to the ground. To do small group work, students had to gather around the large, fixed worktables, sometimes lying on them to get close enough to see what they were working on. There was absolutely no way to form a circle with the 30+ students in each of my five classes.

After experiencing circles in the open spaces and the circular "yurts" of The Ojai Foundation, one student lamented that the rooms at Palms were "cramped up with desks, backpacks everywhere." The reality of most urban classrooms is just this. At the time of this writing, academic classes in LAUSD run at approximately 32–36 students. Rooms have barely enough space to fit student desks or tables with freestanding chairs, so it is often impossible to even form a circle. Add to this the usual 52–54-minute hour and one begins to wonder who these people are who suggest we can do circles in the schools.

Nice idea. Impractical, though.

In some private schools, like Crossroads in Santa Monica and Archer School for Girls in Los Angeles, there are Human Development (HD) departments, with their own space, their own time, and their own staff. In the public school, however, the academic teachers are attempting to bring council to classes given the realities of limited space, limited time, and too many bodies.

In the best of all possible worlds (we can dream, can't we?), the council space should allow students to sit in a circle, equidistant from its center, preferably on the floor with comfortable mats, Backjack chairs, or zafus (round meditation cushions). There should be no obstructions. Students should be able to move in the space and to walk across the circle to pass the talking piece. They should have enough freedom in the space to dance, play, draw, create music, and interact in dyads and other smaller groupings.

Seating should be movable so that other circle forms, like the "fishbowl" and the "spiral" can occur. Perhaps the debate about class sizes can be answered simply: "Only as many students as can sit comfortably in a circle!"

One of the innovations, however, being considered during the pandemic time was to create outdoor classrooms: spaces that break up the concrete and foster a natural environment where things (and children) can grow. Outdoor classrooms present opportunities to learn sustaining human (circle) and environmental practices (permaculture, agriculture, bushcraft, and animal husbandry). Outdoor council circles now exist on many campuses, beckoning passersby to engage heartfully.

If your school doesn't yet have such accommodations, be sure to insinuate yourself at the next building and facilities committee meeting. In the meantime, however, here are a few suggestions:

- On occasion, move the class to a common area. At Palms, we had a small "council room," which used to be a teacher's lounge. We also used the auditorium pit, stage, and foyer, the cafeteria, and various outdoor spaces. Some schools have even built council gardens. (Note: when you move circles outdoors, you are inviting in the natural world—with all its wonder, possibilities, and distractions.)
- If possible, enlist students to move desks to the periphery of the room so that an open space for the circle can be created in the center. We would flip student desks over to stack them.
- Move desks into a circle or consolidate tables in the center or the periphery of the room and create the circle with freestanding chairs.
- Move student desks into three concentric circles and use the *spiral* form.
- *The flower:* Simply place an item on the floor to mark the center of the room and ask everyone to turn to face the center. The talking piece weaves among the petals of this flower.
- *The Virtual Circle*: If the desks can't move, or there are too many, and it is impossible to form an actual circle, use a "virtual," projected circle as described in Chapter 6.

I once attended a lecture by Adolf Guggenbühl-Craig at the C. G. Jung Institute in Los Angeles. There was a podium at the front of the room for the speaker and about thirty rows of chairs extending to the rear of the carpeted hall. For anyone sitting beyond the first 10 or so rows, it would be impossible to see the speaker. I thought, "OK, I'm not here to *see* him. I'm here to *listen*." Once he began, it became clear that there were problems with the sound system. Now many in the room couldn't see *nor* hear. To make matters worse, the room was stifling in the summer heat, so the windows were opened. Because they faced a busy street, this let in a rush of traffic noise, further muting our soft-spoken elder.

The 200+ people in the room were getting restless. I and a few others moved up and sat on the floor of the carpeted area by the podium where we might be able to hear. It quickly became apparent that the majority in the room could not.

After some confusion, I suggested to a friend that we move all the chairs into concentric circles with the speaker in the middle and floor space directly around him for anyone who wished to sit on the floor. She suggested I broadcast this suggestion above the din. Soon, we were packed in close to one another, and, with a bit of leaning in, everyone was able to hear. All who could sat on the floor in concentric circles, while those who needed chairs were able to arrange them in an outer circle.

The conditions at this lecture—the numbers, rigidity of the seating arrangement, the heat—might be familiar to urban teachers adapting to ever increasing class sizes in shrinking accommodations.

The size of the group can certainly make a difference in the classroom as well as in circle. James K. Moffett and Betty Jane Wagner in their book *Student-Centered Language Arts, K-12*, suggest that five is an ideal size grouping for classroom discussions.[1] For councils, Jack Zimmerman and Virginia Coyle suggest 10 to 15 to "provide a comfortable balance between the number of voices and the demands on participant's attentiveness." They also say that "above 20, councils can get unwieldy, so that special forms or time restrictions may be necessary."[2]

At Palms, we had a crew of trained council facilitators to work with student groups so that some classes could split, with the teacher taking one half and the facilitator taking the other. There are problems with this arrangement, however. First, although it provides for the intimacy of smaller groups, the teacher only gets to sit with half of the class at any one time. Second, when an "outside" facilitator is brought in, the circles must be scheduled at a particular time regularly convenient for that person, somewhat limiting the teacher's and the students' ability to call a circle when needed. Third, the students themselves only get to sit with half of their peers. Finally, unless the facilitator and teacher are carefully planning together, each group may be taking up very different issues and activities.

The reality in these times, however, is that a wide enough pool of facilitators or partner teachers to serve schools is still far off. So, in the meantime, here are a few suggestions for dealing with large numbers of students:

- *Concentric circles:* A class of 36, for example, can be arranged with an inner circle of six, a second circle of 12, and an outer circle of 18. On the floor or in freestanding chairs, students in this arrangement can fit in a relatively small space and can hear each other quite well. The talking piece is passed around one circle and then passed in or out to the next.
- *Fishbowl*: The rest of a class as a circle of "witnesses" surrounds a small inner circle, whose number depends on time and the issue to be discussed.
- *Spiral*: Place four to eight chairs or desks in an inner circle. One student begins the process and passes the talking piece to the student on her left. After that second student finishes speaking and passes the talking piece, the first student rises and moves to the outer circle, leaving an empty seat to be filled by another student from the outer

circle. When this student arrives in the inner circle, the next speaker can begin.

- *Small group, student-led circles*: Each circle is an opportunity for students to learn about facilitation, especially if the adult facilitators model "transparent" leadership; that is, if we explain to them *why* we are employing certain prompts, activities, and circle forms and *how* we arrived at these choices. This includes telling them when we are confused or uncertain! Students can learn quite readily to lead their own councils. Initially, it is good to write out directions and assign roles for these small group circles.
- *Small group councils and "the grand council:"* Divide students into groups of four to six. Have them each take up the same prompt or task. Ask that they elect a "witness representative" at the end of their council. These representatives return to a "grand council," an inner circle of six students, surrounded by the rest of the class, who report the process and determinations of each small circle.
- If the class is too large or the room will not accommodate an actual circle, use the virtual circle. You can even employ the fishbowl or spiral: add a particular group of student names to the center. The outer circle designates the "witnesses."

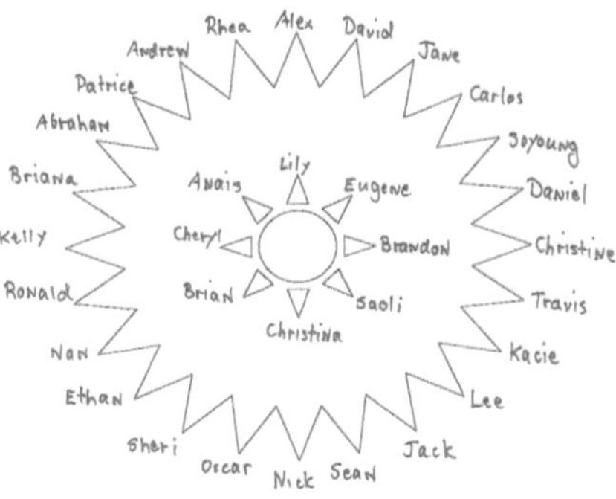

A virtual fishbowl

The Virtual Spiral

Using any number of inner "seats," note on the board, overhead projector, or screen which students are entering the spiral.

Classroom realities provide us with challenges. Still, the value of using a circle-based pedagogy is that the field of heightened awareness creates an intimacy even in the rigid, cramped conditions and time constraints of the typical classroom. Accompanied by mutual respect and elevated concentration, this intimacy can make these conditions feel spacious.

Discipline

A favorite professional development topic for those who have had circle training for education is "council discipline." How will we ever get these kids to stop interrupting and truly respect one another? In modern usage, the word "discipline" connotes the measures we take to keep order and the consequences of stepping outside of that order.

The word also refers to *areas of knowledge* such as in the traditional *disciplines* of art, science, mathematics, language, etc. It is useful to remember, however, that the original meaning of the word comes from the Latin *disciple*—the root of which is *discere,* which means "to learn." In this way, a disciple is "one who learns." So, we might reframe the question about discipline in this way: what can we do to encourage and support students to *want* to learn about what it means to be in circles with others? In other words, *how do we become disciples of the circle?*

The first principle of circle-based discipline is that the facilitator be a "disciple" of the circle. As with any other "discipline," effective teachers must love their subjects. To inspire students to be disciplined in circle practices, we must experience the profound value of the practice in our own lives. We must *walk the talk* of circles.

Consider the fact that *in so many ways we ask children to do things that we ourselves fail to do*: take responsibility, admit your mistakes, respect others, share your things, etc. If we are not living these values, students will sense it and not feel the need to transform their energy in service of them. This is especially true when we are trying to promote the values of *speaking and listening from the heart.* If our speaking contains a hidden agenda and our listening is evaluative, we are not practicing what we preach. I count myself among those deeply in need of practice. This kind of honesty, vulnerability, and suspension of judgment is not in my cultural conditioning.

To be a disciple of circles, capable of conveying to others a desire to do likewise, I *practice with other adults*. What we share in circles with students must be in service to them. What we share in adult circles can be in service of self. In every school where we offer a systemic program, we insist that staff practice circles together, usually in either an open, agendaless fashion or focused on the *educator mysteries*. The staff circles must be strong enough, safe enough, and trusting enough to contain our sharing of *worst practices* as well as best practices. As physicians-in-training must do when a patient dies, we must be able to share our mistakes, failures, and the outright harms we may have caused through unskillful means with our students. Without such a commitment to deep adult practice, the program will be less than effective.

Additional Guidelines for Circle Discipline

- **Initiate early:** Classroom culture is set within the first six hours. Procedurally, every change after that comes as a shock. As discussed in Chapter 7, the circle is a great way to celebrate the *rite of entry* at the start of a new year. Consistency with regularly scheduled circle time is also essential. If there is to be continuity, circle time must reliably come around even when there is conflict or pressure because of upcoming exams or other schedule changes. Doing so conveys the importance of the practice and will result in more familiarity and order. Bear in mind that the shift to circle culture is a radical one. It is not easy for anyone.

- **Community participants:** There will be more about this in Chapter 12, but just to note here that, whenever possible, have at least one other adult in the circle with you. This person sits across from you and provides a reliable, *listening presence* in the circle. Students do not have many exemplars of adults who listen deeply. At first, students will tend to tell their stories to you. Having a second listener directly across from you will begin to move students toward the goal of addressing the entire circle, not just you. This person should also learn to tell age- and context-appropriate, facilitating stories.
- **Keep early circles light:** Remember that the reason we gather in circles is to *enjoy* our time together. A circle that evokes student stories of accomplishments, insights, a naming of people, things, and activities important to them lifts the atmosphere and strengthens the *relational field.* Even if reluctant students only say one word, like their favorite color or animal, the circle will have an uplifting, unifying field. It should go without saying, but it is not a great idea to *introduce* the circle when there is a conflict. We don't want circles to become just *that thing we do when there is a problem.*
- **Don't go into council just because it is circle time:** The circle becomes a council only when participants are ready to bring heightened awareness of self and other to the proceeding. It is a rookie mistake to sit down in the circle and call for a dedication before anyone knows why we have come together. If you are bringing the topic or prompt to the group, it is best to discuss it in circle *before* you formally go into council. Let them know why you chose the topic and see if they are on board with it and might have stories to share. It might be that something other than what you planned is needed. I like to ask the group, "Are we ready to go into council?" If

the body language says yes, then it is time to call for an opening and bring in the talking piece.

- **Keep the sanctity of circle time:** Post a note on the door: *We are in circle. Please don't interrupt unless it is absolutely necessary.* When you convey that circle time is as important as direct instruction or exam-time, students will come to share this value. If you allow for interruptions from the outside, expect the same inside.
- **Involve students in norm setting:** As we saw in the last chapter, when students are involved in developing and refining the agreements of a circle, they are more likely to align themselves with them. Use a question like, "What do you need from me, the other students, and yourself in order to feel safe and comfortable to speak your truth?"
- **Model respect for the talking piece:** Once a council is underway, show the students that you won't speak either unless you have the talking piece. Sometimes this means letting things go somewhat awry before the piece comes back to you so you can comment on what you witnessed (without judgment). I like to tell students that when we are in council, I have to shut up and just listen! They love that idea.
- **Vary circle *forms*, i.e., basic, fishbowl, spiral, web, dyad, response:** No matter how compelling the topic is, if every circle uses the basic form with the talking piece going around the circle, students will be bored. Look back to Chapter 6 to review the forms. To keep your circles fresh, use a variety of forms, even sometimes when the topic or process doesn't call for them. This will keep involvement high and disruption low.

- **Vary circle *modes*, i.e., kinesthetic, intrapersonal, interpersonal, linguistic, spatial (art), musical/rhythmic:** To sustain interest and engagement, offer circle modes *other than linguistic* (*talking*). See Chapter 6 to review the modes.
- **Encourage student ownership of the process:** Every time we facilitate a circle, we are teaching how to facilitate a circle. Be transparent in your choices of topic, form, and mode. Discuss these choices so students can agree, disagree, or revise before you begin. The youngest students love to be responsible for setting up and bringing or creating items for the center. Engage students in norm setting. Encourage student leadership as early as possible as we saw in Chapter 10. Use small group circles so students can facilitate their own.
- **Use a facilitator's piece sparingly:** Trainer Camille Ameen calls this a "pause piece." I like to use something easily seen, like a giant plastic sunflower (though a real one would be better). Raise this piece only to comment on *process, not content.* Sometimes you need to interrupt to tell students about how much time remains or to suggest shifting the form. This piece should not be used as a cudgel to correct a student who might not be speaking to the prompt.
- **Progressive discipline:** The facilitator's piece can be used to bring order. I tell students that when I raise it and say nothing, *something* is not working, intentions or agreements are not being followed. Sometimes simply *raising the piece* will be enough to bring back attention. If it doesn't, at a second level intervention, you can say something like, "I want to remind everyone that *we are in council.*" When I say this, I am addressing the whole circle, not a particular individual. At a third level, I might raise the piece and note *a particular agreement or intention* that is not being followed. If this doesn't restore order, I might raise the piece and *address the individuals*

who appear to be causing the disruption. If the only option is to *remove a student or students from the circle,* this can also be done when you raise the piece, as long as you have provided the protocol for what happens when a student sits out is clear to all. If you ask a student to sit out, have a designated place for them to go. Some teachers make prior arrangements for a student to go to another class. Have an alternative assignment for them; best is a writing opportunity to respond to the prompt being addressed in the circle. Talk to the student alone afterwards to listen to their challenges and determine if there is an adjustment you can make. Talk to the student before the next council, reminding them that today is a fresh opportunity to practice the intentions. Sometimes students simply need to sit out to rest or gather themselves. Whenever you need to remove a student, it should be done with a message that you want them to return when they can follow the agreements, a message that *the circle is not complete without you.*

- **Sometimes let the circle completely spin out:** From time to time, it is valuable to be completely hands off while the talking piece is going around. Don't make any process interventions even when students are side-talking, disrespecting the talking piece and each other, breaking the agreements, etc. Remain externally impassive, non-reactive, and non-judgmental. When the talking piece comes back to you, attempt to describe what you saw and heard. You might even, using nonviolent communication (NVC), say what you are feeling, needing, and requesting. Then, pass the talking piece. Sometimes through the mirror of your objective witnessing, students can see themselves and modify behavior.
- **If it clearly isn't happening, close the circle:** Close without any judgment. Sometimes simply just move on to another activity or lesson. If possible, enlist

the class in discussing what happened and brainstorming ideas and perhaps new intentions or agreements for the next circle.

- **Turn into the skid:** When there is ice on the road and the car begins to skid to the right, counterintuitively we turn the wheel to the right to keep moving forward. Notice where the circle is going and shift the focus to acknowledge the new direction. What the circle needs is of primary importance, not your chosen topic. Model flexibility based on what is happening.

Resistance and Emotional Bandwidth

It is useful to remember any resistance *you* might have had to circle practice: concerns about loss of autonomy, authority, time, other priorities, boundaries between personal and professional, etc. As D. W. Winnicott said, "It is a joy to be hidden, a tragedy not to be found." Often, what we long for we turn away from, usually for fear that it can't be real or can't be sustained. In our individualistic culture, we have indeed "sustained unhealthy, yet functional, ways of surviving without it" as Kenneth R. Lakritz and Thomas M. Knoblauch's express in their book *Elders on Love* (1999). For the word "love" substitute "circle":

"Love is the essential ingredient that makes it possible for us to remain present and to endure human life's suffering and sober realities. Without love, it is difficult to value our lives; our natural response is detachment from life as a means of coping with its intrinsic physical and emotional pain. If we bring our love forward, after long standing patterns of safe retreat, we will inevitably upset that comfortable homeostasis of our life situations and create disturbance and crisis in our usual (and often destructive) ways of adapting to love's absence. Thus, we must be respectful of the potentially overwhelming experience of opening to love's energy when we have sustained unhealthy, yet functional, ways of surviving without it."[3]

When the Palms Council Project was gaining some notoriety in the LAUSD, administrators from other schools would come to see what it was all about. When we sat in a circle, regularly a few would sit side-saddle, half in and half out. That was over 30 years ago, and the good news is that now school leaders are much more open and embracing of social-emotional learning, and we understand that to teach it we must live it. How do we increase our own emotional bandwidth, our ability to feel more across the whole spectrum of human emotion? I have found only one way: to be with others who are willing to feel deeply, to express ecstatic joy, to openly grieve losses, and to allow their hearts to break. In other words, to have a consistent adult circle practice.

Resistance among young people by the time they are adolescents is equally if not more profound. Like oppressed people, youth often come to devalue the truth of their own experience. They receive messages that they don't understand what is happening to them. When we invite them into deep dialogue, they often don't trust that what they have to offer is of value or that anyone would care to hear it. Paulo Freire puts it this way in reference to oppressed or marginalized people:

"With no experience of dialogue, with no experience of participation, the oppressed are often unsure of themselves. They have consistently been denied their right to have their say, having historically had the duty to only listen and obey. It is thus normal that they almost always maintain an attitude of mistrust towards those who attempt to dialogue with them. Actually, this distrustful attitude is directed also toward themselves. They are not sure of their own ability. They are influenced by the myth of their own ignorance."[4]

With a bit of reframing, we can begin to see what we perceive as resistance to be self-preservation on an emotional level. Doing so allows us to soften our judgments about teachers and students who distance themselves, sometimes forcefully, from participation in circles. *Our singular goal in this work is to help young people to value and express the truth of their own experience and to value and be receptive to the experience of others.*

Sometimes resistance to circle practice comes from a healthy recognition of one's own limitations as to emotional bandwidth. When we do create safe spaces for young people and offer them the opportunity to speak from the heart, they will sometimes take us up on it. When we adults become privy to the inner lives of children, we are likely to have to bear witness to their losses, their fears, and their concerns about their personal future and future of the planet. The weight of this can be overwhelming. I have found only one way, besides doing my own inner work, to expand my capacity to be present, to allow my heart to break and still listen from the heart when the circle is filled with sorrow. That is *to be in the company of others who are willing to let their hearts break*; that is, to sit in circle with peers and tell the stories I am hearing from the youth. My experience tells me that when broken hearts come together to share the causes and the feelings they evoke, we grow a bigger heart. With this bigger heart, we can return and return again to the circles. As Joanna Macy says, "Don't apologize for the sorrow, grief, and rage you feel. It is a measure of your humanity and your maturity. It is a measure of your open heart, and as your heart breaks open there will be room for the world to heal."

Sustaining a School-Based Program

At Palms Middle School, the flagship public-school program where 2,000 students participated weekly in one of 100 circles, the practice has vanished. This loss was the product of three things: letting go of adult practice; relying on outside facilitators; and a change in leadership. Once Monica Chinlund and I moved into the LAUSD headquarters, the teacher coordinating the project determined that there was no need for adult councils, that it would just be something teachers did with the students. Without ongoing adult practice, the circles lose their authenticity, and without the adults meeting regularly to experiment with forms and prompts and to address issues that arise in the community, the circles lose their freshness, immediacy, and responsiveness. At Palms, a great effort was made to train outside (non-teacher) facilitators so large classes could be split. This created a dependency that could not be sustained without significant fundraising every year. When funding dropped in certain years, some teachers felt it was impossible to conduct circles with the whole class.

Some teachers were also given the option to have two facilitators so they would not have to take responsibility for leading. The result was that they never learned to facilitate with their own classes. We found that this "facilitator model" was not sustainable without a pool of trained and experienced adults and financial resources that in general are not available in the public schools. Finally, a change in leadership to a principal who was limited both in her willingness to understand the history and practice and to listen for any extended period was the final piece that diminished the once thriving program. A few teachers have continued to use the practice in their classrooms, but it is no longer systemic in the Palms Middle School community.

Systemic Practice

What does it mean to have a school that fully embraces circle ways? First, the school must value and articulate the centrality of circle practice at the school in discussions, on its website, in advertisements, etc. Circle practice should not be considered an expendable extra just when there is nothing else pressing. If fact, when there are "high-stakes" events like state-mandated testing, when big changes are to be implemented, or when there are challenges in the community, the first and best thought should be to *bring it to the circle.* Circle practice must be an inviolable part of the weekly schedule and circles for staff, parents, and community *must be calendared in advance.* In the same way that some schools offer Sustained Silent Reading (SSR), where *everyone* on campus drops what they are doing to be with a book, the school must commit fully to circle practice.

The single most important element in the establishment of a circle-based culture at the school is for students to see parents and staff engaged in circle practice. Children rarely have exemplars of adults who listen with compassion and speak authentically with an awareness of the impact of their words on others. In cultures that embrace circles, that is not the case.

Modern parenting can be quite a lonely enterprise. In times past, parenting was the responsibility of *every adult* as each child was seen as a gift to all in the community. At Circle Ways, we are re-creating a kind of village atmosphere with the school as its center. We now offer a training for parents/caregivers and grandparents. After a first year of Circle Ways facilitators leading these monthly parent/caregiver circles, generally a group of engaged participants emerge, and we offer a facilitator training for them. They learn to use the mysteries process to determine the most salient topics in the parent body. In that second year, we mentor this group as *they* lead the parent circles. Before the third program year begins, we team with these parents to co-lead a training for new interested parents. Then, the process sustains itself.

Community Resources

Another important consideration is that the school have a regularly updated *community resource list* and clear guidelines for when these agencies and services must be called into play. When people are offered the possibility of speaking their truths in a safe, public setting, they tend to take you up on the offer. This can mean having to bear witness to and act upon issues of abuse, drug and alcohol use, suicidality, etc. This fact alone is often enough to dissuade school leadership from developing a systemic practice. However, when students learn circle ways beginning with the games and dances of pre- school, by the time they reach adolescence they have learned that *if* they speak their truths into compassionate listening, the school community will rally in support. All staff should know the outside agencies that support families in crisis and what the protocols are when a child needs support.

Scheduling

Countless times over the years I have heard teachers say that circle time is wonderful, but they don't know how they will get the space in curriculum delivery to devote an hour a week to circle practice. I like to ask this question: is it not possible to have one thirtieth of the time students spend in school be devoted to being in circle? Creative administrators and teachers always find a way to make it happen. In some cases where rigid bureaucracies are at play in the system, circle time must be connected to learning standards. If that is so, then my hope is that you will find it quite easy to link standards in any discipline to the practice. It is especially relevant to communication arts, social studies and history, and health and sex education.

With the younger grades, the scheduling issue is easy as students often only have one teacher throughout the day. Nonetheless, circle time should be offered at the *same time every week*. This gives the teacher an opportunity to say to students, "That's something we can take to our circle!" In addition to this reliable weekly time, circles are offered as needed, as desired or as called by the children.

Scheduling in the upper grades becomes a bit more complicated. In some schools, an hour or two is carved out of the schedule, and circle time is a class unto itself, offered at the same time once a week. There are also "advisory" classes that meet every day to keep a focus on deepening relationships with each student and providing individual guidance. One of those class hours per week can be devoted to circle. In many schools, the schedule does not allow for a carve-out period or advisory. When this is the case, we recommend *rotating the practice* through different departments by grade level and then adding a few minutes from other classes to the instructional time for those classes. For example, in a high school, the circles can be scheduled in the social studies classes in ninth grade, health classes in the tenth, communication arts in the eleventh, and government in the twelfth. Circle process is also a natural fit in certain elective classes such as Leadership, Community Service, Business Management,[5] etc.

"Training"

I put this section title in quotes because what we do at Circle Ways when we offer a workshop is always more of a taste or an orientation and experience of the many forms and modes of circle practice for the classroom and school community. I even like to call what we do a "remembering" because *circles are a natural way to learn that we have simply forgotten.* The real "training" happens when you begin to engage students, staff, parents, and community in the practice.

We recommend that *all* members of the staff, including clerical, custodial, food service, and security are involved in the introductory workshop. Regular staff circles are critical to systemic implementation. Circles can never be seen as something we do only with the children. If that is the case, they will not trust the process. The *best* way to have students acquire the practice is for them to see the staff modeling it! At Palms, we would leave the library doors open when we held a staff circle so students could come by and "discover" their teachers doing exactly what they are asked to do.

As we saw in Chapter 9, all so-called "restorative" practices rest on the foundation of the relationships built through consistent circle practice. Again, if there is no relationship, there is nothing to restore. In fact, when we work to establish a systemic program, we do not offer the second level workshop, "Foundations of Restorative Practices," until staff have completed a full year of circle practice with students. While there is a desire to learn the conflict mediation aspects of circles to deal with "problems," we prefer to have the school gain experience with the joys and challenges of circles before we offer processes for reconciliation.

In the first few years of establishing a systemic practice, some schools bring us in to provide teacher coaching and co-facilitation of adult circles with members of a school-based Circle Leadership Committee (CLC). We also provide restorative mediation for schools that are just getting started. The purpose of training, however, is to become fully independent of the trainers. (Same for teaching.) Every circle you lead must be led transparently; that is, explicitly giving the circle your thought process for choices of topic, prompt, form, and mode. Every circle you lead is a *training* for those in the circle. We are not looking to create dependency. One way we promote independence is by supporting a CLC.

The Circle Leadership Committee

On every campus that embraces circle practice, there are always a few staff members who are naturals, people who have a capacity to "read the field" and make choices that serve the immediate needs of the participants. Comprised of a few staff members, parents, and even students in upper elementary and above, this group becomes the go-to for staff who need support or are looking for ideas for their work with students. The CLC keeps track of the *relational field* of the school. They take note of the need to bring ceremony to achievements, festive occasions, themed days, and holidays. They also provide structure for processing loss, major changes in the school, as well as local, national, and global events that impact the atmosphere of the school. Recall the story of the beginning of the Palms Council Project in the aftermath of the acquittals of police for the Rodney King case in Los Angeles. This group will also process the information that comes through the feedback loop created by a box (or online document) where staff can anonymously submit "concerns and celebrations."

Addressing Concerns and Celebrations

In Peter Senge's book *The Fifth Discipline*, he notes, "The gap between vision and current reality is also a source of energy. If there were no gap, there would be no need for any action to move towards the vision. We call the gap creative tension." As Victor Frankel puts it, "Between stimulus and response, there is a space. In that space is our power to choose our response. In our response lies our growth and our freedom." Sometimes that space goes unnoticed or unacknowledged. It represents the information that remains below the surface in an organization. This information, however, is critical for growth and improvement of the organization as well as the well-being of its members. In engineering as in all complex systems, there are closed and open feedback loops. An open loop allows a system to correct itself. Sometimes just acknowledging the issues that were underground will instigate positive change. To create such a loop in the school, we suggest placing two boxes in a common use area, one marked *celebrations* and the other, *concerns.* A slot on the top of each box allows participants to insert index cards with anonymously written notes. This can also be done online as long as the contributions can remain anonymous. The process described here is easily adapted for the classroom, with students and the teacher contributing to the box or document.

Celebrations involve the relationships and things we value at the school, things we take pride in, even the little things: a colleague earning a degree, getting married, the birth of a child, receiving a grant, completing a marathon, noticing a colleague who has done an act of kindness, etc. *Concerns* can be big problems, conflicts and challenges, or simply the small frustrations that make work difficult. *Concerns* are not about blaming anyone or sharing in a way that might be hurtful. We suggest that contributors consider how they and the persons of concern might feel when the card is shared, being sure that what they write is something they want heard and being mindful about how they express it.

The process works like this:

1. The CLC collects the cards before each team meeting. The cards are shared with staff. Sometimes the team can anonymously share all the concerns and celebrations as they were written. Some might need to be amended before they are shared so that the issue of concern is emphasized and not identified with any one individual or group.

2. The feedback is sorted into three categories:
   a. Issues that can *easily be addressed.* The team can note these actions in a staff or school newsletter, a PA announcement, or in a staff meeting.
   b. Issues that *need further discussion* either in administrative, departmental, or full staff councils.
   c. Issues that given current resources and regulations cannot be changed.

3. For issues that need further discussion, as usual in the development of circle prompts, look for the inherent topic in each celebration or concern.
4. The team creates prompts from the celebrations and concerns they deem the highest priority. Prompts are structured to elicit direct experience with the issue rather than opinions.
5. In a staff meeting or staff council, the prompts are offered. The object of these councils, particularly those involving a concern, is not to agree but to come to a shared understanding. If a particular action is determined, intentions for its enactment are shared and responsibilities accepted. Celebrations are noted and then followed by a brief popcorn council to honor a particular person or to share reflections on an achievement or event.

Community Participants

A community participant (CP) is an adult who commits to regularly attend classroom circles, primarily to provide *a listening presence* and to share authentic, developmentally appropriate, "facilitating" stories when the talking piece comes.

CPs are vital to the success of a school circle program. The presence of listening adults, in addition to the teacher, provides students with a sense that they are not just responding to prompts from the teacher but that *what they have to say is being received and valued by the adult community.*

Ideally, these adults are community elders—parents, grandparents, non-teaching school personnel, local business owners, and other service providers, any adult who has a stake in the well-being of the school.

CPs are *not* facilitators. They may work with the facilitating teacher to plan or take a role in the facilitation of sessions, but they are primarily there to anchor the groups by modeling deep listening.

As with any adult who will have direct contact with students, there must be some kind of screening process. Often, teachers will invite adults whom they feel will be suitable CPs. Announcements may go out through the parent group and then the CLC can screen these people.

CPs receive a three-hour training that focuses on the following objectives:

- To develop attentive listening skills—suspending judgment, the desire for a specific outcome, or the need for the council to be "good."
- To understand the developmental level of the students with whom they will be sitting.
- To learn to tell authentic, appropriate, and "facilitating" stories, ones that makes it easy for the students to tell their own stories.

Schools and individual teachers can make their own determination as to whether parent CPs are placed in their own child's circle. In the early grades, having a parent in the council with his or her child might be fine, but in the upper grades and in secondary school, this is rarely done for obvious reasons. When a parent does serve as a CP in their child's class, every effort must be made so that the other students do not experience this as providing preferential treatment to that child. Likewise, these students must agree to have their parent participate.

As with teachers who practice circle with their students, CPs should also be involved in regular adult circles where they can speak about their experiences in the student circles. Additional training may also be valuable, including developing the CP's ability to read the interactive field of the circles—the verbal, non-verbal, and energetic aspects of the dynamics. Often sitting across the circle from the facilitator, the CP offers valuable perspective in a debrief.

Online Circles

The writing of this book coincided with the devastating global pandemic of COVID-19. A pandemic virus that spreads through human contact or proximity brings with it a challenging paradox: *at a time when we fear human contact, we most need human connection.* Ironically, this book which addresses how to bring deeper connections to others in the schools and deeper understanding of content came in part at a time of "physical distancing," the closing of schools, and the necessity of moving learning online.

A news report from Italy—after nearly the whole population of Wuhan, China, the first "hotspot" of the virus, was put under quarantine—said "consider a phone call as good as a hug." Nothing replaces physical presence. So much is missing when we only see faces in boxes on a computer, the connections only as reliable as the internet. With virtual circles, however, we can stay safe and still connect with others in a meaningful way, and we also can expand our circles to include people from around the world.

We have been conducting virtual circles online with participants around the world for many years. Here in Los Angeles, sometimes just traveling across town is an obstacle to circling up. As many schools moved online, teachers did not have to give up circle practice —for social-emotional and academic learning—just because students are not able to come to school. We even noticed a doubling down on circle practice in recognition of the trauma all had experienced during this time.

The image below is from a recent virtual online circle conducted via the Zoom platform. The "children's fire" at the center is a reference to indigenous wisdom that reminds us to make all our decisions with an awareness of their effect on the children ... for seven generations. "Keep the children always at the center of your circles," we say to the adults.

The Children's Fire

The process for conducting a virtual online circle is quite simple. We send a diagram showing the names of all participants (and in this case, their locations) arranged in a circle. As usual, we have a way to open the circle (ringing a bell, clapping hands, lighting candles, making dedications, etc.). After opening, anyone can begin by checking in, telling a story, or speaking to a pre-determined topic. The virtual "talking piece" proceeds clockwise from person to person based on the order of names in the diagram. At the end of each participant's sharing, they say, "I pass the talking piece to" (naming next person in the diagram). Participants can also "pass" by saying so.

After a round using the *basic form* (the talking piece going around the entire circle), the *web form* can be used for additional shares by having any person say, "I'm picking up the talking piece," and then returning it to the virtual "center" so another person can pick it up. Another online option is "roulette," where the speaker chooses the next speaker randomly. If the person chosen does not wish to speak, they can "pass" and choose the next to receive the virtual talking piece. After the sharing is complete, *witnessing* (each participant saying what stayed with them from what someone else said), *harvesting the wisdom of the circle* (reflecting on what can be gleaned from what everyone has said), and *check-out* (saying what you're taking with you from the circle) can be conducted by returning to the *basic form.*

In a moment, we will take up conducting circles that focus on experiences of the pandemic. First, here are a few gleanings from our experience. Obviously, the lack of physical presence severely limits our ability to play and to read social cues. When our experience of a person is limited to a box, one among many, on a screen, much non-verbal communication is lost. We have found that movement activities and games that engage students in mirroring one another physically contribute to group bonding, sensitivity to social cues, and empathy. I believe that at the time these activities were more important than any content we might convey. The activities described in Chapter 9 for developing a vocabulary of feelings and needs are useful here. Have one student start a movement that all others mirror by focusing their attention on that student's "square," and then having that student "pass" the movement by calling out the name of another who picks it up and transforms it.

Anything that gets students to "see" each other is useful. Studying and mirroring each other's facial expressions also tune students into subtleties. We play a game called "pass the face." One student makes a funny face and calls out another to mirror it. After copying it exactly, the second student transforms the expression into another and calls out someone to mirror and so forth.

Once, early in the pandemic, my wife and I were walking in our neighborhood, and we came upon a couple with a toddler held in the mother's arms. As I was wearing an unusual mask, Abbe said, "Your mask might scare the child." I moved to let the mask hang on one ear so the child could see that a real human being was behind it. The mother then said, "This generation will become expert at reading feelings expressed only through the eyes and forehead." Such a challenge might well bring about some kind of evolutionary leap!

As I have noted before, using a circle diagram listing all the students' names with an image of something beautiful in the "center" can keep a sense of a physical circle in their awareness. After all, there are real people attached to each one of those squares on the screen. After looking at the diagram, we might close our eyes and try to feel the connections that are there regardless of distance.

The following recommendations can be adapted for online or classroom circles and can even be useful with large groups in an auditorium or in a crowded classroom where you can't move the chairs into an actual circle.

Grades TK-2

For our youngest students, we always follow their lead. If we are hearing them talk about the virus or people getting sick, then we recommend circles that focus on the reality that *everyone gets sick from time to time and that we have the amazing capacity to recover and heal!* If the students are at home, parents can also participate (not by giving advice but by telling an *age- and context-appropriate facilitating story.*)

Begin by noting that you hear them talking about the virus and that some people might be afraid of getting it. Then, ask how many of them have ever been sick and had to stay home from school or stay in bed. Every hand should go up.

The prompt for the circle is something like: *Tell about a time you got sick or got hurt.* It could be just a time you had a cold or maybe you had to go to the doctor or the hospital. It could also be a time you fell and needed a Band-Aid or some other help.

The telling of these stories (even if at this age they are fantasies) has a salutary effect. This is because if we can tell such stories, that means we have healed and because if we hear similar stories from others, we know we are not alone. We sometimes call these "boo-boo stories," and they build resilience in our little ones. A second round can use the prompt: How did you get better?

Since some of the fear associated with these things comes from a sense of having no control over them, it is also important to have students tap into *their own wisdom* about how to stay healthy and prevent disease. Although this does not replace giving them useful information about washing hands, not touching their faces, and keeping distance from others who are sick, it does activate an "internal locus of control" necessary for all behavior change. Advice-giving is not the place we start. First, we build a foundation upon which the advice can be received. To build that foundation in the circle, you can ask simply: *What are some things you know you can do to stay healthy?* After a round of sharing responses to this, *witness* what you heard that you know to be helpful and *add* anything that might be missing.

It is important not to compound the fears expressed by the children, but it is equally important to give them an opportunity to express them. Finally, close with an *intention-setting* round where students say *one thing* they will do, one manageable, short- term objective, to stay healthy. The prompt for this round is something like: *What is one thing you can promise to do today to keep yourself and others around you healthy.* You can close with a group cheer like "Go for it!"

Grades 3–5

By the time students are 8–10 years old, they are certainly aware of information coming from the news and social media. This will likely get into the mix of what they are sharing. With students this age and older, it is good to ask about the information that has already come to them: *What have you heard about the coronavirus and where did you hear it?* Just as we adults were experiencing, there is likely to be misinformation in what the children have heard. Importantly, as circle facilitators, it is not our place to correct them *as they are sharing*. Rather, when it is your turn to share, you can reflect on what you have heard, including what you think might be inaccurate information; but do this in a way that does not demean students for having taken in the misinformation.

With students this age, *accountability* for their intention setting comes into play. After a round of intention setting, call for a round where students share one thing they heard another student say that might be something they also would be able to do. Sharing these things in a context of deep listening raises consciousness, making it easier for students to recall and act on their intentions.

A useful acronym for intention setting around healthy lifestyle choices is SMART: commitments should be *specific, measurable, achievable, relevant, and time-limited.*

If you can, make a list of all the students' stated intentions and distribute the list. When the circle meets again, offer a check-in round on what happened as they tried to keep the intentions they set from last week. Again, there is no shame in not fulfilling an intention. It is an opportunity to look at the challenges and to reset a viable intention.

Also, at this age you can begin to offer reliable secondary sources of information from articles, books, and stories. Once again, this is offered *after* the primary sources of information from students' own experiences have been shared in the circle.

When you use a story, myth, fairy tale, or poem that has a healing motif, you can conduct a circle using this protocol:

1. Read the story or poem aloud one or two times.
2. Ask students to listen only for what interests them, what catches their attention. It might only be a word, phrase, or image. (They are not trying to figure out what the story "means.") Keeping the instruction as simple as this, lowers what educators call the "affective filter" and avoids creating a cognitive load that would require the students to "perform" by interpreting the piece.
3. After opening the circle, do a round with students only saying the word, phrase, image, character, or moment that caught their interest. This is a "*speed round.*"
4. Then, for a "*story round,*" ask students to *tell about an experience in your life that is somehow related to the word or moment you chose.* For example, if a rainy day is mentioned in the story or poem, and that is what caught their attention, they can tell about a memory of a rainy day. If a friend is mentioned, they can tell whatever story comes to mind about an experience they had with a friend.
5. Follow the story round with a *witness round.*

6. Read the piece again. This time, the students will listen not only for their own connections to the piece but also to the connections their fellow students found. (You do not have to give this instruction, it simply happens.) In this way, the piece truly comes alive for them!
7. Harvest the wisdom of the circle by asking: *What can you say now about this story, having heard all of the connections shared by your classmates?*
8. Close the circle.

Grades 6–12

All the above is useful with older students. Even as adults, we like to tell our "boo-boo stories" of hurt and healing. At these ages, students are likely to be even more connected to information from social media and the internet. So, in a round where they share what they know, ask them to *identify the sources* of their information.

It is critical to include a round that invites students to share how they feel and what they think about this information. The intention-setting process described above is very useful for any age.

Mythology, fairy tales, and poetry are no less powerful and useful for older students (or even adults) because they convey universal patterns (archetypes) of healing and resilience and so connect us with a reservoir of human experience that has endured for ages. Some examples are the myth of Asclepius, the mortal and immortal healer, or The Book of Job.

There are of course many poems that speak to illness, healing, and resilience. One might say that any poem, no matter how dark, is a testament to human resilience. If a poet or artist takes up the pen or brush to capture profound loss, fear, or desolation, the act of doing so is itself a testament to the resilience of the human spirit.

As discussed above with younger students, after constructing a foundation of relevance based on the sharing of personal experiences, secondary informational sources (historical and current) can be offered; and subsequent circles can evolve from consideration of those sources as well.

Information about historical epidemics provides context for the current situation. Students can also be directed to current informational sources, such as the CDC website in America. After students access such information, use the same protocols as with the story and poetry circles mentioned above. Ask the students: *What struck you or stayed with you about the information you read about the history of epidemics (or about the current pandemic)?* And carry on from there with their personal associations, thoughts, and feelings. When using these informational sources for circles, remember that the point is not to test for information retention, but rather to explore how the information touches us directly.

There are countless reasons we can be pulled away from circle practice. Given our vertically-oriented systems of dominance and control, what is implied by the egalitarian values of a circle based-worldview is radically countercultural. Circle practice comes from cultures for whom assigning a hierarchy of importance to any individual or group is bewildering and doing so can lead to societal, environmental, and global destruction.

We tend to try to go it alone. That tendency is contrary to what it is to be in circle. My cultural orientation, my default, has led me to only meet my neighbors at the hardware store when we are both looking to buy the same tool! So, while circle practice might not be great for a consumer economy, it does support one of imagination, collaboration, innovation, and durable decision-making in service of posterity.

If you have gotten this far in this book, I suspect you are already implementing or seriously considering moving the furniture from time to time to make our world a little rounder. If you do, you are likely to encounter many resistances, as Rumi says, "a crowd of sorrows, / who violently sweep your house /empty of its furniture." Especially if you have arranged the chairs in a circle. But take heart! You are not alone in hearing the call to return to the ways your ancestors, not so long ago, gathered around the council fire. And, again as Rumi puts it, when we encounter "The dark thought, the shame, the malice–/meet them at the door laughing /and invite them in." He encourages us to "be grateful for whatever comes, /because each has been sent / as a guide from beyond."

For Reflection and Imagination

Look again at the list of reasons *not* to do circles on your classes and with colleagues on page 376.

- Which of these reasons resonate strongly for you? Make a list.
- Then, look over the rest of the chapter and see if there is a strategy you could use to overcome these concerns.
- What concerns do you have that do not appear on these lists, and, if you viewed circles as imperative, how might you design a workaround?

Chapter 11:
Circles and Institutional Realities

1. **Circle Is Essential, Not Extra**
   Especially in times of stress and testing, circle is not a luxury: it supports emotional safety, focus, and connection when it's needed most.

2. **Reframe Common Objections**
   Concerns about time, space, control, or emotional overwhelm are valid, but can also be reframed as opportunities to shift school culture.

3. **Lead with Self-Awareness**
   Circle leadership requires vulnerability, reflection, and a balance between institutional authority and relational equality.

4. **Make Discipline Relational**
   Discipline in circle comes from modeling, consistency, and inviting students to become participants in a shared learning practice—not enforcing compliance.

5. **Get Creative with Logistics**
   Circles can happen anywhere: with limited time, space, or large groups. Flexibility in form keeps the practice alive.

6. **Normalize Resistance**
   Apparent resistance (especially from adolescents) often masks a longing for connection. Circles can gently expand emotional bandwidth over time.

7. **Embed Adult Practice**
   Sustainable programs depend on consistent staff participation. Students won't trust a practice they don't see modeled by adults.

8. **Build Systemic Structures**
   Leadership teams, community participants, feedback loops, and scheduled practice help embed circle deeply into school life, even online or during crises.

12

SCHOOL AS NEXUS, DEEPENING THE PRACTICE: A CIRCLE-BASED WORLDVIEW

LIKE ME, most people reading this book were not born into a circle-based culture. While our ancestors, wherever they came from, conducted all decision-making, celebrations, and cultural transmission for millennia in circles, most of us have lost this way of being and this worldview. For some, like Native Americans and enslaved peoples, this loss was a deliberate act of colonizers and those who believe in the Doctrine of Discovery or what we in the United States call "manifest destiny." Beyond acts of genocide and enslavement, when children are punished for speaking their native languages and people are forbidden their indigenous cultural practices, the damage results in so many of the ills plaguing us now: degradation of the earth, domestic violence, suicide, addiction, famine, and endless wars. And if we don't honestly face the harm done, we will perpetuate it, projecting evil onto the other rather than coming to terms with our own capacity to instigate cruelty, and we will find ourselves as we do now on the brink of our own destruction.

There is an opportunity to heal from the harm. We can return to a worldview that embraces circles. And what are circles after all? Places where we turn respectfully towards one another, where every person, every being, and the Earth are honored and valued for the gifts they bring.

The challenge for teachers and those who see this possibility for healing is that we have not been the recipients of this worldview. *We are, in effect, trying to give the children something we did not receive.* We are uninitiated initiators. Young people have always known when we are asking them to do something we ourselves are unwilling to do, like to be truthful, to take responsibility, to admit our mistakes. When we offer them circles and suggest that these are *safe* spaces where one can speak and listen *from the heart,* they smell the hypocrisy, unless we practice and convey circles with humility and transparency. Since we are the uninitiated initiators, it is even more critical that we have a consistent, adult practice.

It is my hope that teachers who read this will not consider the circles as just something to do with students. It must be something we do, and if we do it well enough, we can offer it to the children.

Coming Back to the School As Nexus

This book began with a call to turn our attention back to the "children's fire" and the injunction to always consider the welfare of the children in every decision we make. This chapter will look at what that means in practical terms.

As they are, *our schools are underutilized.* These public spaces often sit idle at night and on the weekends, except for sports activities and school-related meetings. But the schools are where our children spend most of their waking hours. Students find lifelong friends there. Schools are where parents meet and form lasting and supportive relationships. The same for teachers. Local merchants depend on the families connected to the school. "Land values" are determined by their quality. With the exception, perhaps, of places of worship, *schools provide the closest thing we have to community.* Further, as we diminish our reliance on fossil fuels, local communities must become ecologically and relationally self-sustaining. So, how can we fully utilize these spaces, not just to educate children but to promote wellness and civic engagement throughout the community? And how can deepening a circle-based pedagogy and culture contribute to its thriving?

School-based Hologenic Healthcare

I use the term "hologenic" for its root meaning, "wholeness generating." The word "whole," derived from the Old English "hāl," gives us the words "heal" and "health." The universal symbol of wholeness is, of course, the circle. It should be clear now how circle practice can lead to psychological well-being: breaking down isolation and alienation; valuing personal experience and the experience of others; embracing multiple perspectives and worldviews; repairing relational harm—in effect creating the conditions where we can see others for who they are and *feel* seen for who we are.

The connection between psychological and physical health is well documented. Debates around healthcare as a human right consume political discourse. There is a crisis of healthcare worldwide. But just what is "healthcare," and who can provide it?

My answer to this question is that medical professionals, doctors, and therapists are not healthcare "providers." They are healthcare "educators." Doctors, for example, diagnose, intervene when there is a health crisis, and prescribe medication, diet, and other healthy lifestyle options. But they do not provide "care." Care is provided by the sister who brings soup, the friend who calls to see how you are doing and offers to go for a walk with you, even by the dog or cat that jumps up on your bed to comfort you and helps you learn to relax. In short, "care" is provided by the community.

I want to summarize a formal, biometric, three-year study, funded by the National Institute for Complementary and Alternative Medicine (NICAM) that Circle Ways conducted in collaboration with the USC Keck Medical School here in Los Angeles: "Diabetes Empowerment Council: Integrative Pilot Intervention for Transitioning Young Adults With Type 1 Diabetes."[1]

The study involved groups of mostly Latinx high school students at risk for complications of diabetes. The ten-session process was divided into three parts: council circles, guided imagery, and information about healthy nutritional choices, exercise, and mindfulness-based stress reduction.

Doctors, therapists, and health educators provided options for healthy lifestyle choices. Facilitators trained by Circle Ways guided the circles. As we all know, the best advice is only useful if we act on it. The study therefore focused in part on what is called "adherence," that is, a person's capacity to follow through on what a medical professional has suggested. Cortisol measurements were taken before and after each circle to measure stress levels.

Essentially, the circles focused on *community, intention setting,* and *accountability.* In the circles, students played games, shared stories of the joys and challenges they face, and learned to listen deeply to self and other. Once a degree of bonding and trust occurred, students set intentions for healthy lifestyle actions for each week. For example, some would pledge to cut out junk food for the week, others would define an exercise routine or commit to not sitting in front of a screen for at least one hour before bedtime. In the circle the following week, there was a "check-in," where students could speak of the degree to which they were able to fulfill their intentions. If they fell short, there was no shaming, but they had an opportunity to reframe their intention to make it even more manageable.

The point is this: when we make promises only to ourselves or to one other person, it is easy to make excuses for not following through, but when we know that a community is holding our intentions and wants us to succeed, we are much more likely to accomplish what we set out to do. This is *accountability in a context of care.*

Applications of this process are far-reaching. The reality is there will never be enough healthcare professionals to meet the need. At one under-resourced inner-city school, we brought together a group of parents, all of whom had various health concerns. After building trust in a circle process, a doctor came, listened to the concerns, and offered advice. Using that advice as a starting point, the participants set intentions weekly and checked in just as the students had done in our study.

It seems that the critical missing element in healthcare is *community.* If no one cares, why bother? This process, of course, holds true in many contexts that wish to promote well-being. Parents set intentions for better parenting practices. Educators support one another's professional development. Service providers hear from the communities they serve and then commit to provide what is called for. Merchants listen to the community and strive to produce what is needed. Artists create supportive "salons." Legislators craft bills based on the immediate needs of the people they represent.

And I would like to suggest that *all* these activities occur *on the school campus.* In this way, we might learn to live and be true to the injunction, gifted to us by indigenous peoples, that we make all our decisions with an awareness of their effect on the children ... *for seven generations.*

Sustainable Human and Environmental Practices

The practices we apply to our work in circles also apply to how we view and interact with our local environments. We begin by listening from the heart to what the natural world is telling us. Having worked for 34 years in the LAUSD, I have seen firsthand the environments at many schools. Dilapidated buildings, broken desks, few water fountains (with questionable, if any, filtration systems), unkempt bathrooms, ragged books, meals that we adults would never consume—all here in America, the "richest" nation in the history of the world. When I walk on those campuses, I notice the plant life. How do we expect the children to grow and thrive if even the plant life in their environments does not. I believe that the external world reflects the internal, that the natural world thrives when the people are in right relation with it, and that we suffer internally when the environment around us is neglected. We are all familiar with the statement attributed to God in Genesis 1:26: "Let us make man in our image, after our likeness. And let them have *dominion* over the fish of the sea and over the birds of the heavens and over the livestock and over all the earth and over every creeping thing that creeps on the earth." My friend, Rabbi Arielle Hanien, once told me that the word first translated from the Latin as "dominion" in the King James version of the Bible, in the original Aramaic meant "*in service to.*" Imagine how different things might be if this translation held, how we might view all of nature and our role as its stewards!

The climate crisis is affecting all of us but mostly the world's poor. Hunger is rampant. Refugees are clamoring to move away from war and ravaged natural resources to lands that might prove more hospitable. We understand the impact the burning of fossil fuels has had on the Earth in what has been called the Anthropocene, the last 200 years. About the same span of time that we in the "West" have forgotten how to be in circles.

As we radically decrease our reliance on fossil fuels and face the coming limitations on the transportation of resources, we must diminish our need for imports. There will be an increasing need to source everything locally. And this brings us back to the schools. I know of a few urban schools that now sustain vegetable gardens, fruit trees, and flowers on campus and provide students the opportunity to participate in their care and in the preparation and distribution of foods from them. This should absolutely be the standard.

This moment calls for a repurposing of the land around our schools to become educational centers focused on local sustainability: permaculture, sustainable building practices using only local materials, bushcraft, food cultivation, animal husbandry, and arts inspired by and using materials from the environment. Along with healthcare services, food production, transparent political engagement and decision-making, and transitional shelter for the homeless (as schools often become when there is a disaster), the schools will become exemplars for sustainable, creative, respectful human interactions. In schools that have embraced circle practice, by the time students reach the second grade, *they* are the ones introducing and leading circles with adults in the community. It's hard to resist when a seven-year-old suggests that we learn to listen and speak from the heart.

A Vision of Public Conversation Spaces

Some of our schools have been able to create dedicated circle spaces: round structures, yurts, tree trunks in decomposed granite, etc. When we pass by these places, we remember what they are for, the egalitarian practice of sharing our gifts in circle. Imagine such spaces in our public parks as well. I see youngers, middlers, and elders gathering there. Perhaps there is even a sign as you enter the park that reads, "The elders are gathering today," or "the women, men, or non-binary people will be in circle today."

Just to have the children notice this happening—people listening respectfully to one another—will transform the way they see the world. I imagine a group of elders, retirees, grandparents, regularly meeting. As children play nearby, one kicks a ball close to the circle and hears the considerate tone and sees the quality of attention and listening. They retrieve the ball and go back to their play. Then, somehow, they manage to kick the ball a little closer and more often until they stop to listen. Perhaps they linger. Then, one asks a question, a "mystery," a question from the heart like "Why do people hurt one another?" Instead of receiving *answers,* their inquiries are answered with *stories!*

Deepening the Practice

People who have associated circle practice with the traditions of The Ojai Foundation and Zimmerman and Coyle's *The Way of Council* speak of "living council." To live council is to bring a heightened, compassionate awareness to every interaction, with ourselves, others, and the natural world. Quite a challenge. But if the children grow in a culture that honors and embraces circle practice, if they never lose their connection to others and live the Nguni Bantu term "ubuntu," often translated as "I am because you are," if they see adults engaged in the practice, then living council will be easier for them than it is for us. When we worked with the Marlton School for the Deaf and Hard of Hearing in Los Angeles, we learned that one of the teachers had grown up in Nigeria.

In an interview after the workshop, he said, through an interpreter, "This council is nothing new. In Nigeria, every night in our village, the elders would get together to have council. We children would sometimes come close and listen, and we might even learn something!"

To deepen our practice as teachers, we keep a consistent adult practice. We come together in circle to share what we experience as we try to offer circles to the youth. We are honest with each other about what we might call the "shadow" of our facilitation, aspects of our interaction that are mostly or wholly outside our conscious awareness. We invite one another into our circles with students as "witnesses" who watch our patterns, our tone, the impact our presence has on the students, and what I call our *default facilitation styles*. The default is what we rely upon when we are uncertain of what to do, when we are experiencing fear of what might happen in the circle, when we arrive in uncharted waters. While we always try to listen to discern whether we are serving the needs of the students or our own needs, it is easy to fall into the default and lose our capacity for presence. I sometimes say that for the first ten years of my circle practice with students, I would come up with what I thought was a brilliant prompt, and then as the talking piece went around the circle, I would *vibe* each student to say what I wanted them to say! And when they didn't, I no doubt sent a nonverbal signal of disappointment. Letting go of my "lesson plan" was *not* something I learned in teacher college.

To deepen one's circle practice, one must learn from the circle. When I would first introduce circle to my students, I would set the room up traditionally with desks in rows facing forward, and I would ask, "Where's the teacher?" Students would point to me, and I would give them all the reasons that in this configuration, this culture, I was indeed the teacher. Then, we would rearrange the desks into a circle, and I would ask the same question. While some students would again point to me, there would always be one who would say, "We are all teachers." At first, I would challenge this with, "What have you got to teach me?" Eventually, a student would say something like "I am the only one who knows about my life." "Right!" I would say, "we are all teachers in the circle."

But there is something more that I could not explain. It had to be experienced again and again because our culture has no way of describing what we might call the "third presence" or the "wisdom of the circle." Over time, we learn to hear the voice of the circle itself. Hard as it may be to grasp, the circle itself is the teacher, but this can only happen, that voice can only become clear, when every individual in it values and conveys the truth of their own experience.

This is why Circle Ways uses a circle of multicolored stones as one symbol of the work we do. Each stone is not only its own color but also has a unique shape. Each one is unique and complete unto itself. When our students come to value and convey their unique lived experience, which is something that happens in the context of a circle of curious, compassionate listeners, the wisdom of the circle becomes clearer and clearer. One does not lose one's uniqueness in the circle. It is the gift that one brings. If we can help our students to know that their experience matters, the joys and the challenges, the accomplishments and the losses, the full spectrum of human emotion, then we have created the conditions where that gift can be unveiled.

And when the students have learned to listen to the voice of the circle, how will that serve them in life? What skills will they take with them into the world? The ability to meet any new group, to create safety so all voices are heard and valued, to listen for the unique needs and visions of that group and then create the support and accountability to follow thorough to meet those needs and manifest those visions. This "portable" skill is of value in all endeavors.

To deepen one's practice is to embrace a worldview that sees through the illusion of separateness, that sees the interconnectedness and interdependence of all life. A great deal of unlearning must occur for this way of seeing to come into view. To deepen one's practice is to ask not, "What is the answer to this question?" but "How can I bring this to the circle?" To deepen one's practice is to be in circle with oneself, to listen to the inner "still, small voice," to enter into dialogue and relationship with all parts of oneself, the valued parts as well as the marginalized, rejected, and completely unknown parts. To see the unknown parts, we need the *mirroring* of others and of nature. In dyads with significant others, we ask, "What does *the relationship* need from us to be healthy, vital, and whole?" In a classroom, we ask, "What does *this class* need from all of us to create the best place for learning?" In a school, we ask, "What does *the school* need from us? If it had a voice, distinct from but embracing of our own, what would *it* be asking from us to create a place where all can thrive?" In any environment, in the concrete jungle or the pristine wilderness, we ask, "What does *this place* need from us to be healthy and life sustaining?" In effect, to deepen our practice, we ask, "What will serve self, circle, and the greater good."

In the year of global pandemic we learned of a virus called COVID-19. The root meaning of the prefix "co-," together with the root "vid" yields "see together" or perhaps "co-vision." With all the tragic losses and untimely deaths, together we saw the fragility of human life (and of democracy). We saw that what affects one affects the other. In short, this year brought us all into circle on this round Earth.

Another pancultural symbol is the "wheel of life." Although there are many cultural variants, each recognizes these quaternities: the four directions, the four seasons, and the four phases of life—birth and childhood, adolescence, adulthood, elderhood and death.

As Oglala Sioux elder, Black Elk says:

You have noticed
that everything an Indian does is in a circle,
and that is because the Power of the World
always works in Circles,
and everything tries to be round,
and I have heard this earth is round like a ball,
and so are the stars.
The wind in the greatest power, whirls.
Birds make their nests in circles,
for theirs is the same religion as ours...
Even the seasons form a great circle in their changing,
and always come back to where they were.
Our life is a circle
from childhood,
and so it is in everything
where the power moves.

For Reflection and Imagination

The authenticity of your circle facilitation, and therefore the ability of others to develop trust in your circles, is a product of personal practice, of walking the talk. So ...

- Find one (or two or three or more) willing partners. Set a time for a circle.
- Beautify the space and the center.
- You might chat first about some important topics or simply determine to "check in." (You might also consider determining some norms or agreements about how you plan to be in the circle.)
- Decide on a prompt together.
- Open your circle.
- Using a talking piece, speak and listen from the heart. Embrace silences. Allow time to reflect on what you hear and consider what needs to be said.
- Conduct a witnessing round.
- Close the circle.
- Harvest: Discuss any takeaways, pearls and nuggets, as well as what the next circle might pick up where this one left off.
- Repeat as often as you can.
- Keep the "children's fire" burning.

Chapter 12:
School As Nexus, Deepening the Practice: A Circle-based Worldview

1. **Live Circle as a Worldview**
   Circle is a holistic way of being that centers mutual respect, relational learning, and interdependence with all life.

2. **Model What We Invite**
   As educators who weren't raised in circle culture, we must develop our own authentic, consistent circle practice to lead with humility and honesty.

3. **Reimagine the Role of Schools**
   Schools can become thriving centers of community health, sustainability, civic dialogue, and social care.

4. **Heal Through Community**
   Circle fosters wellbeing by providing connection, accountability, and a sense of belonging, which are often missing from institutional healthcare and social systems.

5. **Grow Through Reflection**
   Deepening practice requires awareness of our default habits, letting go of control, and listening for the emergent voice of the circle itself.

6. **Remember Our Interconnectedness**
   A circle-based life recognizes that healing, learning, and transformation happen in relationship with self, others, nature, and future generations.

RESOURCES

Organizations that offer circle training with fidelity to the lineage expressed in this book:

GLOBAL

Ways of Council (an international hub for all things Council)
website: waysofcouncil.net

USA

Circle Ways
website: circleways.org
email: info@circleways.org
tel: +1 310 502 7214

School of Lost Borders (youth and adult wilderness rites of passage)
website: schooloflostborders.org
tel: +1 760-938-3333

Restoring Lifeways
website: restoringlifeways.org

Circles of Resilience
website: circlesofresilience.net
email: circlesofresilience@gmail.com

The New England Council Collective
website: necouncilcollective.org

The Topa Institute
website: topa.institute
email: contact@topainstitute.org

UK

CircleWise CIC
website: circlewise.co
email: info@circlewise.co
tel: +44 7891 062769

Ancient Healing Ways
website: ancienthealingways.co.uk
email: pippa@ancienthealingways.co.uk

True Circles
website: truecircles.com
email: dave@truecircles.com

CZECH REPUBLIC

Učíme (se) v kruhu (Learning in circle)
website: vkruhu.cz
email: ucimese@vkruhu.cz
tel: +420 608 838 064

GERMANY

Eschwege Institute
website: eschwege-institut.de/en/
email: info@eschwege-institut.de

HUNGARY

Way of Council
website: wayofcouncil.hu
email: info@wayofcouncil.hu

ISRAEL/PALESTINE

Amutat Maagal Hakshava
website: hakshava.org
email: hakshava.info@gmail.com

Diwan Siti
website: diwan-siti.com

Itaf Awad
website: itafawad.com

The Uriel Center
website: urielcenter.co.il

IRAN

Dayereh
email: Dayereh.iran@gmail.com

PORTUGAL

Aprender em Círculo (Learning in Circle), a project of Florescer – Associação de Educação Global
Website: aprenderemcirculo.pt
email: info@florescer.pt

NOTES

1. Invitations to the Circle: History and Rationale

1. Donald A. Grinde and Bruce E. Johansen, *Exemplar of Liberty: Native America and the Evolution of Democracy* (Los Angeles: American Indian Studies Center, University of California, Los Angeles, 1991).
2. Olga Louchakova M.D., "Awakening to Spiritual Consciousness in Times of Religious Violence: Reflections on Culture and Transpersonal Psychology," in *Ways Through the Wall: Approaches to Citizenship in an Interconnecting World* (Glasgow: First Stone Publishing, 2005), 32–46.
3. Jack M. Zimmerman and Virginia Coyle, *The Way of Council* (Las Vegas: Bramble, 1996), 5.
4. Bonnie Benard, *Resiliency: What We Have Learned* (San Francisco: WestEd, 2004).
5. Now, Democracy. "Dr. Gabor Maté on ADHD, Bullying and the Destruction of American Childhood." *Democracy Now!*, 24 Nov. 2010, www.democracynow.org/2010/11/24/dr_gabor_mat_on_adhd_bullying. Accessed 26 Mar. 2026.

2. Rearranging the Furniture

1. Christina Baldwin and Ann Linnea. *The Circle Way: A Leader in Every Chair*. Berrett-Koehler Publishers, 2010.
2. Wayne Liebman. *Tending the Fire: the Ritual Men's Group*. Ally Press, 1991.
3. Jean Shinoda Bolen. *The Millionth Circle: How to Change Ourselves and the World: the Essential Guide to Women's Circles*. Conari Press, 2003.

3. Commonalities: Circle Basics

1. Marshall B. Rosenberg, *Life-Enriching Education* (Encinitas, CA: PuddleDancer Press, 2003).

4. Circle Facilitation

1. Paulo Freire, *Pedagogy of the Oppressed*, trans. Myra Bergman Ramos (New York: Continuum, 1970; repr., 2003), 80.
2. Marshall Rosenberg, *Nonviolent Communication: A Language of Life: Life-Changing Tools for Healthy Relationships* (Encinitas, CA: PuddleDancer Press, 2015).
3. Marshall B. Rosenberg, *Life-Enriching Education* (Encinitas, CA: PuddleDancer Press, 2003).

4. Kurt Lewin, *Resolving Social Conflicts; and, Field Theory in Social Science* (Washington, DC: American Psychological Association, 1997).
5. Jaquelyn McCandless, Teresa Binstock, and Jack Zimmerman, "Starving Brains, Starving Hearts, What Does It All Mean?" in *Children with Starving Brains: A Medical Treatment Guide for Autism Spectrum Disorder* (Thousand Oaks, CA: Bramble Books, 2003).
6. Rupert Sheldrake, *Morphic Resonance: The Nature of Formative Causation* (Rochester, VT: Park Street Press, 2009).
7. Camille Ameen, *Bringing Circle to Students with Special Needs*, typescript, September 1, 2009, author's private collection, Los Angeles.

5. Forming Circle Prompts: The Facilitator's Art

1. David Bohm, *Science, Order and Creativity* (London: Routledge, 2016).
2. "Developmentally Appropriate Practice in Early Childhood Programs Serving Children from Birth through Age 8," *National Association for the Education of Young Children*, 2009, accessed April 24, 2015, http://naeyc.org/.
3. "Josephson Institute of Ethics: Training, Consulting, Keynote Speeches, Materials for Ethical Workplaces," *Josephson Institute of Ethics*, accessed January 18, 2015, http://josephsoninstitute.org/index.html.
4. Christopher Peterson and Martin E. P. Seligman, *Character Strengths and Virtues: A Handbook and Classification* (Washington, DC: American Psychological Association, 2004).
5. Kahlil Gibran, *Sand and Foam: A Book of Aphorisms* (New York: A. A. Knopf, 1926).
6. Casey Miller and Kate Swift, *Words and Women* (Garden City, NY: Anchor, 1976).
7. "Ecclesiastes," in *The New Oxford Annotated Bible with the Apocrypha: An Ecumenical Study Bible*, ed. Herbert G. May and Bruce M. Metzger (New York: Oxford University Press, 1977), 807.

6. Circle Modes and Forms

1. Valerie Strauss, "Howard Gardner: 'Multiple Intelligences' Are Not 'Learning Styles,'" *Washington Post*, October 16, 2013, https://www.washingtonpost.com/.
2. "Multiple Intelligences Oasis – Howard Gardner's Official MI Site," *Multiple Intelligences Oasis*, accessed March 16, 2015, http://multipleintelligencesoasis.org/.
3. Howard Gardner, "A Case Against Spiritual Intelligence," *The International Journal for the Psychology of Religion* 10, no. 1 (January 2000): 27–34.
4. Micael Gonzalez, *Psychospiritual Group Work: The Impact of a Talking Circle Training Program on Emotional and Spiritual Intelligences* (PhD diss., Institute of Transpersonal Psychology, 2012).
5. "Richard Schwartz, Ph.D.," *The Center for Self-Leadership*, accessed March 20, 2015, http://www.selfleadership.org/about-richard-schwartz.html.
6. James J. Asher and Carol Adamski, *Learning Another Language through Actions: The Complete Teacher's Guidebook* (Los Gatos, CA: Sky Oaks Productions, 1982).

7. Stephen W. Porges, *The Polyvagal Theory: Neurophysiological Foundations of Emotions, Attachment, Communication, and Self-Regulation* (New York: Norton, 2011).
8. Viola Spolin and Max Schafer, *Theater Games for the Classroom* (Evanston, IL: Northwestern University Press, 2003).
9. Susan Kaiser Greenland, *The Mindful Child: How to Help Your Kid Manage Stress and Become Happier, Kinder, and More Compassionate* (New York: Atria Paperback, 2013); and *Mindful Games: Sharing Mindfulness and Meditation with Children, Teens, and Families* (Boulder, CO: Shambhala, 2016).
10. Augusto Boal, *Theatre of the Oppressed*, trans. Charles A. McBride and Maria-Odilia Leal McBride (New York: Theatre Communications Group, 1985; repr., 2002), 126–30.
11. John Seed and Joanna Macy, *Thinking Like a Mountain* (Philadelphia: New Society Publishers, 1988).
12. Stephen Scott, *Vikings of the Sunrise: Fantasy on the Polynesian Star Navigators* (New Albion Records, 1996).
13. Annie Dillard, *Pilgrim at Tinker Creek* (New York: Harper Perennial, 1988).
14. Donald A. Grinde and Bruce E. Johansen, "Vox Americana," in *Exemplar of Liberty: Native America and the Evolution of Democracy* (Los Angeles: American Indian Studies Center, University of California, Los Angeles, 1991).

7. Circles in General Classroom Use

1. Arnold van Gennep, *The Rites of Passage*, trans. Monika B. Vizedom and Gabrielle L. Caffee (Chicago: University of Chicago Press, 1960), 10–11.
2. Walter Pauk, *How to Study in College* (Boston: Houghton Mifflin, 1974).
3. Daniel Goleman, *Emotional Intelligence: Why It Can Matter More than IQ* (New York: Bantam, 1995).

8. Circles and Traditional Academic Disciplines: Language Arts, Social Studies, Mathematics, and Science

1. Antonio Machado, trans. Robert Bly, *Times Alone: Selected Poems of Antonio Machado* (Middleton, CT: Wesleyan University Press, 1983), 113
2. California State Board of Education, *History–Social Science Content Standards for California Public Schools: Kindergarten Through Grade Twelve* (Sacramento: California Department of Education, 2000), Kindergarten Introduction, "Learning and Working Now and Long Ago," https://www.wccusd.net/cms/lib/CA01001466/Centricity/Domain/1140/H-SS_StandardsK.pdf
3. Benjamin S. Bloom, Taxonomy of Educational Objectives: The Classification of Educational Goals (London: Longman Group, 1969).
4. Joanna Macy, *World as Lover, World as Self* (Berkeley, CA: Parallax Press, 1991).
5. Paulo Freire, *Education for Critical Consciousness*, trans. Maya B. Ramos (New York: Continuum International Publishing Group, 2003).
6. Paulo Freire, *Pedagogy of the Oppressed*, trans. Myra B. Ramos (New York: Continuum, 2003).

7. Rebekah Caplan, Writers in Training: A Guide to Developing a Composition Program for Language Arts Teachers, Grades 7–12 (Palo Alto, CA: Dale Seymour Publications, 1984).
8. National Council for the Social Studies, accessed August 22, 2020, http://www.socialstudies.org/.
9. John Dewey, Democracy and Education: An Introduction to the Philosophy of Education (New York: Macmillan, 1916), 5–6, Kindle edition.
10. Hyemeyohsts Storm, *Seven Arrows* (New York: Ballantine Books, 1989).
11. Augusto Boal, "Colombian Hypnosis," in *Games for Actors and Non-Actors*, trans. Adrian Jackson (London: Routledge, 1992), 51–55.
12. Babak A. Ardekani, Khadija Figarski, and John J. Sidtis, "Sexual Dimorphism in the Human Corpus Callosum: An MRI Study Using the OASIS Brain Database," *Cerebral Cortex* (2012): n.p., accessed May 31, 2015, https://academic.oup.com/cercor.
13. Harrison Owen, *Expanding Our Now: The Story of Open Space Technology* (San Francisco: Berrett-Koehler, 1997).
14. Marianne Mille Bojer, Heiko Roehl, Marianne Knuth, and Colleen Magner, *Mapping Dialogue: Essential Tools for Social Change* (Chagrin Falls, OH: Taos Institute Publications, 2008).
15. David Bohm and Lee Nichol, *On Dialogue* (London: Routledge, 2004).
16. Paul Showers, *The Listening Walk*, illus. Aliki (New York: HarperCollins, 1993).

9. Circles in the Relational Arts

1. David Bohm and Lee Nichol, *On Dialogue* (London: Routledge, 2004).
2. "SEL Competencies," *CASEL*, accessed September 24, 2014, http://www.casel.org/social-and-emotional-learning/core-competencies/.
3. Marshall Rosenberg, *Nonviolent Communication: A Language of Life: Life-Changing Tools for Healthy Relationships* (Encinitas, CA: PuddleDancer Press, 2015).
4. Deborah Heifetz, "The Map to Compassion: A Systems-Based Model of Human Needs," *Journal of Awareness-Based Systems Change* 3, no. 2 (2023): 41–74.
5. Nana Veary, *Change We Must: My Spiritual Journey* (Honolulu: International Zen Dojo, 2001).
6. Anna Halprin and Rachel Kaplan, *Moving toward Life: Five Decades of Transformational Dance* (Middletown, CT: Wesleyan University Press, 2015).
7. Carol A. Dahir and Chari A. Campbell, *Sharing the Vision: The National Standards* (Herndon, VA: ASCA, 1997); and Carol A. Dahir, Carolyn B. Sheldon, and Michael J. Valiga, *Vision Into Action: Implementing the National Standards* (Herndon, VA: ASCA, 1998).
8. Peter A. Levine, *Waking the Tiger: Healing Trauma* (Berkeley, CA: North Atlantic Books, 1997).
9. "Controversial Issues," Learning Resource Center at Palo Alto College, http://www.accd.edu/pac/lrc/issues.htm.
10. See Restorative Response Baltimore, https://www.restorativeresponse.org/; California Conference for Equality and Justice (CCEJ), https://www.cacej.org/; and Restorative Justice for Oakland Youth (RJOY), https://rjoyoakland.org/.

11. Rupert Ross, *Returning to the Teachings: Exploring Aboriginal Justice* (Vancouver: Langara College, 2016).

10. Following Their Lead: What Students Want to Know and The Role of Circles in Rites of Passage

1. Bonnie Benard, *Resiliency: What We Have Learned* (San Francisco: WestEd, 2004).
2. Rebekah Caplan, *Writers in Training: A Guide to Developing a Composition Program for Language Arts Teachers, Grades 7–12* (Palo Alto, CA: Dale Seymour Publications, 1984).
3. Rainer Maria Rilke, *Letters to a Young Poet*, trans. Stephen Mitchell (New York: Vintage, 1986), 34–35.
4. Adam Waters, MFT, "Non-Conforming Gender Identities" (lecture, The Ojai Foundation, Ojai, CA, July 21, 2016).
5. American Psychological Association, *Individuals with Intersex Conditions* (Washington, DC: American Psychological Association, 2006).
6. "An Adorable, Accessible Way to Explain a Complicated Concept: The Genderbread Person," *The Genderbread Person*, June 13, 2019, https://www.genderbread.org.
7. Jem Bendell, "Deep Adaptation," *Professor Jem Bendell*, last modified May 7, 2020, accessed May 26, 2020, https://www.jembendell.com/.
8. Joanna Macy and Chris Johnstone, *Active Hope: How to Face the Mess We're in without Going Crazy* (Novato, CA: New World Library, 2020).
9. Molly Bang, *In My Heart* (New York: Little, Brown, 2005).
10. Sara Fanelli, *My Map Book* (New York: HarperCollins, 1995).
11. John Seed and Joanna Macy, *Thinking Like a Mountain: Toward a Council of All Beings* (Gabriola Island, BC: New Catalyst Books, 2007).
12. Luigi Zoja, *Drugs, Addiction, and Initiation: The Modern Search for Ritual*, trans. Marc E. Romano and Robert Mercurio (Boston: Sigo Press, 2001).
13. Arnold van Gennep, *The Rites of Passage*, trans. Monika B. Vizedom and Gabrielle L. Caffee (Chicago: University of Chicago Press, 1960), 10–11.
14. Steven Foster, *Sun Bear: The Book of the Vision Quest: Personal Transformation in the Wilderness* (New York: Prentice Hall, 1987).
15. Rupert Ross, *Returning to the Teachings: Exploring Aboriginal Justice* (Vancouver: Langara College, 2016).
16. Eugenia W. Collier, "Marigolds," in *Black American Short Stories: One Hundred Years of the Best*, ed. John Henrik Clarke (New York: Hill and Wang, 1993), 354–62.

11. Circles and Institutional Realities

1. James Moffett and Betty Jane Wagner, *Student-Centered Language Arts, K–12* (Portsmouth, NH: Boynton/Cook Publishers, 1992), 51–52.
2. Jack Zimmerman and Virginia Coyle, *The Way of Council* (Las Vegas: Bramble Books, 1996), 12.
3. Kenneth R. Lakritz and Thomas M. Knoblauch's *Elders on Love* (New York: Parabola Press, 1999), xvii.

4. Paulo Freire, *Education for Critical Consciousness*, trans. Myra Bergman Ramos (London: Continuum International Publishing Group, 2005), 120–21.
5. Peter M. Senge, *The Fifth Discipline: The Art and Practice of the Learning Organization* (New York: Doubleday, 1990); and C. Otto Scharmer et al., *Presence: Exploring Profound Change in People, Organizations, and Society* (New York: Doubleday, 2008).

12. School As Nexus, Deepening the Practice: A Circle-based Worldview

1. Marc J. Weigensberg, Cheryl Vigen, Paola Sequeira, Donna Spruijt-Metz, Magaly Juarez, Daniella Florindez, Joseph Provisor, Anne Peters, and Elizabeth A. Pyatak, "Diabetes Empowerment Council: Integrative Pilot Intervention for Transitioning Young Adults with Type 1 Diabetes," *Global Advances in Health and Medicine* 7 (2018): 1–8, https://doi.org/10.1177/2164956118761808.

www.ingramcontent.com/pod-product-compliance
Ingram Content Group UK Ltd.
Pitfield, Milton Keynes, MK11 3LW, UK
UKHW041633190726
13854UKWH00006B/2464